1814 - THE CAMPAIGN FOR FRANCE

The Wounded Eagle

F.-G. HOURTOULLE

with Jacques GARNIER

Uniform plates by André Jouineau
Maps by Jean-Marie Mongin and Denis Gandilhon

Translated from the french
by Alan McKay

HISTOIRE & COLLECTIONS - PARIS

FORWARD

Battles in Italy such as the Mincio have been excluded from this study because they were too far away from the centre of operations.
Napoleon was relying on the army in Italy's retreat, led by Prince Eugene, Viceroy of Italy, to reinforce Augereau and break the communication channels of the Allied armies in Champagne.

This book includes a simplified summary of this campaign; it is centred on the actors who took part in the drama of 1814.

The information comes from a host of excellent works: Houssaye in his 1814 insists on the political details and describes the battles and their strategic consequences for the headquarters. Lachouque is very complete, but is a little confusing and difficult to follow. He is very useful in his work on the Guard.

Von Koch, published in 1816, gives the state of the opposing armies perfectly and the battles are described by an eye witness. I have delved into this fundamental book for the make-up of the different corps, principally the Allied ones.

Tranié and Carmignani also provide excellent illustrations.

In 1816, J. Guerre published a history of the Lyon campaign which was very complete.

Ronald Zins also proposed a very good work with his 1814. J. Paul Escalettes did the same thing for Toulouse which is studied in detail.

To these must be added the re-edited books by Teissèdre, which include memoirs of participants and accounts of the places where the fighting took place.

The Cossacks of the Guard formed a regular and well-trained unit, unlike the sotnias of the other Cossacks and the Bashkirs.
(Private Collection)

Histoire & Collections
© 2005

1814 - THE CAMPAIGN FOR FRANCE
The Wounded Eagle

CONTENTS

The French Campaign of 1814 did not start at Leipzig. But on the evening of 19 October 1813, Germany had been lost and the Emperor was obliged to withdraw his troops over the Rhine into France. De Wrede, at the head of his Austro-Bavarian troops, tried in vain to block this retreat, but he was swept aside on 30 October by the remnants of the French army corps. The Russian steppes had however engulfed the Grande Armée. It was re-formed within a few months but Napoleon's armies had been trounced on the battlefields of Germany. Once faithful in victory, yesterday's allies had now started to defect and turn their guns, victorious the day before, on their former companions.

The Wounded Eagle

Capitaine Adjudant-Major Guindey of the Grenadiers à cheval of the Guard would never see France again. He fell at Hanau beneath the horses of the Bavarian Chevau-Légers, surrounded by the corpses of his one-time allies whom he had cut down, before himself being overwhelmed. When he passed away, the brilliant Maréchal des Logis of the 10th Hussars who in 1806 had killed Prince Louis-Ferdinand of Prussia at the battle of Saalfeld in single combat, took with him the lights of an Empire which was foundering.

When Napoleon reached Paris, the last French soldiers were crossing over on to the left bank of the Rhine. How many were there? 50 000? 60 000? Their greatly reduced strength was only matched by the pitiful state they were in. Hunger and typhus carried them off quicker than cannon balls or bullets. But the enemy was on their heels and already they had to turn and face him. The army corps, very often reduced to regiment strength, took up their position on the Rhine, their gaze once again turned towards the East.

In November, Maréchal Victor occupied Alsace with 5 000 men. Morand was in Mainz with 12 000 men. Maréchal Marmont and his 15 000 bayonets covered Napoleon as far as Koblenz whereas MacDonald with less than 9 000 men protected the Rhine up to the Dutch border, itself watched over by General Maison. Behind this thin curtain, there were 10 000 horsemen spread out among four corps, together with just as many old moustaches of the Imperial Guard. Finally at Sedan, 6 000 Polish troops, the faithful among the faithful, were having difficulty reorganising. France did have other troops but they were committed on other fronts.

*The Emperor
is still standing.*

(Pen drawing by P. Benigni. Musée de l'Empéri)

On the Spanish border, Soult was in command of 60 000 experienced men to the west, and Suchet was in command of 25 000 just as war-hardened men to the east.

In Northern Italy, Prince Eugene had 50 000 Franco-Italians on the Pave. But most important of all, a lot of French soldiers were being besieged in the numerous garrisoned strongholds in Germany and Poland: Danzig, Glogau, Torgau and Magdeburg, and Hamburg where Davout was organising a vigorous defence. The Emperor had left them there because he had not yet given up hope of campaigning in Germany once again. This situation did however deprive him of 150 000 men who were holding out against only second-hand troops.

Back in Paris, the Emperor showed great determination and energy, and used all available means to create a new army. He used conscription for a part of the 1815 levy; he levied 300 000 men from the 1811 to 1814 classes; he recalled the men from all the other classes. He created cohorts of National Guardsmen, intended to replace the troops called upon to join the battle corps: some of these would take part in the fighting directly, sometimes with great courage. But after twenty years of war, France was exhausted. Campaigns and battles had cut huge swathes into the population. Out of the 900 000 men taken into the army, less than half were able to return to take up their places beneath the Eagles. Some did not return to the army in time, before the end of the fighting. Raising troops was one thing; equipping, arming and training them was quite another.

France no longer had the wherewithal to do all that. Big depots had been organised in the German strongholds. Large quantities of weapons, ammunition and equipment had been stocked there. But these strongholds were now way behind enemy lines and nothing had really been organised in France, so much did the prospect of French soil being invaded seem remote. So France was transformed into huge arsenal, producing everything and anything that could be of use to the soldiers, and as quickly as possible: rifles, cannon, ammunition and harnesses. All this was sent in a continuous stream to the newly created depots where the new recruits rallied to get equipped before joining their army corps. Training was done on the way, but it did not take long to learn how to charge with fixed bayonets. The French economy had been bled dry, but Napoleon nevertheless took drastic measures enabling him to get his hands on the resources necessary to finance this campaign. He even went as far as to pay from his own pocket.

With a final jolt, France readied herself to fight off the invasion. What Napoleon lacked was the time needed to assemble the fruits of his enormous activity and to prepare for the struggle. Of course, the Allies had understood that they could not afford to give their adversary any respite; they therefore went into action at the end of December 1813.

Above, from left to right and from top to bottom.
Stein, the Prussian Baron; the Austrian Prince, Metternich; Maréchal des Logis Guindey and Armand de Caulaincourt, Duc de Vicence.
(RR)

The Allies gather together to consult.

Having already won in Saxony, the Allies had chased the remnants of the French Army right up to the Rhine. Prevarication and endless arguments followed on after the pride and the jubilation of victory. They had beaten Bonaparte. Knowing the losses they had inflicted upon him, they knew that he had his back against the wall. But over the last thirty years, all of them had been beaten if not humiliated, by this remarkable man. He had taught all of them that sometimes defeat could appear just at the very moment they thought victory and its laurel wreathes were there for the picking. All of them were frightened.

The Sovereigns who met at Frankfurt on Main were all for an overall winter's halt to military operations. The King of Prussia and the representatives from Austria wanted to go for this cautious option, even (if) Frederick-William II wanted to get hold of Alsace, Lorraine, Burgundy and even Champagne. Bernadotte did not wish to engage personally in operations on his native soil. He cherished the ambition of obtaining the French crown and was supported in this ambition by the Tsar; but he did not want his return to be associated with a campaign of blood and ashes. Alexander dreamed of conquering Paris, in order to avenge the taking of Moscow barely a year before. But he nevertheless gave in to the general atmosphere and waited patiently. The English wanted Antwerp, but played for time. Only the hotheaded Blucher ranted and raved about this lack of enthusiasm, encouraging the Allies not to give Napoleon any respite. It was the hussar in him speaking, for he knew that it was not a good thing to let an enemy on the run have time to re-form.

But for the moment, it was time to negotiate. Metternich made an offer of peace: France had to return within its 1792 boundaries. It was a good offer considering the situation; but Napoleon took his time answering and did so badly. He gave his new Minister of Foreign Affairs, Caulaincourt, the task of "doing something which had not yet been done: obtaining good peace conditions after a series of setbacks". Caulaincourt let Metternich know that the Emperor was ready to negotiate along the lines of the proposals which had been put forward. At the beginning of January, the Duke of Vicence went to Saint-Dizier where he learnt that a conference was to be held at Chatillon-sur-Seine, but not before 3 February. But the Allies had already taken their decision on 10 December: they proclaimed that they were not at war with France but only with he who was an obstacle to peace in Europe: the Eagle had to be struck down. They decided to launch a winter campaign against France. Since mid-November, Schwarzenberg, Commander-in-Chief of the Allied troops

had already started reorganising his troops. 200 000 men were massed on the banks of the Rhine. More than 150 000 others were to join them progressively. But setting up such an operation required a hitherto unheard of logistics effort for these armies who were more used to fighting on their own soil than far from home. And so it was only on 20 December 1813 that the invasion started. Napoleon had only had one month's respite.

The enemy is on the border

When they started the campaign, the Coalition Forces were spread out all along the borders of the hard-pressed Empire.

In Spain, Wellington was advancing at the head of 140 000 English, Portuguese and Span-

*On 24 January 1814, before joining the Army, the Emperor entrusted the
National Guard with the protection of Marie-Louise and the Aiglon, his heir. (RR)*

ish troops. He had re-conquered the whole of the Iberian Peninsula. He had to keep up the pressure and advanced towards south-western France. He was thus able to immobilise Soult and Suchet who could only divert 20 000 men from their strength; these men only reached Champagne and Lyons - for the troops who had been detached from the Army of Aragon - in February.

In Italy, Bellegarde was in command of an army of 75 000 men. Prince Eugene's retreat had enabled him to reach the Piave. But whilst facing the Viceroy of Italy's Franco-Italian troops, the Austrian had at the same time to cover against the arrival of a Neapolitan army which Murat could lead up to the Po.

From the North Sea to Switzerland, more than 350 000 men were advancing: Austrians, Russians, Prussians, Swedes, English, Bavarians, Wurtemburgers; the entire European Coalition was getting ready for the kill.

In the north was the army group under Bernadotte, the Royal Prince of Sweden who, after having being responsible for the Saxons' underhand defection at Leipzig, had notions of himself being chosen as the Emperor's successor. This group included naturally enough the Swedes, Bülow's Prussians and Winzigerode's Russians. Walmoden was also there with Swedes and Russians. His task was Hamburg. Graham's English moved up to Antwerp in support.

In the centre, Field-Marshal Blücher, the most virulent of them all, wanted more than anything to advance "nach Paris". He was in command of the Army of Silesia. He was later reinforced by Winzigerode's and Bülow's corps who were entrusted to him after being detached from the Army of the North. Blücher had divided his army into three main corps: York's Prussians, Sacken's and Langeron's Russians and finally Kleist's German corps. The overall strength was 130 000 soldiers.

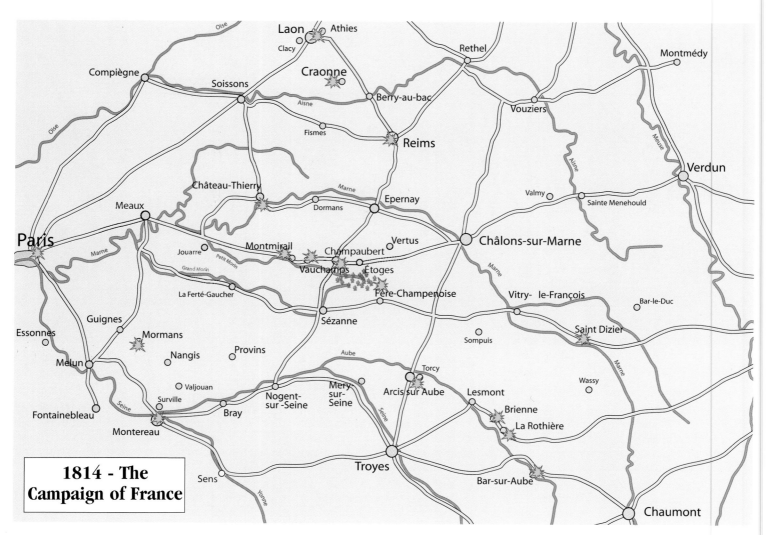

During the night of 31 December 1813 and 1 January 1814, the Army of Silesia led by Blücher crossed the Rhine. (RR)

In the south, near the Swiss border, under the command of the Commander-in-Chief of the Coalition Forces, Field-Marshal the Prince of Schwarzenberg, there was the Grand Army of Bohemia. Regrouping Austrian, Russian, Bavarian and Wurtemburger corps, as well as elements from Hesse and Baden, this was the Allies' main massed manoeuvring element. The Tsar and the King of Prussia marched with this army, accompanied by their respective Guards. The total strength of this ensemble was 200 000 men.

The Emperor's Bayonets

To cover the north-east, on 21 December, the Emperor had to spread out his forces in the following way.

To the North, in Holland and around Antwerp, Maison took command, replacing Decaen. With him in the 1st Corps were Molitor's, Ambert's and Carra-St-Cyr's divisions, Castex's cavalry, as well as Barrois at Antwerp and Roguet with the Tirailleurs of the Guard.

Near Mainz, Marmont commanded the divisions of his 6th Corps: Ricard and Lagrange. At his disposal, he also had the 2nd Cavalry Corps entrusted to Sebastiani and Bourdesoulle. Their total strength was some 150 000 men. Morand commanded the garrison in this stronghold, with

four divisions from the 4th Corps: Dumas, Guillemot, Durutte and Semellé; in all 12 000 men. MacDonald was in Cologne with the 11th Corps - the Charpentier and Brayer divisions, almost 9 000 men. In and around Strasbourg, Victor mobilised the National Guardsmen and local resources with the help of Generals Desbureaux, Schramm and Boursier. He was soon to be joined by Grouchy, commanding the cavalry. Moreover he had the 2nd Army Corps with the Dufour, Dubreton and Duhesme divisions at his disposal together with the 5th Cavalry Corps of Milhaud who had Piré, Collaert and Lhéritier under his command. The marshal also had to watch over the Swiss approaches along which the main body of Schwarzenberg's Army of Bohemia would arrive. He had only 5 000 men. Under Mortier's orders, the Guard gathered together progressively near Metz and Trèves. The Old Guard comprised Friant's and Curial's divisions. The Voltigeurs of the Young Guard formed three groups under Generals Meunier, Decouz and Boyer de Rébeval. The Tirailleurs were also in three groups under Generals Barrois, Roguet and Rottembourg. The light cavalry under Lefebvre-Desnoëttes comprised the Lancers and the Chasseurs of the Young Guard, the heavy cavalry under Guyot comprised the Chasseurs, the Dragoons and the Grenadiers à cheval. Three recently-formed regiments of scouts joined later. The outcome of many of the battles depended on the worth of these 10 000 elite troops.

The curtain is torn

On 21 December, Schwarzenberg accompanied by the sovereigns, entered Switzerland and crossed the Rhine at Basel, clearly violating the Confederation's neutrality. The French present in the town did not resist this mass. The invasion started. The Army of Bohemia marched towards Alsace and the Vosges in the north, Langres and Dijon in the centre, and Berne and Geneva in the south. On 1 January, it was Blücher's turn to cross the Middle Rhine at Mannheim, Koblenz and Mainz. Confronted with this flood of troops, the marshals retreated without giving battle because they thought that their forces were not up to slowing the enemy down. For the whole of the month of January – which was put to good use by Napoleon to reorganise his armies – the Allies' progress seemed to be inexorable. Alone in the north, Carnot and Maison did their duty. On 24 January, Napoleon entrusted the Regency to Marie-Louise and recommended her to the National Guard, named his brother Joseph Lieutenant-General to the Emperor and said good-bye to his son. On the morning of the 25th, he left to join the army at Châlon. On the 26th he was at Vitry-le-François. The marshals at last had their leader; the ship which had been adrift was no longer without its captain.

The time to go over to the attack had come.

Above: **18 October 1813, after the Battle of Leipzig, Napoleon heads home to France.** *(RR)*

Below: **During the night of 31 December 1813 and 1 January 1814, Sacken's Corps crossed the Rhine at Mannheim.** *(RR)*

FIRST BATTLES

THE BATTLE OF BRIENNE

29 January 1814

On 27 January, Blücher had concentrated Sacken's and Olsufiev's corps at Brienne. He was waiting for Landskoy and Schwarzenberg who had joined the Army of Silesia whose reinforcements were moving up: de Wrede, coming from Joinville,

*Above: **The Battle of Brienne and Blücher's Headquarters. For Napoleon, this fight marked the beginning of the French Campaign.**(RR)*

*Bottom: **The Emperor at Brienne.**(RR)*

arrived from the east and came out of the woods towards Morvilliers supported by Wittgenstein. In the rear, York arrived from Commercy. Blücher had borrowed Pahlen's cavalry and attached it to Wittgenstein's. Giulay and Wurtemberg were within reach, as was Barclay with the reserves.

On 28 January, Napoleon decided to march on Brienne; the peasants helped the soldiers push the cannon and gave them supplies.

On 29 January Brienne was attacked. Grouchy sent Briche's and Lhéritier's dragoons, supported by two batteries, to attack Pahlen who fell back behind three of Scherbatov's battalions to the right of Sacken with Wassilitschikov, who destroyed the Lesmont Bridge.

Victor arrived, pushing Duhesnme forward. Behind him Ney hurried up. General Chataux set off to go round the position. He passed by the park at the head of the 37th and 56th of the Line and took the castle at Brienne. During the assault, Blücher was almost caught. Pahlen and Wassilitschikov charged the Duhesme column capturing eight cannon.

Casken and Olsufiev tried to take the castle, to no avail, because they came up against Baste's brigade division from Decouz's division. Both French generals were killed during the confrontation. The Prussians managed to stay in the town in spite of a heavy barrage from the French artillery.

Napoleon entered the castle accompanied by a priest who was his former teacher and to whom Roustam gave a horse. On the way, they were attacked by a band of Cossacks. The Emperor was saved by Gourgaud who killed one of the attackers; Berthier was thrown to the ground.

On 30 January, in the morning, the Russians fell back. Napoleon got Grouchy and Duhesme to advance in the fog; they took Dienville and la Rothière. The Prussians regrouped at Trannes and waited for Giulay and Wurtemberg as well as Colloredo and de Wrède.

When they arrived, these reinforcements attacked. The following day the two enemies remained facing each other improving their positions.

THE BATTLE OF LA ROTHIÈRE

1st February

On the evening of 31 January, Blücher did not make the mistake of going over to the attack by himself. Napoleon was in the castle at Brienne but decided to fall back on Troyes before the Allied armies could gather and overwhelm him with their sheer numbers. The transport train and the wounded headed for Lesmont in the middle of the night. Ney's Young Guard followed, followed by the other corps. The bridge at Lesmont was to be destroyed after the army had crossed it.

But on 1 February the Allies, now almost totally regrouped, launched an attack in spite of appalling weather conditions. They all wore a distinctive white armband.

Gérard was at Dienville, to the right of the French line. Victor was in the centre of la Rothière held by Duhesme. Marmont who had moved up was at Morvilliers. Ney who had been called back was to be found at Breugné and Oudinot was on his left. The cavalry was behind Victor's corps.

De Wrède faced Marmont. He moved up towards Morvilliers and Chaumesnil; Rechberg repulsed Joubert's brigade, from whom Spleny captured three cannon and 100 prisoners. Marmont had to abandon Morvilliers. The Bavarians were supported by Wittgenstein who was at Soulaine in front of the Der forest. Giulay and Sacken attacked Dienville and la Rothière; Wurtemberg attacked Chaumesnil and la Giberie and carried the Petit-Mesnil. Barclay de Tolly remained at Trannes with the reserve.

Colbert and Krasinsky beat Lubeskoy but were pushed back by Wassilitchikov whose cavalry's flanks were charged by Piré and halted. But 24 artillery pieces were captured off the Guard. The regiments coming from Spain however were en route: Treillard's dragoons with Generals Ismert, Ormancey and Sparre as well as Leval's and Pierre Boyer's divisions.

Napoleon sent Guyot and one of Meunier's brigades to his left which was weakening; but his seven cannon were captured by Frimont together with a hundred or so prisoners. The Emperor decided it was high time to retreat with the protection of the Rottembourg division in Oudinot's corps. Milhaud came up in support but had to give in to the Wurtemberg chevau-légers which captured six of his artillery pieces. Despite the support from this brigade of the Young Guard,

*Top: **The Battle of Brienne.***

*Above: **On 1 February, at la Rothière, the Wurtemberg Dragoons from the Crown Prince's Regiment drive in the French line.** (Knötel/RR)*

Marmont was unable to recapture Morvilliers.

On the French right, Gérard fought well and his Marie-Louises held Dienville until midnight. In the centre, Duhesme and his Young Guard worked miracles in la Rothière. But he had to fall back from the village, overwhelmed by sheer numbers. The village of la Rothière from which Duhesme had been driven had to be retaken if a good withdrawal was to be made towards Lesmont. It was Marguet's 2nd brigade of the Rottembourg Division, supported by Colbert which carried out this mission successfully, using the 7th and 8th Tirailleurs and four cannon. Sacken was almost captured. Marguet was killed and Oudinot moved up in support with his 1st Brigade. Guyot's, Piré's and Colbert's cavalry was sent to free them. They were pushed back towards Brienne-la-Vieille and Beugné Farm. The Guard lost twenty-four cannon in spite of a charge by Nansouty togeth-

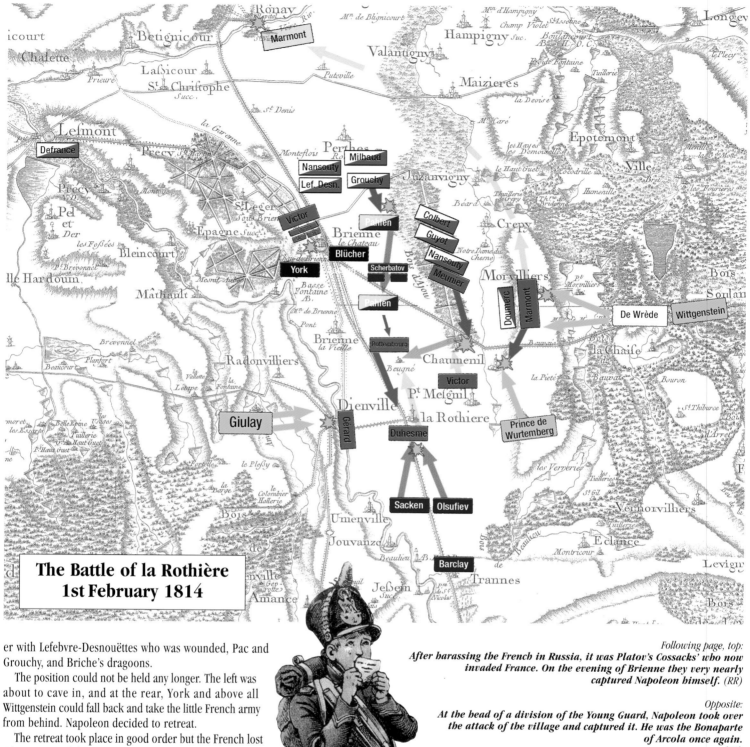

**The Battle of la Rothière
1st February 1814**

er with Lefebvre-Desnouëttes who was wounded, Pac and Grouchy, and Briche's dragoons.

The position could not be held any longer. The left was about to cave in, and at the rear, York and above all Wittgenstein could fall back and take the little French army from behind. Napoleon decided to retreat.

The retreat took place in good order but the French lost 54 cannon and 6 000 men among which 2 400 prisoners. Generals Marguet and Forestier were killed. Lefebvre-Desnoëttes was out of action -replaced by Colbert - and regained Versailles. The Allies' losses were heavy too but they had won. 32 000 French had confronted 150 000 enemy.

The retreat was carried out at night and in good order. While Marmont was fighting at Rosnay to take the bridge, Ney took up the rearguard on the Lesmont Bridge with the Meunier division and the Chasseurs à pied of the Old Guard.

The bridge was only destroyed when the last troops had crossed. The Allies lost contact with the French army which moved off towards Troyes, managing to get two steps ahead of the enemy.

At their end, the Allies got together in the castle at Brienne on 2 February. Their victory the previous evening and their overwhelming numerical superiority made them forget that they had a genius for an opponent in front of them.

The impatient Blücher got permission to march on Paris along the valley of the Marne with his Army of Silesia. Schwarzen-

berg moved along the river Seine. Clausewitz later criticised the Allies who, because they had finally united, could have crushed the French army on this particular occasion; they also ought not to have split up, with Blücher choosing the valley of the Marne convinced that he could beat MacDonald and reach Paris first and leaving Schwarzenberg to follow the Seine valley and contain Napoleon; but the Supreme Commander was always slow and undecided, and it took him a week to cover the 45 kilometres to Troyes which he only reached on 8 February. chose his target: to attack Blücher who was now divided, isolated and marching towards Paris, offering Napoleon an unhoped-for opportunity to prove his strategic genius.

THE ALLIED TROOPS

THE ARMY OF BOHEMIA

Headquarters

The Supreme Commander of the Allied armies and of the Army of Bohemia in particular was Field-Marshall Schwarzenberg. The Sovereigns were also present but they had no "official" authority concerning the military operations. However, their presence was not neutral and the Supreme Commander followed their "advice" on several occasions.

General Radetski was the Chief-of-Staff. The Quarter-Master was Langenau. The Commander of the Artillery was Reisner.

1st CORPS: BUBNA'S VANGUARD

These are the divisions which crossed Switzerland. They formed the vanguard; they were Austrian and belonged to the Army of the South. They will be dealt with in the operations against Augereau and the Army of Lyon.

PRINCE LUDWIG OF LICHTENSTEIN'S
2nd AUSTRIAN CORPS

● WIEDRUNKEL'S DIVISION

In fact this division was commanded by Lichtenstein himself.

— The Prince of Coburg's Brigade

Gradiscain's Regiment
1st Valachian Regiment
Kienmayer's Hussars

— Second Brigade

Archduke Rainer's and Archduke John's Regiments

Longueville's Brigade
Vogelsang's Regiment
Archduke John's Dragoons
Reuss's Regiment

● GRETH'S DIVISION

— Klopstein's Brigade

The Venceslas-Colloredo and Kaunitz Regiments

— Beck's Brigade

Bellegarde's and Strauch's Regiments
Total: 24 battalions, 12 squadrons and 64 cannon.

AUSTRO-HUNGARY- INFANTRY

1806-model
regimental flag.

Fusilier from the Froon
Regiment, IR N°54,
Count Colloredo's 1st Army,
Baron Wimpfen's Division.

NCO, (Prima Plana) from Devaux's
Regiment IR N°45,
Count Colloredo's 1st Army,
Baron Wimpfen's Division.

Fusilier from Argenteau's
Regiment, IR N° 35,
Count Colloredo's
1st Army, Baron
Wimpfen's Division.

Fusilier from
Erbach's Regiment,
IR N° 42,
Count Colloredo's
1st Army, Baron
Wimpfen's Division.

Officer in
Czartoryski's
Regiment, IR N°9,
Count Colloredo's
1st Army, Prince
Wiedrunkel's
Division.

Officer
of the Regiment
of the Line,
IR N°30, Count
Colloredo's
1st Army,
Prince Wiedrunkel's
Division.

Fusilier and Grenadier
from Gynlay's Regiment,
IR N°60
(Hungarian Regiment),
Count Colloredo's
1st Army, Prince
Wiedrunkel's Division.

André Jouineau © Histoire & Collections 2005

DE GUILAY'S 3rd AUSTRIAN CORPS

● CREENVILLE'S DIVISION

— Hecht's Brigade

The Warasdin-George Regiment
Klenau's and Rosenberg's Chevau-Légers
The Hohenloe-Bartenstein Division

— Spleny's Brigade

The Mariany and Ignatius Giulay Regiments

Grimmer's Brigade

The Kollovrath and Froelich Regiments

● MARIASSY DIVISION

— Pfluger's Brigade

Archduke Ludwig's and Wurzburg's Regiments

— Salins Brigade

The Kotuliski and the Emperor's Regiments
Total: 25 battalions, 13 squadrons and 56 cannon.

THE 4th WURTEMBERG CORPS

This corps was commanded by the Royal Prince of Wurtemberg.

● THE ROYAL PRINCE ADAM OF WURTEMBERG'S DIVISION

— Walsben Brigade

2nd Dragoon Regiment
2nd Chasseurs Regiment

— Jett's Brigade

4th Chasseurs Regiment
5th Cavalry Regiment

● KOCH'S DIVISION

— Doering's Brigade

2nd and 7th Infantry Regiment

— Hohenloe Brigade

4th and 6th Infantry Regiments

Above, from left to right:
General Count Bubna of Litic; Feldzügmeister Count Guilay and the Cavalry General Frimont. *(RR)*

Below, from left to right:
Prince Eugen of Wurtemberg and Field-Marshal Count Radetsky, Chief-of-Staff of the Army of Bohemia. *(RR)*

● FRANQUEMONT'S DIVISION

— Stockmayer's Brigade

3rd and 9th Infantry Regiments

— Misany's Brigade

10th Regiment of the Line and Tirailleurs

● DOERING'S DIVISION

This division only arrived at the end of February, but it was mentioned at Montereau.

— Spitzenberg's Brigade

1st Regiment of the Royal Guard
5th and 8th Infantry Regiments
3rd, 4th and 5th Militia Regiments

— Lalance's Brigade

6th, 7th and 8th Militia Regiments
Total: 24 battalions, 16 Squadrons and 48 cannon.

MARSHAL DE WRÈDE'S 5th AUSTRO-BAVARIAN CORPS
FRIMONT'S AUSTRIANS

● HARDEGG'S DIVISION

— Mengen's Brigade

3rd Chasseurs Battalion
Schwarzenberg's Uhlans

— Gerambe's Brigade

Sczekler's Regiment
Archduke Joseph's Hussars

Some of Schwarzenberg's Austrian Uhlans. (RR)

AUSTRO-HUNGARY- INFANTRY

Sapper from Archduke Régnier's Regiment, IR N°11, 2nd Army, Prince Ludwig of Lichtenstein's Division.

Fusilier from Vogelsang's Regiment IR N°47, 2nd Army, Prince Ludwig of Lichtenstein's Division.

Grenadier from Reuss's Regiment, IR N° 17, Count Colloredo's 1st Army, Baron Wimpfen's Division.

Grenadier drummer from Kaunitz's Regiment IR N°20, 2nd Army, Prince Ludwig of Lichtenstein's Division.

Officer from Bellegarde's Regiment IR N°44, 2nd Army, Prince Ludwig of Lichtenstein's Division.

Fusilier from Strauch's Regiment IR N°24, 2nd Army, Prince Ludwig of Lichtenstein's Division.

Officer in Vanceslas Colloredo's Regiment IR N°56, 2nd Army, Prince Ludwig of Lichtenstein's Division.

Fusilier wearing a greatcoat, from Kaunitz's Regiment IR N°20, 2nd Army, Prince Ludwig of Lichtenstein's Division.

André Jouineau © Histoire & Collections 2005

AUSTRO-HUNGARY- INFANTRY

**NCO from Jordis's Regiment IR N°59,
Count de Wèdre's 5th Army,
Count Spleny's Division.**

Chasseur.

**Bannat's Frontier Regiment
(Grenzer Regiment), Count Colloredo's
1st Army, Hardegg's Division.**

**Warasdin Kreuz's Frontier Regiment
(Grenzer Regiment),
1st Light Division.**

**Vallachia-Illyrian
Frontier Regiment
(Grenzer Regiment),
2nd Light Division.**

**Officer, Vallachia-Illyrian
Frontier Regiment
(Grenzer Regiment),
2nd Light Division.**

**Brooder's Frontier Regiment
(Grenzer Regiment),
1st Light Division.**

**Sczekel's Frontier Regiment
(Grenzer Regiment),
Count de Wèdre's 5th Army, Count
Hardegg's Division.**

André Jouineau © Histoire & Collections 2005

AUSTRO-HUNGARY- CHEVAU-LÉGERS and DRAGOONS

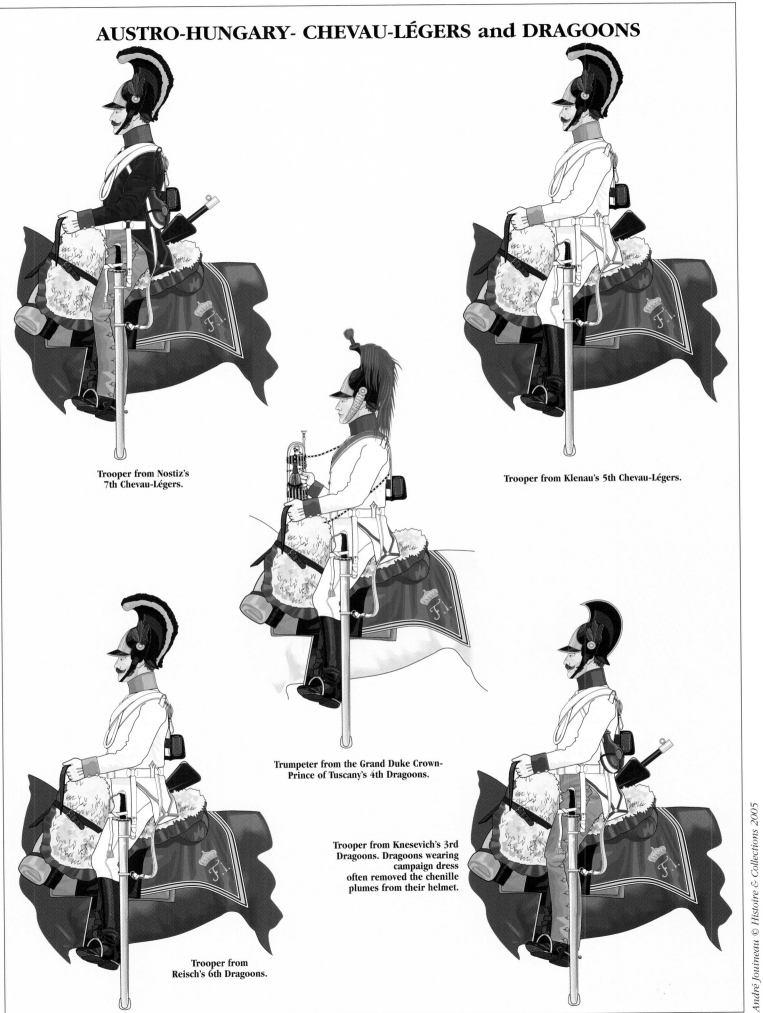

Trooper from Nostiz's 7th Chevau-Légers.

Trooper from Klenau's 5th Chevau-Légers.

Trumpeter from the Grand Duke Crown-Prince of Tuscany's 4th Dragoons.

Trooper from Knesevich's 3rd Dragoons. Dragoons wearing campaign dress often removed the chenille plumes from their helmet.

Trooper from Reisch's 6th Dragoons.

André Jouineau © Histoire & Collections 2005

AUSTRO-HUNGARY - HUSSARS and UHLANS

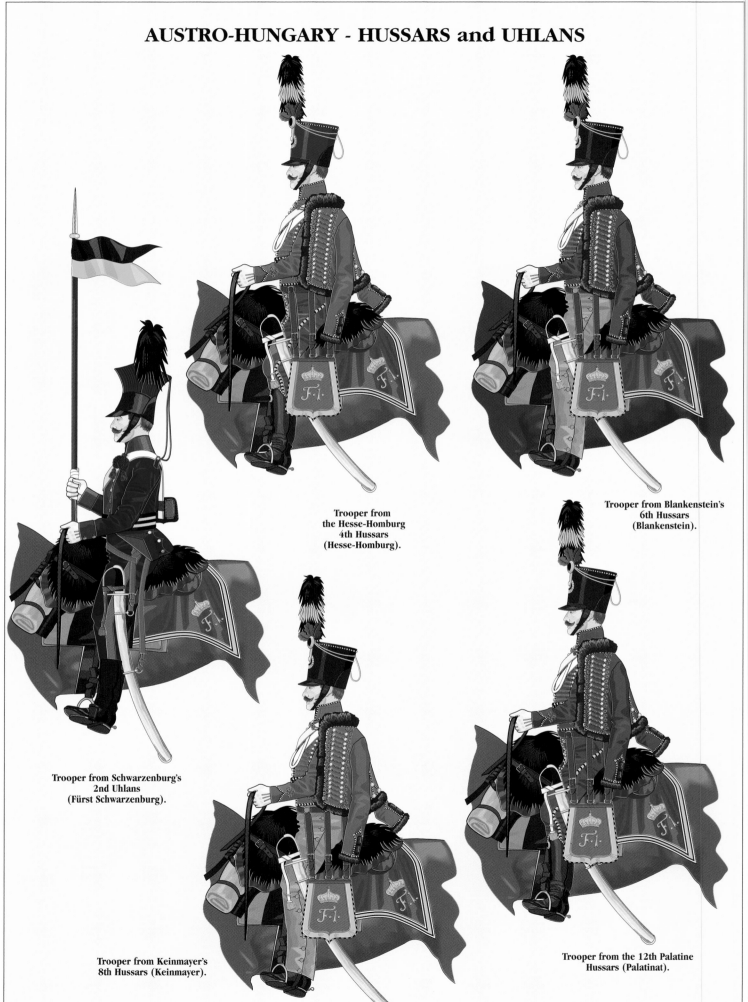

Trooper from Schwarzenburg's
2nd Uhlans
(Fürst Schwarzenburg).

Trooper from
the Hesse-Homburg
4th Hussars
(Hesse-Homburg).

Trooper from Blankenstein's
6th Hussars
(Blankenstein).

Trooper from Keinmayer's
8th Hussars (Keinmayer).

Trooper from the 12th Palatine
Hussars (Palatinat).

André Jouineau © Histoire & Collections 2005

AUSTRO-HUNGARY- CUIRASSIERS

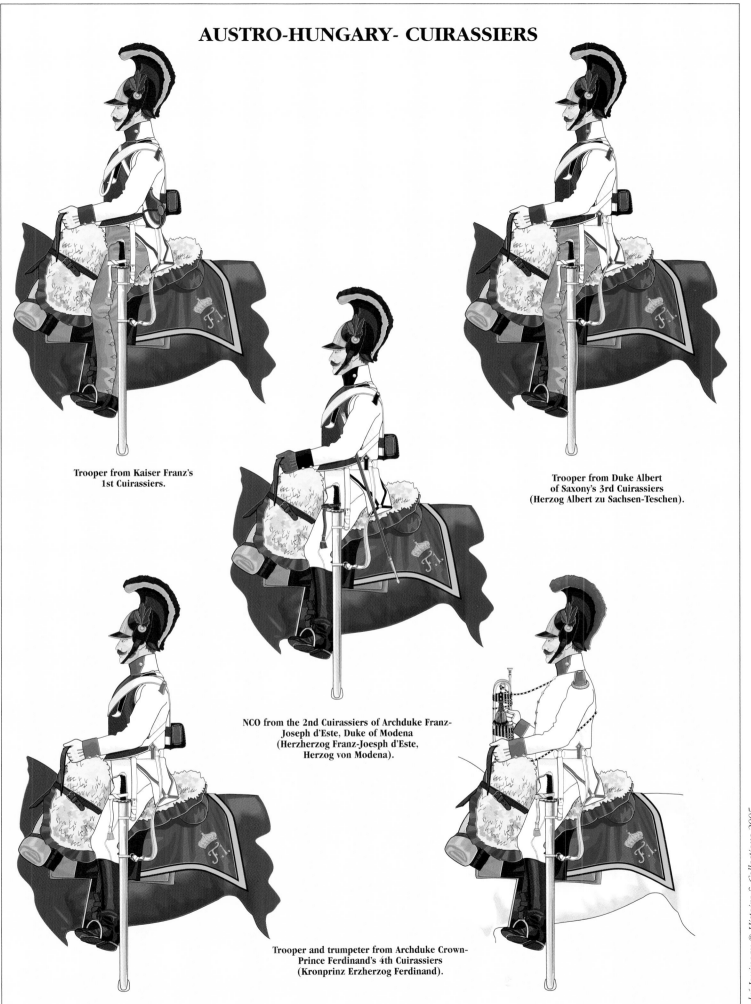

Trooper from Kaiser Franz's
1st Cuirassiers.

Trooper from Duke Albert
of Saxony's 3rd Cuirassiers
(Herzog Albert zu Sachsen-Teschen).

NCO from the 2nd Cuirassiers of Archduke Franz-
Joseph d'Este, Duke of Modena
(Herzherzog Franz-Joesph d'Este,
Herzog von Modena).

Trooper and trumpeter from Archduke Crown-
Prince Ferdinand's 4th Cuirassiers
(Kronprinz Erzherzog Ferdinand).

André Jouineau © Histoire & Collections 2005

AUSTRO-HUNGARY- ARTILLERY and ENGINEERS

General.

Surgeon.

Pontoneer.

Pioneer.

Wagon driver.

Artillery server.

Gunner.

Gunner wearing a coat.

WURTEMBERG - INFANTRY

NCO from Prince Paul's
1st Infantry Regiment.

Officer from Prince Paul's
1st Infantry Regiment.

Drummer from Prince Paul's
1st Infantry Regiment.

Soldier from Prince Paul's
1st Infantry Regiment wearing
campaign dress.

Soldier from Duke William's 2nd
Infantry Regiment.

Soldier from the 3rd Infantry
Regiment.

Soldier from the 4th Infantry
Regiment.

Chasseur from the 1st Battalion.

André Jouineau © Histoire & Collections 2005

Two indispensable figures among the German troops: William of Wurtemberg (left) and the Bavarian General, de Wrède - once the "faithful ally" of the French (right).
(DR)

● **SPLENY'S DIVISION**

— **Volkman's Brigade**

Archduke Rudolf's and Jordis's Regiments

— **Minutilli's Brigade**

Sczekler's Hussars and Knesevistch's Dragoons
Total: 11 battalions, 26 squadrons and 48 cannon.

DE WRÈDE'S BAVARIANS

● **RECHBERG'S DIVISION**

— **Wieregg's Brigade**

1st, 2nd and 7th Chevau-Légers Regiments
1st Regiment of the Line

— **Prince Karl of Bavaria's Brigade**

3rd Infantry Regiment of the Line
10th Militia Regiment
2nd Battalion of Light Infantry

— **Maillot's Brigade**

2nd and 10th Regiments of the Line
2nd Light Battalion
11th and 15th Militia Regiments

● **BECKER'S DIVISION**

— **Elbracht's Brigade**

3rd and 6th Chevau-Légers Regiment

— **Pappenheim's Brigade**

4th Regiment of the Line
5th Light Battalion
4th and 9th Militia Regiments

— **Zollern's Brigade**

6th Regiment of the Line
11th Light Battalion
13th and 14th Militia Regiments

● **LAMOTHE'S DIVISION**

— **Diest's Brigade**

4th and 15th Chevau-Légers Regiments

— **Habermann's Brigade**

7th and 11th Regiments of the Line
Lower Danube and Iller Mobile Legions

— **Deroy's Brigade**

5th, 8th and 9th Regiments of the Line
5th and 6th Militia Regiments
Total: 45 battalions, 14 Squadrons and 76 cannon.

WITTGENSTEIN'S 6th RUSSIAN CORPS
Pahlen III Vanguard

● **RUDINGER'S DIVISION**

— **Delianov's Brigade**

The Grodno and Sumz Hussars

(continued on page 26)

Fusilier from the 4th Wurtemberg Infantry Regiment seen from the rear.
(Aquarelle by H. Boisselier, DR)

The 4th Wurtemberg Infantry Regiment.
(Aquarelle by H. Boisselier, RR)

Drummer • Drum-Major • Officer • Fusilier • Feldwebel • Fusilier wearing marching uniform

WURTEMBERG - CAVALRY

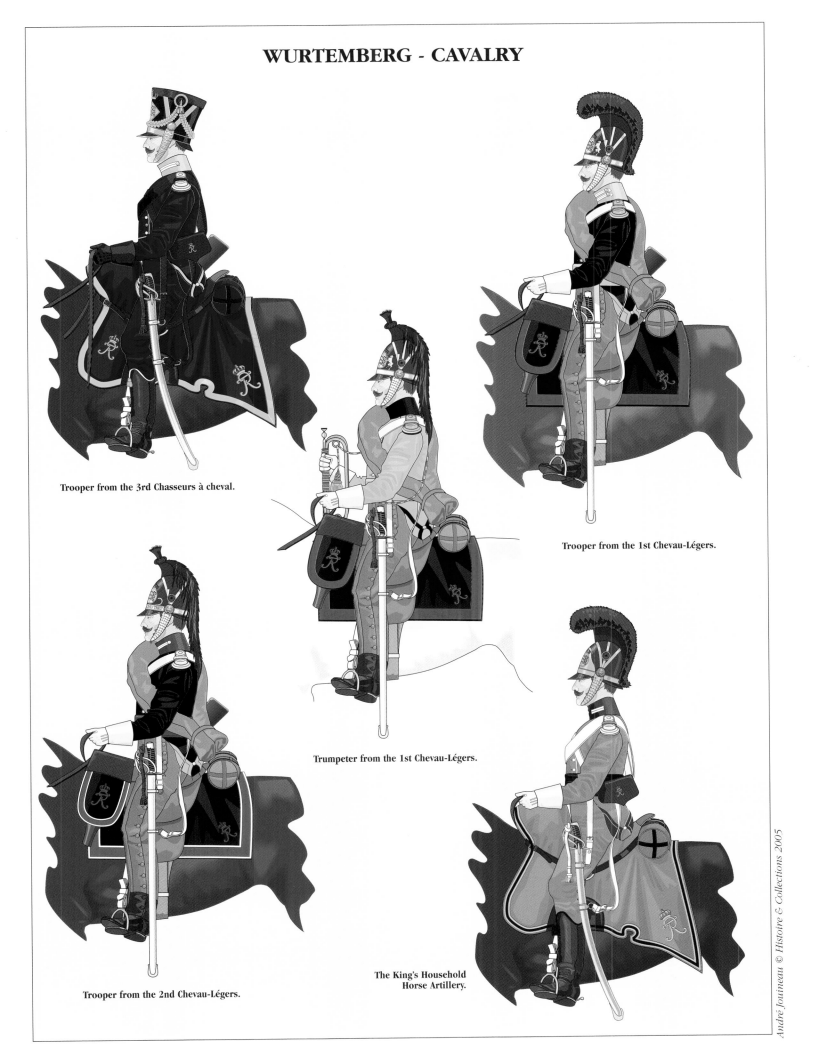

Trooper from the 3rd Chasseurs à cheval.

Trumpeter from the 1st Chevau-Légers.

Trooper from the 1st Chevau-Légers.

Trooper from the 2nd Chevau-Légers.

The King's Household
Horse Artillery.

André Jouineau © Histoire & Collections 2005

BAVARIA - INFANTRY

Corporal from
the 3rd Infantry
Regiment.

NCO from the Chasseur Company
of the 6th Infantry Regiment.

Officer from the 6th Infantry
Regiment.

Drummer in the 3rd Infantry
Regiment.

Soldier in the 7th Infantry
Regiment.

From left to right:.
De Wrède Chasseur.
Bernclau Chasseur.
Gunner.

24

André Jouineau © Histoire & Collections 2005

BAVARIA - CAVALRY

Trooper from the 2nd
von Thurn and Taxis
Chevau-Légers

Trooper from
the 1st Chevau-Léger
Regiment.

Trooper from
the Prince Royal's
3rd Chevau-Léger Regiment.

Trooper
from the train.

Trumpeter from the Prince Royal's
3rd Chevau-Léger Regiment.

Trooper from
the 7th
Chevau-Léger Regiment.

Above and Opposite, from left to right: General Count Wittgenstein commanding the 6th Corps, General Count Pahlen commanding the vanguard, and Grand-Duke Constantine.
(RR)

— Dechterew's Brigade

The Lubni and Oviopol Hussars
The Tschuyugev Hussars

● ILOWAISKI'S DIVISION

(under Mussin-Puchkin)

Wlassov II Cossacks, Ilowaski 12th,
Rebikov 3rd, Tscernuschkin 2nd and the Jaroslav Volunteer Cossacks
Total: 30 squadrons and 8 cannon.

BATTLE CORPS

● MESENSOV'S DIVISION

— Malanov's Brigade

Perm and Mohilev Regiments

— Nabokov I Brigade

Swesk and Kaluga Regiments

— Wlastov Brigade

23rd and 24th Chasseurs Regiments

● HELFREICH DIVISION

— Loelin's Brigade

The Tinginsk and Estonian Regiments

— Roth's Brigade

25th and 26th Chasseurs Regiments

● SCHACHAFSKOI'S DIVISION

— Wolf's Brigade

Morum and Tschernigov Regiments
21st Chasseurs Regiment

— Schilwinski Brigade

Revel and Siliginsk Regiments
20th Chasseurs Regiment

● PISCHNITZKI'S DIVISION

— Treffurt's Brigade

Tobolsk and Volhinia Regiments
34th Chasseurs Regiment

— Reitenitz's Brigade

Kremenschung and Minsk Regiments
4th Chasseurs Regiment
This brigade as attached to Headquarters as were the Ingrelia Dragoons, the Irtuch Hussars, the Bug Cossacks and a battalion of Militia.
Total: 24 battalions and 6 squadrons, with 64 cannon.

GRAND DUKE CONSTANTINE'S AND BARCLAY DU TOLLY'S RESERVES

Chief-of-Staff: Sabajenev Quartermaster: Diebitsch
Artillery: Jaschwilli Divisions attached to the General Headquarters

● REISNER'S DIVISION

26 artillery companies and workers

● LANGENAU'S DIVISION

One Pioneer Battalion and one Pontoneer Battalion
Headquarters Guards
Headquarters Dragoons and Militia

● PROHASKA'S DIVISION

— Rheinwald's Brigade

The Devaux and Froon Militias

— Herzogenberg Brigade

The Reuss-Galtz, Vogelsang, Erbach and Albert Giulay Militias

THE CROWN-PRINCE OF HESSE-HOMBURG'S INFANTRY

BARON BIANCHI'S DIVISION

— Hirsch's Brigade

Hiller's and Colloredo's Regiments

— Haugwitz's Brigade

The Hesse-Homburg and Simbschen Regiments

— Quallemberg's Brigade

The Esterhazy and Davidovitch Regiments

● WEISSENWOLF'S DIVISION

— Fursten Mayer's Brigade

The Tzarnotz, Berger, Oklopsia and Obermayer Regiments

— Weigel's Brigade

The Habenay, Portener, Fischer and Ruber Grenadiers

● Trautenberg's Grenadiers Division

— Klenau's Brigade

The Frimm, Moessel and Puteany Grenadiers

— Luz's Brigade

The Posmann, Lany and Gromada Grenadiers
Total: 26 battalions and 76 cannon.

RAJEVSKI'S RUSSIAN GRENADIER CORPS

● Tschoglikov's Division

— Knieschnin Brigade

The Ekaterinoslov and Araktschov Regiments

— Sulima's Brigade

Taurid and Saint-Petersburg Regiments

— Jemelianov's Brigade

Pernau's and Kexholm's Regiments

● Paskievitch's Division

— Pissarev's Brigade

Kiev and Moscow Regiments

— Damas' Brigade

The Astrakhan and Fanagor Regiments

— Posnikov's Brigade

The Siberian and Little Russian Regiments
Total: 12 battalions and 48 cannon.

RUSSSIA - INFANTRY OF THE GUARD

Preobrajenski battalion
standard with the award
of St George
and straw yellow
flag shaft.

Semenovski battalion
standard with the award
of St George
and black flag shaft.

Ismailovski battalion
standard with the award
of St George
and white flag shaft.

Guards' Colonel flag.

Guards' Colonel flag.

Lithuania:
battalion flag.

Finnish Chasseurs
battalion flag.

NCO from the Sailors
of the Guard.

André Jouineau © Histoire & Collections 2005

Above and opposite, from left to right and from top to bottom:
General Yermolov in command of the Russian and Prussian Guards, Lieutenant-General Sacken with the vanguard; General Gortschakov, General Kapzewitch, General Korf and Generals Wassilitchikov and Langeron who commanded one of the corps in the Army of Bohemia. This French émigré had already faced his compatriots at Austerlitz and in Russia.
(RR)

JERMOLOV'S RUSSIAN AND PRUSSIAN GUARDS

● **Rosen's Division**

— **Potemkin's Brigade**

Preobrajenski and Semeniovski Regiments

— **Shrapowitz's Brigade**

The Ismailovski Regiments
The Chasseurs and Sailors of the Guard.

● **The Alvensleben Division (Prussian Guard)**

1st and 2nd Grenadier Regiments
Chasseurs of the Guard Regiment
The Duke of Baden's Guards Regiment

● **Udom's Division (mentioned with Olsufiev)**

— **Richter's Brigade**

Finnish and Lithuanian Regiments

— **Scheltuchin II Brigade**

Guards Regiments and the Pavlowski Regiment
Total: 28 battalions and 44 cannon.

THE GALLITZIN II CAVALRY RESERVES

● **The Depreradovitch Guards Division**

— **Arseniev's Brigade**

Chevaliers-Gardes
Horse Guards

— **Rosen's Brigade**

Cuirassiers of the Guards and the Empress's Cuirassiers

— **Prussian Guards Brigade**

Life Guards and Light Guards Cavalry

● **Kretov's Division**

— **Stahl 2 Brigade**

Ekaterinoslav and Astrakhan Cuirassiers

— **Leontiev Brigade**

Gluchov and Pleskov Cuirassiers

● **Duca's Division**

— **Pratassov's Brigade**

The Saint-Georges and Little Russian Cuirassiers

— **Levachov's Brigade**

The Old Dubno and Novgorod Cuirassiers

● **Oscherowski's Light Division**

— **Tschailikov's Brigade**

Dragoon, Hussar and Uhlan Regiments

— **Jefremov's Brigade**

The Don and Black Sea Cossacks

The Don and Black Sea Cossacks

NOSTITZ'S AUSTRIAN CUIRASSIERS CORPS

(blockading Besançon)

● **Klebelsberg's Division**

— **Auersperg's Brigade**

The Grand-Duke Constantine and Sommariva Regiments

— **Desfours' Brigade**

The Emperor's and Lichtenstein Regiments

● **Lederer's Division**

This division was sent to reinforce the Army of the South which confronted Augereau.

— **Rothkirch's Brigade**

Archduke Franz's and Prince Ferdinand's Regiments
Kutalek's Brigade
Duke Albert's and Lorraine's Regiments

Total: 36 squadrons and 24 cannon.

(continued on page 36)

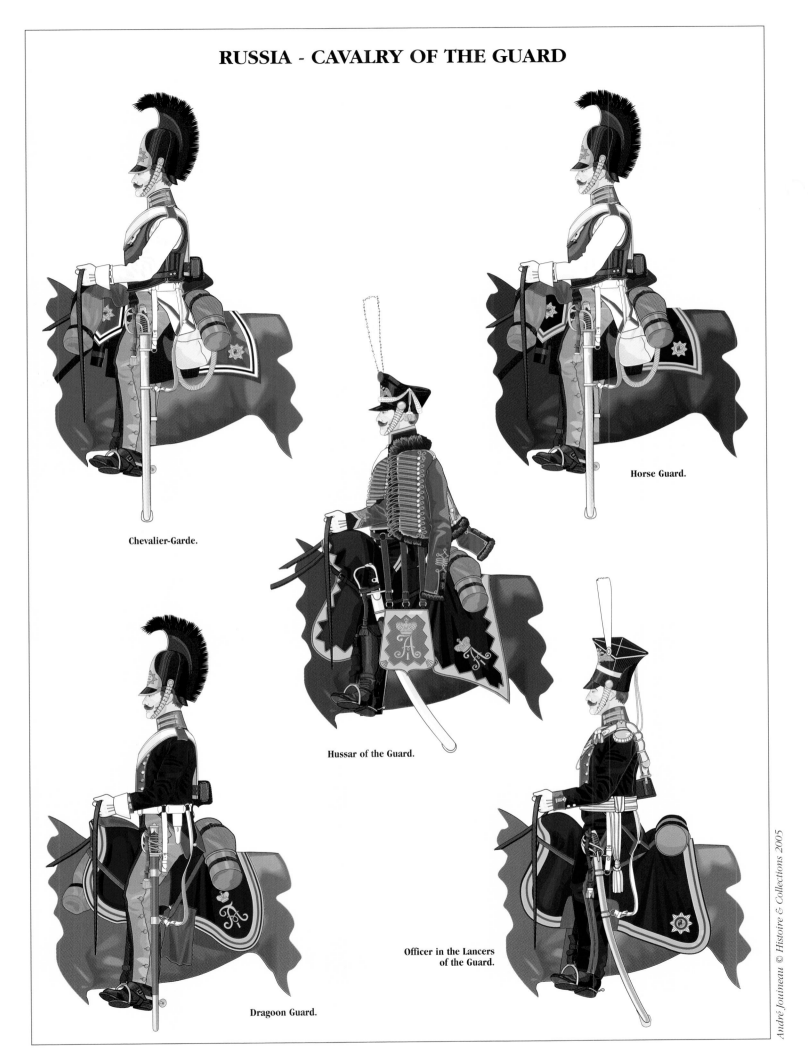

Chevalier-Garde.

Horse Guard.

Hussar of the Guard.

Dragoon Guard.

Officer in the Lancers
of the Guard.

RUSSIA - INFANTRY

Ekaterinoslav Grenadier.

St Petersburg Grenadier.

Tauride Grenadier.

The Pernovsk Regiment received a flag of St George on 20 September 1809.

Kexholm Regiment.

Sophia Regiment.

RUSSIA - INFANTRY

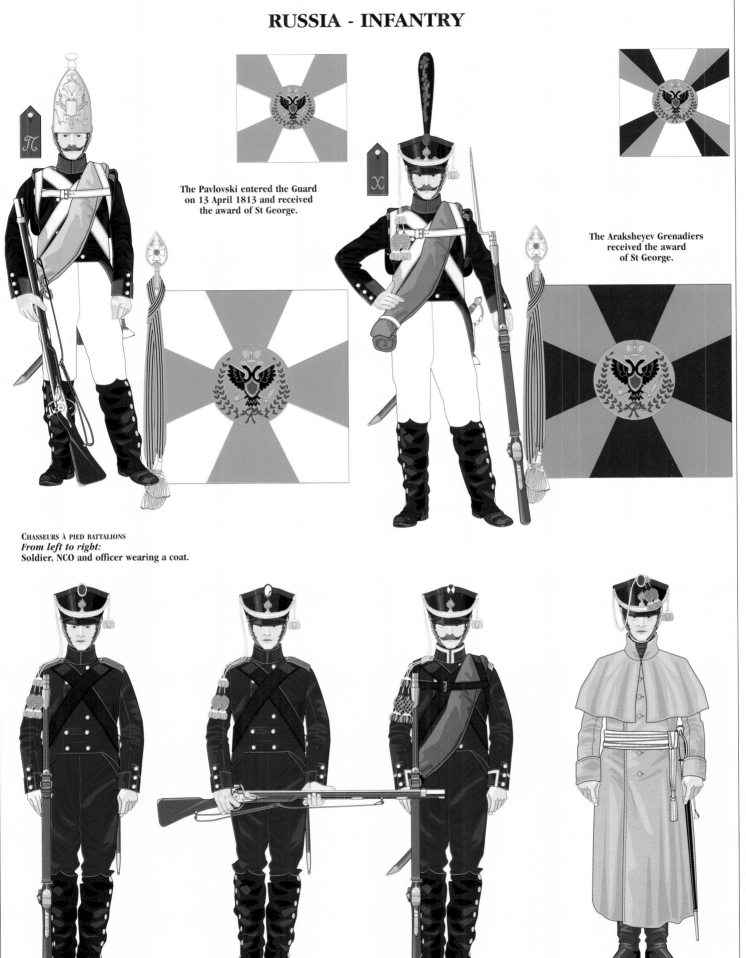

The Pavlovski entered the Guard
on 13 April 1813 and received
the award of St George.

The Araksheyev Grenadiers
received the award
of St George.

CHASSEURS À PIED BATTALIONS
From left to right:
Soldier, NCO and officer wearing a coat.

André Jouineau © Histoire & Collections 2005

RUSSIA - INFANTRY

Moscow Regiment.

Alexopol Regiment.

Fanagoria Regiment.

Tchernigov Regiment.

André Jouineau © Histoire & Collections 2005

RUSSIA - ARTILLERY

ARTILLERY OF THE GUARD

Artillery officer.

Gunner.

Horse Artillery.

ARTILLERY OF THE LINE

Trumpeter in the Horse Artillery.

Gunner.

Horse Artillery.

André Jouineau © Histoire & Collections 2005

RUSSIA - CAVALRY

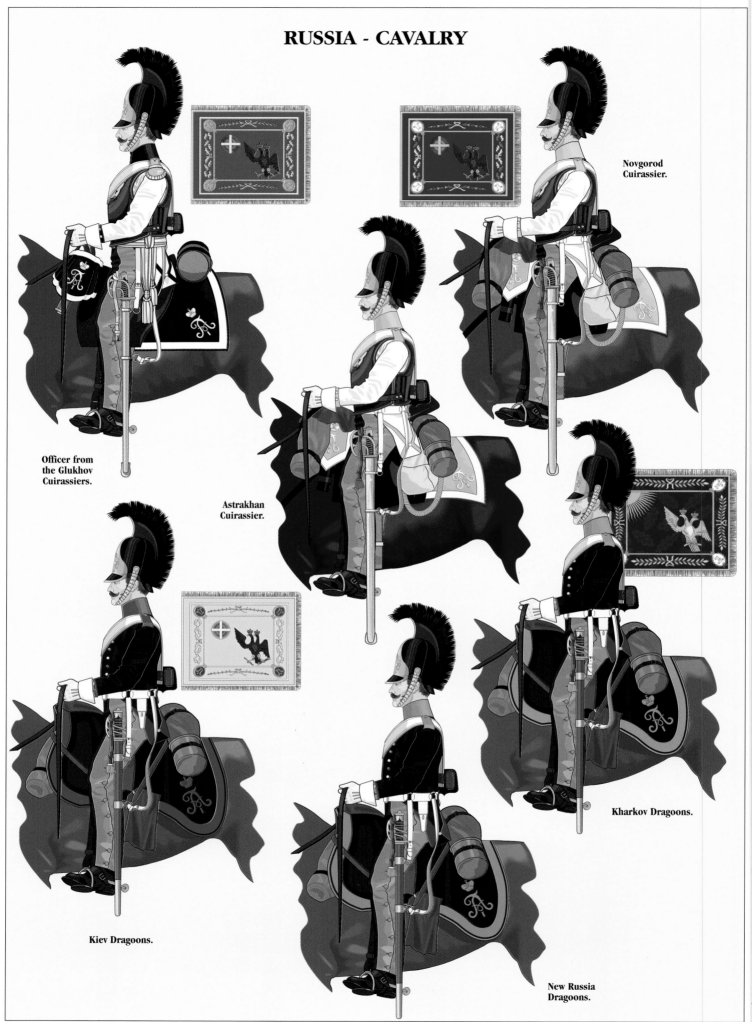

Officer from the Glukhov Cuirassiers.

Novgorod Cuirassier.

Astrakhan Cuirassier.

Kharkov Dragoons.

Kiev Dragoons.

New Russia Dragoons.

André Jouineau © Histoire & Collections 2005

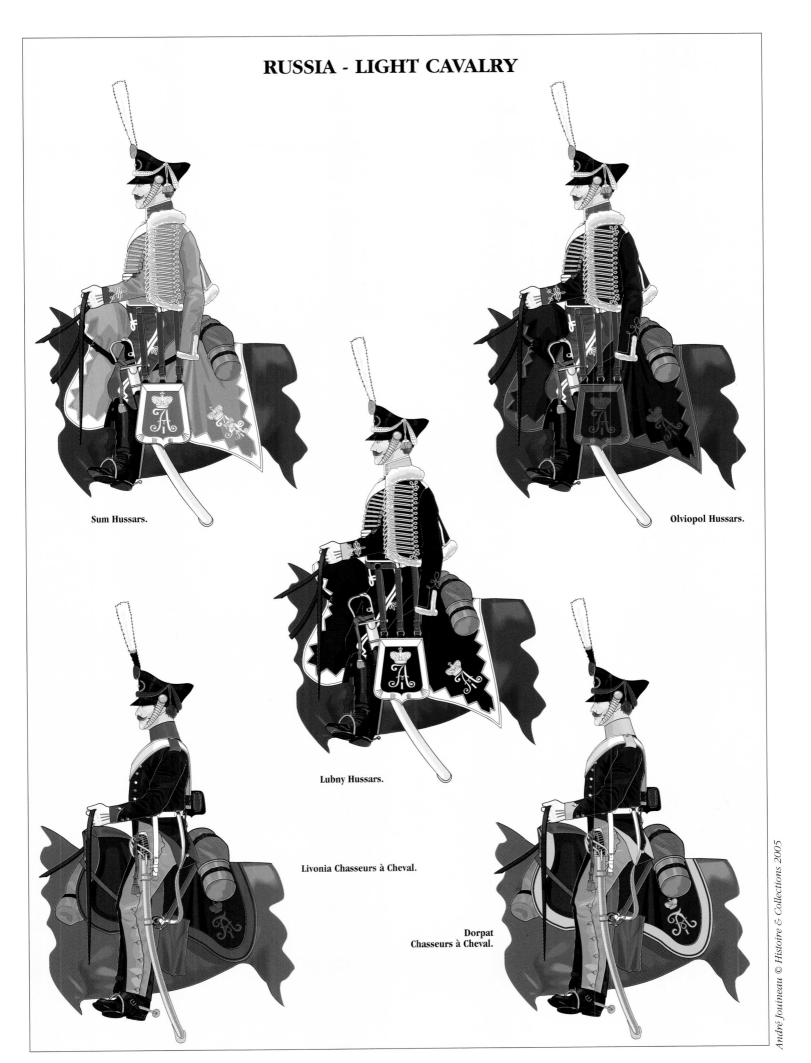

Sum Hussars.

Olviopol Hussars.

Lubny Hussars.

Livonia Chasseurs à Cheval.

Dorpat
Chasseurs à Cheval.

General Platov, Ataman of the Don Cossacks. (RR)

PLATOV'S COSSACKS

— Kaisarov's Brigade

The Grekov 8th, Ilovaiski and Hetman's Regiments

— Grekov 3rd Brigade

Kostin 8th and Black Sea Regiments

— Seslavin's Brigade

Sumz's Hussars
Laral's 4th Cossack Regiment, Toepter's 1st,
Orenburg's 3rd and Jagodin's 2nd Regiments,

— Prince Scherbatov's Brigade

The Gorin I, Elmursin and Schaltonoschkin Regiments.
This brigade was with Sacken with the Vanguard.

— Schevachov's Brigade

Serpukov's Uhlans
The Kireva and Tabunzikov Cossacks
3rd Bug and 1st Tula Regiments
This brigade was attached to Barclay de Tolly's Headquarters.
Detached Service Squadrons
Serpukov's Uhlans
Little Russian, Tchernigov and Pultava Cossack Volunteers
2nd and 11th Baskir Regiments
The corps was accompanied by 30 cannon.

Stroganov's Division (au blocus de Hambourg)

— Cossack Brigade

9th Baskirs
Jakontov's Volunteers
Polish Uhlans

— Schletuchin's Brigade

The Pensa and Sarantov Regiments

Glebov's Brigade

6th and 31st Chasseurs Regiments
18 heavy and light cannon.

In all, the Army of Bohemia totalled about 160 000 men and 550 cannon.

THE ARMY OF SILESIA

This army was commanded by the Prussian Field-Marshal Blücher. The Chief-of-Staff was Lieutenant-General Gneisenau and the Quartermaster was General-Major Muffling.

It was made up of Russian and Prussian troops shared out among four corps which have already been detailed when the battles of Champaubert, Montmirail and Vauchamps were dealt with.

● York's Prussian corps

had a strength of 20 172 men of which 5 280 were cavalry, with 104 cannon.

● Kleist's Prussian corps

had a total of 21 626 men of which 5 280 cavalry, with 112 cannon.

● Langeron's Russian corps

had a strength of 27 832 men of which 4 200 cavalry. It also had 136 cannon. This corps started the campaign with a strength of 19 000 men but was considerably reinforced several times and eventually reached a total of 42 000 men.

● Sacken's Russian Corps

had a strength of 18 912 men of which 4 400 were cavalry with 126 cannon.

In all, the Army of Silesia made a force of nearly 70 000 infantry, 20 000 cavalry and 174 cannon. It was sorely tried and even sometimes trounced, but it was reinforced with Winzigerode's and Bülow's Corps during the campaign which were detached from the Army of the North. On 14 March, Marshal Blücher commanded 109 000 men and 30 000 cavalry.

Other forces did not take part directly in the fighting in the Champagne area, but were assigned to blocking various strongholds. The troops from Baden in Count Hochberg's 8th German Corps were used to blockade the Lower and Upper Rhine strongholds. Their two divisions were commanded by Generals Stockorn, Neuenstein and Schoeffer; they had a strength of 14 battalions and 8 squadrons.

Below and from left to right:
Tsar Alexander I and General Count Barclay de Tolly,
one of the important elements of the Allied disposition.
(RR)

RUSSIA - COSSACKS

Officer
in the Ukrainian
Cossacks.

Bug
Cossack.

Don Cossack.

Black Sea
Cossack.

Don Cossack.

Ural Cossack.

PRUSSIAN LANDWEHR INFANTRY
1. 3rd Neumark Landwehr
2. 4th Neumark Landwehr
3. 1st Westphalian Landwehr
4. 5th Westpahlian Landwehr
5. 2nd Silesian Landwehr
6. 1st Silesian Landwehr

7. 1st Pomeranian Landwehr
8. NCO in the 2nd Elbe Landwehr
9. Drummer in the 3rd Elbe Landwehr
10. Officer in the 3rd Elbe Landwehr
11. Officer in the 1st Pomeranian Landwehr
(Author's Collection)

PRUSSIAN INFANTRY OF THE LINE
12. Musketeer, 10th Rgt. (1st Silesian)
13. Fusilier, 19th Rgt. (2nd Westphalian)
14. Musketeer, 1st Elbe Rgt.
15. Fusilier, 14th Rgt. (3rd Pomeranian)
16. Musketeer NCO, 6th Rgt. (1st West Prussian)
17. Officer, 1st Elbe Rgt.

18. Lieutenant, 19th Rgt. (2nd Westphalian)
19. Fusilier, 7th Rgt. (2nd West Prussian)
20. Musketeer, 9th Rgt. (2nd Pomeranian)
21. Drummer, 2nd Silesian Rgt.
22. Fife-player, 1st West Prussian
(Author's Collection)

PRUSSIA - INFANTRY OF THE ROYAL GUARD

Soldier from the 1st
Regiment in full dress.

NCO from
the 1st Regiment
in full dress.

Musician.

Soldier from
the 1st Regiment
in campaign dress.

Officer from the 1st Regiment
in campaign dress.

Senior officer from the 1st Regiment
in campaign dress.

Chasseur à pied.

Gunner.

André Jouineau © Histoire & Collections 2005

PRUSSIA - INFANTRY

Fusilier from the 6th
Infantry Regiment,
1st West Prussian.

Fusilier from the
10th infantry
Regiment, 2nd
Silesian.

Officer and soldier
from the Tirailleur
Battalion of Silesia.

Fusilier from the 6th
Infantry Regiment,
1st West Prussian,
wearing a greatcoat.

The flag of the 6th Infantry Regiment,
1st West Prussian.

The flag of the 11th Infantry Regiment,
2nd Silesian.

The flag of the 1st Infantry Regiment,
1st West Prussian.

André Jouineau © Histoire & Collections 2005

PRUSSIAN LANDWEHR CAVALRY
*In the background, troopers from the
2nd Silesian, 2nd Kurkmark, 1st
Westphalian, 3rd Silesian, Elbe, 5th
Neumark, 2nd Neumark and 2nd
Pomeranian Landwehrs.
1. Cavalry officer from the 1st Silesian
Landwehr. 2. Cavalry officer of the 1st
Kurkmark Landwehr*

*3. Cavalry officer of the 3rd Silesian
Landwehr
4. Cavalry officer from the 1st Neumark
Landwehr
5. Cavalry officer from the 1st
Pomeranian Landwehr
6. Trumpeter from the 1st Pomeranian
Landwehr*
(Author's Collection)

PRUSSIAN UHLANS
*7, 8 and 9. Officer, Trooper and
Trumpeter from the 4th Squadron of the
6th Uhlan Regiment (formerly the
Bremen Volunteers)
10. Trooper from the 1st Squadron of the
7th Uhlan Regiment (ex-Hellwig Hussars)
11. Trumpeter from the 1st Squadron of the 7th
Uhlan Regiment (ex-Hellwig Hussars)*

*12. Officer (1st, 2nd and 3rd Squadrons)
of the 6th Lutzow Uhlan Regiment
13. Officer from the 1st Squadron of the
7th Uhlan Regiment (ex-Hellwig Hussars)
14. Trumpeter from the 6th Lutzow
Uhlan Regiment
15. Trooper (1st, 2nd and 3rd Squadrons) from
the 6th Lutzow Uhlan Regiment*
(Author's Collection)

Above, from left to right and top to bottom:
General Count Zieten, General York, Count von Wartburg, General Bülow, Field-Marshal Blücher commanding the Army of Silesia, General Count Kleist and Prince Charles of Mecklemburg-Strelitz. *(RR)*

VOLUNTEER CHASSEUR DETACHMENTS
1. NCO and trooper from the 5th Brandenburg Dragoons.
2. Trooper wearing a litewka, from the 2nd Prussian Dragoons. 3. Officer from the Queen's 1st Dragoons. 4. Dragoon from the Queen's 1st Dragoons. 5. Trumpeter

wearing a kollet, from the 6th Neumark Dragoons.
6. Trooper wearing a litewka, from the 6th Neumark Dragoons. 7. Trumpeter wearing a litewka, from the Queen's 1st Dragoons. 8. Officer wearing a kollet, from the Queen's 1st Dragoons *(Author's Collection)*

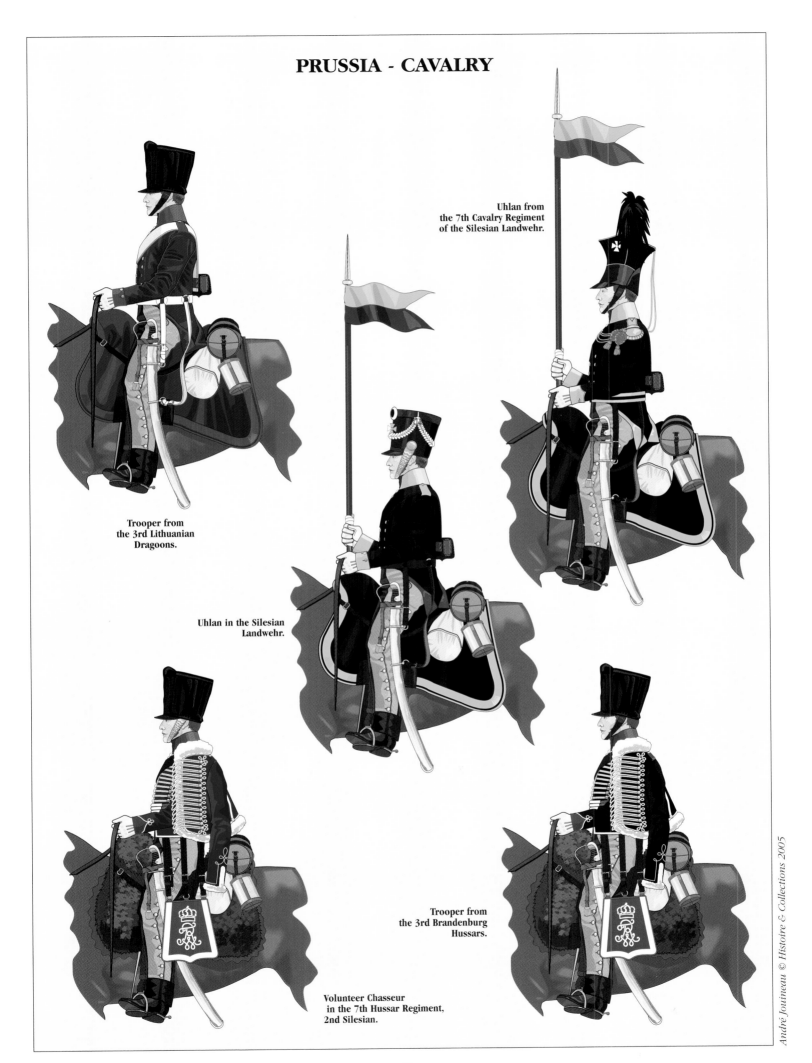

PRUSSIA - CAVALRY

Uhlan from
the 7th Cavalry Regiment
of the Silesian Landwehr.

Trooper from
the 3rd Lithuanian
Dragoons.

Uhlan in the Silesian
Landwehr.

Trooper from
the 3rd Brandenburg
Hussars.

Volunteer Chasseur
in the 7th Hussar Regiment,
2nd Silesian.

André Joutineau © Histoire & Collections 2005

Above, from left to right and top to bottom:
General Tettenborn, Major-General Baron Lutzow,
Crown-Prince Frederick-William of Prussia, General Clausewitz,
General Müffling, Lieutenant-General Horn, Frederick-William III,
King of Prussia and General von Hardenberg. *(RR)*

Below and opposite:
These Prussian soldiers have been taken, like most of the portraits
of Prussian senior officers (shown above and on previous pages),
from little cards for collecting, found in cigarette packets at the beginning
of the 20th century. *(Author's Collection/RR)*

PRUSSIA - CUIRASSIERS

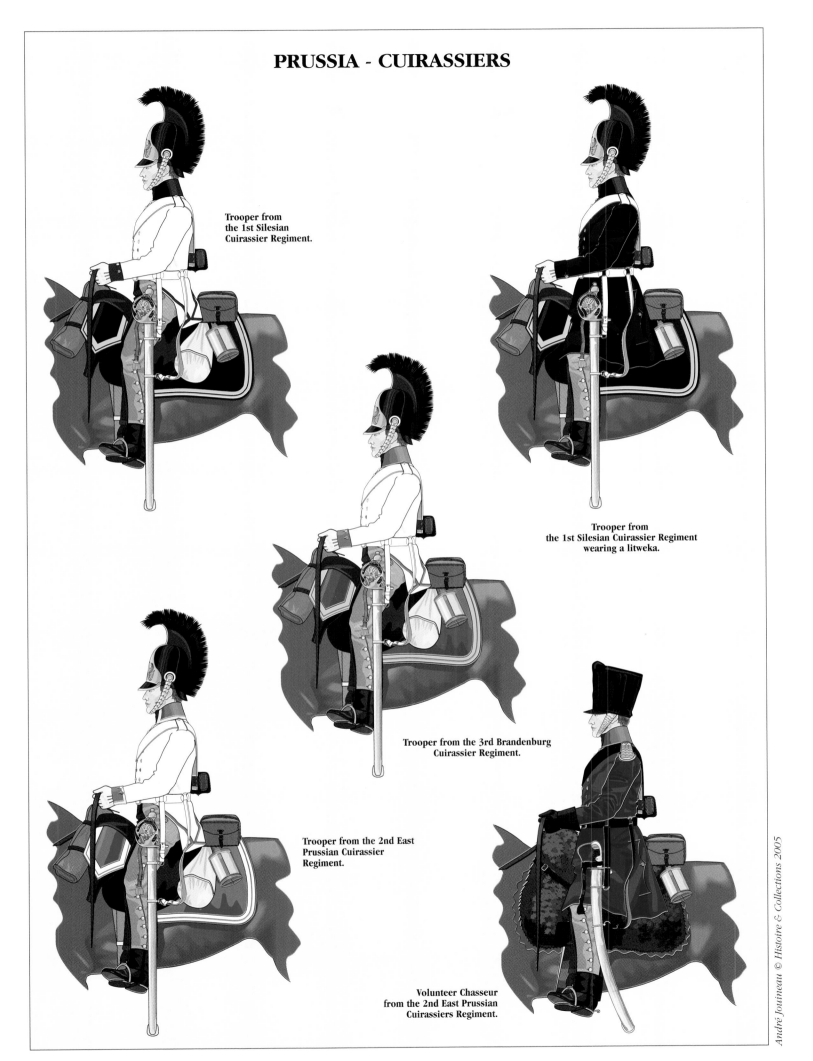

Trooper from
the 1st Silesian
Cuirassier Regiment.

Trooper from
the 1st Silesian Cuirassier Regiment
wearing a litweka.

Trooper from the 3rd Brandenburg
Cuirassier Regiment.

Trooper from the 2nd East
Prussian Cuirassier
Regiment.

Volunteer Chasseur
from the 2nd East Prussian
Cuirassiers Regiment.

André Jouineau © Histoire & Collections 2005

PRUSSIA - INFANTRY RESERVE and LANDWEHR

Soldier and NCO from
the 5th Infantry Reserve Regiment.

Soldier from the 7th Infantry
Reserve Regiment.

Soldier from the 10th Infantry
Reserve Regiment.

Soldier from the 11th Infantry
Reserve Regiment.

Elbe Landwehr.

Pomeranian Landwehr.

Silesian Landwehr.

Artillery soldier and officer.

André Jouineau © Histoire & Collections 2005

THE TIME OF VICTORIES

THE BATTLE OF CHAMPAUBERT
10 February 1814

After having crossed the Aube at Lesmont, Napoleon reached Troyes with the Guard; the other corps were nearby. He decided to move towards Blücher via Nogent-sur-Seine and Sézanne. He left only Victor and Oudinot to watch over and slow down the Army of Bohemia.

Blücher, fed up with Schwarzenberg's dilly-dallying, decided to thrust ahead with his Army of Silesia directly towards Paris following the river Marne. He had sent York's and Sacken's corps beyond Montmirail and Olsufiev's corps was following him. The weight of the French attack would fall upon this Russian corps.

This ninth corps of Olsufiev belonged to Langeron's Russian corps attached to the Army of Silesia.

The battle

Napoleon was at Sézanne with his staff where he had regrouped: Nansouty and the Cavalry of the Guard and Marmont's 6th Corps, together with Maurin's and Grouchy's cavalry. Defrance joined them with Doumerc's Cuirassiers, Dragoons and the Young Guard with Ney. He decided to beat the individual corps which Blücher had not had the foresight to concentrate.

Marmont had been sent to keep an eye on things in the direction of St-Prix. He returned saying that the bridge was practicable and not very well guarded by the Russian soldiers under Olsufiev who were on the Montirail road. Olsufiev's 9th Corps was at Champaubert and was marching alone to Montmirail.

In the early hours of the morning, Napoleon arrived and launched the attack. Ricard was sent along the road to the village of Baye; he was supported by Maurin's cavalry which moved up on his right. Lagrange's division headed for the village of Bannay with the Pelleport Brigade in the lead ahead of Joubert's Brigade, Doumerc's Cuirassiers supporting them on the left. Olsufiev had sent Udom II with four battalions of Chasseurs and six artillery pieces to defend Bannay. He had almost no cavalry and felt quite isolated; but he wanted to stay nevertheless and accepted the fight.

Lagrange's men fought hard to try and take Bannay. Colonel Ghézéner who had taken some men from the 37th Light with him was pushed back. Lagrange was wounded. Ney had to intervene with the Young Guard of the Meunier division so that the two villages were taken in the middle of the afternoon. Friant was behind the Prince of the Moskova. Maurin and Picquet with their lancers had moved up on the right to block the Etoges road.

On his side, Doumerc had moved up to the left, towards Fromentières to hold the Montmirail road. Olsufiev put his troops with Generals Poltoratzki, Anensur and Juchov, and the Nashburg and Apsheron Regimentsn in front of Champaubert where his cannon were assembled.

An attack by Picquet and some lancers started a panic.

47

Above:
Champaubert: Commandant Morell
of the 4th Cuirassiers taking four cannon. (RR)

General de Girardin, Berthier's aide de camp was sent with some service squadrons to join Doumerc so that they could attack together. The Russian squares, which had been formed, were broken and pushed towards the small lakes of the Désert and towards the woods. Girardin was promoted to Major-General for these deeds. The road to Epernay was occupied by Grouchy's light cavalry. The Russians were surrounded and chased into the woods as mentioned in the report by Capitaine Guillaumet of the 6th Light.

Captain Guillaumet's hunt

It says: *"He was ahead in order to attack Baye when musket fire started in the middle of the wood. Marmont asked Capitaine Guillaumet to take three companies, and go and explore the woods and come back quickly. The captain left with three officers and 26 soldiers only, because of the losses suffered due to fatigue and fighting every day. The wood was small, but very thick. I placed my men in a single line of battle five*

A young Frenchman captures two Russian Grenadiers.
(Drawing by JOB/DR)

or six feet apart and got them to walk 400 paces intending to bring them about to the right to join the Etoges road where I could hear rifle shot. I shouted the order as loud as I could: "To the right, wheel!" at the same time as we were shot at very keenly by the enemy hidden in the undergrowth; two of my corporals were killed; since the shooting stopped as quickly as it had started, this suggested that the enemy had been surprised and had fired all at once. I did not hesitate and ordered "Forward, bayonet charge, no quarter!" Fifteen or so of the enemy were killed and the others cried for mercy. They were Russians who gathered together after having thrown down their bags and weapons. There were so many of them that I thought it wise to move them as far as possible from their weapons as quickly as possible, since they could have picked them up again had they realised that there were ten or twelve times more of them than us.

Night was falling and we had to get out of this wood with our prisoners as quickly as possible. I therefore sent an intelligent officer, Lieutenant Lecomte, to look for a way out which would lead us

General Ricard. (RR)

General Lagrange. (RR)

rapidly to the Etoges road, along which we could hear our artillery moving. This officer returned very shortly and told me that there was a hunting path thirty paces in front of us which seemed to lead out onto the big road. There were a colonel and twelve officers among the prisoners whom I put at the head of the column; only one of them spoke a bit of French, so I took advantage of the fact to tell him to warn his soldiers that I had given my men orders to tear apart with their bayonets any prisoner who tried to escape during our march. Having taken these security measures, I got my column walking and less than twenty minutes later, we reached the Etoges road which we went down in order to join the Duke of Ragusa whom we found on the slope, where we had left him with our division in battle order.

Not seeing us return, the Marshal and General Ricard, after hearing the shouting and lively firing were furious with me. They thought that I had been caught with my 28 men. They called me and had the regimental march sounded, but as I did not have any drums with me, I could not answer them. Finally, when I got close enough for them to hear me, I answered: "Here I am!"

Maréchal Marmont and General Ricard were angry with me.

"Where did you get to? We told you!"

"Don't get angry, Sir; I've brought you some company."

When we reached the Duke of Ragusa, I showed him the Colonel, the twelve officers and the prisoners who were following us. The scolding turned into congratulations; the marshal wanted to count the prisoners himself. He found, not counting the officers, 360 Russian NCOs and men.

"Captain, go with your 26 men", the Duke of Ragusa told me, "and take your prisoners to the Emperor; he is quartered at Champaubert. Ask him for the rank of Battalion Commander, you can't fail to get it this time!"

Capitaine Guillaumet reached Champaubert with his column of prisoners in front of the Emperor's quarters. He was received with a lot of fuss and attention by General de Montesquiou but he was not allowed to see the Emperor who was at that moment dining with General Berthier and General Olsufiev who had been made prisoner shortly before.

Olsufiev, the Russian General. (RR)

But the Duke of Ragusa arrived. "Well, did you speak to the Emperor?"

"No, Sir", I replied. "The General here will not allow me to."

"Indeed", answered the General at the entrance to the Emperor's quarters. "The Marshal may enter but not the Captain."

So the Duke entered alone. The Emperor seeing him said: "Ah, there you are, Ragusa! You must be hungry, sit down. What's going on, outside at the entrance?"

"Sire", the Duke answered, "It's the brave captain of Carabiniers Guillaumet who has just arrived under your windows with a whole Russian battalion which he captured with 28 men in the Champaubert wood."

"Ha, Ha," said Napoleon with satisfaction. "It's good that he's a captain of Carabiniers". At the same time he got up from the table, took a torch and looked out of the window at the 360 prisoners.

Turning to the Duke, the Emperor asked, "What regiment is that officer from?"

"From the 6th Light Infantry", was the answer.

"It's a good regiment, it was with me at Marengo; and what do you want for this officer?"

"The rank of Battalion Commander, Sire, which has been requested for two years now."

"Good, have him promoted tomorrow," the Emperor said gaily.

Seeing him so well disposed, the Duke of Ragusa asked for the rank of Major for the Battalion Commander Philippe which he obtained without any difficulty and the following day we were promoted, both of us, to our new rank within our good old 6th Light."

The six officers, whom the captain had under his orders during the Champaubert business, were all decorated with the Légion d'Honneur. General Montesquiou invited them all to supper at headquarters. The meal was rather frugal consisting only of a dish of rice since there was nothing better at the time. It was the best invitation which we could have received since several of us had not eaten anything for twenty-four hours."

Colonel Zaeppfel was the colonel of the 6th Light, appointed on 25 December 1812. The 3rd battalion joined Guillaumet's 2nd, the whole being commanded by Major Philippe, still in the Ricard division with 15 officers and 197 men.

The strength of the regiments gathered together to make up the divisions which campaigned in 1814 was very weak. Colin's studies are very precious in helping us to understand which elements were present; on the other hand Martinien's give us useful information as to the losses suffered. This research enables us to improve our knowledge of the order of battle, which are nevertheless still confusing because of the continual movement and endless reorganising that occurred during these tragic weeks.

Bordessoulles and Piquet

About this particular subject, Madame Mathieu asks a double question because the names of both Bordessoulle and Picquet appear on the monument at Champaubert. She has doubts about their presence at the battle and gives her reasons.

After careful research I have found arguments to the contrary as follow:

The blue house at Champaubert, where the Emperor spent the night of 10-11 February 1814. (RR)

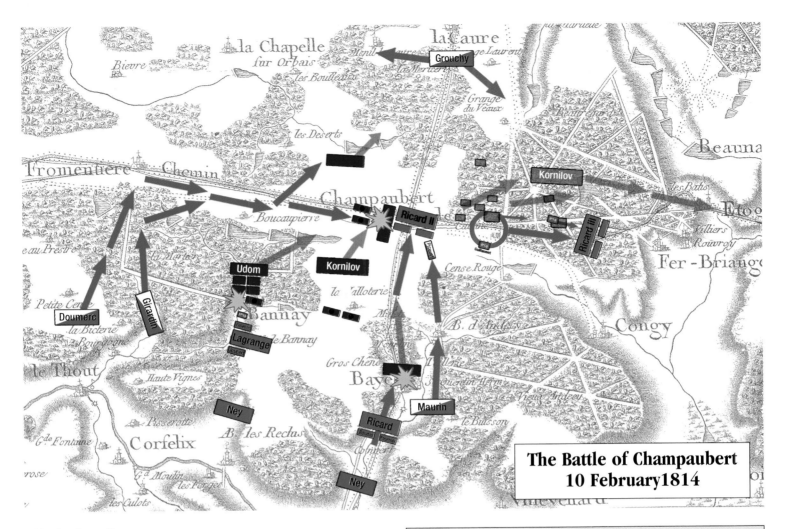

The Battle of Champaubert
10 February 1814

For Bordessoulle

It seems that Bordessoulle was sent to the depot at Versailles to prepare and train the next two temporary divisions which had assembled there. He was given command of them on 3 January. Maurin was with him and was appointed at the same date.

The confusion may originate in the fact that General Bordessoulle was already under the orders of Doumerc in the 1st Cavalry Corps in 1813. But Doumerc gave him command of these regiments when he took the reinforcement divisions to Rheims; at the same time Bordessoulle kept direct command of the heavy division. Six does not give an accurate answer, since he states that Bordessoulle was present at Champaubert under the orders of Milhaud who was not however mentioned as being present at this battle.

It seems to be difficult however to decide one way or the other, since everybody talks about Doumerc's Cuirassiers at Champaubert, including all the witnesses; later Doumerc apparently kept his command until March since Bordessoulle only arrived at that moment to take over command of the corps.

For Picquet

Madame Mathieu bases her arguments on the fact that he was in command of the first brigade of the Defrance division which was obvious; but she forgets that a few pages earlier she had quoted a letter from Napoleon to Mortier saying: *"The Emperor orders you to take up a position at Sézanne. You will have General Defrance under your command who will also take up position at Sézanne and set up his line of communications with us on the Champaubert road. The Emperor has ordered elements to be sent towards Arcis-sur-Aube. You will have an aide de camp let me know what time he can leave here to join us if we are to be engaged."*

Picquet was well and truly present and he must have left with his Lancers of the Line including the 5th and 8th Regiments. His participation at Champaubert was therefore most likely and Six mentions him as being present at the battle; Curély also mentions him as being present at this battle. In any case, a lot of changes were made in the command of the cavalry and they are very difficult to follow.

In order to have a good idea of the small numbers making up the so-called divisions, it is worth consulting the figures given by Colin and quoted by J.-P. Mir with the regiments. Lagrange's division only numbered 4 477 men and Ricard's division 2 917 on the eve of the Battle of Champaubert.

Langeron's Russians

This French émigré's command was made up of the following corps:

SAINT-PRIEST'S 8TH CORPS

● GURGALOV'S DIVISION
— Turgenev's Brigade:
Ekaterinenburg and Rilsk Regiments
— Karpenkov's Brigade:
Galetz and Polotzk Regiments
— Bistram II Brigade:
1st and 33rd Chasseurs
● PILLAR'S DIVISION
— Kern's Brigade:
Resan and Beloserk Regiments
— Schertov 1st Brigade:
Brest and Wilmanstrand Regiments
— Sablin Brigade:
30th and 48th Chasseurs

OLSUFIEV'S 9TH CORPS
(or Alsufiev, according to Koch)
● Udom II Division
— Poltorotski's Brigade:
Apsheron and Rashburg Regiments
— Juskov's Brigade:
Yakutsk and Rjäsk Regiments
— Melnik Brigade:
10th and 38th Chasseurs
● Kornilov's Division
(or Kalnielov according to Koch)
— Mussinpuschkin's Brigade:
Vitepsk and Kaslovski Regiments
Colonel Anensur's Brigade:
Kolivan and Kurinsk Regiments
— Tichanowski's Brigade:
12th and 22nd Chasseurs
The 9th Corps had 32 cannon but no cavalry.

The Laurels at Champaubert

If one admires the Emperor who turned out to be just as effective when things were going badly as he was when he was winning, the same has to be said for his administrative work, which was carried out under Berthier's management and kept the celebrated files of his boss – whose sense of organisation and administrative drive were still quite astounding - up to date.

The military quality of the veterans has also to be admired; they were formidable elite soldiers, the terror of their enemies, unconditional in their support for their idol.

Finally the conscripts have to be praised, too; they came out from their countryside backwaters, were thrown into the fiery furnace of war without real clothes, without training, without even knowing how to load a rifle; they were nonetheless instructed by the old hands during the successive battles. They knew how to sacrifice themselves to defend their country from the invading Allied hordes. Their patriotism was wonderful and everywhere they showed their

"Laissez m'en un l'Ancien"
(RR)

willingness to try and equal the terrible old hands who, in the end, adopted them as worthy of being "Grognards".

At Champaubert they won, but many of them were to die in Champagne. In this battle, the Allies were finally driven back up against the Desert lakes where many got stuck. Surrounded and unremittingly hacked down by the cavalry, having no way out either to Etoges or to Montmirail, or Epernay, Olsufiev thought he had found a way going from the Epernay road to the east, but Grouchy, the commander of the cavalry, surrounded the Grande Laye wood with the support of Ricard whose 142nd entered Champaubert first. The Russians who had been chased into the woods surrendered. Olsufiev and Poltorasky were captured as well as two generals, a good number of colonels and officers; apparently it was the Chasseur Cristil from the Elite Company of the 16th Chasseurs who captured Olsufiev. He was awarded the Legion d'Honneur. The soldiers of the 9th Corps were chased to the Grands Grès lakes where many drowned or got stuck.

In all, the Russians lost 1 500 men killed and wounded, and about 3 000 prisoners. Flags, three generals, twenty or so cannon and caissons were captured. Only General Kornilov together with Udom managed to get out with 1 500 men, their flags and their cannon, and reach Blücher at Vertus. Olsufiev's corps almost ceased to exist. The French 6th Corps was one of the great actors in this series of confrontations which is sometimes called the "Battle of the Five Days". At Champaubert it faced the isolated Olsufiev. Maréchal Marmont, Duke of Ragusa was one of the important men of the French Campaign. Under his command were:

MARMONT'S 6th CORPS

THE RICARD DIVISION

This division had already fought at la Rothière.

Ricard: General in 1806, Major-General in 1812, wounded in front of Paris. Followed the King to Ghent. Pair de France in August 1815. GdCxLH and St Ferdinand in 1823, retired in 1831. Died in 1843.

The two divisional brigades, famous at Champaubert, Montmirail, Vauchamps, Rheims and Fère-Champenoise were commanded by Fournier and Boudin

● The Boudin Brigade

Boudin de Roville, General in 1813, wounded at Montmirail, suspended in March 1815, GdOLH in 1825, retired in 1835, died in 1843.

— The 6th Light

Colonel Zaepffel, Baron in 1809, appointed colonel on 25 December 1812. Mentioned at Vauchamps. Reunion in 1814; served in Paris in 1815. Maréchal de Camp in 1823 at Bayonne. In Belgium in 1832. CrLH in 1833, Order of Leopold, retired in 1853 and died in 1865.

The regiment which came from the 81st of the Line started the campaign with 197 men. The 3rd Battalion went to join Guilaumet's 2nd, the whole being commanded by Major Philippe, still in the Ricard Division.

— The 9th Light

The Battalion Commander Négrier, mentioned at Méry, Soissons, Craonne, Fère-Champenoise.

Fririon, Battalion Commander in the 9th Light, OLH in 1813, aide de camp to Lacoste, killed at Montmirail. The regiment fought at Brienne, la Rothière, Champaubert, Montmirail and Vauchamps. The regiment's strength was 130 men.

The 16th Light

Colonel Cornebize, appointed since 1813, was in the 1st of the Line. Chevalier in 1810, CtLH in 1814; served in 1815, Baron in 1815. Maréchal de Camp in 1825, retired in 1826; he died in 1846.

The regiment came from the 91st of the line and started the campaign with 199 men and was mentioned at Champaubert, Vauchamps, Rheims and Paris.

— The 138th of the Line

Colonel d'Albignac. Baron in 1813. Ney's aide de camp. Temporarily replaced Boudin who was wounded. Maréchal de camp in October 1814. Deputy for the Calvados department in 1815. In Spain and GdOLH in 1823.

The regiment was represented by its 3rd battalion only. It was mentioned at Brienne, la

Rothière, Champaubert and Montmirail where the division was reduced from 2 900 to 1 500 men. After Vauchamps, there were only 80 men remaining out of the 108 present a week earlier. They were sent to Paris. The 4th and 5th Battalions were in Luxemburg.

— The 142nd of the Line

Its commanding officer, Colonel Camescasse was probably killed at Leipzig. According to Smith, he was replaced by Facon.

The regiment sent 95 men who took part at Rosnay, Nogent, Champaubert and Montmirail.

— The 145th of the Line

Colonel Dolisie, OLH in 1813. He remained in Koblenz where he died on 22 December.

This regiment sent 261 men and was at la Rothière, Champaubert, Montmirail and Vauchamps where two officers were mentioned in despatches.

● Fournier's Brigade

Fournier, General and CtLH in 1813. Champaubert, Montmirail, Vauchamps. Wounded in front of Paris having gone over to the Lagrange division; served at Marseilles in 1815; put on half-pay and retired with the rank of Honorary Lieutenant-General in 1826.

— The 2nd Light

Colonel Verdun, CrLH in 1814, served in 1815, Baron in 1822, retired in 1826

The regiment sent 112 men who served at Champaubert, Montmirail, Méry, Craonne and Paris.

— The 4th Light

Colonel Langeron was made the provisional commander a brigade on 13 February 1814. The regiment was at Champaubert, Montmirail, Vauchamps then with Souham in Paris. It sent 136 men. The regiment was changed into the 79th of the Line.

— The 22nd of the Line

The regiment sent a battalion of 281 men.

— The 40th Light

Colonel Jaquemet. Took part at the Battle of Trafalgar aboard the Formidable, was captured and exchanged. OLH in 1812, in the regiment in 1813. At Montmirail he replaced Boudin who had been wounded. Retired in 1816. On 22 March 1814 he was replaced by Monneret who was with the Army of the Pyrenees with the rest of the regiment, in the Fririon brigade of the Foy division.

The regiment sent the 223 men of its 3rd Battalion to Champagne.

— The 50th of the Line

This regiment was in the Army of the Pyrenees. Only one detachment of 190 men was present in Champagne.

— The 69th of the Line

Colonel Hervé, Chevalier in 1809, OLH in 1812, retired in 1815.

This regiment was incorrectly given as being present here; it was with the Army of the Pyrenees with which it fought at Orthez and Toulouse. Only the 3rd Battalion, comprising 97 men, was regrouped with elements coming from other regiments. They fought at Brienne and Rosnay after la Rothière where they were behind Dufour. At Champaubert, they took Baye then entered Champaubert. They were among the heroes of Montmirail, attacking as they did Marchais five times, finally taking it

The Navy Artillery Regiments distinguished themselves all during the campaign.
(J. Girbal. Author's Collection)

with the help of Lefebvre and Bertrand who brought up four battalions of the Old Guard. Worn out and having suffered almost 50% losses, they were sent to Montmirail to re-group. On 14 February they attacked at Vauchamps.

— The 136th of the Line

Colonel Comte d'Aubremé was a Belgian. Reunion in 1812, wounded and mentioned at Montmirail. Went over to the Army of the Netherlands and became a General. Served against the French at Waterloo. Lieutenant-General in 1825, made a noble by William I.

The regiment had a strength of 582 men.

— The 144th of the Line

Colonel Ruelle wounded at Leipzig and at Fère-Champenoise. Served in Belgium in 1815. Maréchal de camp in 1832, retired in 1848, GdOLH in 1836. Died in 1865.

306 men were sent; they fought at la Rothière on the Dienville bridge alongside the 145th of the Line, Champaubert, Montmirail, Vauchamps, Laon, Fère-Champenoise and Paris.

● Clavel's Brigade

— The 2nd Naval Artillery Regiment
Colonel Deschamps: OLH in 1813, Baron in 1814, killed at Craonne.

Colonel Pons, appointed 29 February. OLH in 1813, wounded at Brienne. Retired in 1822. Mayor of Perpignan.

There were 29 officers and 205 men in Champagne.

Colonel Schouller with the rest of the regiment was with the Army of the North where Maison sent him to Maubeuge which he defended for three months against the Duke of Saxe-Weimar. He served in Belgium in 1815, was Maréchal de camp in 1832. GdOLH in 1847. He was retired in 1848.

— The 4th Naval Artillery Regiment
Colonel Rouvroy: appointed Colonel in 1805, Baron in 1813, CtLH on 26 February 1814. Killed in front of Paris on 30 March.

The regiment numbered 19 officers and 153 men who were mentioned at Champaubert, Vauchamps, Etoges and Paris. Detachments were at Langres and Arras.

The four Naval Artillery Regiments who were stalwart and numerous distinguished themselves brilliantly during the whole of the campaign.

— The 132nd of the Line
Colonel Cailhassou was in command of the regiment since 1813 but he was cut off in Mainz. The Two-Sicilies at Naples in 1811, LH in 1813, served in the Var in 1815, was promoted to Chevalier in the same year. CrLH in 1852; Mayor of Toulouse.

The regiment with its 380 men was at Saint-Dizier in January, la Rothière on the Rosnay Bridge, at Champaubert, Vauchamps, Berry-au-Bac, Laon, Rheims, Méry, Fère-Champenoise and Paris.

The Major, second in command, was Gibon: OLH in 1804, Réunion in 1813, wounded at Brienne. In Belgium in 1832, CrLH in 1833.

LAGRANGE'S DIVISION
Lagrange was a general in Egypt in 1799, Major-General in 1800, la Rothière, Rosnay, wounded at Champaubert, Vauchamps. Inpsector of the Gendarmerie in the West in 1815. GdCxLH in 1821. Pair de France in 1831, retired in 1832, died in 1853..

● Joubert's Brigade

Joubert, Egyptian Campaign, General in 1811, Brienne, la Rothière, Champaubert, Vauchamps, Fère-Champenoise. Viscount in 1822, retired in 1835.

— The 23rd Light
Colonel Peyris, OLH in 1809, Chevalier in 1810, wounded at Romans on 2 April. Retired in 1826 with the rank of Maréchal de camp then again in 1848.

This regiment came from the 94th of the Line. It was part of the Army of Aragon but was detached from that of Lyons. 76 men joined the 6th Corps in Champagne. They were at la Rohière and Rosnay, Champaubert, Vauchamps, Etoges, Meaux and Paris.

— The 24th Light
Colonel Plazanet, OLH in 1808, wounded at Bar-sur-Aube, retired in 1816. The regiment lined up 530 men at the beginning of the campaign. It was mentioned at Brienne, la Rothière, Montereau, Bar-sur-Aube, then with Duhesme at Arcis-sur-Aube.

— The 37th Light
Colonel Jacquet commanded the regiment in 1813. OLH in the same year. He served in the Jura in 1815, died in 1820. It had been commanded however by Colonel Ghénézer since 1 January.

Ghénézer, called Frederic, was born in Riga, mentioned in Spain. Campaigned with the 6th Corps. CtLH in 1814. Colonel of the 104th in 1815 with Rapp at Strasbourg. Naturalised and retired in 1816.

The regiment was mentioned at Champaubert, Vauchamps, Meaux and Rheims; it comprised only 72 men.

— The 1st of the Line
Colonel Baron de Saint-Martin fought in America in 1777-1781, had commanded the regiment since 1807. Baron 1809, OLH in 1812. Maréchal de camp in August 1814. Served in 1815 and was retired afterwards.

The 194 men of the regiment were at Brienne, Champaubert, Montmirail, Vauchamps, Laon and Paris.

— The 15th of Line
Colonel Levavasseur, LH in 1804, wounded in Spain in 1823 then appointed colonel and Maréchal de camp in the same year. CtLH in 1815, rescinded then reappointed in 1829. Retired in 1832.

In Spain, the regiment sent 340 men who fought at Sens, Vauchamps and Bar-sur-Aube.

— The 16th of the Line
This regiment was in fact with the Army of Lyons; it may have sent a contingent of 129 men.

— The 70th of the Line
Colonel Dumareix, Baron in 1809, OLH in 1811.

According to J.-P. Mir, the 70th of the Line sent 229 men but in the regimental history, it seems that the regiment sent its 3rd Battalion with 112 officers and 420 men, together with the 4th Battalion with 11 officers and 436 men to begin with.

It took part in la Rothière, Champaubert, Vauchamps, la Ferté-sous-Jouarre, Soissons, Laon, Rheims, Fère-Champenoise, la Ferté-Gaucher.

— The 121st of the Line
This regiment was made up of a battalion of 400 men.

● Pelleport's Brigade

Pelleport. Baron in 1809, General and Couronne de Fer in 1813. La Rothière, Champaubert, Vauchamps, Meaux on 28 Frebruary. Not on active list in 1816. Viscount in 1822, Lieutenant-General in 1823. GdCxLH in 1826, Peer of France in 1841. Reserve in 1852.

— The 1st Naval Artillery Regiment
Colonel Maury was in command since 1813. He was wounded and mentioned in despatches at la Rothière then mentioned again the following day at Rosnay which he captured, then at Vauchamps and at Etoges during the night attack, took many prisoners. In Paris he was congratulated by Marmont. Baron in 1814, CtLH in 1815, killed at Ligny.

The regiment numbered 508 men.

— The 3rd Naval Artillery Regiment
Colonel Bochaton. OLH and Baron in 1813, wounded twice at Brienne then at Sézanne; Brienne, Montmirail, Vauchamps, Paris Champigny and Buzenval. In the Alps in 1815. Maréchal de camp in 1832. GdOLH in 1847.

The regiment was made up of 543 officers and men.

— The 62nd of the Line
Colonel Regnault, CtLH in 1813.

The regiment was from the Army of the Pyrenees but it was nevertheless mentioned in Champagne with two battalions numbering 228 men

At Champaubert, Olsufiev's Corps was crushed.
(RR)

General view of the Battle of Montmirail. (RR)

THE BATTLE OF MONTMIRAIL
11 February 1814

With the Russian 9th Corps annihilated, the Emperor turned to Sacken who was advancing towards Montmirail.

The battle

After the first magnificent victory at Champaubert, Napoleon had cut the Army of Silesia in two. He then tried to eliminate the Sacken and Yorks corps which had ventured too far forward. As these two corps tried to join up with Blücher, who was at Vertus (with Kleist and Kapsevich), they converged on Montmirail to turn back towards Etoges and Vertus.

Napoleon regrouped his forces in the vicinity of Montmirail. He left Marmont however with the Lagrange division and the 1st Cavalry corps at Vauchamps to counter any attempt at an attack on the part of Blücher.

The Emperor sent Nansouty forward as the vanguard with part of the cavalry of the Guard under his command, supported by Fournier's brigade from the Ricard division. These men had rested at Fromentières and were guided by Alfred de Montesquiou who knew the country well.

Nansouty reached Montmirail in the middle of the night and dispersed the 300 Karpov Cossacks who were there; they had been sent forward by Sacken who was himself towards Vieux-Maisons. He then climbed the heights of Montcoupot which overlooked the terrain and sent scouts along the road which Sacken would use when he came. They went and explored the Grénaux, the Chouteaux, Marchais and on the Chateau-Thierry road they headed towards le Plenois. Some of them went also towards Pomesson to watch over the Petit Morin valley.

The various troops coming up in support followed each other through Montmirail.

The first to pass was Edouard de Colbert's division with its red lancers, followed by the Poles of the Line and the Chasseurs. This division had just received 600 cavalry as reinforcement consisting of Kirmann Mamelukes, Chasseurs of the Guard of which the 2nd Regiment in which Capitaine Parquin served commanding a company, and the 2nd Scouts of the Young Guard. Behind was the Laferrière-Levesque Division with its Grenadiers à cheval, the Chasseurs and the Dragoons. After that there was Guyot's division formerly commanded by Lefebvre-Desnoëttes (replaced after he was wounded at Brienne). It included the Polish Krasinski Lancers, the Chasseurs à cheval, Letort's Empress's Dragoons and 41 Grenadiers à cheval. Ricard with Boudin's 2nd Brigade went to join Fournier at the Tremblet (or Tremblay). Friant who was expected at 8 o'clock arrived with his Grognards who consisted of Petit with his Grenadiers à pied and Cambronne with his Chasseurs à pied.

Ney, who should have been coming with his Young Guard, had left it to get its cannon unstuck and followed Napoleon by himself to take part in the fighting where his help was invaluable. The Emperor ordered Oudinot to send the Leval and Rottembourg divisions towards Montmirail as quickly as possible; likewise he asked MacDonald to follow Sacken towards la Ferté-sous-Jarre. But the two marshals were too late for there to have been a great victory.

The battle can be split into two large phases: the fighting against Sacken who came back towards Montmirail along the Jouarre road, and the fighting against York who was coming from Chateau-Thierry.

The struggle against Sacken's Russians

York's Prussians were in the process of pillaging Rozay. York had contacted Sacken to suggest a common operation but the two men hated each other and the Russian, who was very sure of himself, answered that he could probably get along very well by himself with his 20 000 men without any help.

Sacken started by occupying the village of Marchais, the Grenaux Farm and the Chouteaux, as well as la Chaise and the Bailly Wood as far as le Plenois. His right was covered by the Courmont Wood.

He placed a battery of two six-pounders facing les Chouteaux. He put his twelve 12-pounders in reserve and on his left he placed two heavy batteries, behind the cavalry. Marchais was very strongly occupied.

THE FRENCH

● **The Infantry of the Line**
Marmont stayed with the Lagrange division at Vauchamps, watching Blücher. Only the Ricard division took part in the battle and brilliantly.
● **The Cavalry of the Line**
This was represented only by Saint-Germain's heavy division.
THE IMPERIAL GUARD
was present and played a very important role.
● **The Infantry**
The Old Guard under Friant (4 750 men)
The Grenadier Guards of the 1st Regiment under Petit and the 2nd Regiment under Christiani (2 437 men)
Cambronne's Chasseurs, i.e. the 1st and 2nd Regiments (2 136 men)
Michel's division made up of Fusiliers, Flankers and the Turin and Florence Velites (3 878 men)
Ney was present but without his Young Guard which was getting its cannon out of the mud.
The Leval division only arrived for the end of Vauchamps.
● **The Cavalry** under Nansouty
— **COLBERT'S DIVISION**
- **Chasseurs and Mamelukes:** 25 officers and 297 men

- the **2nd Chevau-Léger Lancers:** 15 officers and 247 men
- the **2nd Scouts:** 12 officers and 241 men
- the **Poles of the Line:** 6 officers and 149 men
— **GUYOT'S DIVISION** he replaced Lefebvre-Desnoëttes who was wounded (Young Guard)
- **Chasseurs à Cheval:** 511 men
- **Grenadiers à Cheval:** 401 men
- **2nd Scouts:** 313 men
- the **Empress's Dragoons:** 460 men
- **Polish Chevau-légers:** 600 men
- **Light Artillery:** 300 men
— **LAFERRIÈRE-LÉVÊQUE** (2 228 men)
- Chasseurs
- Dragoons
- Grenadiers à Cheval
— **DEFRANCE** (1 061 men)
The 3rd and 4th Guards of Honour
and the **10th Hussars** under de Curély with Picquet

Parquin arrived with reinforcements, Kirmann's Mamelukes and his one company of Chasseurs, on 10 February.

Napoleon sent the Ricard Division to attack Marchais with its four divisional guns. This attack was repulsed and was repeated five times with the help of only one Guards battalion. They were all driven off by the Russian 6th Corps which initially comprised the Pskov, Vladimir, Tambov and Kostroma Regiments plus two companies of Chasseurs and the Ludovkin Cossacks with 6 cannon. But these French attacks kept running up against an enemy which was getting numerically stronger by the minute because the Russian 6th Corps kept feeding the garrison with reinforcements. The cannon in the first battery got stuck in the mud and the rest of the artillery was lined up on the western slope of the ravine situated behind the village. The Cossacks had managed to slip into Pomesson where the fighting lasted until nightfall. The men in the Ricard division rallied Tremblet; they were exhausted by the effort they had made.

The Emperor waited impatiently for the arrival of the 2nd Guards Division commanded by Michel with Mortier, followed by the Defrance Division which arrived towards 3 o'clock.

The Russian 11th Corps occupying the centre of the road advanced and captured the Grenaux Farm. It progressed towards le Tremblet in order to attack Ricard. Towards 3 o'clock, Mortier arrived with Michel and Defrance. The arrival of this reserve reassured Napoleon and he could now launch his attack.

First operation: the Grénaux Farm

It was Ney who directed the attack against the Grénaux farm with the Friant division marching in a column. Parquin who witnessed the scene reports:

"This position was the most difficult point to capture, supported as it was by formidable artillery... Maréchal Ney dismounted and sword in hand at the head of six battalions, had the fire-pans opened because he wanted to make a bayonet charge; this he did and was very successful. The Russians abandoned the farm, their guns and their caissons." This was confirmed by Baron Fain.

Seeing the strength of this attack, Sacken sent some cavalry to take the column on the flank... it was Henrion's men who with the Chasseurs of the Guard saw this threat coming. Henrion immediately ordered: "Column halt! Form a square, arms ready, aim, fire!" As the cavalry was only ten paces away, it was engulfed in fire and turned tail, leaving behind it a large number of bodies. General Henrion got his soldiers back into an attack column and without them reloading, attacked the redoubt which was overrun in spite of the desperate defence by the gunners who fell by their guns. "The Emperor came over to Henrion to congratulate him on his magnificent manoeuvre."

Second Operation: Marchais

Napoleon was irritated by the position of the Russians of the Stawitski division, which was dug in in the village of Marchais. He ordered Ricard to attack again but Ricard answered that Boudin was wounded and Fournier unhorsed, and that his men were worn out and greatly diminished by the great number of their losses. Maréchal Lefebvre and General Bertrand were sent to their help with two battalions of the Old Guard. They attacked Marchais from the north.

Ricard's conscripts, rested and encouraged came out of le Tremblet and moved over to the north-west corner of the village where the greatly disputed "Cour d'Airain" farm was situated. It was this fight which Horace Vernet painted. He had come up to see this terrain which was still intact. Surrounded on all sides, the Russians sounded the retreat. The men climbed down the clock tower which was riddled with cannon shot or came out of the houses. They were massacred and the village was filled with bodies and blood. 400 bodies were removed from the "Cour d'Airain". The Ricard division which had a strength of 1 600 men at the beginning had only 800 at the end of the battle, in other words 50% losses. This was compared to a total loss for the army of 2 000 men.

With these two covering points taken, Napoleon launched his cavalry to support Friant who was advancing towards La Meulière and la Haute-Epine. These cavalry charges were well described by two participants.

Dautancourt's Narrative

Dautancourt explains: *"The Guyot division which I was in, was given the order to move up near the Emperor, on a level with Marchais after les Granges... almost on a level with la Chaise. The Emperor ordered General Guyot to have the old Dragoons of my brigade charge against the enemy which had cut the road. This order was given to me immediately with another one telling me to leave the Grenadiers where we were; only one Grenadier followed me. This was Rousselet, my ordnance sergeant.*

In the field I formed up the Dragoons in columns by platoons, and with me at their head, we set off along the road... In the short time it took us to cover the distance separating us from the enemy we reached le Grénaux... Beyond these houses, a ravine starts which continues west of Marchais and along which runs a little stream which joins the Petit Morin below Pomesson... In spite of terrible fire from the enemy we reached the line and we got to the rear of his right wing which occupied Marchais. The Russians were thus pushed around and threw themselves to their left beyond the ditch which lined the road; some of them escaped across the plain on the left towards a little wood. I was at that moment on the heights beyond the ravine. From this position I could tell the enemy's centre from their right. They nevertheless tried to rally to the left of the road (this was the Epine au Bois Wood)... We moved forward but this infantry was completely routed; it did not wait for us and scattered into the wood..."

SACKEN'S RUSSIANS

(RR)

The quartermaster was Count Rochechouart
SCHERBATOV'S 6th INFANTRY CORPS
● **The 7th Division of Tallisin II**
— **Krischiknikov Brigade**
Pleskov and Moscow Regiments
— **Augustov Brigade**
Sophie and Liebau Regiments
— **Dietricht Brigade**
11th and 36th Chasseurs
● **Bernodossov's 18th Division**
Blagowenzenko Brigade
Vladimir and Dnieprov Regiments
— **Freudenrich Brigade**
Tambov and Kostroma Regiments
— **Metscherinov Brigade**
28th and 32nd Chasseurs
    THE 11th CORPS OF LIEWEN 3RD
● **General Sass's Division**
— **Sokolowski Brigade**
Jaroslav, Crimea and Bialistok Regiments
— **Sevilanov Brigade**
Oshotsk and Kamschatka Regiments
— **Haschlestischev Brigade**
8th and 39th Chasseurs
● **Stzawitsky's Division**
— **Levandowski Brigade**
Vilna and Odessa Regiments
— **Alexeyev Brigade**
Tiraspol and Simbirsk Regiments
— **Kollogribov Brigade**
49th and 50th ChasseursWith 72 cannon for this corps of 26 battalions
    WASSILITSHIKOV'S CAVALRY CORPS
● **Landskoi's Hussar Division**
— **Wadolski Brigade**
Aschtirsk and Marienpol Hussars

— **Kaslowski Brigade**
Alexandria and White Russia Hussars
● **The Dragoon Div. of Panchulidzev II**
— **Uschakov Brigade**
Courland and Smolensk Dragoons
— **Umanez Brigade**
Tver and Kinbur Dragoons
● **The Karpov II Cossacks**
Lukovkin with the Kutainikov 4th, Karpov 2nd, Sementschenko, Lukovkin and Grekov Polks
The 2nd Kalmuks, the 4th Ukraine and the Saint Petersburg Volunteer Cossacks
● **The Artillery**
N° 10, 13 and 18 Heavy Batteries
N° 24, 28, 34 and 35 Light Batteries
The Corps therefore numbered 20 squadrons and 54 cannon.

Kleist's corps and Kapsevich's division from the Langeron division were moving up behind this corps with Blücher's headquarters.

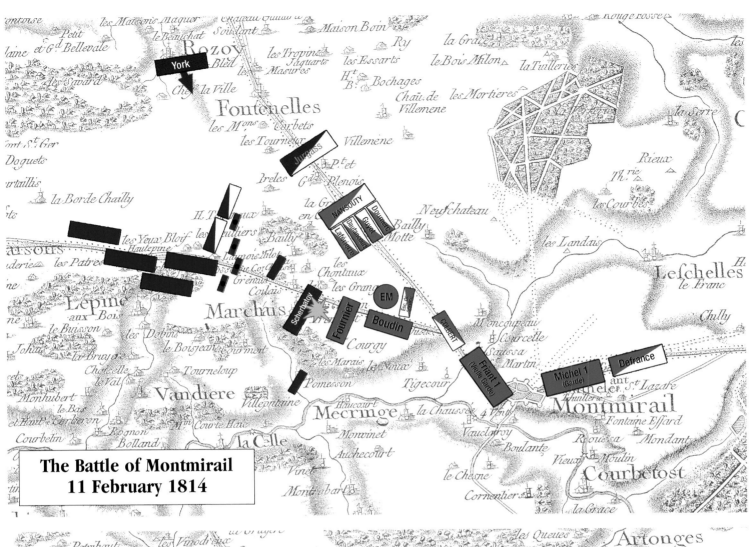

The Battle of Montmirail
11 February 1814

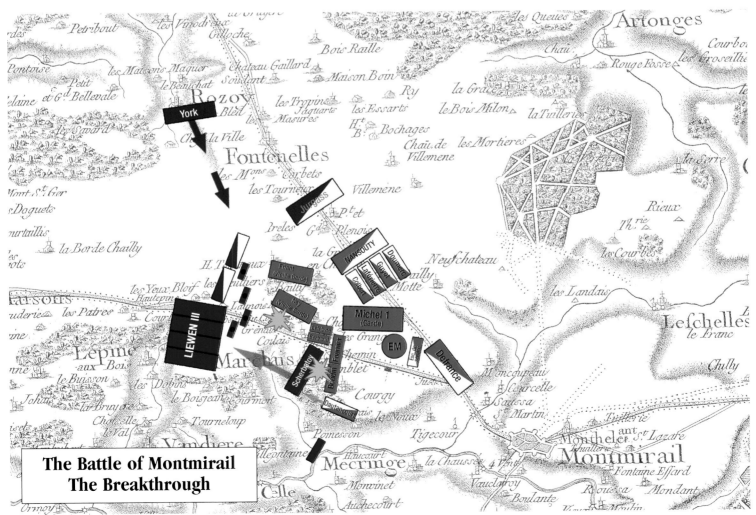

The Battle of Montmirail
The Breakthrough

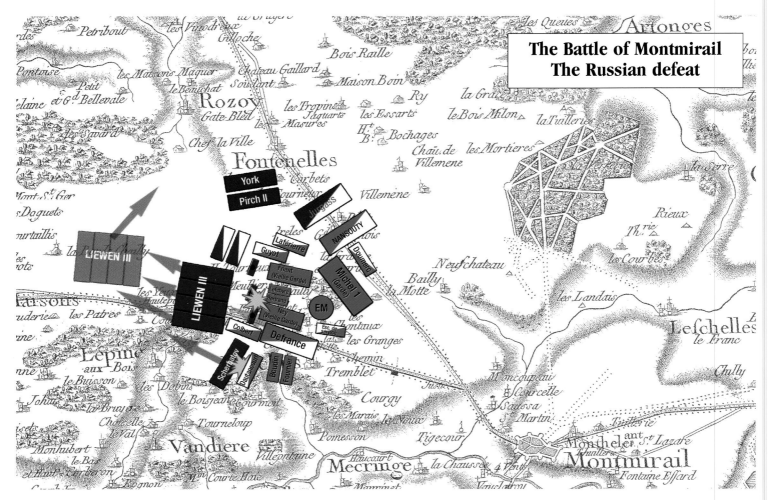

*Montmirail: the Grénaux Farm seen from the entrance to the yard –
a photograph taken at the very beginning of the 20th century; and a shot
taken now from the fields at the rear of the buildings.*
(Photos Jacques Garnier and DR)

At the moment when the fleeing infantry abandoned Marchais and tried to climb the western slope of the ravine, they ran into Dautancourt's Dragoons. He continues: *"It was a nice sight to see the Russians running out of Marchais situated on the left bank of the ravine, go and cross it in front of a little wood called… the Courmont Wood… Their last hope of retreat had to be taken from them and I was about to give the order along those lines when the Dragoons' Squadron Commander (M de Saint-Léger, a good and brave officer) made the same proposal himself. We went off to the left at the bottom of the ravine, near the wood and totally behind Marchais, in order to cut off the escape route which a lot of infantry had already used. They were rallying near some houses called "le Bois Jean"; but some of the Dragoons had entered the wood using a path which came out along the same way by which we were arriving; a few of those intrepid soldiers even went down into the ravine which in truth was not very deep there; they took and butchered anybody who turned up. At the same time, when we came out of the wood, we fell upon those who were rallying. We overran them and the Dragoons, who only stab with their sabres, turned the spot into a real butcher's yard. I nevertheless ordered my men to stop the carnage and rally their squadrons, now that I was sure that the enemy could not escape us; those who remained on the left bank of the river were being chased by our infantry and were surrendering."*

What De Ségur saw

De Ségur who had just arrived with his Guard of Honour gives his version of this fight: *"After two hours, the Emperor seemed to give ground to the Russians on his left and to threaten them with his right wing on the plain. His aim was to draw their forces gathered in the centre from both sides simultaneously. In this manner he lured Sacken with hope on one side, and fear on the other. Sacken believed his plan of attack was going to triumph so he weakened his centre at la Haute-Epine and at l'Epine-aux-Bois to reinforce his right and consummate his victory. In the same way, he reinforced his left wing to maintain his communications on this side with York. It was just what the Emperor expected him to do. It looked just as if the Russians were actually following his instructions and that both sides were obeying his orders.*

Only Friant and four thousand old soldiers remained in the reserve but only half of them were enough. When Napoleon gave the signal they launched themselves into the attack and rushed the Haute-Epine. All those who tried to stand up to them fell and the rest were thrown over their artillery; the forty Russian guns fell silent, the firing stopped.

Then it was hand to hand fighting and soon our bayonets came out of this bloodbath triumphant. With this stroke of genius, the Russian centre was driven in and Sacken was suddenly beaten. He had Liexen move up to la Haute-Epine and towards the plain, but he exposed the flank of this column and the Emperor threw his cavalry of the Guard against it. Grenadiers, Lancers and Dragoons sabered the men in this column which was destroyed. The Russian right wing was driven back up against the ravine at Marchais where a tributary of the Petit-Morin flowed towards Pomesson. But Tallizin replacing Sherbatov who was ill, was obstinate and continued his advance.

While Lefebvre was finishing off the attack at Marchais and its Cour d'Airain with his two battalions, the Guards of Honour formed up into columns and were sent to attack the venturesome Russian right wing."

This charge completed Dautancourt's with his Dragoon Guards.

The Struggle against York's Russians

If the fighting with the Prussians finally got mixed up with the fighting with the Russians, it was later, however, since York only intervened when Sacken asked him for help after deciding to retreat. He asked for a diversion so that the Prussians

The battlefield at Montmirail as it can be seen at the very beginning of winter nowadays at the beginning of the 21st century. Nothing has changed, or very little… (Photo Jacques Garnier)

could get their numerous artillery pieces and miscellaneous caissons out and on the way towards Chateau-Thierry.

York moved slowly protecting his eventual retreat by sending his two heavy batteries towards Chateau-Thierry with one of the infantry brigades, probably William's 8th. He left Vittori and went down to Fontenelle which he reached at two o'clock.

These movements were described by Colin.

"When he saw Sacken retreating and following his request [for help], York advanced. He disposed Jurgass's cavalry near le Plenois where the cavalry, who were stuck in the mud, had to face up to Nansouty's cavalry, which itself had got stuck. Colbert's cavalry supported Friant's merciless advance which continued to push the Russians back against Viels-Maisons. They pushed them further, supported by the Guards of Honour.

When they passed through Presle, the Prussians threatened le Grénaux. So Napoleon directed Mortier to fight the Prussians with Michel's division.

It was Pirch who was leading, but he had kept a battalion of Grenadiers from the

The Guards of Honour are about to charge and salute the Emperor.
(H. Charpentier and RR)

Above: **The fighting at the Cours d'Airain.** *(RR)*

Bottom:
On the evening after the battle, the prisoners were presented to Napoleon.
(RR)

corps, a battalion of the 5th Landwehr and the men of the 13th Silesian Landwehr, in the second line as reserves. While they passed through the Bailly Wood, they were shot at by Friant's men and attacked on the flank by Michel's; two battalions blocked their forward progress. These were the 2nd and 4th Lights who were in the Bailly Wood. The senior officers were decimated and Pirch was wounded after having committed his reserve battalions. He fell back behind Horn's Brigade which was in turn committed towards Presle. Night was falling and York decided to retreat towards Chateau-Thierry where he had left his reserve. Sacken took advantage of the fact to let his artillery slip through towards Viffort then Chateau-Thierry where his soldiers took part in the fighting which bears the name of the battle of Chateau-Thierry."

Napoleon was forced to wait until the following day before starting chasing the defeated enemy because his troops were too exhausted.

The Ricard division was the most affected and went to Montmirail where it rested and regrouped. The Curial division arrived there with its first battery which they had managed to get unstuck with difficulty, the second being still bogged down; Curial had left the 8th Voltigeurs of the Guard to bring it in. Michel and Mortier advanced against the Prussians and Pirch was wounded.

The losses at Montmirail

The result was quite clear: 26 cannon and 260 carriages were taken, 4 500 men were out of action, killed, wounded or captured.

The French lost 1 800 men. Colonel-Major Malet of the 2nd Chasseurs of the Guard died as did the Adjudant-Commandant Allemand of the Headquarters Staff. General Michel was replaced by Christiani. The Battalion Commanders Deschamps and Bertrand of the Fusiliers-Chasseurs were killed. In her Appendix B Madame Mathieu gives a list of the soldiers who were killed at Montmirail or during the following days. This list is precious since it gives the regiments which were present, apart from the Guard.

YORK'S CORPS (or the 1st PRUSSIAN CORPS)

Chief of Staff: Colonel Valentini
Quartermaster: General-Major von Schack
— 1ST DIVISION OF VON PIRCH
● **Lieutenant-Colonel Hiller's Brigade**
1st East Prussia Grenadier Battalion
Corps Grenadier Battalion
West Prussia Grenadier Battalion
● **Lieutenant-Colonel Losthing's Brigade**
Silesian Grenadier Battalion
5th Silesian Landwehr
13th Silesian Landwehr
2nd Hussars of the Guard
East Prussia Regiment and its detachment of Chasseurs
6-pounder Battery N°2
— C. DE MECKLEMBOURG 2nd DIVISION
● **Colonel Lobenthal's Brigade**
1st East Prussia Regiment
2nd East Prussia Regiment
6th Silesian Landwehr
Mecklembourg-Strelitz Hussards
— VON HORN'S 3rd DIVISION
● **Zeppelin's Brigade**
Guards' Infantry Regiment
● **Roudlich's Brigade**
4th Silesian Landwehr
15th Silesian Landwehr
Brandenburg Hussars

— WILLIAM OF PRUSSIA'S 4th DIVISION
● **Bork's Brigade**
Brandenburg Regiment
12th Reserve Regiment
● **Second Brigade**
14th Silesian Landwehr
2nd Hussar Regiment of the Corps
— JURGASS'S 5th CAVALRY DIVISION
● **Colonel Count Henckel-Donnersmark's Brigade**
Four squadrons of West Prussia Dragoons
Plus a detachment of Chasseurs
Four squadrons of Lithuanian Dragoons
Plus the detachment of Chasseurs
● **General-Major von Katzler's 2nd Bgde**
Brandenburg Uhlans
1st New March Landwehr
● **Major von Bieberstein's 3rd Brigade**
3rd Silesian Landwehr
1st and 10th West Prussia
Horse battery N° 1 and 2
● **Colonel von Schmidt's Artillery Reserve**
Horse Batteries N°3 and 12
N°1 and 2 12-pound batteries
In all 104 cannon for the corps
● **Transport pool n°18**
and 2 companies of pioneers.
In all a total of 20 000 men according to Nikitin.

THE BATTLE OF CHÂTEAU-THIERRY
12 February 1814

The victory at Montmirail had to be consolidated by pursuing the two defeated opponents. Once his troops had recovered, Napoleon set off on 12 February, all the more quickly as he had learnt that Blücher was now positioned at Vertus in strength and the threat to Marmont was quite clear if he was left alone at Vauchamps.

Preceded by Colbert's division, Napoleon went first to Viels-Maisons where he left Friant; he took his Grenadier Guards from him, however. Then he returned to the Chateau-Thierry road.

Dautancourt gives the details.

"On the 12th, we only mounted at 8 a.m. and we marched on the road, towards Viels-Maisons. From that village, which had been burnt and sacked by the enemy, we turned sharply right and took a road across country which led to Montfaucon and then to Chateau-Thierry. This road, which follows the left bank of the stream which flows south and joins the Petit-Morin, was just like all the country roads at that period of the year: muddy and very difficult to use; it was therefore clogged up with wagons which were stuck in the mud, enemy baggage which the enemy had abandoned and two or three artillery pieces. These wagons were loaded with the loot the enemy barbarians had pillaged: each one contained furniture, beds and their curtains, women's clothes, and finally even all types of clocks… Others contained bread and brandy and these were distributed, although I did order the officers to keep an eye on this. Apart from these things these were also new rifles and I had some taken for the Dragoons and the Grenadiers who did not have any."

For his part, Mortier had passed Fontenelle and pushed Katzler, who retreated without fighting, back to a position at les Caquerets on a level with Viffort. Behind this York had established a second line of defence on a level with les Noues (Grande and Petite), behind the muddy stream, but in front of this line which was formed by his two mounted brigades astride the road. Jurgass's cavalry was in the rear to which was attached the Russian cavalry behind the Prussian infantry, which made up the left wing. On the right, Heidenreich's Russian cavalry had taken up its positions with three cannon.

Napoleon attacked

Madame Mathieu's text makes it plain. "Sacken drew back his troops behind this line of defence towards Chateau-Thierry. Napoleon joined Mortier who was waiting for him. He decided to set up a battery of eight guns, positioned the Laferrière and his own Guards of Honour on the right wing to cut York off from the Epernay road. On his left wing he grouped the Colbert division and the Cavalry of the Guard.

The Guards of Honour started by driving off the enemy Tirailleurs beyond the stream where several got stuck; then Ségur sent Capitaine Carabène with the 3rd

Krakus reconnoitring.
(J. Girbal. Author's Collection)

Squadron of the 1st Regiment (Picquet's Brigade) to a suspicious-looking wood towards Viffort; they attacked a ten-gun battery of which only three were defended; they cut down the servers and took 34 prisoners. This was the moment when the soldiers of the Old Guard crossing the brook assaulted the village of les Caquerets where they forced their way through fighting hand to hand. Moreover, von Katzler was threatened by the cavalry and decided to fall back towards the bigger part of the Prussian army. The village was occupied by the "Grognards". They reached the Petite Noue.

Napoleon was in Montfaucon and joined Colonel Griois who pushed his cannon forward and who wrote: *"While the gunners were rushing about to get the guns firing, the oakum around the ammunition in a caisson, which had been placed too near one of the artillery pieces, caught fire. We did not notice this and continued riding forward until I noticed the smoke coming out of the caisson. I immediately stopped everything and the gunners managed to tear the burning oakum away before the fire got to the ammunition.*

The explosion would have certainly caused casualties among the gunners and I would have been one of the first victims."

Dautancourt passed les Caquerets, crossed the stream and the little Petite Noue ravine also and reached the vast plain which leads to Nesles; this was a well-ploughed-up plain where horses "got bogged down up to the hams". Mortier took the les Noues Farm then

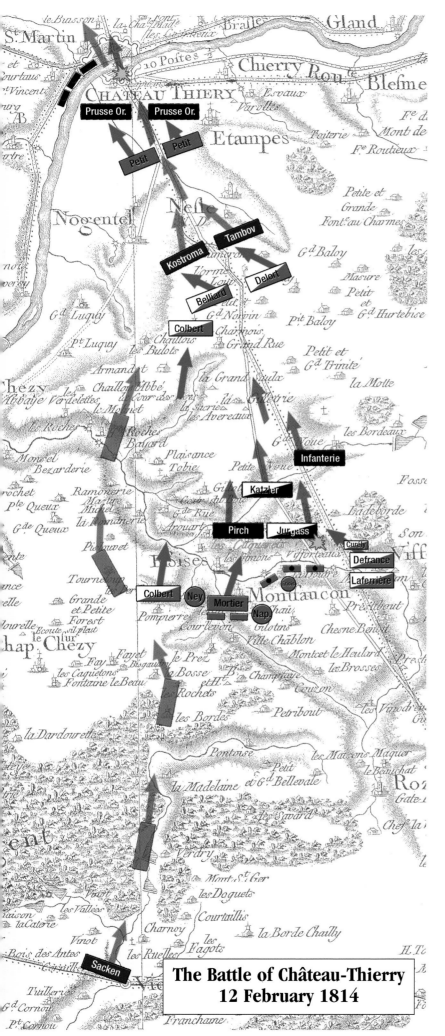

**The Battle of Château-Thierry
12 February 1814**

the la Trinité Farm where the enemy had dug in. Jurgass returned to Nesles with Russian cavalry behind him. The Prussian infantry retreated under the fire from our cannon and was only supported by the Brandenburg Hussars. Picquet's brigade was attacked by Jurgass but in a magnificent charge, the Hussars of the 10th led by Curély, pushed the Landwehr squadrons and the West Prussia Dragoons aside; they then slaughtered their way through the Prussian infantry. This got Curély his promotion to General. He had applied the principles of his former commander Lasalle. Picquet and his Guards of Honour continued this brilliant action pushing back all the enemy cavalry. He was supported on the left by Colbert's cavalry, itself supported by the service squadrons led by Belliard, and on the right by Laferrière's cavalry which Picquet let through.

Last Shots.

Alone on the left, Heindenreich still held out with the Tambov and Kostroma Regiments. Belliard's charge, supported by Letort's Dragoons, drove in the Russians and their General and their artillery were captured.

Dautantcourt admired Letort's action which broke into a 7- or 8-battalion Russian square; Griois' cannon fired on the fleeing soldiers who tried to reach the bridge leading to Chateau-Thierry. Enemy soldiers sheltering in the woods surrendered fearing they might be massacred by peasants exasperated by their abuses. Prince William of Prussia formed up two squares with the 2nd East Prussia Regiment which had succeeded in crossing the bridge among the fleeing soldiers. He tried to get them to attack but Napoleon sent two battalions of Grenadier Guards with their commanding officer, General Petit. Part of the Prussian contingent was captured or put out of action, the rest were able to cross the bridge which was then destroyed. York set up a twelve-gun artillery battery which he had left in the town and they fired over the Marne protecting the approaches to the bridge which was burning. Drouot was given the task of rebuilding the bridge. Planat, his aide de camp, was with him. Firing broke out from in front and Planat was wounded in the legs and taken to cover. This shooting had to be stopped. One soldier swam across the river to bring back a boat which was on the other bank. He was helped by brave inhabitants and succeeded. As soon as the boat approached, an officer and fifteen men crossed over onto the other bank and charged, pushing back the enemy who quit the town which they had sacked and in which they had committed many atrocities.

Napoleon appointed Letort and Bourmont (for his action at Nogent) Major-Generals, and also handed out rewards. A Brigadier from the 3rd Cuirassiers, two Cuirassiers from the 4th, Osowski from the 3rd Scouts or Krakus who had captured 18 prisoners with 8 Lancers and Nélis from headquarters, were all awarded the Legion d'Honneur.

The Leval Division which had been called up in support when it was at La Ferté-Gaucher announced its arrival at Viels-Maison, but this was well after the battle.

Mortier, followed by the division under Christiani – this general had replaced Michel who was wounded – set off on the Soissons road chasing the fleeing enemy.

The men rested at Chateau-Thierry, but there was bad news from Marmont: he was being threatened by Blücher who seemed to want to attack with Kleist's and Kapzevich's corps. Marmont retreated towards Fromentières in the direction of Montmirail, waiting for support. Among those who joined him was Dautancourt's brigade. Dautancourt himself gives the make-up of this contingent.

He had at his disposal.

Some old Dragoons with 19 officers and 387 Dragoons of which 100 were on duty with the Emperor.

Some old Grenadiers: 35 officers and 480 Grenadiers of which 100 were on duty with the Emperor.

That day the Allies lost 3 000 men of which there were 1 800 prisoners, and three cannon on top of those that were abandoned and many wagons were also taken. General Heindenreich was captured.

After the town was regained, Mortier chased the enemy who were on the road to Soissons. Many rewards were handed out by Napoleon which were put forward by Mortier who mentioned: Cicéron from the Turin Velites; Leglise from the Fusilier-Grenadiers; Saint-Charles, Chief of Staff; Pompéjac from the Fusilier-Chasseurs was wounded as were two of his Battalion Commanders, Bertrand and Deschamps who died at Montmirail; the marshal's two aide de camps: Chevreau and Levesque. Yvan decided to look after Mortier who was wounded and to get him to rest. Likewise, Ségur proposed Capitaine Carabène who captured 13 cannon of which 10 were abandoned, and fifty men.

A lot of Légions d'Honneur were awarded to worthy soldiers.

It was now that the penultimate battle of this succession of great victories leading to Montereau was fought. This was the Battle of Vauchamps.

It was now that the last of the great victories of what has come to be called the "Battle of the Five Days" was fought: the Battle of Vauchamps.

Vauchamps: the French break up the Russian squares one by one. (RR)

THE BATTLE OF VAUCHAMPS
14 February 1814

The battle

Because he did not dispose of enough forces to oppose the Prussians, Marmont asked the Emperor for help. He sent the old Prussian Marshal his decorations which he had forgotten at Etoges. He recalled Ricard who was resting but who only brought 800 men with him to make up Lagrange's 2 500 infantry. General von Ziethen commanded the Prussian vanguard in which there was Colonel Blücher, the marshal's son. Their presence was signalled near the Essarts Wood, beyond Mondant and Chilly.

Napoleon got his troops on the march to go to Montmirail first. To help Marmont, he sent Curial's division which was in Montmirail with its cannon, now out of the mud; Friant's Old Guard; Leval's division which was at Viels-Maison; and the Meunier Division.

First Clash

Grouchy gathered his cavalry and went round the future battlefield by the north, passing by Hautefeuille and Serrechamp. Marmont first attacked towards les Essarts Wood which concealed Colonel Blücher's vanguard; he approached Vauchamps, entered the village, and drove off a counter-attack led by Ziethen with two battalions of the 1st Silesian Landwehr Regiment. Grouchy charged a battery in les Essarts Woods and captured two guns; he then chased the fleeing gunners towards the road. Napoleon launched the service squadrons into Vauchamps led by Squadron-Commander Labiffe. The cavalry of the Guard joined with Marmont's escort to drive back an attempt to sally from the village. The occupants of the village were made to flee as were the two battalions of Neumann's Chasseurs. Laferrière who was on the right wing took part in this fighting. On his side, Ziethen sent the 7th Landwehr to try to retake his cannon. He saved the surviving gunners, but Curto held on to four cannon and five caissons. Two companies descending from Corrobert were dispersed. In this fighting, the 1st Silesian lost 1 758 men in all including 25 officers, with almost 800 prisoners. Neumann's Chasseurs held out for a while; some of them sought shelter in the Villeneuve Farm, next to the Perchis Wood.

Dautancourt is precise on this fact: "...the enemy which was in Vauchamps had just left and we were marching towards them. On the left-hand side of the road we were stopped for a moment by enemy infantry which had been left behind and which let us know it was there by shooting at us. My regiment's Polish Chevau-légers, led by Krasinski who were at the head of the division replied with their Tirailleurs.

I stopped my brigade and approached... But the firing drove me back. Those people could not escape from us and while I was moving round the property, some men from the 2nd Chasseurs turned up and in a moment had climbed over the walls. Some Chevau-Légers who had dismounted entered with them and got hold of this small band of enemy who, because they defended themselves, were cut to pieces, most of them. General Krasinski himself took part in this attack and entered with the infantry. A few men tried to get away from behind, I had them stopped."

The Prussian survivors who held Vauchamps tried to get through to Blücher at la Riquetterie, but the Marshal had fallen back on Fromentières.

Guyot's cavalry, with Dautancourt and Krasinski then headed for Janvilliers.

On the right wing, Laferrière-Levesque first drove back the Landwehr onto the Russians. Two Chasseur regiments were in position; these were the 7th and the 37th; they had formed up into a square. But the terrain behind Vauchamps, near a small lake which has since then disappeared, was not very favourable for cavalry charges which it slowed down. The Russians drove off the French cavalry.

Kleist arrived on the enemy's right wing and placed his 10th Brigade in front of Janvilliers from where von Pirch chased the French who had managed to get there. The 12th Brigade was positioned in front of Bièvre. Grouchy's cavalry reached la Marlière. Blücher immediately sent Haack to his right and placed a battalion in the Sarrechamps Farm which

Field-Marshal Blücher. (RR)

General Kleist. (RR)

61

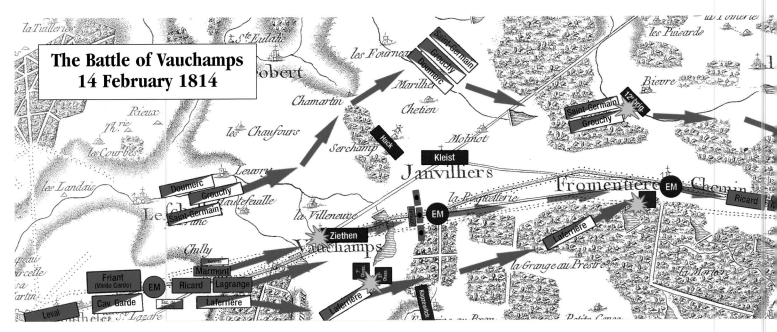

The Battle of Vauchamps
14 February 1814

he fortified as much as he could. On the left wing, the Russians under Kapzewich sheltered at Fontaine au Bron where they received reinforcements in the form of the 1st Silesian regiment.

Grouchy sabres Blücher

Napoleon advanced slowly in order to give Grouchy enough time to get round the enemy right wing. The Emperor got Drouot's artillery – which meant thirty artillery pieces - to advance however and thus weaken the enemy. It was two o'clock and Blücher decided to retreat, abandoning the battalion left at Sarrechamps. He had to protect Etoges which Udom had reached. Blücher and his staff were with the Russian rearguard battalion which was attacked by Laferrière. The latter had to charge three times to drive in the square from which 80 men were captured.

On the enemy's right wing, Kleist had placed Haak and two battalions of the 12th Brigade with the objective of blocking Grouchy, who was getting his Dragoons ready to attack Champaubert, leaving le Mesnil and la Caure on his left. This cavalry did not have its artillery because Couin had not been able to bring it up quickly enough; but the charges followed one after the other and the enemy headquarters staff was only able to get away by sheer luck. Marmont decided to carry on to Etoges at nightfall and fell upon some very surprised enemy troops. Two battalions had branched off towards Féribranges and had reached Etoges from the south. They were men from the 1st Naval Regiment of Lagrange's division (followed by the 130th of the Line). One of the naval gunners made Prince Urusov prisoner after stabbing him with a bayonet; he was captured with 600 men and 8 cannon. Grouchy who had taken part in this movement reported 1 200 prisoners, which Marmont reported as well.

The Glory of Vauchamps

In what was a great battle, the Prussians lost more than 6 000 men of whom 2 000 prisoners, the Russians more than 2 000 as well as 15 cannon. Several flags (mainly Prussian) were captured. The Army of Silesia, trounced, was fleeing towards Chalons.

The Prince of Prussia relates that: *"The French cavalry and infantry got through our ranks, mixed up with the Russians without firing a single shot, knocking us out with rifle butts, hacking with their bayonets, stabbing my men with their sabres; my men were driven back towards the edge of the village where I managed to rally them and continue the retreat up to Bergères-les-Vertus."*

Napoleon returned to Montmirail to stay at the Duke de Doudeauville's Castle; he was the brother-in-law of the Duke of Montesquiou; he got busy rewarding the soldiers their officers had mentioned in despatches.

Grouchy first congratulated his corps commanders Doumerc and Saint-Germain, then asked for his aide de camp to be promoted to Colonel and for the others: Pont-Bellanger, Fontaine and Vial, to be promoted to the rank of Squadron Commander (Fontaine was general Dommanget's aide de camp) and to Sub-Lieutenant for Emeringue of the 8th Chasseurs; for Mangenet and Arbulot of the 4th Cuirassiers, the Legion d'Honneur.

Marmont cited and proposed Capitaine Descrivieux of his own Staff and Colonel Maury of the 1st Naval Regiment who was made a Baron.

In a report by Dautancourt concerning Guyot's division, he says: *"Night fell and although*

it was pitch black, our cavalry charged the squares with the greatest spirit, drove them in and cut them to pieces, whilst the service squadrons (Poles and Chasseurs) charged from the front and created a great bloodbath. General Lion received a scratch. The enemy retreated in great disorder, abandoning their artillery and a large number of prisoners."

40 000 rifles were recovered on the battlefields; they were distributed to the National Guardsmen. On the Allied side, morale was low and disorder had set in. York complained about his soldiers without shoes and somebody said: *"How do you get hold of shoes in a country where everybody wears clogs?"*

So Blücher who was at Chalons was given some shoes. York complained particularly about the build up of wagons - of which there were more and more -cluttering up the army and slowing it down. York was also heard to say that he had the feeling he was leading not soldiers but *"a band of brigands"*. Their pillaging and atrocities made the peasants react very violently.

After this series of very brilliant victories, the effort had to be channelled against the Army of Bohemia which was moving towards Paris; this was all the more necessary as the treachery of Sens had forced Allix to leave, and he did not get on with Pajol. Napoleon's next objective had been decided for some days now: Montereau and its two bridges. However, Grouchy and Marmont were worried by the arrival of de Wrede's Bavarians towards Montmirail; but this corps withdrew towards the Army of Bohemia without fighting.

Marmont was therefore left at Montmirail and Etoges where he got hold of a further 630 prisoners, who had come out of hiding in the woods. Everybody was directed towards la Ferté-sous-Jarre. In this little town, the bridge had been repaired and the first orders received concerned the artillery at Chateau-Thierry where

General Vincent kept the 150 Guards of Honour. Ney was with Meunier's and Durial's divisions, waiting for Leval's division with whom he then marched. Drouot followed with the Old Guard and its artillery; Leval's division followed with Saint-Germain's cavalry under Grouchy's command.

This was followed by the cavalry of the Guard for which, replacing General Lion, Dautancourt had had to leave his brigade to take command of the service squadrons furnished by the Old Guard regiments. He noted down their strength. With Napoleon there were:
- with the Polish Lancers: 6 officers and 69 men
- with the Chasseurs à cheval: 5 officers and 90 Chasseurs
- with the Empress' Dragoons: 5 officers and 92 men
- with the Grenadiers à cheval: 6 officers and 96 Grenadiers

Ney was at Montmirail, but he moved to Meaux quickly with the column of prisoners and General Urusov, escorted by the 113th and its Colonel. Napoleon was hurrying towards Meaux where he arrived at the Trilport Bridge which MacDonald had had blown up, like the one at la Ferté-sous-Jouarre; the Emperor crossed over in a boat and galloped to Meaux with a few Polish Lancers and Chasseurs and set himself up in the bishop's palace. Repair work started on the Trilport Bridge but nobody had expected Napoleon to arrive so soon.

Grouchy arrived at la Ferté and Marmont discovered that there were lots of Cossacks near Montmirail; he chased these adventuresome troops from the town, beat and drove back General Diebitsch. When Grouchy visited him, Marmont said *"he [Diebitsch] was a General who had qualities but also two faults: a lack of resolution and the inability to take a decision".*

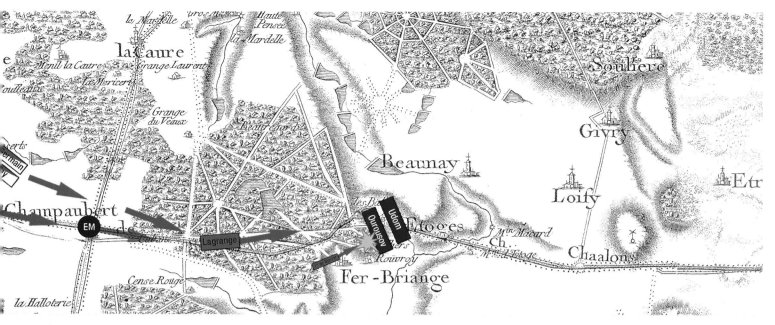

And Now…

With the "Battle of the Five Days", Napoleon beat Blücher's Army of Silesia; but Blücher was able to regroup at Châlons-sur-Marne and be reinforced by Winzigerode's and Bülow's corps. The old Prussian Hussar was just waiting for the opportunity to get the Corsican caught in a pincer movement between his Army of Silesia and the Army of Bohemia.

Napoleon had to choose between two strategic options: he could either chase Blücher, without giving him time to re-form; or he could attack Schwarzenberg who was worried by the French army's latest successes and had therefore called a halt to his march on Paris which he could resume whenever he wanted.

Taking advantage of his central position, the Emperor chose to leave only Marmont facing the Army of Silesia and launched himself against the Army of Bohemia hoping to be able to deal with it before Blücher came back.

On 17 February, Napoleon started his journey towards Montereau. He drove back and dispersed any enemy he met on the way as far as Provins; then he went to Nangis. The Spanish Dragoons under General Treillard arrived. The Emperor gave battle at Mormans where his cavalry was brilliant in action and Victor got as far as Salins before going to Montereau; this was to be the fourth of the brilliant victories which were due to his personal genius and to the quality of the troops he commanded. In order to understand this manoeuvre at Montereau properly, one has to go back a bit in time in order to see how Schwarzenberg had progressed in the meantime.

On 10 February, while Napoleon was sorting Blücher out, Schwarzenberg had started to move westwards on both banks of the Seine and the Yonne. Wittgenstein and de Wrede were advancing towards Nogent-sur-Seine and Bray. The Prince of Wurtemberg entered Sens. Barclay de Tolly's reserve and the Lichtenstein Light Cavalry were between Troyes and Nogent. Platoff's Cossacks marched from Joigny towards Montargis and towards Orléans. On 11 February, Wurtemberg entered Sens. The French who were posted as observers out in front facing the Allies fell back to the Yères. The Allies' march on Paris seemed to be irresistible. Fortunately, the news that Blücher was having problems reached Schwarzenberg. This bad news continued and the Coalition sovereigns met at Nogent where they decided to stop their advance, and even to fall back, while waiting to find out exactly what was going on. On 14 February, after Vauchamps, Napoleon decided not to waste any more time and got ready to attack Schwarzenberg. The greatest difficulty was to find out exactly where this new opponent was. He had to make a choice.

Should he launch himself at the head of the meagre forces (about 20 000 men) he had at his disposal against this large army's flank, by the shortest route (Montmirail and Provins)? Or should he go and give his marshals a hand with a frontal attack?

He chose the second option. As soon as he was able to reach the marshals – leaving Grouchy and Leval nevertheless to cover Paris – he announced what his objective was to be: Montereau. In order to study this battle, we went, my friend Jacques Garnier (for whom this is one of his favourite subjects) and I, to visit the bridges and the lie of the land and brought back several interesting photographs.

KLEIST'S CORPS

(RR)

He joined Blücher at Vertus for the Battle of Vauchamps alongside Kapzevich.

● **KLUX'S DIVISION**
— **Schalensee's Brigade**
1st West Prussia, 6th Reserve
Silesian Tirailleurs
— **Second Brigade**
1st Pomeranian Landwehr and Silesian Uhlans
● **PIRCH 1ST DIVISION**
— **Jagov's Brigade**
2nd West Prussia, 7th Reserve

— **Second Brigade**
3rd Pomeranian Landwehr
7th Silesian Landwehr Cavalry

● **ZIETHEN'S DIVISION**
— **Colonel Leptov's Brigade**
1st Silesian Regiment
10th Reserve
Silesian Tirailleurs
— **Second brigade**
2nd Landwehr of the Electoral Marches
New March Dragoons
Prince Augustus' Division
— **Funk's brigade**
2nd Silesian Regiment
11th Reserve
— **Second Brigade**
2nd Landwehr of the Electoral Marches
New March Dragoons
Roeder's Division
— **Wrangel's Brigade**
East Prussia Cuirassiers
Brandenburg Cuirassiers
— **Haake's Brigade**
Silesian Cuirassiers
2nd Silesian Hussars
Silesian Landwehr Cavalry
— **Mutius' Brigade**
8th Silesian Landwehr Cavalry
1st West Prussia Landwehr

7th of the Electoral Marches
Kapzevich's 10th Infantry Corps
These troops were part of Langeron's corps. They joined Blücher at Vertus and fought at Vauchamps.
● **URUSSOV'S DIVISION**
— **Schindschin's Brigade**
Archangelgorod Regiment
Schlusselburg Regiment, Old Ingrelia Regiment
— **Sutkov's Brigade**
7th and 37th Chasseurs
● **TURTSCHANINOV'S DIVISION**
— **Schapskoi Brigade**
Viatka, Starokolsk, Olonez Regiments
— **Wassilttschikov's Brigade**
29th and 45th Chasseurs

KORF'S CAVALRY CORPS
Koch also placed these cavalrymen in Langeron's Corps

Real Numbers given by Koch.
In order to estimate the strength of those present, Koch gives the following estimates:
For an Infantry Battalion
For the Prussians, a battalion meant about 400 men. This estimate was brought up to 600 men according to Plotho, although this difference is subject to debate.
For the Russians, a battalion was 500 men strong.
For a Cavalry Squadron
For the Prussians this meant 120 men in a squadron.
For the Russians it was 100 men per squadron.
For the Artillery
To serve one gun, Koch counted 15 men for the Prussians and 12 for the Russians without counting the train.

● **BARASDIN II DRAGOON DIVISION**
— **Gerngros Brigade**
Mittau and New Russia Dragoons
— **Pohr's Brigade**
Moscow and Kargopol Dragoons
— **Emmanuel's Brigade**
Scharkov and Kiev Dragoons
Pantschulidsev 1st Chasseur Division
— **Denisiev Brigade**
Tchernigov, Arsamas and Seversk Chasseurs
— **Pahlen II Brigade**
Livonia and Dorpat Chasseurs

● **WITTE'S COSSACK DIVISION**
— **Scherbatov's Brigade**
1st, 2nd and 3rd Ukraine Regiments
— **Grekov 8th Brigade**
7 Cossack Regiments

THE BATTLE OF MORMANS
17 February 1814

As a result, on the morning of 17 February, Napoleon came out of Guignes by the Nangis road. Victor's corps (Duhesme's and Chataux's divisions) led the march. It was supported by Gérard's two divisions. The little army was supported on the right by Milhaud's cavalry and on the left by that of Teillard. Oudinot and MacDonald were coming up behind.

Meanwhile de Wrède headed for Bray. Wittgenstein was the vanguard and already some of his Hussars were at Fontainebleau. Hardegg had reached Moret and Pahlen was in front of him. The latter, warned that the French were approaching, had formed up into a column with two regiments of Cossacks, Soumy's Hussars and Tchuguyev's Uhlans. In front of Mormans, Victor met the vanguard of Wittgenstein's corps, commanded by General Pahlen. Indeed Wittgenstein had delayed obeying the order to interrupt the offensive, and had continued his forward march, only to find himself left "high and dry". The attack was very sudden. While the French cavalry went round the town, Gérard and the 32nd of the Line entered Mormans using their bayonets. The Russians were expelled from the town and Drouot's artillery cut swathes through them. Hardegg's division was drawn into the rout. The Allied infantry tried to protect its retreat by forming up two squares.

But the French cavalry broke them up and got them to surrender. With Pahlen, Revel's and Selenginsk's regiments were wiped out and the Smolensk, Estonia and the 25th Chasseurs lost a lot of men. The cavalry and the artillery suffered a great deal. Wittgenstein was able to fall back on the Bavarians at Nangis, Provins and Bray but with the loss of 4 000 men.

Napoleon gave all his time and energy to taking advantage of this opportunity so that he could reach the Seine before the Allies did and beat them one after the other before they had time to re-group. He therefore directed Oudinot to the left towards Provins and Nogent, MacDonald to Donnemary and Bray where de Wrède had withdrawn, leaving a few Bavarians at Montereau.

Supported by Gérard and the cavalry corps, Victor moved to the right towards Villeneuve where he met Lamotte's Bavarian division near Valjouan withdrawing in the direction of Montereau. Covered by the artillery, Gérard deployed and attacked from the front with the 86th of the Line, while the rest of his corps turned the enemy. Assailed by Gérard's infantry and Doumerc's cavalry, Lamotte's division was badly mauled and was close to surrendering. However, Victor used his cavalry badly and did not pursue the enemy towards the bridges at Montereau; he stopped at Salins. Napoleon was furious and on the following day, he would recall that the Duke of Bellune had not had the capacity to reach and take control of the bridges in time.

Napoleon formed three columns. On the right, Chataux, in the centre Gérard with the Paris reserve, on the left Duhesme. These infantry divisions were flanked on the right by Milhaud with Piré and Briche, and on the left by Kellermann with Lhéritier who had come from the Vth Corps, and Trelliard and Ismert. The Guard set itself up at Nangis. Meanwhile General Pajol's corps also headed to Montereau. Its part in the battle will be discussed later.

It is necessary to analyse the results of this first part of the manoeuvre.

It was true that two victories were won on 17 February but they were not really complete. Wittgenstein's, de Wrède's and Wurtemberg's corps staggered (one could even say scattered) as they were on the right bank of the Seine were certainly beaten; but they had not been cut off from the Seine, they had not been "kicked into touch". Worse, the Allies were now warned of Napoleon's arrival and they started to make their preparations. To sum up, the shot had missed its target. Who was responsible for this?

Victor, whose flabbiness increasingly irritated Napoleon? Napoleon himself who should have realised that a frontal attack would oblige the enemy to fall back on their supporting forces?

Could it have been the disproportion between the sizes of the two armies which made working out a true manoeuvre difficult? In spite of everything, Napoleon did not give up hope; he still thought he could complete his manoeuvre successfully by seizing the bridges at Montereau and by taking the enemy corps - in position at Bray and Nogent-sur-Seine - from behind, from the left bank of the Seine.

THE BATTLE OF MONTEREAU*

18 February 1814

What was the situation on the morning of 18 February 1814?

Warned as we have seen of the French attack, Schwartzenberg decided to concentrate on the left bank of the Seine to gain the necessary time for this movement and left the Prince of Wurtemberg's corps at Montereau with orders to guard the bridges and to stop the French from crossing them.

At Nogent, Wittgenstein was able to cross the Seine and held the passage facing Oudinot. De Wrède's Bavarians had also crossed the river at Bray and MacDonald had been unable to force the passage. Some Bavarians were in Montereau and took part in the battle.

Wurtemberg held Montereau. The town was built between the left bank of the Yonne and the Seine. The Saint-Maurice suburb was on the right bank of the Seine at the foot of the small but steep Surville hill. There were two stone bridges, one over the Seine and the other over the Yonne.

Since his orders were to defend the bridges at all costs, Wurtemberg thought that it would be prudent to take up a position on the Surville plateau. He was obviously taking a risk, having his back to the river with a very inadequate escape route in the case of his having to withdraw.

The actors get into place

Wurtemberg disposed his troops as follows.

On the west of the lay-out, on the Valence road the 2nd and 4th Wurtemberg Chasseurs Regiments were deployed (1 200 sabres with one squadron assigned to the right wing) with two squadrons of Archduke Ferdinand's Austrian Hussars.

The village of Villaron/les Ormeaux formed a salient in the Allied lines. Wurtemberg positioned Stockmayer there at the head of three Chasseur battalions, 2 battalions of the 3rd Light and one from the Colloredo Regiment.

* With the participation of Jacques Garnier.

Schaeffer was at Surville with two Colloredo battalions; Zach's 15th Regiment was in front of the village. A 12-gun battery was fortified at the north-west of the Surville parc. Doering's brigade was to the rear of les Ormeaux, the 2nd and 7th Regiments were on the Villaron

Napoleon remained an artilleryman at heart. Here he is serving a Horse Artillery canon and saying to his worried entourage that "the cannonball which is supposed to kill me has not yet been smelted…" (RR)

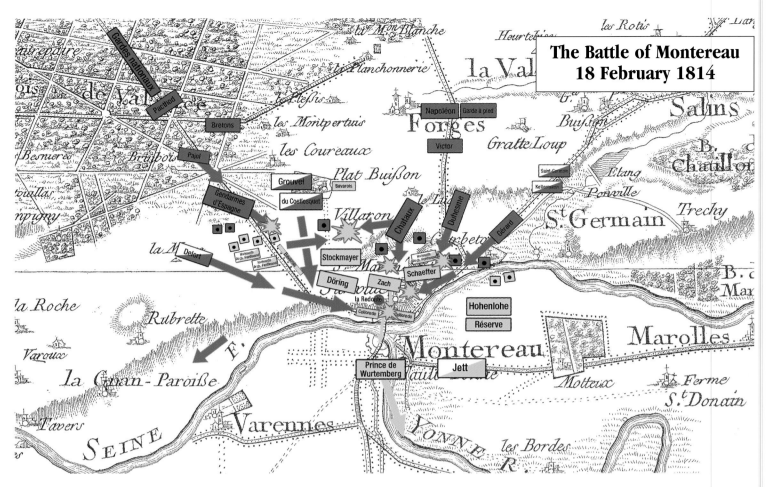

road. One of Zach's battalions and one from the 9th were set up with artillery at Saint-Martin. A screen of Landwehr made up the frontline.

To the east Courbeton was occupied and a battery protected the way out of Bellefeuille. A squadron of Ferdinand's Hussars was there.

THE 4th CORPS OF THE PRINCE OF WURTEMBERG

This corps was made up of Wurtemberg and Austrian troops. A few Bavarians also took part in the battle. It was commanded by the royal Prince of Wurtemberg.

Chief of Staff: Colonel Boyer de la Tour
Commanding the cavalry: Lieutenant-General Prince Adam of Wurtemberg
Chief of Staff of the cavalry: Colonel von Bismark
Commanding the artillery: General Count Franquemont
Chief of Staff of the artillery: Colonel Bangold
● **THE VANGUARD**
— **General Walsleben's Cavalry Brigade**
Archduke Ferdinand's Austrian Hussars
(5 squadrons, 900 men)
5th Wurtemberg Chasseurs à cheval Regiment under Colonel de Mylius (4 squadrons, 600 men)
General Baron Stockmayer's Infantry Brigade
9th Chasseurs à pied under Count Lippe
(2 battalions)
10th Light Infantry Regiment under Colonel Landesberger (2 battalions)

BATTLE CORPS
● **LIEUTENANT-GENERAL BARON KOCH'S INFANTRY DIV.**
— **General von Döring's Brigade**
2nd, 3rd and 7th Infantry Regiments (all with 2 battalions)
One six-gun 6-pounder artillery battery
— **General Prince Hohenlohe-Kirchberg's Brigade**
4th Infantry Regiment (2 battalions)

6th Infantry Regiment under Colonel Himoff
(2 battalions)
One six-gun artillery battery and two Austrian position batteries from Bianchi's corps, 12 guns
— **Major-General Schaeffer's Austrian Brigade**
15th Regiment under Colonel Zach (3 battalions)
Colonel Prince Joseph Colloredo's Infantry Regiment
(3 battalions)
One six-gun 6-pounder artillery battery and one six-gun 12-pounder battery
— **General von Jett's Cavalry Brigade**
Duke Ludwig's 2nd Chasseurs à cheval Regiment (4 squadrons)
Prince Adam's 4th Chasseurs à cheval Regiment (4 squadrons)
3rd Dragoon Regiment (4th Squadrons)
One six-gun Horse Artillery battery
Certain elements of this 4th Corps did not take part in the battle.
— **General Hirsch's Austrian Brigade**
2 two-battalion regiments
This brigade was attached to the 1st Corps; it took up position in Montereau and in the evening retreated towards Cannes.
● **COUNT IGNAZ HARDENBERG'S AUSTRIAN DIVISION**
Made up of General Raigecourt's single brigade, it comprised infantry, cavalry and Cossacks. It took Moret on 15 February.
This 4th Corps regrouped 15 000 infantry and 3 000 horses.

Further back one of Doering's battalions was in the tile factory in the Saint Nicholas suburb. The Wurtemberg cavalry was supported by Bavarian infantry under Bianchi, spread out in the tile factories all along the Paris road; they were accompanied by a battery.

A lot of artillery (54 guns) was spread out along the whole of the frontline from St Martin's Farm on the right of the Paris road on the left.

The forward positions were placed at Forges, Garde-Loup, le Luat, les Coureaux, le Plat Buisson and the small valley of le Four à Chaux. They were eventually driven back to Surville. On the right bank of the Seine there was a general reserve under the Prince of Hohenlohe. It was made up of a brigade of infantry (4th and 6th of the Line) in front of the Chateau of Motteux, twelve squadrons of cavalry and two artillery batteries in the Saint-Maurice suburb with Jett.

Facing this disposition was Maréchal Victor under orders to command the initial attack. He could only muster his own corps and Pajol's, about 15 000 men.

Victor's 2nd Corps comprised the 5 000 men in the Duhesme and Chataux divisions, as well as the Lhéritier Dragoons. Gérard's reserve division (4 500 men regrouping Dufour's and Hamelinaye's divisions) reinforced this corps.

Pajol's corps was made up of 1 500 cavalry from the Delort, Du Coëtlosquet and Grouvel brigades, 800 Gendarmes who had returned from Spain with Capitaine Dourtre (their worth meant that they were attached to the Guard) and 3 700 National Guards from the Pachtod Division. They came mainly from Brittany and Eure-et-Loire. They were supported by 16 light artillery pieces. These men were not of equal worth. The Spanish Gendarmes were elite troops, the National Guardsmen were not well-equipped, but were used to guns, could shoot and were spirited enough. The problem was mainly with the cavalry. They were young and lacking in experience; some of them had never ridden a horse till two weeks earlier. Most of them did not know how either to lead a horse or to handle their weapons. Neither did they know how to ride their horse holding the reins with one hand and their sabre with the other.

The battle can be split into two distinct phases: the *"observation round"* between 8 a.m. and 2 p.m. then the decisive attack from 2 p.m. onwards.

The First Phase: Observation

Coming out of the Valence woods, Pajol went to the Dragon Bleu and took the Plat Buisson and les Coureaux before marching towards les Ormeaux, behind Villaron (the older name for les Ormeaux, apparently?)

In order to make up for the incomplete victory at Villeneuve and catch up on lost time, Victor debouched out at 9 a.m. in front of the enemy positions. The 2nd Corps marched in the lead: the Chataux Division went to attack Villaron which it took. Unfortunately it had to

fall back due to the intense fire from the Prince of Wurtemberg's artillery with resulting heavy losses, among whom was their General, killed in the Saint-Nicolas suburb near the bridges. After this action which failed, the struggle continued without advantage for either side. It was 1 p.m.

The Duhesme Division arrived in turn and took up the attack, supported by the second brigade from Chataux's division which tried to go round the enemy left wing. Chataux, Victor's son-in-law, died in this action which failed anyway. The struggle continued without advantage for either side. It was 1 p.m. It was at this moment that Gérard arrived from Salins with his two divisions.

Meanwhile from 4 a.m. onwards, Pajol's corps got moving, with Delort in the lead followed by the rest of the cavalry then the infantry. It marched from le Chatelet to Valence without being worried. It was barely slowed down by the presence of some Austrians when it went through the Valence Wood. The first problem occurred when they came out of the Valence wood where the road reaches the Dragon Bleu and La Marre Farm. Moving towards the Surville plateau, the vanguard was greeted by shots from a six-gun artillery battery. Pajol took his fighting formation with the Spanish Gendarmes, the Breton Guards and the artillery in the centre, 8 battalions and two brigades of cavalry on the left wing and 7 battalions and one brigade of Chasseurs on the right wing. 15 battalions remained in reserve in the wood.

In spite of the artillery fire, this attack had more opportunities than Victor's and succeeded in advancing to the beginning of the slope towards Montereau when Gérard entered the line. Napoleon had just dismissed Victor and replaced him by Gérard who was much more dynamic.

Pajol took les Coureaux and le Plat Buisson and continued to advance. As soon as he arrived, Gérard realised that the opposing artillery would resist any French advances for as long as it was not reduced. He therefore had the 40 guns he had available moved up and they silenced the Allied shooting. In order to accomplish its mission the French artillery had advanced a bit too far; Wurtemberg realised this and launched a counter-attack led by General Doering (2nd and 7th Wurtemberg Infantry). Berthier's aide de camp, Lecoulteux, was captured.

The joint action of the French gunners firing shot at the attackers and the 500 infantrymen charging with fixed bayonets threw Doering back. At the same moment, Pajol's left wing succeeded in taking the Villaron-les Ormeaux parc from behind and drove out the defenders. It is worth mentioning that this attack was guided by M. Moreau, the Mayor of Montereau (For Koch, Doering who became a Major-General did not arrive before the end of February).

It was now 2 p.m. The keenness of Pajol's and Gérard's attacks had enabled the situation to be re-established. The arrival of Napo-

The Bridges at Montereau, seen from the Surville Heights. (Photo Jacques Garnier)

The bridges over the Seine and the Yonne, the targets of the French move. (RR)

leon on the battlefield followed by two battalions of the Old Guard allowed the real attack to begin which then entered the realms of legend.

The Second Phase: the Battle

The Emperor immediately ordered the Surville plateau to be attacked and organised his army in four columns.

The first was placed on the road to Paris under Pajol; the second by Villaron towards les Ormeaux, the third against the Chateau and the last through Courbeton with Gérard. The Guard was in front of Forges which had been already taken. Wurtemberg started to withdraw. Schaeffer was ordered to defend the Chateau; Gérard who had taken command started by neutralising the enemy artillery. At 4 p.m., the Prince of Wurtemberg left Surville but the enemy retreat was carried out in disorder through the streets of Montereau where everything was incredibly clogged up. The inhabitants shot at the runaways. Pajol, who until then had been firing grapeshot at the enemy masses with his artillery, ceased firing. He ordered General Delort to gallop with his brigade to the bridges in Montereau, down the steep slope of the road which went into the town. He told him he would be following him at the

General Gérard, one of the heroes of Montereau. (RR)

same speed with the du Coëtlosquet and Grouvel Brigades. Lefebvre took the staff and Napoleon's escort with him and followed.

General Delort, answering the officer who brought the order from Pajol, said "In truth, I believe they must be mad to make me charge with cavalry like that." He nonetheless had them bare sabres, formed up his brigade into columns by platoons and started to trot, then to gallop. Half way down the slope he ordered them to charge. *The brigade rolled down the hill like an avalanche"* (Pajol) bowled over everything in its path, went straight through the firing from two battalions of the Colloredo Regiment, posted in the first houses of the town. The enemy had mined the bridges but the suddenness of the charge did not give them time to light the fuses. Delort's column crossed the bridges. The enemy fled in all directions, followed by Gérard's infantry.

At the head of his other two brigades, Pajol followed at the same speed. When he crossed the bridge over the Seine, a mine exploded without causing the bridge to collapse completely. Pajol's horse was killed under him, his fall reopened some of his old 1813 wounds and he had to be taken to Paris for treatment. His corps was disbanded and spread out among the others. To console Victor, Napoleon entrusted him with the Charpentier and Boyer de Rébeval Divisions. Pachtod went with Oudinot.

The cavalry had advanced so fast that it now found itself out on a limb from the rest of the army. It would be in danger should the enemy rally and turn back. Fortunately, the panic was so great that Wurtemberg did not think to take measures for such an operation, especially as the very irritated inhabitants were also taking part in the battle with any means at their disposal. Hohenlohe protected the runaways who tried to rally.

Napoleon was to say, *"Among my generals there's only Pajol who knows how to lead a cavalry charge."* It has to be said that Lasalle and Montbrun were no longer around and that Murat had changed sides…

One of the explanations for this success apart from the intrinsic worth of both Delort or Pajol, is given by the latter's son in his book about his father.

"You had to have General Pajol's boldness to risk a charge like that with two-week old cavalry; you had to know what could be expected from each man when a formidable hurrah drew the whole mass of men forward. With old horsemen who mastered their mounts it may not have been successful. With young inexperienced people obliged to hang on to the reins and to the saddles, one had to expect what in fact happened: one released a flood of horses, mad with pain from the spurs and the bit. Once the three brigades were launched, even if one had wanted to it would have been impossible to stop them at the front so violent was the impetus from the rear."

Meanwhile on the other side of the plateau, the Guards' and Gerard's infantry pushed the runaways in front of them. The artillery of the Guard peppered them with shot. Even Napoleon was seen to aim a canon, answering the man who advised him not to take unnecessa-

ry risks with *"the cannonball which is for me has not been cast yet"*. This legend is debatable. The defenders of Surville, defeated, were in full flight running down the steep slopes leading to the bridges.

The day nonetheless cost the French 2 580 men out of action. On the other side the enemy lost 3 000 killed or wounded with just as many prisoners, 4 flags and 6 cannon. Zach was captured with 200 men before the bridge by a sub-lieutenant of the 133rd who was awarded the Légion d'Honneur for his action. The two Colloredo battalions were wiped out in front of the bridges they were protecting.

Wurtemberg's resistance nevertheless permitted Colloredo's corps which had ventured as far as Fontainebleau to get away. On 21 February, the army moved up the left bank of the Seine heading for Méry; in the evening, Napoleon was at Nogent. His intention was to cross the Seine at Méry and head for Troyes to get there before Schwartzenberg who was retreating. The Emperor hoped to block his line of retreat and to force him to fight facing east before

Below, from left to right:
In the afternoon Pajol, coming out of the Valence Wood, broke up the Wurtembergers and the Bavarians. *(RR)*

During the second attack on Villaron, General Huguet-Chataux was mortally wounded at the head of his brigade. He died in Paris the following 8 May. *(after Siméon Fort, Musée de l'Empéri)*

Leading the service squadrons, Lefebvre supported Pajol's charge. That day, the Marshal handled his sabre just as he did on his first day. *(Composition by V. Huen. RR)*

At Montereau, Pajol and his cavalry made one of the most famous charges of the Imperial period. (C. Langlois, Musée de Versailles, RMN)

he joined up with Blücher. De Wrède left Bray since he had MacDonald and Milhaud in front of him and who followed him.

Alarmed, the whole Army of Bohemia fell back on Troyes which Napoleon reached on 25 February. Oudinot supported by Kellermann and Saint-Germain had Méry as their target. Blücher was also heading for this point. Napoleon was reassured and was going to deal with him.

Once again it was a beautiful manoeuvre but some beautiful battles ended up with a result which was more than uncertain.

The Montereau manoeuvre did not produce the results which were expected because the difficulties were almost insurmountable.

The task was too hard for a small army, diminished and worn out as it was by five days of fighting. The French had however taken the bridges, which was the main thing, and forced Schwartzenberg to retreat.

A legendary cavalry charge

Montereau, 18 February 1814. At about 4 p.m., victory was almost complete. But the Wurtembergers could still blow up the bridges which would make pursuit impossible. It was then that General Pajol launched his legendary charge enabling him to gain control of the bridges before they were destroyed. The General's son relates:

"It was now 4 p.m. and the enemy's retreat was a total shambles through the town of Montereau where the congestion was unbelievable. Pajol ordered his artillery which was posted on the first bend of the road and which was showering the enemy masses crowding up the streets to stop firing. He also ordered General Delort to gallop with his

bled down into Montereau like an avalanche, knocking over anything in front of it without being stopped by the heavy firing from the Colloredo Regiment which had been posted in the first houses of the suburbs to protect the retreat. The Delort column rapidly crossed the bridges over the Seine and the Yonne without giving the enemy the time to blow them up. They passed through Montereau in a flash and the town suddenly found itself rid of the enemy who were fleeing in all directions, vigorously encouraged by the Guards' and Gérard's infantry which were coming up on the double by the Nangis road and the Surville path [1].

It is worth noting that when visiting the same location, it is difficult to imagine this charge. If it followed the road going down into the town, as Pajol relates, then it can only have been along the Valence road, which would confirm Stouff's text [2]. But when it reaches Saint-Nicolas, this road makes a right hand bend which is at so sharp an angle that it is hard to imagine a cavalry charge being able to take it, particularly when it was the older road which came out almost at right angles to the road along to Saint-Nicolas. Campana wrote: "Pajol sent the order to General Delort to charge down the steep slope which goes down to the Saint-Nicolas suburb" [3]. In his sketch concerning the charge, he noted down a route which was almost parallel with the former Valence road, but further east… Could it be the old Avenue de Surville and the old Chemin de Boulains? It was by that route that Tondu-Nangis thought a cavalry charge had been made, but by "Chasseurs of the Guard and the 5th Chasseurs Regiment…" He added "In my youth I sometimes heard old men of the suburb and in particular my own great-uncle Grandjean, tell of this heroic charge; they confirmed, and this may seem unbelievable, that not one horse was hit, not one horseman was wounded." [4]

The old Paris road must have been about thirty feet wide. It is difficult to imagine 1 200 horsemen launching into an attack on such a restricted road. On the other hand, if Generals Bardin and de Brack are to be believed, "a horseman, starting 600 yards from a battery (in our case it is a bridge) which is the object of the attack, and heading there progressively, first trotting then galloping then charging, would reach it in two minutes and 24 seconds, after having controlled his pace as follows: 95 seconds walking, 28 trotting, 13 galloping and 8 at the accelerated charge; during that time he would have a speed of about 3 yards per second". [5]

If one takes the speed of the gallop as being 25 mph, the horseman in the gallop phase would cover a little more than 200 yards. The first bridge being situated at about 300 yards from the bend, it is therefore reasonable to assume that Pajol's cavalry took up the charge on the straight part of the road which runs along the bank of the Seine.

Moreover, from the old Paris road, before the bend to the right, the bridges cannot be seen. Can one really charge without seeing one's objective?

Above, from top to bottom:
The road to Valence which Pajol used to descend upon Montereau.
On this little track, nowadays Rue des Boulais, Lefebvre led the service squadrons' charge. *(RR)*

The Valence Road nowadays.
(Photos Jacques Garnier)

brigade to the bridges in Montereau using the road which goes down into the town. He warned that he would be following him at the same speed with the Du Coëtlosquet and Grouvel brigades. General Delort after having ordered sabres unsheathed and formed his brigade into columns by troops started them off at a trot, then at a gallop. When the column was half way down the slope, he ordered the men to charge. The brigade tum-

1. Pajol Général en chef par le general de division comte Pajol, son fils ainé. Pâris Firmin Didot, 1874, Tome III, p. 146.
2. L. Stouff, Le lieutenant-general Delort d'après ses archives. Paris Berger-Levrault, 1906, p.88
3. Squadron Commander Campana, La campagne de France 1814. Paris Charles Lavauzelle, 1922, p.123
4. La bataille de Montereau par Tondu-Nangis père, témoin oculaire. Montereau, Zanote, 1910, p.56 (this work has been republished by Teissèdre)
5. General Bardin Dictionnaire de l'armée de terre, Paris Perrotin, s.d., t.2., p.1175 (General Bardin was in the Imperial Guard during the First Empire). General de Brack Avant-postes de cavalerie légère, souvenirs, Anselin, 1831.

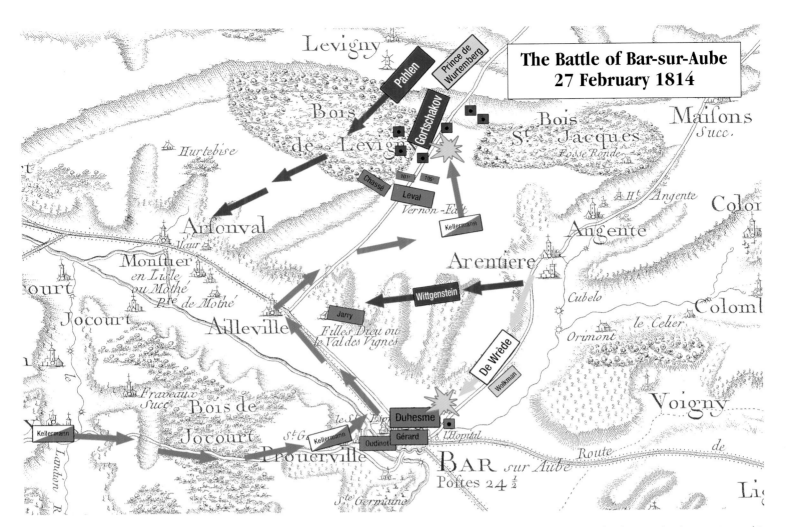

THE BATTLE OF BAR-SUR-AUBE

27 February 1814

On 26 February, Napoleon was at Troyes. The Army of Bohemia was retreating towards Langres but for his part, Blücher was still obsessed with Paris and moved on towards Sézanne. Napoleon decided to go and attack him from the rear while Marmont and Mortier blocked him [in front]. He led Victor's corps taking with him Ney and the Young Guard, Friant and the Old Guard, the Pierre Boyer Brigade and the Arrighi Division. Roussel d'Hurbal's cavalry also marched along with the 2nd and 3rd cavalry divisions of the Guard. This army comprised about 35 000 men.

To cover the line of the Aube, he left MacDonald and Oudinot, giving overall command to MacDonald. Gérard was at Bar with two divisions. Moreover there were Leval and his 5 000 veterans from Spain, Pachtod and his 4 000 National Guardsmen and Rottembourg with 2 600 men plus Chassé's Brigade with 2 500 men. Saint-Germain's and especially Kellermann's cavalry were at hand, ready to move up.

Misled by Blücher's over-optimistic reports, Schwarzenberg stopped his retreat and turned to face in the direction of Bar-sur-Aube.

Oudinot was warned that the Allies had taken up their offensive again. He then hesitated as to whether or not to fight, protecting his possibilities of withdrawal. In the end, this prevarication made him position himself badly and in doing so, he made three mistakes.

His first mistake was to leave his artillery at Magny-Fouchard; the second was not to have occupied the heights on his left with Leval's division; the third was to have put Pachtod, who was at Dolencourt, as well as the cavalry in the wrong place, especially Saint-Germain's which was waiting three kilometres away at Moutiers; only Kellermann, who was at Spoy, was near enough to intervene. After first taking the wrong dispositions, Oudinot then showed himself to be indecisive. He took the following dispositions:

Duhesme was at Bar-sur-Aube under Gérard who was ill but who had kept a few cannon. Leval was at the foot of the Vernonfait heights with Chassé on his left. Rottembourg was in the second line with his Tirailleurs among which the 7th and 8th Regiments.

Schwarzenberg had now decided to march on Paris and sent Pahlen as vanguard with Lubny's Hussars and some Uhlans, together with Tschulugev's Cossacks from the Rudinger Division. He directed Pahlen towards Armentières, Vernonfait and Arsonval with the Schafschaskoi Division. Montfort who was towards Vernonfait recaptured the heights with the 101st

and 105th, driving back the Russian 23rd and 24th Chasseurs; but they were in turn driven out by Gortschakov who arrived with the Kaluga and Mohilev Regiments.

Oudinot was facing Wittgenstein who had 21 000 men at his disposal with the Schafchafskoi Division and the Prince of Wurtemberg who arrived on the Troyes road with the Pitschinitzki Division; Prince Gortschakov with the Mezensov and Helfreich Divisions was behind him. De Wrède attacked Bar-sur-Aube with nearly 6 000 men, with Wolkmann and his Austrians. Kretov's 1 700 Cuirassiers from the reserve supported them. The Allies had 48 cannon. Monfort with the 101st and 105th of the Line retook the heights towards Vernonfait, driving back the 23rd and 24th Russian Chasseurs; but he was in turn driven back by Gortschakov who arrived with the Kaluga and Mohilev Divisions. The Leval Division had to re-take this dominant position, but deprived of its cannon, it wore itself out in futile charges against the batteries drawn up by the enemy.

Wurtemberg's column coming from Levigny, pushed Chaussée's Brigade back. It took the arrival of Pinoteau to re-establish the situation. He was wounded in the action.

Kellerman who had come up from Spoy crossed the Aube at the Saint-Esprit ford and with a brilliant charge led by Jacquinot and the Spanish Dragoons, pushed back Gortchakov's cavalry which had arrived on the plateau.

Wittgenstein re-centred his troops and Ismert with his 4th and 16th Dragoons tried to charge him three times, in vain. The lack of artillery was a disaster for the French: none of the actions could be supported. Schwarzenberg who had been slightly wounded, sent two cavalry brigades in support together with Wolkmann's Brigade from de Wrède's Corps.

Wounded, Wittgenstein sent a column of eight battalions to attack the Filles-Dieu crest which was held by Bellair and Jarry. The French had to pull back. Finally Pahlen, joined by the Cossacks and the Tsuyugev Uhlans, started to outflank the French on their left.

This turning manoeuvre and de Wrède's attack on Bar-sur-Aube with nine battalions forced an overwhelmed Oudinot to pull back. In the town, Duhesme held out with the help of his artillery but when he received the order to pull out, he formed a brigade into a square with his cannon and reached Ailleville and Spoy.

The French retreated towards Vendeuvre and Troyes where Oudinot was joined by MacDonald. Gérard abandoned Bar-sur-Aube by the Dolencourt Bridge. The line along the Aube was lost.

At Bar-sur-Aube, Oudinot lost 2 500 men killed or wounded and 460 prisoners. The heaviest losses were mainly from the Leval Division which was one of the best the army had. The enemy lost 2 000 men at most. The French had been 13 000, the Allies 40 000.

The fighting at Bar-sur-Aube.
(Peter Hess, RR)

This battle was in fact one of many countless struggles which took place against the overwhelming mass of enemy troops. They took Troyes and continued their march on Paris. MacDonald who had supreme command of the Corps, joined by that of Victor who had held out in Laubressel, now had the task of stopping the Army of Bohemia.

On this day, several generals distinguished themselves:

Monfort: appointed General in 1811, Baron in 1813 and CtLH the following year. He was wounded at Bar-sur-Aube as well as at Arcis. He served in the Jura in 1815 and was put on the available list in 1821.

Bellair: General in 1813, he was also GdOLH. He took part in the Battle of Waterloo and was retired in 1825.

Pinoteau was appointed General in 1811, was made a Baron in 1813 and OLH in 1814. He was wounded at Bar-sur-Aube. He was exiled in 1816 after having defended Belfort during the Hundred Days. **Jarry** replaced Jan de la Hamelinaye, who was ill, on 14 February 1814.

A Month of Glory

The month of February had seen the Emperor stabilising a very compromising situation. At the head of a small army, a mix of old "moustaches" and young beardless conscripts, for support he relied on marshals who were not always enthusiastic, but whose divisional commands showed that their enthusiasm was just as strong as that of the Marie-Louises.

After the Battle of la Rothière, the Allies were separated and Napoleon was able on the one hand to trounce the Army of Silesia bit by bit and on the other hand to push the Army of Bohemia back to Chaumont by taking advantage of his central position.

But when the Emperor was absent, the marshals did not fight as well as when he was with them and their under-strength army corps could only delay the progress of the Allied armies. The behaviour of Oudinot at Bar-sur-Aube is a perfect example of this.

THE INCIDENT AT MEAUX
(around 27 February)

Guillaumet who had taken command of the 6th Light following his exploits at Champaubert reports: *'We were very satisfied to see lots of young millers from the flour mills on the Oise River coming to mingle, all covered with flour, with the Tirailleurs, bringing their own weapons and taking part in the fighting which was going on around Meaux. The contrast with us was remarkable because we were covered with mud and blackened by powder, whereas they were as white as their flour. What must our enemies have thought of these new opponents who were shooting at them wearing cotton hats?"*

The surviving soldiers from the 2nd Battalion were attached to his battalion which comprised about a hundred men. They fought at Berry-au-Bac where Ricard's division was mentioned, then at Craonne on 7 March. Then they returned to Paris. They escorted an artillery convoy, arriving at Saint-Denis on 26 March.

Two other details concerning uniforms are to be noted. A decree decided to levy conscripts in the Marne and Aisne departments who would be equipped with blue tunics called "Gauloises", with shoes and a shako; later on it was added that even shakoes taken off the enemy could be used for the conscripts.

BLOODY MARCH

THE SOISSONS AFFAIR

2 March 1814

*Above: **The Russians attack Soissons.** (RR)*

*Below: **General Béruyer wearing the uniform of a Colonel of the 21st Chasseurs in 1808.** (RR)*

Napoleon's strategic "acrobatics" got Blücher into a very difficult position. The old fiery Prussian was pushed back when he attempted to cross the Ourcq and was under pressure from Marmont and Mortier. Meanwhile, on 2 and 3 March, Napoleon had the bridge at la Ferté-sous-Jouarre repaired over which he was going to head towards Chateau-Thierry. Blücher was thus cornered in a pocket. Indeed, the Aisne was a large obstacle with Soissons blocking the route of the retreat which he had decided upon with Kleist's and Yorck's corps, with Kapsevich's forming the rearguard. He was waiting impatiently for reinforcements from the Army of the North: Winzingerode and Bülow who were marching towards Soissons and who had been attributed to him. Behind them Langeron was advancing with Saint-Priest in the lead. On 2 March, Winzingerode and Bülow reached and invested Soissons.

The situation inside Soissons

In Mid-January, three generals had been sent to fortify this town.

Rusca: Italian campaign, Major-General in 1799, CtLH in 1804, Baron in 1811. Commanded the town but was killed defending it on 14 February.

Danloup-Verdun: OLH in 1807, General in 1811, replaced Rusca, served with Lecourbe in 1815, retired in 1825.

Berruyer. General on 18 January 1814 at Soissons, wounded at Ligny in 1815 then he was put on leave.

With them was **Colonel Prost**, Chief of Staff to the Army Engineers who had come to reinforce the town's defences. Chevalier in 1809, OLH in 1814, retired as Maréchal de camp in 1825.

On 10 February, a new general was appointed to Soissons: **Moreau.** General in 1803, Baron in 1810, GdOLH in 1813, capitulated on 3 March, arrested, saved by Dupont, the man of Baylen. Served in the Indre in 1815 then was retired.

With him there were: **Strolz.** Artillery Colonel in Joseph's Guard in Naples and in Spain. LH in 1806, Battalion Commander in Saint-Hillier's Engineers.

Colonel Kozynski from the Vistula Regiment, LH in 1811, Baron in 1812, wounded on 2 March at Soissons recapturing the outskirts. He returned to Poland in 1817.

Bouchard: Adjudant Commandant in 1807, Chevalier in 1810; he arrived in Soissons on 2 March

The garrison was made up of a Vistula Battalion of 700 men and 300 men from the town guard. The town's artillery consisted of twenty guns of which ten were

A terrible event which occurred much too frequently at the end of this winter: Cossacks cutting up the French Light cavalry.
(Cossack Museum, Private Collection)

4-pounders, served by 140 Old Guard and Coastguard gunners. A brigade of National Guardsmen, with 2 500 men, came up from Orléans on 28 February, but it never got there. It was in Paris on the 2nd.

The fortifications were improved but not completed and the bridge was not mined as was ordered. Moreau claimed that the powder had not been delivered.

On the 2nd, Winzingerode arrived by the Rheims road and Bülow by that from Laon. A negotiator was sent but the town would not receive him and opened fire. Leroux, a gunner, took out three Russian guns. But the enemy drew up forty 12-pounders which fired at the ramparts and several parts on the bastions were destroyed.

A Russian column attacked the ramparts but was repelled by Kozynski who was wounded. The firing continued and lasted for another 12 hours without breaching the walls; the damage was repairable.

Bulow sent them an aide de camp, Captain Mertens. He was received by Moreau

Nansouty and Pac forcing the way through at Berry-au-Bac. (RR)

who required a guarantee from somebody really in authority. Mertens returned with a letter from Bulow confirming the Russians' agreement. The garrison had only lost 23 killed and 120 wounded but Mertens threatened, that as honour was satisfied there could now be a surrender with full military honours, if not...

Moreau hesitated. He considered the town already lost and that he would not follow the formal orders he had received. He asked for time to think, to convene a meeting of the defence committee. He climbed the 354 steps to the top of the church tower to observe the enemy but since night had fallen he could not have seen very much.

At two in the morning the counsel was in full discussion; Kozynski, Saint-Hillier and Strolz were more for resisting further; Bouchard alone was for surrendering. They decided to ask for a 24-hour delay.

Colonel Lowenstern, sent by Winzingerode arrived and threatened them again. Moreau stated the conditions he wanted to see applied. They were granted very quickly and the Frenchman went off to sign in spite of a very violent reaction on the part of the soldiers but also from the inhabitants. Indeed the approaching canon announced Napoleon's arrival. Moreau realised that he had made a huge blunder and could already see himself being shot.

At about 5 o'clock, Blücher arrived with Sacken's vanguard but for all that did not congratulate his generals for having saved him. Proudly Blücher played down the danger he had been in. He rallied his corps towards Soissons where Bülow had already prepared a second bridge and by 4 March, there were four usable bridges.

Unaware of the capitulation, Napoleon and Marmont continued to advance. At Fismes he learnt the news; the Emperor was furious and ordered those responsible to be arrested and presented for immediate court-martial and then for them to be shot. The commission retained just Moreau, but only gave its verdict on 24 March which saved the general, because it was Dupont, of Baylen fame, who finally got him pardoned. The loss of Soissons caused all Napoleon's clever strategic plans to collapse and marked the real turning point of the campaign. Thiers compared *"Soissons to Waterloo"*.

CRAONNE, L'AISNE

7 March 1814

The shameful capitulation at Soissons enabled Blücher to cross the Aisne and escape probable defeat. Napoleon decided to pursue him because Schwartzenberg was much slower moving, and because Blücher feared the Corsican Ogre all the more. But the Emperor had first to cross the Aisne himself. He sent out scouts and some Dragoons returned confirming that the river could be crossed at Berry-au-Bac where they had seen only a small number of enemy soldiers. Nansouty and Pac were immediately sent to safeguard the crossing there.

Some Cossacks and their two cannon were driven back to Corbeny. Colonel Gagarin was captured but his name was mentioned erroneously on the Rheims monument as having been killed in the town. The staggered corps columns followed, crossing over at Berry-au-Bac. The French vanguard went as far as Vaucler Abbey but discovered a mass of troops set out in battle order on the Craonne plateau which hindered further progress towards Laon. Napoleon was warned and came up to see these enemy troops and thought that it was the rearguard of the Army of Silesia which had found a marvellous position which was easy to defend. Indeed this plateau between the Aisne and the Ailette was situated 450 feet above the rivers. It was made up of a great plateau, 450 feet wide behind a farm called Heurtebise. A path led to this farm and linked up with a little road which edged along the plateau and which was called "le Chemin des Dames" (of notoriously sad reputation in the 1914-1918 war). This road climbed up to the plateau and crossed it. It had been traced so that the Ladies of France staying at the Chateau de Bove could go and visit N. de Narbonne. It went from Corbeny, and Vaucler Abbey was just nearby, on the north of the plateau. The Lette flowed along the plateau parallel to the Laon road.

An Impressive Position

Blücher had disposed Voronsov (who was in command) and his troops on this plateau, supported by Sacken. A big line of artillery with 36 cannon was positioned in front of the infantry, drawn up in several deep ranks.

In the front line there were Bekendorf on the far right at Jumigny with Krakowski, Harpe and Wuitsch, with Benkendorf between Jumigny and Ailles. In the second line there was the Laptiev Division with the 44th Chasseurs in Ailles. The third line was made up of Stroganov between la Bovelle and Paissy. Wassilitschitkov's cavalry was on the right between Cerny and Troyon, on the road. In Heurtebise Farm, about which a lot has been written, there were only Chasseurs. On the right there were 4 cavalry regiments and twelve cannon. Thirty other guns protected the left wing. The total strength of Voronsov's troops was 16 500 men. Sacken had 13 500 men in reserve. To make up this strength, Blücher had entrusted Winzingerode with some cavalry which had to go round and tackle the French columns on the flanks. 22 000 Allies opposed 22 500 Frenchmen. The terrain was awful because of the thaw and the paths leading up to the plateau were very difficult to climb. Napoleon had found one of his old friends at la Fère, a M. de Bussy who turned up and who knew the lie of the land very well. The Emperor took him on as guide, made him an aide de camp, a Colonel and gave him the Légion d'Honneur. A certain Wolf, a former Sergeant in the la Fère Regiment also turned up with important news from the towns on the Rhine.

First Wave

Having seen what the situation was on this 7 March, Napoleon decided to attack on the

The voltigeurs from the Light Cavalry shooting at the Cossacks. (Private Collection)

wings. While the artillery arrived on the plateau and started to engage its Russian counterparts in order to fix it, Ney who had arrived by the left bank of the River Lette and had climbed by Vaucler, moved forward to Ailles and attacked from the North. The Prince of the Moskova disposed of the 3 700 men of Meunier's and Curial's divisions reinforced by the Pierre Boyer Brigade.

He had to attack the enemy left wing through the little valley of the Lette. When he arrived on the top of the plateau his conscripts were riddled with shot and he had to fall back into the Vaucler ravine from which he called for reinforcements and tried to rally his soldiers. He had attacked too soon, without waiting for the other staggered corps to come up. He drove off the occupiers of Vaucler towards Heurtebise where two battalions of Chasseurs were dug in, who held out then set fire to the farm before regaining Benkendorf's frontline. Napoleon sent him Victor who arrived with Boyer de Rébeval's division. At the very outset of the action, Victor was wounded. He was at first replaced by Rébeval but he was in turn wounded so Mortier and Charpentier directed the attack. Grouchy and Roussel d'Hurbal with his Dragoons climbed up by the Heurtebise path. They were wounded when they arrived there, then it was the turn of Laferrière-Levesque who had his thigh blown off and had to be amputated. Letort replaced him helped by Testot-Ferry but they were driven back.

Voronsov got his left, weakened as it was by the attacks of the courageous Young Guard, to pull back, but Ney in his ravine now only had 2 000 exhausted men including the 1st and 2nd Voltigeurs. So it was Drouot who came to their rescue with two batteries of Guards Horse Artillery. He helped the conscripts who had lost several pieces, taken out by the Russian gunners, and showed them how to use their cannon. Like on many other occasions before, his calm and his experience turned the tables on what could have been a very dangerous situation.

Second Attack

After this rather unpromising start, Napoleon was able to put together a combined attack

The Russian General, Woronzov and General Charpentier commanding a division of the Young Guard. (RR)

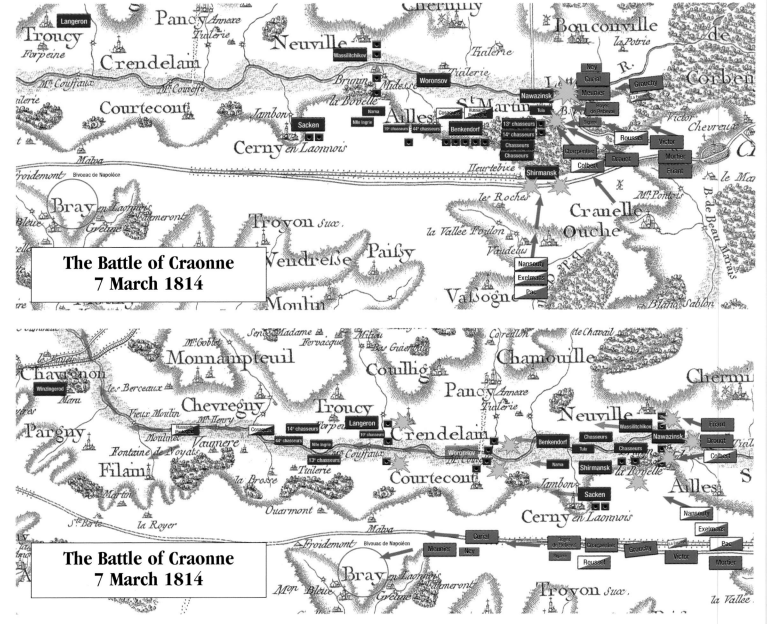

The Battle of Craonne
7 March 1814

The Battle of Craonne
7 March 1814

thanks to the arrival of Charpentier. He attacked in the centre with Friant, Colbert and Drouot who continued to give of his best without thought for himself. Ney was able to attack the left with Charpentier and pushed back the Russian battalions. He was supported by Grouchy's Dragoon's fiery charges which reduced to silence the Russian batteries who had been giving the Young Guard such a hard time. The resistance from the 19th Chasseurs and the Schirwansk Regiment supported by two Paulogrod Hussar squadrons halted Ney in front of the Saint-Martin Wood. On the left it was Nansouty who, advancing by Vassogne les Roches and the Heutebise path and leading the cavalry of the Guard with Pac and Exelmans, took up the attack even though he did not have any artillery. These brilliant cavalrymen broke up the enemy ranks.

But the Russians held out. They were waiting for Wintzigerode and only gave away a little bit of ground whilst nevertheless inflicting heavy losses on the French. The Schirwansk Regiment and the 2nd, 6th, and 19th in particular were outstanding.

At the beginning of the afternoon, the Grenadiers and the Chasseurs à cheval of the Guard, supported by Charpentier's infantry, together with Colbert and Friant, charged the enemy's line in the centre. This attack enabled a big Guards artillery battery to deploy and set itself up; this cut down the Russians. Blücher called his corps back to Laon which upset Voronsov who wanted to continue because Wassilitchikov's charges had stopped the French. The role of Heurtebise Farm has been played up and the Chasseurs who were occupying it set fire to it when the French attacked.

Wintzigerode, slowed down by the state of the terrain and the bottlenecks, had been unable to intervene in time. Voronsov under pressure from the French attack, decided to start retreating on the plateau, protected by a battery of cannon set up at Cerny then by a second screen consisting of 24 guns 1 400 yards further back. The Allies fell back in the direction of Laon in staggered moves, first to Cerny, then Troncy and finally to Cavignon and Filami where they stayed for four hours. The Russian artillery pieces were finally reduced to silence by the indefatigable Druout; the pursuit started and was followed through vigorously till nightfall. Blücher only regrouped his army at Laon.

Finally, this battle was theoretically a victory. But at what price? There were 6 000 French casualties. Victor, Grouchy and four general were wounded, Cambronne four times. The 14th Voltigeurs had lost 30 officers out of 33 present in the field in the morning. Boyer de Rébeval had lost a third of his strength, i.e. 63 officers and 1 584 men killed or out of action. Charpentier's division had lost more than 1 500 men. Meunier had only 6 000 men left. The Young Guard had paid a heavy price; only Curial was not too badly affected. No prisoners had been taken, no guns captured. On their side, the Russians only reported a loss of 4 500 men and two generals killed or wounded.

The Russians fell back, and the French advanced towards Braye where the Emperor settled for the night. He was surprised by the extent of the losses but he was still under the impression that he had only beaten a rearguard, and his intuition drove him to go for the attack as usual. Blücher had to be beaten and driven away. Then he would go and take his Rhine garrisons, get Maison down from Belgium and Augereau up with his army from Lyon, thus threatening the line of operations of the Army of Bohemia. But his lieutenants' morale was very low. They were seeing their meagre regiments frittered away; they preferred peace and holding on to their privileges and what they had already obtained.

The Emperor was at Braye, covered by the Old Guard and Letort's cavalry. Ney had got as far as Chevergny. It was nevertheless surprising that Napoleon should want to take Laon where an army of at least 84 000 men was concentrated, when he only had 24 000 at most. Only Marmont was able to join him the following day with his 9 500 men.

Bonaparte had never been one to take into account the numerical strength of his adversaries. But at the time, the exceptional quality of his troops and their enthusiasm compensated for the lack of numbers. Nevertheless at Craonne, the conscripts had shown what they were worth.

THE BATTLE OF LAON
9 March 1814

On 8 March, Napoleon got news of the Congress held at Chatillon. The Allies sent him an ultimatum: either he accepted their conditions or he could propose new conditions which were more acceptable. If not the Congress would be dissolved and a struggle to the bitter end would start. The Emperor made his choice. He ordered Caulaincourt to gain time so that he could win a brilliant victory. He decided that Blücher had to be beaten and it would be at Laon. He got his troops on the move.

He had at his disposal Ney's troops including Meunier's and Curial's brigades as well as the Pierre Boyer Brigade; Friant and the Old Guard who were at Chavignon; Victor who brought with him the Boyer de Rébeval and Charpentier Divisions; Charpentier replaced Victor who was wounded at Craonne; finally Mortier with the Christiani, Poret de Morvan Divisions with Boulnois' cavalry.

Marmont was to join them towards Athies on the right wing with his 6th Corps, the 1st Cavalry Corps, and the Arrighi Division; in all about 20 000 men

Preliminary attacks.

At Laon, in order to open a passage, they had first to go through the gorge at Etrouvelles which was surrounded by marshes and which had resisted the first attempts the day before. Napoleon decided to attack during the night.

Charpentier, who came from this area, advised him to go round this position using a path which debouched near Chivy. The Emperor agreed and sent Gourgaud, his ordnance officer, off in front along the road with two battalions of Chasseurs à pied and two squadrons of Chasseurs of the Guard. Boyer de Rébeval had to attack the gorge with 400 elite soldiers at one in the morning; Gourgaud had to signal that he had reached his objective.

Ney moved up himself towards Chivy, and then let the cavalry led by Belliard through on their way to try to get into the town. Some peasants had offered to help guide Boyer de Rébeval's troops which had to attack without making any noise, with fixed bayonets. A battery was set up to cover them.

They forced their way through and Ney advanced and attacked Chivy, running up against three Russian regiments. It was about 5.30 a.m. Belliard came up followed by Gourgaud who had arrived at last. The Dragoons entered Sémilly, mixing with the fleeing soldiers; they tried to get further but they were driven off and ended up in Leuilly which they occupied. Snow had fallen during the whole of the night and thick mist covered the countryside. Seeing Laon heavily fortified Napoleon sent Poret de Morvan to attack Ardon. Ney entered Semilly with the Pierre Boyer Brigade driving out Clausewitz who held the village and who received two companies from the 5th Reserve Regiment as reinforcements, but he was unable to re-take the village.

Ardon was taken and the soldiers just reached the walls of Saint-Vincent. Napoleon still thought he was tackling the rearguard, whereas in fact he had the Army of Silesia totalling 90 000 men facing his 35 000.

Blücher was not alone!

Blücher was satisfied because he had got the Army of Bohemia away from the Emperor whom everybody feared so much; his formidable position would enable him to hold out, thanks to his obvious numerical superiority.

He deployed his troops in the following way.

He set up 30 artillery pieces in front of Semilly; they also threatened Clacy. Towards Ardon, he placed four 12-pounders and two howitzers plus a battery. Towards the Rheims road, there were six Russian guns at the Sauvoir Wood, supported by a Russian battery and a Prussian half-battery.

He spread out his infantry thus: In the town there was a battalion of East Prussian Grenadiers and one from the New Marches Regiment plus two other battalions from the regiment in the rear. In front of Semilly, Clausewitz still had a Battalion of the 4th East Prussian and two and a half battalions of the 4th Reserve. At the bottom of the Soissons road, there was a battalion of the 4th Reserve and two battalions of the 4th East Prussia. On the Ardon side there was a battalion from Colbert's regiment of which two companies were suppor-

At the head of the Young Guard,
Marshal Ney attacked the Semilly suburb and took it. *(RR)*

ting the Sauvoir battery, together with two battalions of the 9th Reserve as back-up and a battalion from the New Marches Regiment, as well as two regiments of Pomeranian cavalry. He put a battalion of the 9th Reserve at Vaux. As reinforcements, between the Marie and Rheims roads, he positioned one of Colbert's battalions, two light batteries and the 3rd Cavalry Corps. The strength of Bülow's 3rd Corps was 16 900 men; his battalions were in and around Laon. In all 25 000 men and 72 cannon were positioned in Laon and its environs. The cannon were disposed around the town under the command of General Holtzendorf. On the right wing, Wintzingerode had his infantry placed in two ranks preceded by two batteries in front of Thierret Farm. Most of his cavalry was at Avin Farm and at Molinchart.

On the left wing, Blücher had massed a large number of troops, including York's 1st Corps in the front line; Kleist's 2nd Prussian Corps and three Hussar regiments were placed further back at Chambry. Prince William's division had two battalions in Athies covered by 1st Corps artillery and the Silesian Hussars. Pirch's division held the Rheims road with three battalions at le Sauvoir, with a brigade in reserve. Kleist was covered on his left by the reserve cavalry and 24 guns, and in the rear by two cavalry regiments. The artillery reserve with light guns was behind Athies and York.

These corps formed a mass of more than 25 000 men.

As a general reserve, the Prussian Marshal had placed Sacken's corps with 13 000 men on the la Fère road and Langeron's corps of 25 000 men behind Laon.

In front of these masses, the French columns seemed quite puny. This was the case with Marmont who hurried up with his 9 500 men towards Athies. Blücher feared a trap and let Napoleon attack in order to judge his strength for himself.

It was 11 o'clock when the Emperor arrived, expecting Marmont to arrive on his right wing. At 11 p.m., Gougaud, at the head of a detachment of the Old Guard, with the 14th Tirailleurs and the Flankers, was sent to go round the marshy gorge between Etouvelle and Chivy; he was delayed by the bad terrain. Ney attacked during the night and took Chivy and joined up with Gourgaud. Beillard with Roussel's division progressed but was halted in front of Laon by heavy artillery fire; he occupied Ardon and Leuilly however, then Semilly defended by Clausewitz. Boyer joined him. Poret de Morvan also set himself up in Ardon, but they were driven out by Bülow and Woronsov who were in turn pushed back into Laon by Roussel and Grouvelle. Curial and Charpentier were launched upon Clacy and Montmarie took this village. Bülow counter-attacked and took Ardon where Poret de Morvan was wounded.

Marmont was advancing on the right; so Blücher got Sacken and Langeron to advance in order to reinforce his left. At midday Marmont finally arrived; with him he had 1 400 men and

10 cannon, Arrighi's 4 000 men whose artillery was served by sailors, and Bordesoulle's cavalry. He arrived in front of Athies and Vaux after having driven off some cavalry under Blücher's son and Katzeler. Arrighi and Lucotte threatened Athies and entered the burning village.

The First Ragusades?

Maréchal Marmont no longer believed in victory and if the article under the heading of "Marmont" in the "Fastes de la Légion d'Honneur" is to be believed, there were some doubts as to his behaviour.

In June 1834, M. Dineur, Administrator of the Rhin-et-Moselle department published *"les Trahisons de 1814"* (the Betrayals of 1814). He relates that Marmont was in command at Koblenz where he had placed Ricard with his division. His corps was spread out to Mainz and Spire on the right of the line held by MacDonald. At that time, the Allied and the French guards faced each other on opposite banks of the Rhine; the redoubts and the batteries set up by Ricard were of no use when the Allies moved up.

M. Dineur claims that *"the gunners had been withdrawn and that Marmont had taken care to remove all the obstacles; and that it was exactly at that very spot that the Coalition forces landed in force."*

Apparently Marmont discussed with Ricard how they would retreat. When leaving for Mainz he stopped his carriage and ordered the artillery officers to remove their cannon. General Ricard had agreed to carry out this retreat and this done immediately, with both the artillery and the troops in his division, but without even waiting for the enemy to make the slightest attacking move; the inhabitants found themselves handed over to, and invaded by, the Russians. MacDonald often said that he gave up his position on the Rhine because his right wing had been laid completely bare.

M. Dineur adds that at the time, while the evacuation of France was being discussed between the Emperors and Lord Castleread on 21 March 1814, M. de Polignac turned up and apparently said that everything had been arranged, prepared and finalised, and that the conspirators in Paris had done their job well.

There then follows the hardest attack. I quote this surprising passage, relating an event which took place certainly later, near Paris towards 24 March.

"On 24 March, Maréchal Marmont went over to the enemy disguised as a peasant; he stayed with the Lancelot brothers, farmers in the village of Soudé-le-Grand; there he removed his clothes and marshal's insignia; he left his fully-equipped horse; he put on a peasant's tunic and hat; he then asked the two farmers an hour before dawn to lead him to the line of his forward positions. Having gone beyond that line, the two

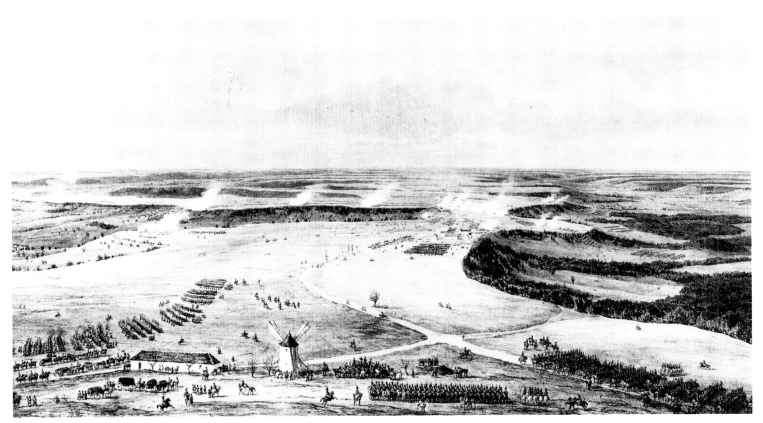

A general view of the Battle of Laon. (RR)

farmers told him that he was in danger if he went any further because the enemy sentinels were out in front. 'You are wrong' was his answer, 'Besides, I know now how to get back to the village by myself'. The enemy detachment presented arms: did the soldiers recognise him in spite of his disguise? The two men were even more surprised when the whole of the enemy forward position was called up to let the disguised marshal through. About an hour later, the troops which Marmont had abandoned, were attacked by the Russians who captured the village of Soudé-le-Grand. A Russian cavalry picket at once hurried to the two farmers' house which Marmont had left barely an hour before; these cavalrymen took as their loot only the coat, the hat and the fully-equipped horse that the marshal had left behind and with which he reappeared, to take up his position a few miles away in front of Vitry at the head of the French army which was ignorant of where he came from and which under his command withdrew in front of the Russians and marched to Paris."

In a note at the bottom of page 387 of this second volume, he recalls also that General Souham, who took part in this affair at Essonnes, had also been compromised in the Pichegru conspiracy. He was at first dismissed then reinstated but he was not well-disposed towards Napoleon.

Besides, following this reproduction of the assertions of M. Dineur, the author relates the subsequent days preceding the abdication; General Castex, Ledru des Essarts and Lucotte were not incriminated. This story was perhaps made up, but Marmont never reacted in any way against such a publication.

The Debacle at Athies

Let's get back to Laon. Perched on the top of their hill, the Prussians occupied la Mouillée Farm. Marmont pushed them back into Athies with Bordessoulle's help. While trying to go round Athies, the French were stopped in front of the Chauffour battery. Arrighi, with Lucotte entered Athies which the Prussians had set on fire before leaving. Napoleon had not been advised of Marmont's arrival. He was waiting for him so that he could attack, but Marmont stopped because of the night. He had his troops camp a few yards from a formidable mass of men and went off to sleep at the Chateau of Eppes "showing unforgivable carelessness".

"Human nature in him had reached the limits of its ability to resist", said Foch in his lecture on this battle, held when he was a Lieutenant-Colonel. When night had

fallen completely, the Prussians attacked in four columns among which Ziethen's who fell upon Bordessoulle. Fabvier who had left alone to join Napoleon with two battalions, came back to oppose Kleist. He disengaged the road to Rheims so as to enable the fleeing troops to get through. Marmont's corps was routed and lost 2 500 prisoners, 41 cannon and 131 caissons. The Emperor, informed of this on the morning of the 10th, still had thoughts of attacking even then, but Blücher who was getting more sure of himself now attacked, even though he was still ill. He had Marmont pursued to Rheims and attacked in front of Laon by York and Bülow with Wintzingerode. Napoleon resisted then gave up and withdrew, reaching the Etouvelle gorge. Ney and Semery made up the rearguard; the Russians and the Prussians, cautious when facing such an adversary, did not pursue him. The retreat was carried out without hitches. Two Cossack regiments were surprised and pushed back. The little French army had lost 6 000 men captured or out of action, without counting Marmont's losses and it had lost the battle.

Foch in his very good lecture from which we have used a lot of extracts, said in his summing up *"In him, the Conqueror finally killed the Sovereign."* It was the twilight of the heroes, before the end at Waterloo.

Napoleon at Laon. (RR)

*Surprised all bedded down in the middle of the night,
Marmont's 6th Corps was routed and suffered heavy losses.*
(RR)

THE BATTLE OF RHEIMS
13 march 1814

After the carnage at Craonne and the defeat at Laon, Napoleon now had a greatly diminished army and was obliged to fall back on Soissons guarded by commandant Gérard.

At Rheims, after 5 February, General Rigau had had to fall back with the approach of the Army of Bohemia. He left Miteau, commander of the National Guard in command and evacuated his wounded towards Soissons leaving Rheims with 50 men. Blücher sent Major Falkenhausen with 500 cavalry to occupy the city where a committee had been set up. Major Schoeling enjoined the town to surrender and announced the arrival of Wintzingerode's corps.

The committee took in the Cossacks, putting up their demanding officers who formulated their demands. The Russian vanguard arrived with Woronzov and Strogonov arrived on 16 February; the Russians and Prussians shared quarters. To warm themselves, the occupiers cut down the trees along the promenades.

They had 60 cannon and more than 500 carriages. From his headquarters in Chalons, Blücher threatened the town with reprisals which were explained in detail. On 25 February, Wintzingerode was sent towards Soissons. Some Cossacks of whom there were many, committed all sorts of exactions. After Soissons had capitulated, Napoleon decided that he had to pursue Blücher in order to get him further from the Army of Bohemia, and Rheims seemed to be the perfect centre from which to launch this offensive. So on 4 March he sent Corbineau with two battalions and Delort's cavalry and surprised the over-confident Russians.

Corbineau took 200 or 300 prisoners. Legend has it that Prince Gagarin just had the time to get away though in fact he had been captured at Berry-au-Bac. Exelman's cavalry reached the fleeing soldiers at Berry-au-Bac, cutting down 45 of them. The people of Rheims were happy at the arrival of the French. Corbineau tried to drum up a bit of resistance and reinforced the town's defences. He sent Delort back keeping only 100 horsemen as scouts. Two of his eight cannon were sent to Berry-au-Bac where Napoleon was at that moment; Napoleon was not pleased with the inhabitants of the town who had welcomed the enemy too warmly; the local committee tried to justify itself. But on 6 March, Saint-Priest, an émigré, had to evacuate the hospitals to Nancy in order to disengage Vitry.

Wintzingerode arrived with York. On 7 March, Saint-Priest was ordered to go and arrange things with the town.

On 7 March, Tettenborn presented himself before the town. He waited for Yagov who arrived with 8 Landwehr battalions, three Russian regiments from the 3rd Corps as well as several squadrons of Kiev and Pantshulichev Dragoons. Saint-Priest was at the head of 7 000 men.

The same day, Prince Galitzin, one of Blücher's lieutenants came up and demanded the town's surrender; Corbineau answered with his cannon. So Saint-Priest sent a battalion to set fire to Saint-Brice and threaten the Mars Gate. Napoleon had detached the Defrance Division towards Rheims because Saint-Priest, whom Corbineau had driven back to Epernay, was returning to the town. So Defrance had to go to the help of the town.

De Ségur takes up the tale.

"On 7 March, the eve of the Battle of Craonne, at daybreak, at Berry-au-Bac, at the moment when the Honour Guards Division was mounting to follow the Emperor, Napoleon had learnt that Saint-Priest, who had been driven back from Rheims to Epernay by Corbineau had returned to the town which he was about to capture. The Emperor having our regiment at hand sent it immediately to help Rheims. We left on the double... The journey seemed long for the Guards. In our anxiety, with every sound of Russian gunfire, we feared we would arrive too late; our gaze would scan the horizon. So, reduced to 800 sabres by a lot of our number being assigned elsewhere and a host of wounded horses, as soon as we saw 1 000 to 1 200 enemy cavalry in battle order in full view of the town on some heights, we attacked them.

In order to get in front of them, we had to leave the main road to our right and deploy to the left on the plain. The 1st Brigade carried out this movement; to my great surprise, mine received the opposite orders. We were sent to the right of the main road. There, pushed into a muddy impasse with no other obstacle but the ground itself, with the Vesle to the right, a deserted side of the town to the front and surrounded on all sides by muddy ditches, we found ourselves trapped.

I took the responsibility myself for disobeying my orders. This was such a bad position that in order to get out of it,

join and support the other brigade, mine would have had to pass in full view of the enemy one by one across the ditches of the great road. The sight of the big charge getting ready, excited the Guards and we arrived in the nick of time. The Russians had more cavalry than us and they overlooked us from the heights which run from Cernay to the

80

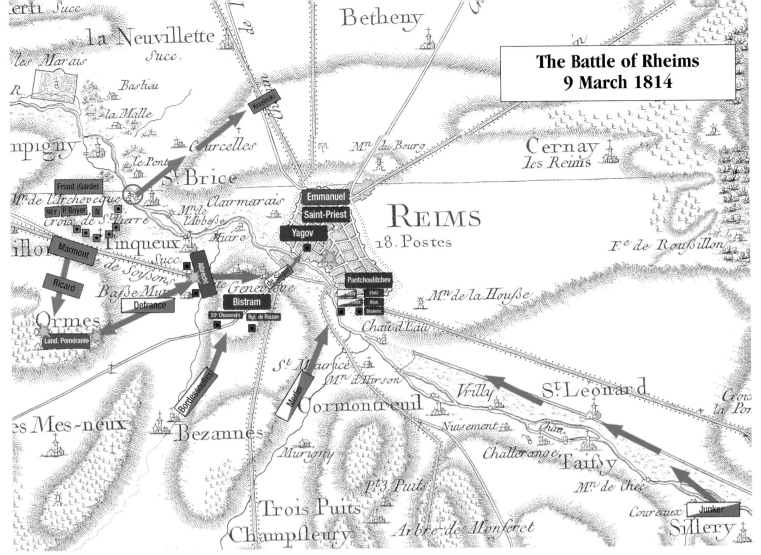

Bourgs windmill. They turned tail immediately and left us the position, from which they could have seen how weak we actually were. Encouraged by this success we finished reconquering the hill when the sight of 8 000 Russians and 20 cannon stopped us.

Their scouts, already skirmishing with some of Corbineau's infantry and some brave citizens of Rheims who had left the safety of their walls, had reached the walls of the town where, after the Russian cavalry, the Russian infantry was itself also surprised by our arrival and the cries of "Long live the Emperor!" from the townspeople and went briefly onto the defensive. It was only a short respite. In order however to take advantage of it and the protective screen which hid our lack of numbers, we had to be crafty. I was in the lead; I had the ranks doubled up and spaced out to make us seem more numerous, and had myself surrounded by a swarm of Tirailleurs to impress the enemy and not lose the initiative. There was nothing else I could do; and yet what could we hope to gain from all this subterfuge, when a single step forward would have revealed everything? Already, for fear of getting too involved in the fight, we even had to slow down seeing how much our Tirailleurs were getting carried away and how keen the furthest forward of the Rheims National Guardsmen were. Indeed there were still four hours of daylight left and it needed the enemy to make just one move to dislodge us, to count us, to push us back to the Aisne, and another one to drive in the gates of the town which Corbineau and only a hundred or so infantry were defending."

The enthusiastic population was shouting *"Long live the Guards of Honour! Long live the brave Hussars of the 10th!"* The Russians withdrew their lines outright, but General Saint-Priest set fire to two workshops and fifty houses situated outside the city walls, *"conduct worthy of a renegade"*.

On 10 March, Tettenborn entered Epernay whereas some Cossacks invaded Saint-Brice and started burning and looting everything as was their wont. Saint-Priest, billeted on the Vesle received reinforcements: Yagov brought up 26 battalions – 15 000 men with 2 400 cavalry. Pantshulichev arrived with the Eletz, Rilsk and Ekaterinburg regiments, a regiment of Chasseurs à cheval and two batteries.

They were given information by some royalists in Rheims and the result of Laon was known to them. It was decided to attack from several sides; Corbineau tried as well as he could to dispose his National Guards and his 18 cannon together with Colonel Jaquemart's men from the 5th Voltigeurs, General Lacoste and Colonel Régnier.

Saint-Priest entered the town after it had resisted as well as it could. Corbineau sought refuge with M. Comeyras who hid him until 12 March. The Allies pillaged the town. Saint-Priest

The Vesles Gate through which the Guards of Honour entered Rheims. (RR)

did try to impose some form of order but the damage was already done.

Napoleon learned of Corbineau's failure but considered that possession of the town was essential to prevent the two Allied armies communicating with each other. So he reacted as quickly as possible and called Marmont to Rheims, together with Sebastiani and his 2 000 cavalry, Ney, the Guard and the Defrance Division – about 30 000 men of which 7 000 were cavalry, and a hundred or so cannon.

Marmont was also ordered to have Berry-au-Bac guarded. At Ormes, Ricard, Pelleport and Bordessoulle beat the Pomeranian Landwehr whose fleeing soldiers were attacked by Picquet's brigade from Defrance's division. Saint-Priest was taken completely by surprise and the runaways flocked into the town; he therefore ordered General Bistram to position himself to the south of the Sainte-Geneviève plateau with the Riazan Regiment, the 33rd Chasseurs and a battery. He also asked Count Albrecht to block the Soissons road against Defrance. Yagov was ordered to block the west with a 24-gun battery on the mountain and with troops as far as the Vesle.

The Guards of Honour charge at Rheims. *(Engraving by Philippotaux/RR)*

Napoleon did not move for an hour, waiting for Ney and Friant. When they arrived, he sent Ney on to the Soissons road supported by Defrance, Sebastiani, Colbert and Exelmans. They marched towards Trinqueux.

More to the south, Bordessoulle headed to Berzannes and cornered the enemy so that Merlin with a regiment of Cuirassiers could capture them.

The French artillery was lined up in front of Croix-Saint-Pierre, supported by the Old Guard and the Pierre Boyer Brigade and the Cavalry of the Guard (Delort, Colbert and Exelmans).

Ricard reached the suburb separating the Allies, with the Russian division and its artillery to the north and the Prussians to the south. Alarmed, Saint-Priest rode up with all his glittering staff between the road and Trinqueux. One of the French Guards batteries seeing this group fired a shot at it and seriously wounded the General in the shoulder. The gun-layer was the one who had already killed Moreau. Panshulichev who had been wounded when he fell from his horse nevertheless came up to take command but was unable to rally his men. Napoleon got some cannon to advance and continue firing. He launched Ricard into a bayonet attack along the Soissons road. He sent Defrance to turn the enemy left and capture the Sainte-Geneviève plateau which was still held by two Russian batteries and two battalions, from behind.

The Glory of the Guards of Honour

De Ségur could see the entrance to the suburbs at the rear of the plateau, but the enemy cavalry had positioned itself so as to screen the outer side of this suburb; covered behind this screen, the artillery rushed into place.

He relates in his memoirs that:

"I got the order to throw these 800 horsemen back into the town with only one squadron from my brigade. I set off immediately, not doubting for a moment that the rest of our division and Bordessoulles' 1 500 sabres would support me against the infantry whose retreat I was about to cut off.

So we charged, outnumbered eight to one: the enemy cavalry took fright, did not dare hold and rushed towards the suburb, but found it clogged with artillery, so they had to turn round with their backs to the houses and face us. We got there at the same time as they did. There, separated from them by only the ditch and the width of the road, I halted in order to rally. Some shots were exchanged.

Seeing nothing coming up to support us against the Russian infantry marching up to enter the suburbs behind me, I sent messages three times asking the others to hurry up and move up, on which depended both the taking of Rheims and this rearguard.

Finally, let down by our Tirailleurs and under pressure from the situation, I ordered my men to charge. On hearing this command the Guards, Squadron Commander Andriau in the lead, jumped straight over the ditch and crushed the Russian Lancers against the wall they already had their backs to. Instead of defending themselves, the Russians only

thought of escaping into the town. They offered their flank to our sabres.

I had my men stab with their swords. A good many of the enemy perished and the rest escaped, only to run into the cannon and caissons which our charge had caused to flee precipitously inside the town. But the barricade which had been set up across the suburb had prevented the artillery from retreating; cannon and hooked-up caissons were piled up any old how against this obstacle and formed a confused, motionless mass. It completely blocked the way. The enemy Lancers, pushed onto and over this obstacle, lost their heads. There were scenes of despair and fear which were difficult to describe. Some dropped their weapons and holding up their arms asked for mercy; others turned and defended themselves in desperation."

De Ségur then mentions the Guards wounded or killed by the Russian infantry whose bravery he noticed. In particular he mentions Colonel Count Briançon-Belmont, defended by Maréchal des Logis Fresneau, but who was killed; Midshipman Lanneau, with eleven bayonet wounds, who later went on to become a Colonel. Fatally wounded, de Ségur's horse doubled up with the pain, thus saving its rider from a bayonet wound; the officer was however unsaddled and hit in the back. He hid in the ditch and dragged himself towards the town accompanied by a wounded Guard.

Defrance and Bordessoulles arrived followed by Ricard who ran into Bistram who was bringing up four regiments and two well-protected cannon. The gate of the town still had to taken, but Marmont used his cannon well even though they were badly shot up by the Russian artillery. Napoleon wanted to have done with it all, so he sent Squadron Commander Juncker with 150 cavalry to attack and take the Sillery Bridge. He eliminated two Cossack squadrons but ran into large detachments of Russians. Exelmans succeeded in repairing the Saint-Brice Bridge and sent Krasinski's Poles across; they pushed back Karpenjo who was leading Yagov's vanguard, and Emmanuel. At eleven in the evening, Ricard took the barrier at the Vesle Gate and Bordessoulles came up to help him take the town.

The Last Smile of Good Fortune

The Allies lost 900 killed, 2 000 wounded and 2 500 prisoners, 11 cannon, 100 caissons and a bridging team. After the defeat at Laon, there was rejoicing in the town and this victory was good for the troops' morale. For Marmont, in his memoirs, it was *"the last smile of good fortune"*. The following day a grand review of the troops was ordered. The men had a thorough wash during the two days' rest intended for this purpose. General Léry of the Army Engineers was ordered to repair the defences of the gates of Rheims. He was Maréchal Kellermann's son-in-law and he was given the grand Cordon of the Légion d'Honneur on 27 December 1814. Napoleon quit the town on 17 March. Marmont went to Fismes where Mortier joined him with Roussel's cavalry, which was left as Rheims' only defence, waiting for a possible return of Curial and the possible support of Belliard.

Wintzingerode recaptured Rheims after a heavy artillery bombardment and left it on 21 March for Epernay. Blücher arrived on the 23rd.

Above:
The death of Colonel Briançon-Belmont in the streets of Rheims.
(J. Girbal. Author's Collection)

Opposite:
The Trophies.
(Painting by Maurice Orange/RR)

Comte Philippe de Ségur. *(RR)*

The Russian General, Saint-Priest. *(RR)*

*Above: **Napoleon at Arcis-sur-Aube.** (J.A. Baucé. Musée des Beaux-Arts at Troyes)*

*Below: **The Austrians attack the Grand-Torcy in vain.** (Knötel/RR)*

ARCIS-SUR-AUBE
20 and 21 March 1814

CamOn the evening of 13 March, the Imperial Army was still in a central position between Blücher who was moving towards Rheims and Scwhartzenberg who had stopped falling back towards Chaumont, had beaten Oudinot and Gérard at Bar-sur-Aube and had taken up his march on Paris again. His corps were already at Sens and Nogent-sur-Seine. In order to protect his southern flank the Austrian Field-Marshal had sent Bubna's corps to reinforce the army facing Augereau at Lyon.

The Army of Bohemia consisted of more than 100 000 men. Napoleon knew that now, and chose to hit south in the direction of Troyes, thus cutting the Army of Bohemia, and withdrawing to Chaumont and the eastern strongholds. In case this manoeuvre failed, he could rejoin his garrisons through Vitry-le-François and Saint-Dizier. But he needed more information and he lost three days waiting for it. He only left on the 18th for la Fère-Champenoise then Arcis. He crossed the Aube on 19 March.

But Schwartzenberg had felt this move coming and withdrew his corps hastily. When Napoleon arrived at Arcis, the Allies had regrouped and could either continue to fall back towards Chaumont and Langres which was what the Tsar advised, or turn round and face the French. To present the Battle of Arcis-sur-Aube, it is interesting to consult three different versions: those of Houssaye, the historian, and Generals Griois and Koch.

Houssaye's Version

Schwartzenberg stopped hesitating and decided to face Napoleon who had crossed the Aube at Plancy. The French therefore had a river at their backs and with the Army of Bohemia in front that could be concentrated on a level with Arcis with a very clear numerical superiority. The various corps were called up: Wurtemberg, Giulay and Rajewsky; de Wrède's was also present, covering the right wing.

Napoleon thought he only had a very large rearguard in front of him, ready to be attacked.

The day of 20 March

Sebastiani who was the vanguard with Exelmans and Colbert drove off Kaizarov's Cossacks and Frimont's Bavarians who then fell back. He continued on his way to Arcis which he entered at 11 o'clock. He was followed by Ney with Janssens' and Rousseau's divisions. They occupied Arcis where, from the right bank, Defrance and Mourier (Berckheim's heavy cavalry brigade) arrived. They were joined by the Emperor with his service squadrons towards one o'clock. Sebastiani had placed himself in a covering position on the left bank and Ney set himself up ay Torcy-le-Grand, covering Arcis. He placed Janssens in the village and Rousseau in reserve. Napoleon was still convinced that the enemy only was only a rearguard and waited for his reinforcements which were marching with Lefebvre-Desnoettes and the 2nd and 3rd cavalry corps. A reconnaissance had only found a few Cossacks. Sebastiani was more anxious and went forward with two squadrons and discovered a mass of cavalry consisting of Kaisarov Cossacks and Frimont's 56 squadrons. Having been given permission, Sebastiani decided to attack, the best form of defence.

Colbert who was leading, was slowed down by light enemy batteries, then driven back by a flanking attack on his lancers. This retreat forced them back onto Exelmans' cavalry, creating disorder and soon panic and "run for your life".

"Which of you will go past me?"

Napoleon who was at Torcy, rode up with his

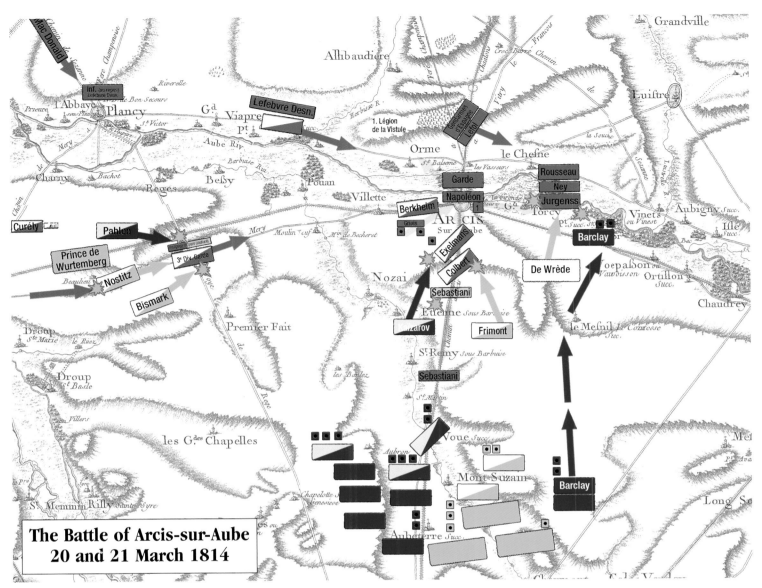

The Battle of Arcis-sur-Aube
20 and 21 March 1814

escort amidst the fleeing troops, sought shelter inside the square of a Vistula battalion which resisted three charges; then he reached the bridge and sword in hand, shouted "Which of you will cross before me?" This appearance stopped the runaways. He rallied them and sent them back forward, but they were out-numbered three to one; moreover 72 artillery pieces were lined up in front of them. On the left there was Ney who stood up to a terrible attack from the Austro-Bavarians who took the village from Janssens, but Ney engaged Rousseau, who recaptured it. The enemy attacks succeeded each other, supported by their mass of artillery. The Old Guard arrived in time. Napoleon sent Ney a battalion of Grenadiers and two of Spanish Gendarmes who were already the heroes of Montereau. To give them a boost of courage, Napoleon rode his horse towards a smoking shell which had just landed. The explosion threw Napoleon over and killed his horse.

Napoleon was unscathed and imperturbably remounted another horse and lined up his three fresh battalions exalted by such bravery. In Arcis, the enemy cavalry was whirling around, running up against the Guards' squares upon which they foundered. Towards Torcy, Barclay de Tolly and his reserves had come up to support the attackers. The Prince of Wurtemberg's vanguard was approaching Méry which the French Grenadiers à cheval and the Chasseurs of the 3rd Division of the Guard had left, to escort a bridging team taken the previous day leaving only Curély in Méry. Generals Nostitz, Pahlen and Bismarck rushed against this Guard. The defence was magnificent. The Old "Moustaches" fought against two regiments of Wurtemberg Dragoons, a division of Austrian Cuirassiers and two light batteries. Curély came to their help with his Horse Artillery but they were forced to move back towards Mery.

The Lions of Torcy

Meanwhile, part of the Russian reserves was sent towards Torcy to support de Wrède who had engaged the Austrian regiment of Archduke Rudolph which was driven off. He therefore attacked with Habermann's brigade, Rechberg's division, and then Lamotte's. Barclay was then also sent to him taking Tschuglikov's Grenadiers, the 2nd Russian Cui-

rassiers Division, the 6th Cuirassiers Brigade and two position batteries. Ney repulsed their assaults until midnight, reinforced by the Vistula Regiment and the Spanish Gendarmes. Janssens was seriously wounded and was replaced by Lefoi. The Bavarian General Habermann was killed. Towards 7 or 8 o'clock, Lefebvre-Desnoettes arrived with 1 500 cavalry having left his worn-out infantry behind him. Towards 10 o'clock, thus reinforced, Sebastiani tried another attack. He pushed back the Cossacks and the Hussars who were on the left of the troops attacking Torcy and fell upon Frimont's cavalry which fled in disorder. The other enemy regiments intervened pushing the French back behind Nozay, where they rallied; they stayed awake, mounted, bridles in their hands. The Allies took up their positions for the night at the rear of the battlefield.

Defrance's division and Mourier's brigade were not really engaged. The French losses amounted to 1 800 men and those of the Allies to 2 500 Austro-Bavarians and about 500 Russians. This battle was all to the credit of the French who held out for eight hours against these overwhelming odds, fighting at two to one, if not more.

Griois' Version

20 March 1814

"After three days' rest which I sorely needed, I left Rheims and came to bed down at Epernay with the rest of the staff. M. Moët put the Emperor up. His cellars, which I visited, were magnificent and contained a huge number of bottles of Champagne.

I left on the 18th with General Sebastiani and the cavalry of the Guard and we headed for Arcis, to flank our troops on the right.

When we reached the river Aube which we crossed at Plancy, we ran into the enemy. They wanted to stop our advance. They resisted for only a short time and we continued to advance, pushing before us swarms of Cossacks who were supported by a few artillery pieces, which rallied when they found a favourable position and started jeering at our vanguard units. But a few well-placed artillery shots soon stopped them and as soon as they saw our squadrons set off they cleared off, galloping out into the plain…

On 20 March we arrived in Arcis-sur-Aube early. Some troops still holding on to positions around the town withdrew when we approached. The Emperor arrived a short while after us with the first corps of his infantry. He went over to the different points to reconnoitre the lie of the land, called me over and ordered me to re-establish a bridge which the enemy had destroyed over a small but deep and very muddy river on the way out of town on the Saint-Dizier road.

I had rebuilt the bridge when, towards midday, lively artillery and musket fire could be heard on the Méry road. I mounted my horse and joined General Sebastiani very quickly; he occupied part of a raised plateau on the left of the road some distance from Arcis. Firing was coming from the whole length of the line. I noticed some disorder among the Polish Lancers with whom the 5th Company was positioned on the far right; swarms of Cossacks and light cavalry were putting them under great pressure. I suggested to the General that I might go over there and galloped over. When I arrived, some of the platoons on the wing had been cut off and dispersed and the rest were starting to break up and withdraw. My company, whose forward position was getting very critical, had stopped firing and was leaving. I had them slow their movement down because it looked too much like flight and I ordered a staggered retreat, one half of the battery firing while the other moved back.

The operation started off quite steadily at first and our shot worked against the enemy cavalry which surrounded us. But the squadrons of Lancers who were riding on a level with us, were pushed about by new enemy cavalry troops and let themselves be cut into, then they finally broke up completely. In this confusion, three cannon were overtaken by the enemy and taken; several gunners were taken or killed, others were wounded.

It was only with great difficulty that I got myself out of the fray by throwing myself to the left on the road where Capitaine Laporte followed me with the rest of his company. I was going to go back to General Sebastiani and give him this sad news when I spotted him coming up at the gallop with the cavalry of the Guard. They too must have turned around but were still in good order and the squadrons had not broken up. Soon they came up to me and I can still see and hear Sebastiani; carried away by the impetus and while still galloping, he was shouting to the men to stop and to turn back; all the squadron commanders were repeating the same order, but to no avail.

The impetus had been given and this retreat would have turned into a true rout by the entrance of the town when suddenly this huge mass was stopped as if by enchantment. It had spotted the Emperor, sword in hand, on the main road at the head of his staff. Seeing this, every single one of these brave men only thought of the shame of running away in the presence of the Emperor and of the danger he was in; the squadrons turned around.

Exelmans, at the head of the dragoons turned round and ran into one of the Austrian Hussars who was following too close on his tail and knocked him down; those Austrians who could not stop their horses in time suffered the same fate; our caval-

ry knocked down about everything it ran into: it charged at the gallop against the squadrons it had been retreating in front of just a moment before, and very soon it had taken up its original positions.

During our cavalry's flight, one has to call a spade a spade, I found myself in a very difficult and especially very extraordinary position. On the right of the main road on which I found myself I was only followed by a few ordnance gunners; the Polish Lancers were fleeing in disorder. On the left the Dragoons and the Chasseurs of the Guard were coming up; soon they passed me by. Thus in withdrawing – I had to follow the general movement – I rode surrounded by Austrian Hussars. Only the ditch along the road separated them from me.

Thankfully they never thought of crossing it; they only thought of chasing our cavalry. It was thanks to rather singular circumstance that I owed my salvation. I caught up with our troops at the moment they turned round and there was only the ditch between me and Exelmans when he threw himself round upon the nearest Hussar. It was then that I too saw the Emperor, whose presence alone had stopped our squadrons and got rid of a danger he was ready to face with his staff…

The Emperor only expected to find a part of the Austrian army at Arcis but it was with the whole army that we had to deal with. It was at least three times our size and it forced us to concentrate near the town without being able to break through our lines anywhere or take Torcy which was attacked with great determination. I was in support with my 4th Company and I set up my artillery pieces in a battery until the evening, firing continuously at the enemy soldiers…

On my right there was a company of Coastguard Gunners in their white uniforms; these brave men were under fire for perhaps the first time and they had officers with little experience; they behaved however with great boldness which was all the more remarkable because some sort of fatality seemed to direct all the enemy's shots in their direction; the explosion of several of their caissons which they had left too close to their guns also caused terrible carnage among their ranks and most of their guns were taken out. Squeezed into a circle, whose circumference was held by the enemy, we attracted all the shots in our direction…

Griois then looked for Sebastiani in the darkness and entered the town. He found his Adjudant-Major who had had a dinner prepared which was very much appreciated as was the sleep that followed.

21 March

The two adversaries were lined up but without moving. Towards one o'clock, Napoleon started the retreat while the cavalry of the Guard formed a screen with some of the troops of the Line to cover this movement. The enemy noticed what was going on, and drums sounding, started the attack. Its huge artillery started to fire. The bombardment was terrible but the withdrawal was carried out in good order. Griois staggered his retreat and passed through Arcis without too much difficulty and got into position outside Arcis to protect the last of the rearguard.

Below: **General Chassé gets hold of a drum and beats the charge, leading the 16th Lights and the 26th of the line in an attack on Torcy.** *(RR)*

Centre: **General Chassé, a Dutchman in the service of France.** *(RR)*

Bottom: **The Austrians and the Russians charge and push back Colbert's and Exelman's cavalerie de la garde.** *(RR)*

Ney stayed in the town until night-time in the middle of the fires which were set off by the incessant artillery fire. Griois joined Sebastiani in the village of Dosnon on the Vitry road; they left on the 23rd for Vitry. They crossed the Marne at Fignicourt.

They thought that they were going to Vitry to attack but the objective was changed and it was in fact for Saint-Dizier that they were headed. Napoleon had indeed decided to operate on the Allies' rear. He hoped that the Allies would follow him, moving away from Paris. But they had decided to march on Paris, having got rid of Napoleon whom they feared so much.

Winzingerode's corps was left behind to screen the movement and trick Napoleon. The Russian general was beaten but he accomplished his mission in spite of heavy losses.

Griois fired his last shots in this fighting. He complained about the Parisians' lack of fighting spirit and also especially about the welcome they gave to the enemy when they reached the capital.

Koch's Version

It is precious for the details it gives.

19 March

Sebastiani drove the Kaisarov Cossacks from Plancy where the bridge was re-built. Napoleon headed to Méry with his service squadrons. Ney was at Riverelle and marched to Arcis-sur-Aube; the cavalry was at Viapre.

Rajewsky and Giulay had left for Troyes, Wurtemberg was in charge of the rearguard. The bridge at Méry was burnt. These corps were called to join the Army of Bohemia which was now concentrating. Letort captured a bridging team with 13 elements at Chatres then went to les Grez. Napoleon returned to Plancy with his Guard; MacDonald was at Provins but the Emperor called him back to Arcis. Tettenhorn was sent to Chalons to try and join up with Blücher.

20 March

Janssen was positioned on the Lesmont road with his left at le Grand Torcy. Sebastiani was placed on the Troyes road; Letort left for Arcis alone. The Allied corps joined up with de Wrède and Kaisarov. 1 000 Chasseurs, Knesevich's Dragoons and Schwartzenberg's Uhlans formed a line between Pougy and Rameru.

Sebastiani was attacked by Kaisarov who drove Colbert off onto Exelmans who both withdrew in panic but they were stopped on the bridge at Arcis by the Emperor in person. Friant protected the bridge with a square comprising the Vistula Battalion. Volkmann was thrown against Torcy with Archduke Rudolph's Regiment but he was repelled. De Wrède then committed the 2nd Battalion of the 2nd Bavarians, also to no avail. Rechberg followed as did Habermann's brigade but its commanding officer was killed at the same time as Janssens.

Ney got Rousseau's brigade to advance and was given the Spanish Gendarmes and the Vistula Battalion in reinforcement. He forced the Allies to withdraw. His artillery was very effective.

The reinforcements for de Wrède arrived: Tschoglikov' Grenadiers and the 2nd Russian Cuirassier Division followed by the Prussian Guard and the artillery of the Russian Guard.

Lefebvre-Desnoettes had just arrived with 2 000 cavalry but he had left his exhausted Young Guard infantry at Plancy; there were 4 500 of them under Henrion. Thus reinforced, Sebastiani attacked and drove off Kaisarov and the enemy left; but he was stopped by the 2nd and 7th Bavarian Chevau-Légers, the Guard and the 3rd Division of Russian Cuirassiers. The two cavalries watched each other. Wurtemberg who arrived, ran into the French Grenadiers à cheval and the Chasseurs of the Guard who were bringing back the bridging team which had been taken the previous day by Delort. There was fighting with Pahlen's vanguard.

The Olviopol and Grodno Hussars, the Tchernigev Uhlans were on a level with le Premier Fait and the Austrian Wurtemberg Cuirassiers attacked on the right flank. Curély had to come up with his battery to get his comrades out of this predicament. The French cavalry rallied at Méry but at nightfall they were able leave for Plancy leaving the pontoons to Berckheim. Napoleon called up MacDonald, Oudinot and Gérard as well as Saint-Germain and the 5th and 6th Cavalry Corps, because he now only had 18 000 men.

Oscherovski crossed over to the right bank of the Aube, de Wrède was at Chaudrey and Rajewski was at Mesnil la Comtesse. On the left bank there were Wurtem-

berg and Giulay flanked by Kaisarov at Barbuisse; with them were a Russian Grenadier division and 72 cannon.

Sebastiani and Ney screened and protected the bridge at Arcis. Oudinot and Monfort, Maulmond and Chaussé in reserve occupied Arcis and set up barricades. Rottembourg came to their help; a second bridge was put across the river at Villette and the retreat was staggered.

Schwartzenberg was at Mesnil la Comtesse and launched an attack in three columns against Torcy. Leval was wounded and it needed Chassé's exploit to lead on the 16th Light and the 28th of the Line by sounding the charge with the pommel of his sword.

Pahlen and Rajewski forced the French cavalry towards Villette. De Wrède arrived from Lesmont and the Russian light cavalry passed through Rameru and reached Vinet and Luistre.

Maulmond held out in Arcis until 11 o'clock at night then went to Chesne. Wurtemberg and Rajewski went to Dampierre and Luistre parallel to the Vitry road used by the French. A bridge was thrown across the river at Chaudrey. Napoleon lost 3 cannon and 4 200 men of which 800 were prisoners; de Wrède lost 24 officers and 2 000 men.

Napoleon decided in the end to operate against the enemy's rear and to try and reach his strongholds, in particular Durutte who had assembled 20 000 men. The Russians had left Winzingerode who had to get the Emperor to believe that he was the rearguard of the retreating Army of Bohemia, whereas the Allies had in fact decided to march on Paris, both armies together. Vitry was too well-defended, so they turned towards Saint-Dizier which was where the Russian feint had to be set up and it worked very well.

Milhaud and Kellermann reached the army and Lefol replaced Janssens.

FÈRE-CHAMPENOISE

25 March 1814

"The Twilight of the Gods"

After the defeat at Arcis-sur-aube, Napoleon directed his forces towards Vitry-le-François. Since the town was well defended, he crossed the Marne and went off at a tangent in the direction of Saint-Diziers. He ordered Marmont's and Mortier's corps 50 miles away to join up with him. Pachtod's troops who were too far away had to return towards Paris. Once his army had regrouped, the Emperor would rally the strongholds to the east or would fall back on the Aube and the rear of the Army of Bohemia if the opportunity arose.

For their part, the Allies held a council of war at Pougy. A letter from Berthier to MacDonald had been intercepted and Napoleon's plans were now known. They chose to regroup and to act against the flanks of the French army. But on the 24th, a letter captured by the Cossacks revealed to the Tsar that Paris could not go on any longer and that everybody there wanted peace. There were rumblings of discontent. Another council of war was held and it was decided to march on the capital in two columns: Blücher along the Marne, Schwartzenberg along the Seine and the Aube. Winzingerode would screen the move by making Napoleon think that he was being followed.

The following day at Wassy the Emperor had no idea of what the Allies' movements were. Learning of the presence of troops at Saint-Diziers, he decided to go there thinking that the whole enemy army was there. But it was only Winzingerode carrying out his mission. 30 miles away another scene was set to be played out.

The battle of Fère-Champenoise was important but it consisted of two separate fights which complemented each other to turn it into a decisive defeat.

Marmont's and Mortier's fight.

On 25 March, Marmont was in front of Sommesous at Soudé-Sainte-Croix, waiting for Mortier so that they could march together towards Vitry. He was uncertain about the Allies' objective. He could see the Allied army's campfires of the Allied army in the night.

He only had 5 600 men from the Ricard, Lagrange and Arrighi Divisions. Bordessoulle could only muster 1 800 cavalry; he was at Soudé-Sainte-Croix where he left the few companies of Voltigeurs he could afford to sacrifice.

Mortier had 10 800 men. He was at Vatry with the Christiani, Charpentier and Curial Divisions. Belliard's cavalry only comprised the Roussel Division with Grouvel's Brigade and the 7th, i.e. 2 480 cavalry. He joined Mortier at the moment the Allies attacked. They were near Dommartin l'Estrée. Together the two marshals only had 30 cannon.

Facing them the vanguard arrived led by Pahlen and Wurtemberg. They had almost 40 squadrons with 36 cannon and advanced by Soudé-Notre-Dame. Mortier debouched from Vatry (or Vassy) where he left his troops which he then went and got to take them to join Marmont at Sommesous. An artillery duel preceded the Allies' attack which was about to start.

Bordessoulle was knocked around by Dechterev who disposed of the Isumz and Grodno Hussars as well as the Cossacks; he was followed by Kretov who lined up 12 light cannon and

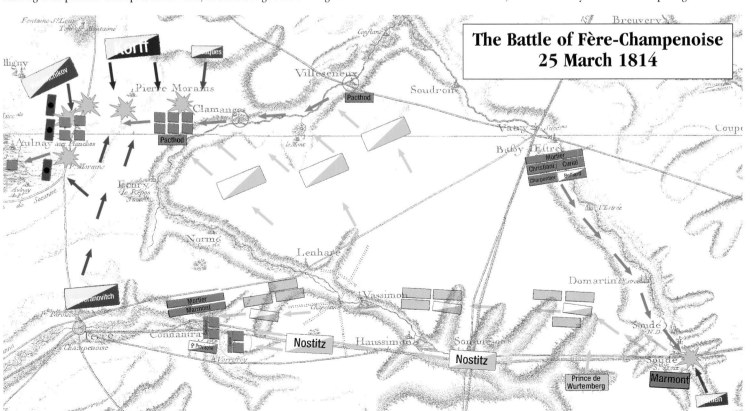

The Battle of Fère-Champenoise
25 March 1814

The village priest at Sézanne imploring God for the souls of the brave. This scene - which is very hypothetical - does nevertheless reflect the French infantry's ardour when faced with the unleashed fury of the Allied assaults. (P. Méjavel. Musée de Chalons-sur-Marne)

1 600 Cuirassiers. Belliard with the Roussel Division was pushed back while trying to bring him help. Behind, Merlin had Latour-Foissac charge with the 8th Chasseurs. The arrival of 2 300 Austrian cavalry worsened the situation; there was Nostitz with the Klenau and Rosenberg Chevau-légers, the Olviopol Hussars, the Tsuschugev Uhlans and a thousand Cossacks. Then came the Guard with Depreradovich and Constantin who took two cannon. The cavalry fled towards the Connantry defile and the infantry made a staggered withdrawal with its squares. Christiani was the rearguard and tried to defend the Connantray ravine. A deluge of hailstones and rain fell upon the combatants who could no longer fire because their powder was wet. The defile in the ravine was difficult to get through and the squares broke up. Jamin and his brigade (from the Charpentier Brigade) were captured, the Le Capitaine Brigade lost its artillery. The arrival of the 9th Provisional Heavy Cavalry Regiment which lined up in battle order with its 530 horsemen stopped the enemy attacks for a moment. 24 cannon and 60 caissons with a transport battalion were captured; the two Marshals had twice to seek refuge inside the squares. The soldiers were fleeing in the direction of la Fère-Champenoise. Suddenly, the troops heard the sound of artillery coming from the Rannes region and this was a breath of fresh hope. The men thought that it was the Emperor coming to their rescue whereas it was in fact Pachtod's column fighting for its life. This at last had the advantage of drawing the Allied cavalry away to go and attack Pachtod, and the Marshals were able to continue their retreat to Provins.

Below, from left to right: **Pachtod's and Ameil's squares attacked by Uhlans after having received a blast of shot.** *(RR)*

The Allies push home their advantage against Marmont's and Mortier's corps which were on the point of collapse. *(RR)*

Moved by the courage of the French, the Tsar *(RR)* **proposed a surrender with honour. The first emissary was shot, but the second managed to convince Pacthod to lay down his arms.** *(RR)*

After capturing two Russian cannon, Sub-Lieutenant Lemaire of the 4th Cuirassier Regiment, had them served by his troopers and fired at the Russians. *(RR)*

Senseless Heroism

The Pacthod and Amey Divisions were at Sézanne. Compans was in command of the town with his 1 500 men. Adjudant-Commandant Noiset had just arrived escorting a very large convoy made up of 100 artillery wagons and 80 carriages full of supplies and clothing with the help of 4 battalions and the 8th Marching Battalion of Cavalry. Pacthod decided to escort them to MacDonald's corps. He had at his disposal Amey's 800 conscripts, his 2 500 National Guardsmen and a weak battalion of the 54th and 16 cannon. Pacthod stopped his column to bivouac at Villeseneux which he thought was out of the danger area.

Suddenly the vanguard from the Army of Silesia appeared led by Korff with 4 000 Dragoons and Chasseurs, 1 500 Cossacks and a light battery. Gneisenau decided to attack this convoy which had just been discovered whilst he was still marching with the main part of the army to Bergères. Faced with this threat, Pacthod formed up his squares and several charges were driven off. Seeing the number of enemy increasing, the French General decided to fall back towards Fère-Champenoise. He had the horses detached from the carriages to reinforce those pulling the cannon and grouped the carriages which were to be abandoned at Clamanges. Thus the French marched towards la Fère-Champenoise, slowly because of the convoy. The enemy took advantage of the fact to try and attack them, alternating firing grapeshot and making cavalry charges. Wassilitchikov arrived and positioned a battery and Dragoons to block the French near Ecury-le-Repos. Delort got this obstacle to move back but Kretov's Cuirassiers, who had given up chasing the Marshals returned and reinforced the Allied troops.

Pacthod, surrounded and overcome by the huge number of enemy formed up six squares. He continued to fight as best he could but there was only one way out: get closer to the Saint-Gond marshes, where the cavalry would not be able to pass so easily. He headed therefore in that direction. Alexander and his Staff came out of la Fère-Champenoise to follow the fight. When they appeared the French thought for a moment that it was their Marshals who had appeared but they quickly realised their mistake. The squares still held out. For a moment, the Russian cannon even fired on Wassilitchikov who responded, but this mistake was corrected quickly. Suffering heavy casualties, the six squares were now reduced to four. They nevertheless continued to advance, driving through the masses of cavalry which had increased with the

Following double page:
Fère-Champenoise:
In full view of the Tsar,
the Cossacks
of the Guard charge
a retreating French
column.
(Private Collection)

Opposite:
The French infantry
defended themselves
as best they could.
It would seem that
the painter has shown
these men as wearing
clean and regulation
uniforms; it is almost
quite certain that this
must have been rare
indeed.
(Private Collection)

arrival of Barclay de Tolly's 25 000 reserve horsemen. Crushed by the grapeshot and the repeated cavalry charges, one of the squares was broken in. The other three held fast and were close to the marshes. Depreradovich however was there blocking their way with 48 cannon.

The Tsar admired this exceptional courage and wanted to stop the fighting; he therefore sent negotiators to obtain a simple surrender. But Colonel Rapatel, Moreau's former aide de camp and now Alexander's ordnance officer was shot down in spite of the white flag of truce. De Ségur wrote about this: "that he found himself face to face with his brother who was in command of the artillery in one of the squares, and when the latter heard his brother enjoining the square to surrender, he replied by letting off a salvo of grapeshot, and the renegade was left lying dead on the ground."

In the end it was Colonel von Thiele who came to beg Pacthod to surrender. The General answered: "I don't negotiate under enemy fire. Have your guns cease fire and will have mine do likewise." The Russian artillery ceased fire. Pachtod whose broken arm hung down all bloody, then surrendered his sword. Delort's square which had run out of ammunition, lay down its weapons and the last square which had been broken did the same. About 500 men reached the Saint-Gond marshes… 2 600 had been put out of action and captured with their generals.

Houssaye discussed Marmont's responsibility: he should have gone to Rheims rather than to Fismes. He would have been wrong to avoid Sézanne afterwards by passing through Allemant. Saved by Pacthod's sacrifice, Mortier and Marmont were able to get to Paris as were Compans and Noiset who was left with him.

A long stop was made at Esternay, but la Ferté-Gaucher was taken and occupied. The cavalry of the Army of Bohemia came up behind Marmont who succeeded in stopping the chase and in getting onto the road to Coulommiers. Mortier who failed in his direct attack on the town, chose to go back to Provins where Marmont joined him. The two Marshals met again finally on the bridge at Charenton on 29 March.

Compans who had been able to pass through la Ferté-Gaucher while it was still unoccupied went to Meaux where he found Vincent and Ledru des Essarts. Together their strength was about 6 000 men who had little inclination to fight. Ledru defined them: "The National Guardsmen are pitiful, badly dressed, badly commanded and not knowing how to hold their rifles which are disgracefully dirty."

The arrival of the Army of Silesia dispersed this last bastion. On 28 March reinforcements enabled a brilliant fight to take place at Claye. Meanwhile, on 23 March, Napoleon was at Saint-Dizier where Caulaincourt joined him, but the Emperor did not want to listen to him.

Above:
The Dragoon Guards charge under Letort and crush
the Russian infantry at St-Dizier.
(RR)

THE BATTLE OF SAINT-DIZIER
26 March 1814

"The Last Victory"

By moving to the east of France, the Emperor had hoped to draw the Allied armies towards him, away from Paris, and then beat them once he had assembled all the garrisons from his strongholds. Durutte had already come out of Metz at the head of 10 000 men after they had stood up to 40 000 Russians.

On 25 March, Napoleon disposed of only Ney, Lefebvre-Desnoëttes, Letort, MacDonald, Oudinot, Sebastiani, the Guard, Milhaud and Kellermann. Gérard and Saint-Germain formed the rearguard which had been harassed since the morning. Ney and MacDonald reported 10 000 enemy cavalry at Saint-Dizier. When he approached the town he discovered the Russians deployed on the right bank of the Marne River. Whether it was the vanguard of the Allied army or an isolated group, this prey was clearly ripe for the taking as far as the French were concerned. So the Emperor turned back and ordered the attack for the following day. Treillard sheltered in Valcourt. Napoleon sent the cavalry to cross the Marne at the Hallignicourt ford. It deployed. Gérard and MacDonald followed it and the army was in line between the ford and Hoiricourt, with the infantry in the second line.

Piré who was in the vanguard, ran into the Cossacks and the Issum Hussars under Tettenborn which he dispersed and pushed back to the Marne. He took Langeron's baggage and 800 prisoners.

Winzingerode tried to reach Saint-Dizier but his column was charged by the cavalry of the Guard which broke it up and chased it to the Trois Fontaines Wood. With the help of Trelliard, Oudinot immediately attacked the town whose garrison fled. He pursued them. MacDonald carried on the pursuit on the left, drove Tettenhorn back into Perthe Wood with Kellermann. The 16th supported Lefebvre-Desnoëttes' charges, helped by the 22nd and six cannon were captured. The Russians lost 1 500 men and 500 prisoners, 18 cannon and a bridging team; there were 600 French casualties. The enemy was retreating. Winzingerode was beaten but he had done his job. It was only on the 27th that Napoleon learned that the Allies were marching on Paris. They had a three days' start on him. What could he do? Finally he decided to head for Paris and also went via Troyes and Fontainebleau.

The Emperor set off on the 27th, with Drouot, Flahaut, Lefebvre and Gourgaud. The army made a forced march to follow. But the tragedy had already been played out before the army reached Paris.

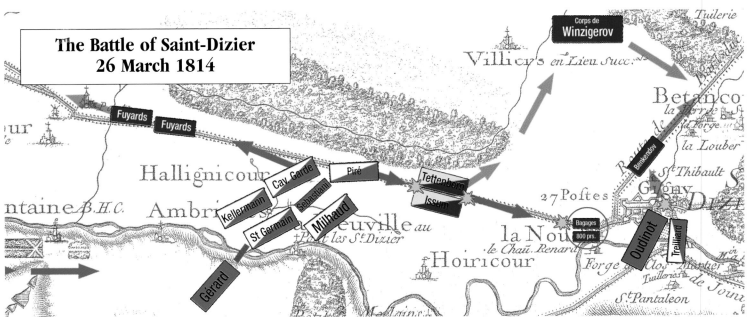

**The Battle of Saint-Dizier
26 March 1814**

THE BATTLE OF PARIS
30 March 1814

Napoleon once said: *"In my position, nobility is only to be found in the riff-raff, and riff-raff are only to be found in the nobility which I have created."*

The answer that a veteran gave when asked what his service record was *"Twenty years of glory and three months of betrayal."*

The battle of Paris was very complicated. But here again, extraordinary courage was shown in spite of the lack of preparation on the part of Joseph. Indeed, the Emperor's elder brother had not been capable either of reinforcing the town's defences, or of mobilising the National Guardsmen, or of planning for the necessary supplies to gain precious time, at least enough for the real leader to arrive.

Napoleon would not have been able to win but he could have at least staved off the final moment for a bit longer, although this would have been without any great hope.

Marmont fought as best he could in Romainville then in Belleville before his defection, which is too long to analyse here but in which Souham played the role of the evil traitor.

Maréchal Moncey

Major-General for the defence of Paris. He ran up against Joseph's and Hulin's apathy, despite all his efforts. His son, Claude Joseph Jannot de Moncey, was his aide de camp. OLH in 1811, Baron in 1813, deputy from 1810 to 1815.

General Hulin

General in 1803, condemned the Duke of Enghien in 1804, Major-General and Governor of Paris in 1807, Count in 1808. Cr of the Couronne de Fer and GdOLH in 1811, wounded by Malet in 1812, GdCx of the Réunion in 1813, exiled and retired in 1815.

General Préval

Commanded the depot at Versailles in place of Roussel d'Hurbal, Lieutenant-General in 1814, Viscount in 1817, Pair de France in 1837, GdCxLH in 1843, retired in 1848, made Senator in 1852.

General Allent

Chief of Staff of the National Guard, appointed General in January 1814, Conseiller d'etat on 25 August 1815 and elected deputy. CrLH in 1825, Pair de France in 1832, died in 1837.

As he came from the Engineers, General Allent was entrusted with the fortifications.

The lack of organisation in the defence of Paris was due above all to Joseph's apathy and the deplorable conditions in three areas.

Insufficient good troops

The National Guard was recruited by the census method, and this only enabled 11 500 men to be put into the line by 16 March; they were divided out between 12 legions. Among these men, only 6 000 had any real military worth. It was a long way from the 30 000 that were expected.

The lack of cavalry also weighed heavily in the outside organisation of the defences. It was not horsemen which Joseph lacked since there were 11 958 of them available, but horses: there were just 3 615 of them.

Inadequate armament

Despite the low number of National Guardsmen levied, the stocks of rifles in the Paris depots were insufficient to arm all of them. As a priority, these weapons had been given first to detachments of soldiers on their way to join the campaigning army; and the rifles recovered from the last victories had not yet been reached the capital. So Joseph had some pikes made and equipped 3 000 men with them... The dearth of clothing and equipment was at least as bad.

The artillery supervised by the ageing **Major-General Lespinasse,** an Arcole and Rivoli veteran, and GdOLH in 1804, still comprised 186 cannon. However, there were not enough gunners to serve them and there were not enough places where they could be set up and even then these were not well-prepared enough for them to be effective.

Colonel Count de Villantroys looked after the pool of the National Guard. He was CtLH during the 100 Days. There were only the 480 men of the Invalides Battalion under Grobert and the 300 cadets of the Polytechnique, organised since 1810, by Colonel Grenier who had lost an arm at Wagram; he was replaced by General Evain.

Inadequate fortifications

Major-General Count Dejean was in command of the Engineers. He was Grand Aigle de la LH since 1805 and the First Inspector of Engineers.

Below, from left to right: **Talleyrand, Prince Orlov – the Tsar's aide de camp – Maréchal Moncey, Joseph Bonaparte, Dejean – Marmont's aide de camp – the Russian Barclay de Tolly, Daumesnil and Caulaincourt.** *(RR)*

Below: **Maréchal Moncey organising and directing the defence of the Barrière de Clichy.** *(By Carl Vernet. RMN)*

Plans for the fortifications had been prepared but never realised for lack of money. Only palisades had been set up to protect from potential Cossack raids. Only Saint-Denis had taken its defence into its own hands, thanks to pressure from the inhabitants and their unpaid but effective labour. Moreover Napoleon had not wanted to fortify his capital and seem pusillanimous and weak; but he had hoped for something better from his brother.

There were zones on the Ourcq Canal which were left practicable.

So, the overall picture was rather disastrous.

The forces available when the Allis arrived

- **The 1 200 men** of the Imperial Guard left to protect the Empress and the Guards' depots.

- **The troops under Marshals Marmont and Mortier** who had fallen back after Fère-Champenoise. Those belonging to Compans and Ledru des Essarts who had come from Meaux and the leftovers of the other divisions which had withdrawn to Paris: Bordessoule, Merlin, Boyer de Rébeval, Arrighi, Michel, Ornano and Belliard.

- **The National Guard** whose twelve legions were spread out around Paris, the firemen, the veterans from the Invalides, the cadets from the Polytechnique and from Alfort.

- **Daumesnil** occupied the Chateau of Vincennes with two Dutch artillery companies.

This made a total of 35 000 to 40 000 men including 5 000 cavalry.

The Fighting on 30 March

The Allies arrived in front of Paris on 29 March and the fighting did not start until the following day. They left a lot of troops in case Napoleon returned:

Bülow surrounded Soissons and Compiègne.

De Wrède and Sacken remained in Meaux.

Large reinforcements were sent to Lyon and Bubna.

Winzigerode continued with his covering mission facing Napoleon's small French army.

Schwarzenberg did however have a lot of troops in front of Paris. He disposed them as follows:

In the vanguard, he placed Helfreich and Kretov.

The centre was commanded by Barclay de Tolly and his objectives were the heights in Pantin and Belleville.

For this he had at his disposal the Russian and Prussian Guards under General Yermolov, as well the Wittgenstein's Corps made up of the Mezensov, Schafschafskoi and Piscknitzki Divisions. Helfreich's Division was also part of this corps but had been placed in the vanguard as previously mentioned.

Pahlen, placed by Koch with Wittgenstein was more to the south ensuring the junction with the troops on Würtemberg's right, moving round Vincennes and then moving up towards Charonne whilst also supporting the west.

*Above: **The pupils of the Ecole Polytechnique acting as artillerymen, distinguished themselves at a number of points on the front.** (RR)*

*Below: **The National Guard furnished scarcely a third of their expected strength. Among these men, half of them had no military fighting value.** (RR)*

Koch made a mistake in his text when he said that the Prince of Würtemberg was under the command of Barclay de Tolly in place of Wittgenstein. This mistake probably arose from a typographical mistake or to a change in the command structure.

On the right, there was the Army of Silesia. Blücher was ill and it was Barclay de Tolly who supervised the attack. His objective was Montmartre and he had the troops of Kapzewitsch, Kalnielnov, Emmanuel and Langeron at his disposal. The latter took part in the move around Paris via St-Ouen, Clichy, the Bois de Boulogne and les Batignolles.

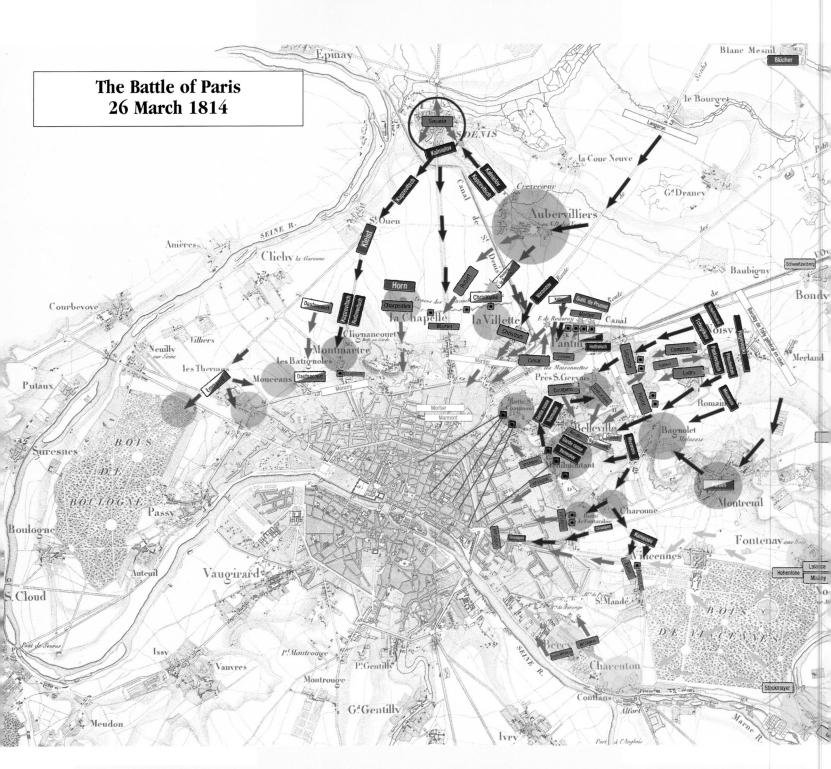

The Battle of Paris
26 March 1814

The fighting on 30 March

Koch has described the fighting of the 30th, establishing five successive phases.

FIRST PHASE

On the Allied side

— **The Helfreich Division** with the **Kretov Cuirassiers** reached Pantin.

— **The Mesensov division** and **Pahlen** marched on Romainville.

— Coming from le Bourget **Langeron** advanced against Aubervilliers.

On the French side

— **The Boyer** and **Michel Divisions** blocked the road to Germany.

— Ledru des Essarts was in the Romainville wood, Compans was at the Pré Saint-Gervais. Mortier left Curial beside Secrétan at les Maisonettes.

— **Marmont** advanced towards Belleville and Charpentier was at the foot of the Buttes-Chaumont (the Chaumont Heights).

— **Christiani** was between la Villette and la Chapelle, supported by Dautancourt, who had replaced Belliard, towards Saint-Ouen then les Batignolles.

SECOND PHASE

On the Allied side, Barclay de Tolly decided to attack.

— with two leading divisions, supported on the left by **Paskevich** between Montreuil and Romainville. The Knieschnin and Tschoglikov Divisions headed for the Beauregard heights with Pitschintzki

and Shasschoskoi. Würtemberg sent a column towards Charenton and Bercy.

— **Pahlen** advanced along the Avenue de Vincennes against Evain and his artillerymen from the Polytechnique.

— **Langeron** attacked Aubervilliers and York's, Kleist's and Voronsov's corps positioned themselves between Pantin and La Chapelle.

On the French side

— **Arrighi** had to abandon Montreuil for Bagnolet.

— **Marmont** succeeded in holding out in the Romainville wood.

— **Mortier** held out and counter-attacked towards Pantin.

— the bridges at Saint-Maur and Charenton were abandoned.

— the National Guards withdrew to the Bercy and Picpus barriers.

— **Ordener** drove off the Russian Lancers.

THIRD PHASE

On the Allied side

— **Mezensov** took Bagnolet.

— **Gortschakov** attacked Charenton.

— **Pitnischki** with the Pleskov and Astrakhan Cuirassiers and the Tschoglokov Grenadiers pushed Compans towards Belleville.

— the Prussians crossed the Ourcq Canal at le Rouvroy and the Russians came out of Pantin.

On the French side

— the Fontarabie Battery and the National Guards held out at Charonne.

— **Marmont** withdrew and held Saint-Gervais where Boyer de Rébeval was positioned.

— **Bordessoulles and Chastel** were in front of the Tourelles heights on the side of Ménilmontant.

— with the Rouvroy battery, Mortier and the Guard stopped the Russians and the Prussians on the canal.

FOURTH PHASE

the simultaneous attack on Ménilmontant, Belleville and Pré-Saint-Gervais

On the Allied side

— **Yermolov** with his grenadiers drove back Sécrétan from les Maisonettes. Secrétan had been left by Curial who had been called to Rouvroy and then la Villette.

— **Prince William of Prussia** with Katzler from York's Corps in support took the canal bridges from the soldiers of the Old Guard.

— **Tschoglikjov and Paskievich** approached Belleville supported by Menzenov and Pahlen.

On the French side

— **Sécrétan and Curial** were pushed back to les Maisonettes and to Belleville.

— **Marmont** kept the upper part of Belleville.

— **Arrighi** gave up Ménilmontant and withdrew towards Marmont.

— the National Guards were thrown out of the Buttes-Chaumont (Chaumont Heights) abandoning their cannon.

— The Mont-Louis Guards, their cannon and Bourdessoulles and Vincent fell back to the barriers of Montreuil.

IN THE PLAIN

On the Allied side

— **Prince William** with Voronzov, Horn and four regiments of Cossacks attacked la Villette and la Chapelle.

— **Langeron** took Aubervilliers and detached a division towards Saint-Denis and pushed Kapzievich, Karnielov towards la Villette and la Chapelle leaving them to hold Savarin at St-Denis where he was still resisting with the 7th Voltigeurs. Emmanuel was sent towards Saint-Ouen and the Bois de Boulogne.

On the French side

— **Mortier** had installed a protected battery on the line of the traces of 1792; it was very effective. He had Colonel Christophe charge, but he was mauled by the Brandenburg Hussars.

— **Curial** abandoned la Villette and Charpentier la Chapelle; they withdrew towards Montmartre.

— **Belliard** was at the foot of Montmartre.

FIFTH PHASE

On the Allied side

— **Emmanuel's** cavalry charged between the Clichy barrier and that of Neuilly.

— **Kapzevich and Rudzevich** moved up to Montmartre.

On the French side

— **Belliard** tried to get Dautancourt and Sparre to charge but in vain, two squadrons rallied towards the Clichy barrier near a battalion of firemen and Moncey. This marshal commanded the cadets from the Polytechnique with their cannon and the National Guards behind their barricades.

When the capitulation was announced the fighting gradually ceased.

98

The French Voltigeurs are engaged against their Allied counterparts in front of Pantin. (Author's Collection)

Opposite, from top to bottom:
Compans' troops defending Pantin.
(by Schommer, Hotel de Ville de Pantin)
The Prussians, under Kleist, attack the Butte-Montmartre.
(German National Museum at Nüremberg)
On the Avenue de Vincennes, the students from the Ecole Polytechnique defend their cannon attacked by Pahlen's Russian cavalry. (RR)

Prince William of Prussia led the crossing of the Saint-Denis Canal and the capture of the battery covering it, then the attack on the 1792 entrenchments commanded by General Mortier.

The left, entrusted to the Prince of Wûrtemberg had to hold the bridges over the Marne and attack towards Charenton, Bercy and Sait-Maur, supported by Guilay. After having taken Bercy, he had also to head for the Barrière du Trone. The brigades that have been mentioned were indeed those of Würtemberg with Hohenlohe in the lead, Stockmayer, Misany and Lalance, which confirmed the presence of this corps on the left wing and not in the centre under Barclay as Koch says.

Barclay sent Rajewski forward; he arrived at Pantin and the Romainville Plateau facing Michel and Boyer de Rébeval, both of whom were wounded. Compans and Ledru des Essarts were on the plateau in the Romainville wood.

Marmont who was to support them moved up by Bagnolet and Montreuil. Rajewski received reinforcements in the form of Langeron when his first attack failed; the Russians were pushed back by the arrival of Marmont and withdrew to Pantin.

Mortier arrived and set himself up in the line up to Aubervilliers. Rajewski launched his Russian and Prussian Guards which were stopped by Chabert de Compans' and Fournier's Brigades from the 6th Corps with Ledru and Fabvier.

Barclay was halted so he waited for Blücher who was still ill and who was coming from Villepinte towards le Bourget with Wurtemberg. When they did arrive, it was Mortier who took the first shock; he had Belliard on his left who covered Saint-Ouen and his right was next to Marmont.

Joseph was in his headquarters in Montmartre where there were still only seven cannon and an insufficient number of National Guardsmen. At midday, seeing the enemy masses arriving from all sides, he left for Blois, fleeing with Clarke and Jérôme. He warned Marmont who was still holding out that *"he authorised him to capitulate"*. He ordered the dignitaries to leave Paris and head for Chartres. In spite of Savary, Talleyrand remained in Paris.

Meanwhile Barclay, replacing Blücher who was still ill, attacked Mortier in front of La Chapelle and La Villette. The Brandenburg Hussars repulsed Dautancourt's and Belliard's cavalry and captured some cannon. Langeron arrived to threaten Montmartre. He sent Kapzevich to attack Saint-Denis on the way, but he ran up against the resistance of this town which had been fortified by its inhabitants and which had 4 cannon and 400 Voltigeurs of the Young Guard commanded by Savarin.

Mortier withdrew to the La Villette barrier where one of Christiani's battalions stopped the attackers. The general offensive was now started, 70 000 men against 6 000.

General Compans vigorously directing the defence of Pantin.
(by Schommer. Hotel de Ville de Pantin/RR)

*Bottom: **The west flank of the Butte-Montmartre attacked by Kapzevitsch's and Rudzewitch's Russians.** (Author's Collection)*

Wurtemberg went round Marmont and succeeded in turning him; Marmont withdrew into Belleville and Ménilmontant. He was supported by Charpentier who was at La Chapelle, under serious threat, and by Curial. Colonel Gheneser got him out with 200 men.

Arrighi was forced back into Bagnolet and Charonne; Vincent arrived to help him. Pahlen in the south had passed Vincennes and avoided the Chateau. He drove back the National Guardsmen and the Alfort cadets and headed for the Fontarabie Heights after having captured Bercy.

Moncey, together with the Polytechnique cadets and the National Guardsmen, set himself up at the Clichy Barrier (Barrière de Clichy) which he reinforced. He held out until the Armistice, helped by some Guards and by the barricades in the Rue de Clichy. Then came the news brought by Dejean who, coming from Troyes, said that Napoleon was on his way, but that he would negotiate directly with his father-in-law; on the other hand Girardin had brought an order to defend Paris and that Napoleon really wanted to fight. Everybody was counting on his arrival!

Over the whole battlefield, the Allies had driven the French back up against the barriers of Paris. A few defenders still resisted fiercely, heroically.

Orlov, Alexander's aide de camp, met with Marmont and they started a cease fire which was to be negotiated. He suggested a meeting where he would be with Mortier at the Saint Denis Barrier.

At the same moment Langeron took Montmartre, Mortier withdrew leaving Marmont alone. Marmont took Orlov to his private house where some of Napoleon's important opponents were gathered except for La Valette and Girardin. Talleyrand then appeared and his treachery "enveloped" the marshal, as Orlov said later.

Marmont thought he was covered by the order from Joseph, but as far as he himself was concerned, Mortier had not received anything. At 2 a.m., Count Paar brought his support to Orlov and the capitulation was decided and signed by the two aides de camp Fabvier and Denys on behalf of Marmont and by the two Allies Orlov and Paar on behalf of the Tsar and Schwartzenberg. The details were discussed and accepted. Marmont had been the arbiter for France. Souham's defection completed this act of treachery.

The battle for Paris was the bloodiest of all the campaign. There were nearly 9 000 French casualties. The Allies suffered more or less the same losses.

In his book on the battle of Paris, Giraud explained his opposition to Bonaparte but also said that Napoleon was ready to invade Paris and had harangued his troops. He reported what Ney said to Napoleon *"You are no longer Emperor, you can no longer command these brave people, and they will no longer obey you. The Marshals are telling you that all is over, that they submit to the wishes of the nation and will no longer bear weapons against their country."*

People mentioned

Sécrétan: OLH in 1812, Baron in 1813, commanded the Chasseurs of the

Guard Depot in Paris, seriously wounded on the Buttes-Chaumont, Major of the 1st Voltigeurs in 1815, retired in 1821.

Chastel: Austerlitz, appointed general in 1811, then Major-General in 1812; CtLH in 1813, commanded the Compans cavalry corps on 28 March 1814, served under Exelmans in 1815 in Belgium, retired in 1825.

Compans: General in 1799, Major-General in 1806, gathered the stragglers at Sézanne and fought on 22 March, at Meaux on the 27th, served at Belleville. GdCxLH in February 1815, refused to serve during the Hundred Days. Pair de France in 1815, voted the execution of Ney.

Chabert: Westphalian General, Jérôme's aide de camp, French General in 1814, commanded a brigade of the National Guards in Paris. CrLH in 1828, retired in 1833.

Greiner: Austerlitz, lost his right arm at Wagram, Baron in 1809, comman-

Above:
The Allied troops enter Paris on 31 March 1814. *(RR)*

Bottom:
On the same day, the Coalition Sovereigns also entered the capital. They had defeated the French army; all they had to do now was to topple its Emperor.
(By P. Knötel. Author's Collection)

ded the Battalion of the Polytechnique cadets in 1810, commanded the artillery of the National Guard on 30 March, Couronne de Fer in 1814, CtLH in 1815, retired in 1816 and then 1836.

Evain: appointed General and Baron in 1813, Lieutenant-General in 1822, retired in 1824, Belgium in 1831. He was naturalised a Belgian citizen in 1832, Minister and GdOLH in 1836, retired in 1843. GdO of the Order of Leopold, died in 1852.

This situation of the French troops has used the original edition of Koch, a Major on the General Staff who was a witness and a historian and who, in his 1819 edition, presented a collection of plates giving detailed tables of the troops engaged and three maps.

Just as we did, he ran into the problem of the discrepancies which appear during the whole campaign, particularly with the French who brought up reinforcements from Paris, Versailles and Spain. These reinforcements were often made up of detachments from the regimental depots or from regiments which had detached smaller elements which were then amalgamated; so much so that regiments were divided and appeared on different fronts and in different corps.

NAPOLEON'S HEADQUARTERS

The make-up of the General Staff is very difficult to present because of all the changes which occurred during the campaign. It is arranged according to the arms and the army corps.

Bertrand: Egyptian campaign, he was made Grand Aigle of the LH in 1809, Grand Maréchal du Palais in 1813, Aide-Major-General in 1814. He was present at Brienne, La Rothière and Champaubert. He was mentioned at Montmirail at the capture of Marchais with Lefebvre. Craonne. He went to Elba, was present at Waterloo and accompanied the Emperor to Saint Helena and witnessed his death. Deputy in 1831, retired in 1832, he saw to the return of Napoleon's ashes in 1840. He was buried next to Napoleon.

Favereau: Bertrand's aide de camp in 1813 and 1815. Promoted to Colonel. Took part in the siege of Antwerp in 1832, appointed Maréchal de camp in 1839, he was CrLH in 1845 and Officer of the Ordre de Léopold in 1833.

NAPOLEON'S AIDE DE CAMPS

Flahaut de la Billarderie: Promoted to Major-General, Napoleon's aide de camp and Count in 1813, he followed the Emperor in 1814, made Pair de France in 1815; was present at Quatre-Bras and Waterloo where he was again aide de camp. Outlawed, he went into exile in England. GdCxLH in 1838, he was Ambassador and Senator in 1852. Grand Chancelier of the LH in 1864, he was awarded the Médaille Militaire in 1866; He was the father of the Duke of Morny.

From 1813 his aide de camp was **Carbonel**; he was made CtLH in 1815 but his promotion was cancelled. GdOLH in 1845.

Montesquiou-Fezenac: Aide de camp in 1814, he was appointed Maréchal de Camp,

Above, left:
General Bertrand,
Grand Maréchal du Palais.
(RR)

Above, right:
General Berthier,
Major General
of the Grande Armée.
(RR)

Opposite:
The Artillery Colonel,
Belly de Bussy, after
a portrait belonging to his great
grand-nephew, M. de Tugny,
(Les Cahiers de la Sabretache. RR)

then Lieutenant-General in 1815, retired in 1816, made GdOLH in 1831 then Pair de France in 1841.

Lebrun: Aide de camp to Napoleon from 1805, he was on the Headquarters Staff in January 1814. Deputy in 1815, he served in Belgium during the Hundred Days. He was made a Peer and Duke of Plaisance on the death of his father in 1824. GdCxLH in 1833, he retired in 1848. Made Grand Chancelier of the LH and awarded the Médaille Militaire in 1853.

Comte d'Astorg: Auguste Colbert's aide de camp in 1807, then Savary's and then Clarke's. He was on the General Staff on 18 February 1814. Dismissed by Napoleon on 15 April 1815, he remained faithful to Louis XVIII whom he joined at Ghent. Served in Spain in 1823. He was a Maréchal de Camp in 1825. CrLH in 1838, Lieutenant-General in 1845, he died in 1849.

Belly de Bussy: An old companion of Napoleon's at La Fère, he joined the Emperor on 6 March to guide him for the attack on Craonne. His help and behaviour got him appointed aide de camp and Colonel on 23 March. He was awarded the LH on the same day. He was at Rheims, Arcis-sur-Aube and Saint-Dizier. Retired in 1830, he died in 1848.

Corbineau: Discovered the way across the Beresina. Napoleon's aide de camp in 1814, he saved his life at Brienne. He commanded the 2nd Cavalry Division of the Guard at Rheims where he was trapped. Wounded twice at Arcis-sur-Aube. He was made a count. Aide de camp to Napoleon in 1815, he followed him to Belgium. Retired in 1824, Pair de France in 1835, GdCxLH in 1838. Had the future Napoleon III arrested in Boulogne in 1840, he retired in 1848.

Dejean: Aide de camp since 1813, he served at Montereau and was made a Major-General in March 1814. Sent to Paris to be with Joseph, he arrived there on 30 March but was unable to prevent the capitulation. He served at Ligny and was then exiled. He returned in 1818; he became a peer on the death of his father. He was in Belgium in 1830. GdCxLH in 1844.

Turenne, Marquis d'Aynac: He was appointed Chamberlain and Count in 1809, Master of the Wardrobe in 1812 and Cr of the Réunion. Peer in 1815, he was at Waterloo. Put on the non-active list in 1816, he was a Ct of the Réunion then GdOLH in 1852, and a Knight of Malta; died in 1852.

The Prince de Savoie-Carignan: Gendarme d'Ordonnance in 1807, he was an Ordnance Officer the following year. Made a Baron in 1810, he was GdOLH in 1823.

Caraman; Lamezan: Captain; **Baron Fain**, secretary and **Roustam** and **Constant**.

MAJOR-GENERAL BERTHIER AND HIS HOUSEHOLD

Girardin, Comte d'Ermenonville: Aide de camp in 1803, he was made a Baron in 1808, then Count in 1810 and General in 1811. A hero of Champaubert where he was promoted to Major-General. Chief of Staff to Grouchy on 13 June 1815. He received the CrSL in 1821 and was GdOLH in 1825. Retired in 1848, he returned to service in 1852, then transferred to the reserve in 1853.

Vicomte Bongard de Roquigny: Napoleon's Ordnance Officer in 1807, he was made a Baron in 1809. He was Berthier's aide de camp in 1812 and 1814. Made OLH in 1813, he was CrLH in 1821. Retired in 1832.

De Galbois: Made a Baron in 1813, served with Berthier in 1813 and 1814. Wounded at Quatre-bras, made GdOLH in 1839.

THE MARÉCHAL'S AIDES DE CAMP

La Bourdonnaye, Marquis de: Ordnance Officer and Baron in 1809, he was Berthier's aide de camp at General Staff Headquarters.

Stoffel, Christophe: Born in Madrid, he was wounded four times in Spain in 1811 and was made OLH in the same year. Made a Baron and Adjudant-Commandant in 1813, he was on the General Staff in 1814. He served during the Hundred Days. Naturalised in 1817, he served in 1823 then commanded the Foreign Legion in Algeria in 1831 and 1832. He retired in 1841.

Stoffel, Augustin: Brother of the above, he was Ordnance Officer at Headquarters in 1814. He was with the 2nd Foreign, made up of Swiss in 1815. Naturalised as a Major, he was in Morée from 1831 to 1833; retired in 1844 as CrLH.

Auguste and François Leroy-Duverger: François was killed at Brienne; **Malaudant** and **Luzignan de Cerze**

General Mongenet commanded the artillery. A Knight of Malta, he was in Egypt with Kléber in 1800. General and CtLH in 1813, he served in the Alps in 1815 and was retired in 1816.

Dufriché de Valazé commanded the Engineers. He was the son of the Convention mem-

A number of regiments which were assigned to other theatres of operations commanded by their Colonel furnished reinforcements for Napoleon's army, often from their depots. These detachments were often under the command of a Battalion Commander. This dispersion explains why the units are difficult to classify.

ARMY GENERAL STAFF

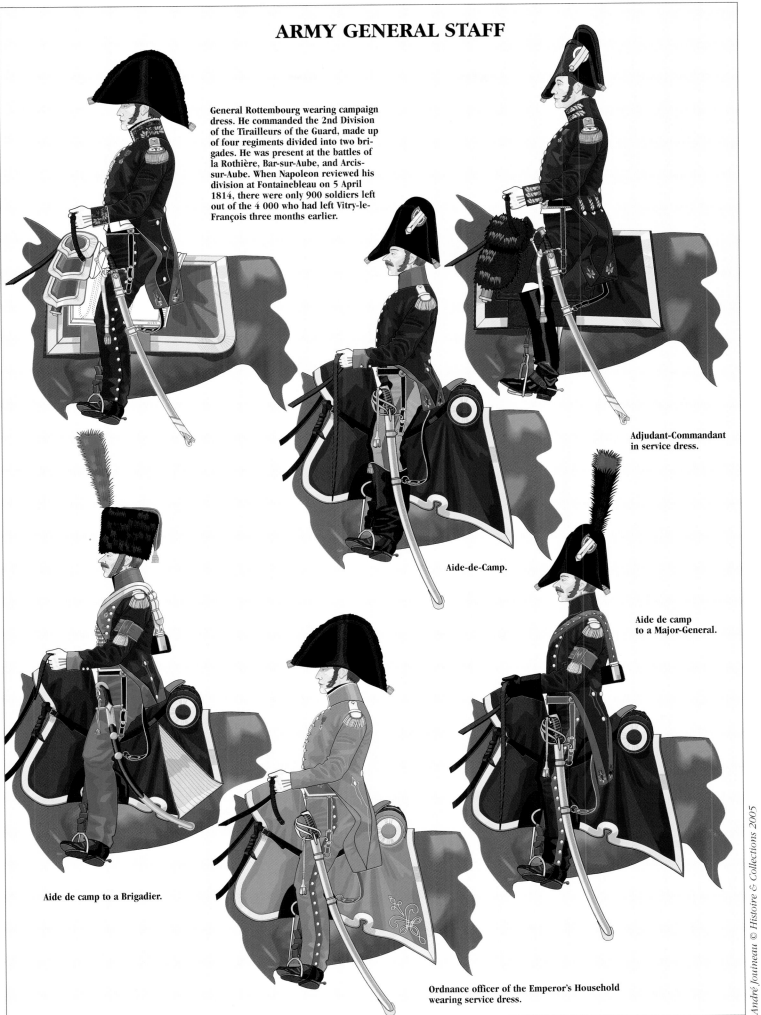

General Rottembourg wearing campaign dress. He commanded the 2nd Division of the Tirailleurs of the Guard, made up of four regiments divided into two brigades. He was present at the battles of la Rothière, Bar-sur-Aube, and Arcis-sur-Aube. When Napoleon reviewed his division at Fontainebleau on 5 April 1814, there were only 900 soldiers left out of the 4 000 who had left Vitry-le-François three months earlier.

Adjudant-Commandant in service dress.

Aide-de-Camp.

Aide de camp to a Major-General.

Aide de camp to a Brigadier.

Ordnance officer of the Emperor's Household wearing service dress.

André Jouineau © Histoire & Collections 2005

De Laroche, Marquis de Fontenelle: Colonel, he was made a Baron in 1813, then CrLH in December 1814. He served in 1815. In the Royal Guard in 1826, he was then dismissed. Appointed Maréchal de Camp in 1830, he retired the following year.

Michal de la Bretonnière: He was made a Chevalier in 1809 and appointed Adjundant-Commandant in 1811. He was on the General Staff in Russia. Baron and OLH in 1813, he stood fast at La Ferté the following year but was unable to hold out. He was in Belgium in 1815 and retired in 1825.

Baillon: Egyptian Campaign, he was a Gendarme d'Elite. He was the Palace Fourrier in 1806 then from 1809 to 1814: he was made a Chevalier in 1812. Squadron Commander in Belgium in 1815, he was promoted to Colonel but this promotion was cancelled then granted again in 1831; he accompanied Napoleon to Rochefort then to the Island of Elba and retired in 1840.

The Neuchâtel battalion whose strength was reduced to an Elite Company was on Ordnance duty with Berthier.

From left to right and top to bottom:
The Aide Major Generals: General Belliard for the Cavalry, General Drouot for the Artillery of the Guard, Maréchal Lefebvre for the Imperial Guard and General Nansouty for the Horse Guards.
General Grouchy commanded the Cavalry of the Line and General Bordesoulle in theory commanded the 1st Cavalry Corps. He only joined the army late in the campaign.
(All photos: RR)

ber and a Polytechnicien. He was at Austerlitz.

HEADQUARTERS "*ADJOINTS*"

Gressot: A Swiss national, he took part in the Italian campaign. Commanded Headquarters on 1 February 1814, then Chief of Staff to Oudinot on 8 February. He was promoted to CrLH in August. He served at Waterloo then was put on the non-active list. He entered the Royal Guard in 1823 and retired in 1833.

Bacler d'Albe: Baron in 1809, he commanded the Cartographical/Topographical (map making) Unit. He was promoted to General and OLH in 1813.

Athalin: Second-in-Command of the Topographical Unit, he was made an OLH in 1813. Commanded Landau's Engineers in 1815. He was aide de camp to the Duke of Orléans in 1817, served in Spain in 1823 and then was aide de camp to Louis-Philippe and Maréchal de Camp in 1830. GdOLH in 1831, he was a Lieutenant-General in 1840 and retired in 1848.

Nillis: A Belgian national, he was naturalised in 1816. He served Austria from 1792 to 1803. He served on the General Staff in 1813, was awarded the LH and was appointed Adjudant-Commandant in 1814. Retired in 1848.

Bonne: Geographical Engineer, he was appointed Maréchal de Camp in 1831.

Babut: Awarded the LH in 1804, he was wounded at Austerlitz. Adjudant-Commandant in 1813, he was on the Staff in 1814. He served in Belgium in 1815. Then was put on the non-active list from 1815 to 1818 and died in 1822.

The General Staff "*Aide Major General*"

Maréchal Lefebvre commanded the Guard. **Nansouty** commanded the Cavalry of the Guard. **Drouot** commanded the Artillery of the Guard. **Grouchy** commanded the Cavalry of the Line. **Belliard** was deputy commander of the Cavalry.

Bailly de Monthion was deputy commander of the Infantry. Count in 1809, he served under Berthier from then onwards. Major-General in 1812, he took part in the Russian Campaign. Chief-of-Staff in 1815, he was wounded at Waterloo. He was made a Pair de France in 1837, GdCxLH in 1843, and died in 1850.

SOUS-ADJOINTS ATTACHÉS

Allouis: Deputy to the General Staff from 1813 to 1814, he was made OLH in 1814. He was a Major then the Adjudant-Commandant in 1815. Baron in 1822, he was promoted to Colonel in 1823 then retired in 1830.

GROUCHY'S CAVALRY

On 20 February due to the weak state of the regiments, the cavalry was reorganised into four corps. Baron Rotwiller, a Major, in his history of the 2nd Cuirassiers, gives the following analysis of the situation:

"The Emperor wanted to save what was left of his cavalry and to reinforce it as quickly as possible. But there were several shortfalls:

- The horsemen had not been instructed and did not know how to look after their mounts.

- The horses had been found hastily and subjected to rapid marches, weighed down by the riders and injured by bad saddles.

- There were not enough cadres, in particular the Non-Commissioned Officers, and the officers were often too young or inexperienced.

- The generals tried to make up for these defects with the quality of their manoeuvres, and they were effective, drawing along their men and carrying out well thought-out charges which stimulated the young recruits."

The losses in Russia and during 1813 had weighed heavily on this arm. The old regiments of veterans of the Guard were exploited to the utmost, but the inevitable losses started to thin out their ranks. Thanks to them there were however some magnificent successes before they finished by being overwhelmed by the sheer numbers of the enemy. The temporary regiments were made up by joining together detachments of various other regiments like for example the 3rd Provisional Regiment which consisted of parts of the 6th, 8th, 9th, 11th and 12th Cuirassiers in just the same manner as in the infantry.

DOUMERC'S CAVALRY CORPS

Doumerc: Took part at Austerlitz and was a hero of the Beresina, he was made a General in 1806. He commanded the 1st Corps at la Rothière and Vauchamps. He served in 1815 before being put on the non-active list and then retired in 1825. He was made GdCxLH in 1832.

Bordessoulle (Tardif de Pommeroux de): He won a Sabre of Honour in 1802 and fought at Austerlitz. He was promoted to General in 1807, made a Baron in 1810, and Major-General in 1812; he had his jaw bone broken at Borodino. He commanded the two divisions which were formed at Versailles on 7 February 1814. On 19 February he was appointed commanding officer of the 1st Corps and fought at Vauchamps, Rheims, Fère-Champenoise on 25 March and at Paris on the 30th. He followed the King in 1815 and was made GdCxLH in the same year. He was elected a deputy. Count in 1816, he was aide de camp to the Duke of Artois then to the Comte d'Angoulême. He was made GdCxSL in 1821, he commanded the Royal Guard in Spain in 1823, at Cadiz. Pair de France in 1823, he retired in 1832.

Bordessoulle was entrusted with organising the new regiments at the Versailles depot and

CHEVAU-LÉGERS LANCIERS

The Chevau-Légers were created from Dragoon regiments. They kept the green background coat and a modified Dragoon's helmet, and added the lance to the equipment and the weapons of the Light cavalry. Their main function was to scout for the Cavalry of the Line regiments.

Trooper from the 1st Chevau-Léger Regiment.

Trooper from the 3rd Chevau-Léger Regiment.

Trooper from the 3rd Chevau-Léger Regiment.

Trooper from the Elite Company of the 4th Chevau-Léger Regiment.

Trooper from the 5th Chevau-Léger Regiment.

7th Chevau-Légers. The three other regiments were made up of two Polish regiments and of the 30th Chasseurs.

Trooper from the Elite Company of 9th Chevau-Légers.

André Jouineau © Histoire & Collections 2005

Colonel Tanski of the 7th Chevau-Légers. This regiment was made up of elements from the Vistula Lancers. (RR)

only went up at the beginning of March to take over command of the corps which Doumerc had commanded until then. The 1st Corps was assigned to Marmont and went to Paris in support. It consisted of 4 351 horsemen on 20 February.

MERLIN'S LIGHT DIVISION

The designation and the make up of the cavalry regiments are debatable and vary depending on the authors. The organisation carried out on 20 February did not clarify matters very much. This reorganisation was necessary because of the reduction in the numbers of cavalrymen present and the extra ones from the temporary regiments following the disbanding of the Pajol Division.

Merlin: Egyptian Campaign where he was an aide de camp to Bonaparte; he was at Marengo and at Austerlitz. Promoted to General in 1813, he was the Major of the 2nd Chasseurs à Cheval of the Young Guard on 25 May 1814. He served in the Nord Department in 1815. Accused of being involved in the Belfort plot he was acquitted in 1820. Lieutenant-General in 1832, he was a deputy in 1834. Made a GdOLH in 1837, he became a count on the death of his father then Pair de France in 1839. He retired in 1848.

General Huber joined the division on 30 March and took part in the battle of Paris. He served under Piré during the Hundred Days. GdOLH and Lieutenant-General in 1823, he retired in 1826.

Wathiez's Brigade

Wathiez: aide de camp to Lasalle in 1807, made Chevalier in 1810 then Baron in 1813. Suspended for disobedience in March 1814, he served with Piré at Waterloo where he was wounded. Lieutenant-General in 1837, GdOLH in 1843 then retired in 1848.

The brigade comprised the 6th, 7th and 8th Hussar regiments (342 men) and the 1st, 3rd, 5th, 7th and 8th Chevau-Léger Lancers regiments (721 men).

The 6th Hussars

The Prince of Savoie-Carignan was their Colonel. He was a Gendarme d'ordonnance then Ordnance Officer to the Emperor. He was made a Baron in 1809. Appointed Colonel of the 6th in 1812, he served during the Hundred Days. Appointed Maréchal de Camp in 1821, he served in 1821 and was made GdOLH in 1823. Buried in Turin.

The regiment's strength was 147 Hussars on 20 February. On 17 March, the 6th Hussars were reinforced with 200 men.

The 7th Hussars

Colonel Eulner: Baron in 1809, he was made an OLH in 1812; retired in 1820 as Honorary Maréchal de Camp. The regiment was mentioned at Vauchamps, Montereau, Rheims, Laon and Paris. There were 71 Hussars on 20 February.

The 8th Hussars

Colonel Turau (called "Thurot"): Wounded seven times, OLH in 1811. Mayor of Hagueneau from 1820 to 1830, died in 1855.

The strength of the regiment was 84 Hussars on 20 February; it was mentioned at Montereau then in the defence of Strasbourg.

The 1st Chevau-Légers

Colonel Jacquinot: Brother of the General; OLH in 1809, fought at Ligny and at Waterloo, retired in 1834.

The 1st Lancers had 121 men on 20 February; it was mentioned at Laon, Rheims, Fère-Champenoise and Paris.

The 3rd Chevau-Légers

At Champaubert, Lieutenant **Sémélé** captured a battery. The regiment was also present at Vauchamps and Troyes.

The 5th Chevau-Légers

Colonel Chabert: Took part in the Russian Campaign, made OLH in 1813. He was replaced in 1815 and retired the same year with the rank of Honorary Maréchal de Camp.

The regiment was formed from the 17th Dragoons in 1811. It consisted of 164 troopers.

The 7th Chevau-Légers

Colonel Tanski was awarded the LH in 1808, was captured at Dresden and replaced by Belinski-Skupiewski who was promoted Colonel in 1815. He went to Elba and fought at Waterloo.

On the accompanying portrait, fawn was more likely to be the colour of the distinctive of the 9th Chevau-Légers; otherwise it should be daffodil yellow as with the 8th (Margerand's article in la Sabretache). This Adjutant probably served in the temporary regiment which included a detachment from the 9th mixed with the 8th on 19 January 1814.

The regiment was formed from the 1st Vistula lancers and comprised 122 troopers. It was disbanded in May 1814.

The 8th Chevau-Légers

This regiment also came from the Vistula Lancers and was amalgamated with the 7th Chevau-Légers, and was in turn disbanded in May 1814. When the cavalry was reorganised, the regiment had 121 men.

Guyon's Brigade

Guyon: Italian and Egyptian Campaigns, he was a general in 1811. He was at Versailles to organise Bordessoulles' divisions and was appointed to the 1st Corps on 26 February 1814. Served under Lecourbe in 1815, made GdOLH in 1825 and was granted leave of absence in 1831. On 17 March 1814, Guyon was replaced at the head of his brigade by Latour-Foissac.

Latour-Foissac: Brigadier, he did not serve in 1815. He was made a Baron in 1816, Viscount in 1817, GdOLH and Lieutenant-General in 1823 and finally CrSL in 1823. He retired in 1832.

In fact this brigade was the combination of two provisional regiments. The 1st Provisional comprised 145 Chasseurs from the 1st, 95 from the 2nd, 107 from the 3rd and 94 from the 6th, in all 443 horsemen. The 2nd Provisional comprised 135 Chasseurs from the 8th, 134 from the 9th, 141 from the 16th and 105 from the 25th, in all 515 men.

This type of combination enabled regiments to be formed which were big enough and capable of carrying out the Emperor's attacks against the huge mass of invading troops. To reorganise the cavalry, Napoleon disbanded the Corps of Pajol who was wounded; this enabled the other regiments to be reinforced.

The 1st Chasseurs

Colonel Huber: Born in Prussian Rhineland, he fought at Austerlitz and was wounded in 1807. Aide de camp to Montbrun in Russia, he was made a Baron, then Colonel in 1813, then General on 15 March 1814. He replaced Wathiez and was present at the Battle of Paris on 30 March. Taken off the active list in September 1814, he served with Piré in 1815 in Belgium. He was made a GdOLH and Lieutenant-General in 1823 in Spain where he was decorated with the order of Saint-Ferdinand. Retired in 1825, he was in the reserve in 1831.

On 25 January, the regiment was present at the capture of Saint-Dizier where Landskoï and Szcherbatov were beaten. On the 29th, it fought at Brienne and on 1 February at La Rothière. The regiment was present at Champaubert, at Vauchamps, then at Mormant with Victor and Kellermann alongside Treillard's Spanish Dragoons. The regiment was at Rheims on 24 March and fell back on Charenton. The regiment numbered 145 men on 9 February. It was reinforced with 103 of Pajol's men and 105 brought up by Bordessoulle. After the 20 February reorganisation, the regiment had 300 horsemen.

The 2nd Chasseurs

Colonel Mathis: Scout with Leclerc in Saint Dominica; with the 7th Hussars under Lasalle at Zehdenick in 1807. OLH, Colonel of the 2nd Chasseurs from 1807 to 1814. Baron in 1809; fought in Russia. Appointed Maréchal de camp in 1815, but this was rescinded and he was retired in 1821. Re-appointed Maréchal de camp in 1831, he was retired in 1832.

In 1813 the regiment had been reduced to 98 Chasseurs. At first assigned to the 5th Cavalry Corps, the regiment went over to the 1st Corps on 26 February. On 9 February, the 95 remaining Chasseurs were incorporated into the 1st Provisional Regiment. It served at Champaubert. The regiment was reinforced and lined up 300 men. On 29 March they were in front of

HUSSARS

Brigadier from the 6th Hussars. In around 1813, the shako rouleau which became generalised in 1815 throughout all the Hussar regiments. The sabretache was made of leather with a copper or brass plate, depending on the colour of the button, bearing the number of the regiment.

Trooper from the 2nd Hussars.

Trooper from the 3rd Hussars. At the end of the Empire, riding breeches were used a lot and were then also worn for full dress.

Trooper from the 5th Hussars.

Trooper from the 10th Hussars.

Trumpeter from the 8th Hussars.

Trooper from the Jerome Napoleon Hussars.

André Jouineau © Histoire & Collections 2005

Paris. In 1815, the 2nd Chasseurs were at Ligny and Wavre.

The 3rd Chasseurs

Colonel Comte de Potier took part in the Russian Campaign where, after being wounded, he was a Brigadier in the "Escadron Sacré". He followed the King to Ghent, was made CrLH in 1820, was awarded the Order of Saint Ferdinand in 1823 and was a Gentleman to the King's Bedchamber.

The 5th Chasseurs

Colonel Baillot: Chevalier in 1809, appointed Colonel in 1811 and awarded OLH in 1813. He was mentioned as Colonel of the 2nd Provisional then with the Army of the Pyrenees. He was most probably in the part of the regiment which was in Spain.

For the campaign, the regiment was under the command of the second Colonel, Beugnat, who was with the part which had joined the Grande Armée, i.e. the 3rd and 4th Squadrons and a company from the 2nd. This totalled 21 officers and 182 men. There were three officers at the depot. On 9 February, the regiment numbered 207 Chasseurs. It was at Mormant on 17 February. The 5th Chasseurs were assigned to Kellermann's 6th Corps on 20 February in Ameil's Brigade. It fought at Bar-sur-Aube on 27 February, Arcis-sur-Aube on the 20 March and Saint-Dizier on the 26th. On 5 April, the regiment was at Fontainebleau.

Beugnat: Wounded at Hohenlinden, present at Austerlitz. OLH in 1811, served at Waterloo and retired in 1816.

The 8th Chasseurs

Colonel Planzeaux: Promoted Colonel on 4 December 1813, he was wounded at Berry-au-Bac on 6 March then fought at Paris on 30 March with Compans. In 1815, he served in Belgium; was appointed Maréchal de Camp in 1831, CrLH in 1932 and retired in 1834.

On 4 December, the regiment only had 7 officers and 83 men left. It was at Brienne, La Rothière, Champaubert and Vauchamps. On 17 March, the strength was raised to 300 horsemen.

The 16th Chasseurs

Colonel Duvivier: a Belgian, he resigned and went over to Wellington; General at Waterloo. Made a Belgian Baron, he retired in 1816. CrLH in 1833, he was awarded several Dutch and Belgian Honours.

The 16th Chasseurs were at Mormant where Piré and Briche were on the left with Kellermann on the right. The regiment also fought at Brienne, La Ferté-sous-Jouarre, Rheims, Fère-Champenoise

The regimental depot was pulled back to Versailles on 27 March with 16 officers and 227 men. The depot had sent a number of detachments of recruits. One of these was at Saint-Dizier on 26 March where Sebastiani with the cavalry of the Guard had found a ford and distinguished himself. On 28 March it fell back on Troyes. Napoleon decided to march on Paris giving up the idea of going to his eastern strongholds. On the 30th, he bivouacked at Sens. On the 31st, the Allies entered Paris. In 1815, the regiment was at Ligny and Wavre.

BORDESSOULLE'S HEAVY CAVALRY

(Doumerc's until 6 March)
The General kept this command for himself.

Thiry's brigade

Thiry: Awarded a Sabre of Honour in 1802 and made CtLH in 1808. Appointed General and Baron in 1809, in Paris in 1815, he retired in 1818.

The brigade was made up of the 2nd, 3rd, 6th, 9th, 11th and 12th Cuirassier Regiments forming the 3rd Provisional Regiment. At the beginning of the campaign it numbered 995 sabres.

The 2nd Cuirassiers

Colonel Morin: OLH in 1809, Baron in 1813. Commanded the 3rd provisional Regiment in 1814 and died in Paris on 20 February of wounds received at Vauchamps. Posthumous CSL. Colonel Labiffe replaced him on 17 March.

Labiffe: Ordnance officer to Napoleon in 1807, OLH in 1809. Appointed Squadron Commander in the Chasseurs of the Guard in 1811, he was awarded the Order of the Reunion in March 1813, and made a Baron in 1814. Mentioned at Montmirail and Vauchamps, he was

made Colonel of the 2nd Cuirassiers in March. Served in Belgium in 1815. On the non-active list in 1815, retired in 1822. The regiment had 13 men and 101 men on 28 January. It was at Brienne with Marmont and with Doumerc at Champaubert. At Vauchamps with Grouchy it made 2 000 prisoners then having turned the enemy it charged the squares and took a further 1 000 prisoners and captured four cannon; but Ney sounded the rally. The 2nd Cuirassiers took part in the recapture of Montmirail but was blocked in front of Soissons on 5 March with Marmont. On 7 March it was at Béry-au-Bac then it moved up to Laon where it was routed at Athies on 9 March by a night attack under Langeron and Sacken. At Fère-Champenoise, the regiment only numbered 125 men.

In a letter dated 2 March from Belliard, we learn that the regiment was reinforced with 624 horsemen on 24 February and a further 300 on the 26th. Moreover, Bordessoulle arrived with 500 men which brought the corps' strength up to 2 663 men. One strange thing was that in this letter, it was learnt that *"Bordesoulle had finally joined the army and taken command of the 1st Corps which until then had been under the orders of General Doumerc."*

The 3rd Cuirassiers

Colonel Préval: Austerlitz, appointed General in 1806, then Baron in 1808; at Versailles on 1 February 1814. Lieutenant-General on 10 May, Viscount in 1817, Peer in 1837, GdCxLH in 1843, retired in 1848, Senator in 1852.

The regiment was at Champaubert, Vauchamps and Fère-Champenoise.

The 6th Cuirassiers

Colonel Martin: OLH in 1808, appointed Colonel in 1811. In Russia he took part in the capture of the Great Redoubt at the Moskova.

The Colonel Second-in-Command was **Lallemant** – not to be confused with General Lallemant. He was the Colonel of the 1st Cuirassiers of the Westphalian Guard, then appointed Colonel of the 6th Cuirassiers on 26 February 1814. Retired in 1819, OLH in 1831, died in 1841. The regiment was mentioned at Brienne, la Rothière, Champaubert and Vauchamps; its strength was 191 troopers on 20 February.

The 9th Cuirassiers

Colonel Habert: LH in 1809, then OLH in 1813, served in the 4th Cuirassiers in 1815 and retired in 1824. He commanded the regiment from 3 September but was mentioned as having been sent to the Army of Lyon, as was his successor, Bigarne. The regimental history however has him taking part in this campaign with Doumerc: only a part of the regiment was with the Thiry Brigade with 11 officers and 133 men.

Colonel Bigarne was awarded the CrLH in 1820.

On 26 January, the 9th Cuirassiers took part in the attack on Saint-Dizier; then it was at Brienne and la Rothière. On 9 February, there were 146 men in the regiment. They fought at Champaubert, Vauchamps, Craonne on 7 March and Fère-Champenoise on the 25th. The survivors were in Paris on the day of the abdication, 11 April; there were only 10 officers and 136 troopers left.

The 11th Cuirassiers

Commanded by Colonel Lefèvre since 1813; OLH in 1814, he served in 1815, retired in 1819 and died in 1835.

This regiment which came from the Carabiniers fought at Brienne, La Rothière, Vitry against de Wrède, Champaubert, Montmirail, Vauchamps, Nangis, Craonne, Laon, Rheims, Arcis-sur-Aube, Fère-Champenoise and Paris.

The 12th Cuirassiers

Colonel Daudes: Chevalier in 1810, Colonel and OLH in 1813; Maréchal de Camp, he retired on 12 May 1815. His appointment was afterwards rescinded then restored in 1831. He retired in 1833. The regiment was mentioned at Champaubert, Montmirail, Vauchamps, Craonne, Arcis-sur-Aube, Saint-Dizier and Paris. On 5 April, Marmont and Souham defected, leaving the regiment with only 13 officers and 82 men.

Laville's Brigade

Laville: Born at Turin he went over from the service of Sardinia to that of France in 1799.

CHASSEURS À CHEVAL

Trooper from the 1st Chasseurs à Cheval. According to the 1812 Regulations the jacket replaced the "à la kinski" coat. However, the skirts of the chasseurs were shorter than those of the Dragoons. The colback was normally replaced by the Grenadier's shako in the Elite Companies.

Trooper from the 2nd Chasseurs à Cheval.

Officer from the 7th Chasseurs à Cheval wearing campaign dress

Brigadier from the 5th Chasseurs à Cheval Elite Company.

Trooper wearing a greatcoat.

Trumpeter from the Elite Company of the 8th Chasseurs à cheval.

Maréchal des Logis from the 4th Chasseurs à Cheval.

André Jouineau © Histoire & Collections 2005

A Trumpeter from the 4th Cuirassiers. All the Trumpeters wore the Imperial Livery after 1812. (RR)

Appointed General in 1813, he was naturalised in 1815. He retired in 1818 then again in 1841.

The brigade was made up of the 7th, 20th, 28th and 30th Dragoons and the 4th, 7th and 14th Cuirassiers.

The 4th Cuirassiers

Colonel Dujon: Sabre of Honour in 1802, fought at Austerlitz, made a Baron in 1810, wounded three times at Epinal; with the Chasseurs of the Guard in 1815, he was retired; GdOLH in 1825, he was retired again in 1830.

The 4th Cuirassiers were at Epinal where the Squadron Commander de Morell replaced Dujon who was wounded. The regiment was at Saint-Dizier on 26 January, Brienne, La Rothière, Champaubert, Vauchamps. With Marmont and Mortier at Fère-Champenoise where Sub-Lieutenant Lemaire recaptured a canon then served two others. Dujon returned on 28 March but was wounded again. On 30 March, the 4th Cuirassiers were at Paris where the 1st Corps was reduced to 895 men. One squadron was in Hamburg and a detachment was in Magdeburg.

At the beginning of the campaign, the regiment had 170 horsemen.

The 7th Cuirassiers

Colonel Richardot: Commanded in fact the 4th Provisional then went over to the 7th. CtLH in 1814, served at Waterloo in 1815, then put on the non-active list. Dismissed in 1815. The regiment was mentioned at Champaubert, Vauchamps, Fère-Champenoise and Paris.

The 14th Cuirassiers

This regiment lost its standard at the Beresina. It was in Paris in 1814. The remains of this unit seemed to have served at Champaubert with Doumerc and 199 horsemen who served in the provisional units.

The 7th Dragoons

Colonel Leopold: Wounded in 1805, then again in Spain in 1808 and 1809, Chevalier in 1810, wounded again at Fère-Champenoise, promoted to OLH in 1814; wounded at Waterloo, retired in 1821.

There were 120 Dragoons in the regiment on 20 February.

The 28th Dragoons

Colonel Holdrinet (called "Clermont"): OLH in 1806. On 28 January he received seven lance wounds from the Cossacks and was taken prisoner. He was replaced on the 30th by Colonel Mugnier who had come from Spain with the 6th Dragoons.

Mugnier: OLH in 1809, Baron in 1813, served in Belgium in 1815, then was retired in 1816.

On 4 January, the 28th had a strength of 8 officers and 66 men. They were under the command of Marmont with Doumerc at La Rothière, on 8 February at Sézanne, on the 10th at Champaubert where the regiment suffered 10 casualties out of the 179 present. They were with Grouchy at Vauchamps and there were only 196 of them left on 20 February.

The depot was at Orléans for the 28th and 30th Dragoons and the 6th Chevau-Légers. The 28th's depot numbered 6 officers and 66 men. Only two squadrons were present at the beginning of the campaign.

Reinforcements came up for the brigade: 6 officers and 88 men for the 7th, and 8 officers and 107 men for the 28th. Then on 26 February, four officers and 55 men left Versailles to join the 28th. On 25 February with Doumerc, the regiment fell back, following Marmont who joined Mortier near Meaux. They held off Sacken and Kleist on the line of the Ourcq on 2 March, but Blücher moved up towards the Aisne where Bülow and Winzigerode took Soissons on 4 March, thus opening the way to Laon. Marmont was routed at Athies near Craonne where the regiment lost Marlinge, the Squadron Commander and ten men. They were at Rheims on 13 March then near Béry-au-Bac.

The 30th Dragoons

Colonel Ordener (the son of the General): Aide de camp to his father, who was in command of the Grenadiers à Cheval of the Guard; wounded at Clichy on 30 March trying to disengage the battery served by the cadets from the Polytechnique. He fought at Waterloo where he was wounded again. He was promoted to Maréchal de Camp in 1831, Lieutenant-General in 1846, GdOLH in 1848, then became count on the death of his father.

On 1 February, the 30th Dragoons were at Morviliers, on the left wing in front of la Rothière. Attacked by de Wrède, they had to fall back on Brienne, acting as rearguard.

Blücher split away from Schwarzenberg and moved along the Seine. Heading for Sézanne, Marmont reached the town on 8 February. On the 10th, they were at Champaubert where Doumerc distinguished himself, then on the 14th at Vauchamps with Grouchy. On the 20th, the regiment only had 196 men left but received reinforcements from Versailles who had left with Wathiez: 8 officers and 107 men. A Squadron Commander of the 9th Cuirassiers brought 18 officers and 259 men on 26 February for the 1st Corps, of which three officers and 16 men were for the 28th.

On 4th March the shameful capitulation at Soissons enabled Blücher to cross the Aisne and move up to Laon, closing nearer to Wintzigerode's and Bülow's Corps which had been put at his disposal. He had already got hold of Pahlen who had been taken from the Army of Bohemia. An attempt was made on Soissons but this met with failure. On the 7th, the regiment crossed at Béry-au-Bac and moved up towards Laon along the Rheims road. It was at Craonne and at Laon. On the 13th, Rheims was taken. On 25 March the 30th Dragoons were at Fère-Champenoise where it lost more than 40 troopers and then retreated towards Paris, arriving in Charenton on the 29th. Marmont, reinforced with Compans' Division, defended Pantin and the Romainville Plateau against Barclay de Tolly and his 50 000 Russians. Chastel's cavalry came up in support of Bordessoulle. The regiment had lost 2 officers and 15 men, killed or wounded. Captain Magnien from Bordessoulles' headquarters brought Napoleon the news of Souham's and Marmont's defection; Bordessoulle took part in this.

SAINT GERMAIN'S 3rd CORPS

Comte de Saint Germain: General in 1805, Baron and Major-General in 1809; under Grouchy since 7 February 1814, fought at Vauchamps; made GdOLH in December 1814. After serving in the Army of the Alps in 1815, he was taken off the active list then given leave of absence in 1818; retired in 1826 then again in 1832.

Laroque: Adjudant-Commandant since 1813, he was Saint-Germain's assistant in 1814. OLH in 1815 he was in the Gendarmerie the following year.

The corps had 2 919 horsemen on 20 February.

MAURIN'S LIGHT DIVISION

Maurin: Former aide de camp to Bernadotte in 1797 then in 1800, he was promoted to General in 1807, then Baron in 1808. Captured by the English in Spain; with Exelmans in 1813, he trained regiments at Versailles; Major-General in February 1814, Cr of the Sword of Sweden in 1814. Wounded at Ligny on 16 June 1815, retired in 1825, he committed suicide on 4 October 1830.

The division's Chief of Staff was **Guichard**. Raised to Baron in 1808, he was mentioned at Rheims, CrLH in 1831, retired in 1832.

Jamin's Brigade

Jamin, Marquis de Bermuy: Aide de camp to Joseph, served with the Royal Guard and was made a Baron in 1811. General in 1814, he was at Versailles on 8 February. Major in the Grenadiers à Cheval of the Guard on 16 March, he remained at Fontainebleau with Napoleon; killed at Waterloo.

CUIRASSIERS and CARABINIERS

Trooper from the 5th Cuirassiers wearing a coat. The 4th and 5th Cuirassiers belonged to General Exelmans' 2nd Cavalry Corps.

Brigadier form the 5th Cuirassiers. The 1812 Regulations added the cavalry carbine which the troopers did not like because they thought it was cumbersome and of no great use.

Officer from the 4th Carabiniers wearing campaign dress.

Carabinier Brigadier.

Trumpeter from the 4th Cuirassiers with the Imperial livery.

Cuirassier wearing cantonment dress and a pokalem.

André Jouineau © Histoire & Collections 2005

Colonel Sourd from the 20th Chasseurs à Cheval at the fight at Laubressel on 3 March 1814. (Musée de l'Armée)

The brigade comprised the 7th, 23rd and 24th Chasseurs as well as the 6th Chevau-Légers Lancers.

The 6th Chevau-Légers (called the "Berry Lancers")

Colonel de Galbois: OLH in 1812, Baron in 1813, commanded the 12th Hussars. He was made CtLH in 1814; wounded at Quatre-Bras, he was off the active list in 1816, appointed Maréchal de Camp in 1831. Served in Constantine in 1837, he was appointed Lieutenant-General in 1838 and GdOLH the following year. Available in 1841, he died in Algiers in 1850.

The regiment was made up from the 29th Dragoons; it was mentioned at Champaubert, where Captain Mathonnet drove in a square with his troop, Montmirail, Vauchamps, Arcis-sur-Aube and Saint-Dizier.

The 7th Chasseurs

Colonel Planzeaux: Mentioned in 1805, wounded at the Moskova, made Colonel of the 8th Regiment but this was formed from the 6th Squadron of the 7th Chasseurs and the remnants of the 4th, 5th, 10th, 13th, 15th and 28th Chasseurs.

Gleize: Egyptian Campaign, he served at Strasbourg with Sémelé in 1815.

The 23rd Chasseurs

It had 203 Chasseurs on 20 February.

The 24th Chasseurs

Comprised 208 Chasseurs.

Dommanget's Brigade

Dommanget: Distinguished himself at Austerlitz where he captured Langeron; Baron in 1810, General in 1811; wounded at the Moskova, CtLH and Couronne de Fer in 1813. He served at Vauchamps, Bar-sur-Aube then during the Hundred Days at Ligny and Waterloo. Arrested for conspiracy in 1817, he was imprisoned for 35 days then released. Retired in 1825, he died in 1848.

The Brigade was made up of the 5th and 9th Hussars, the 11th, 12th and 20th Chasseurs and the 2nd and 4th Lancers.

The 5th Hussars

Colonel Fournier: Brother of the famous Fournier-Sarlovèze whose aide de camp he was in 1807. Promoted to Colonel in May 1813, he was also made a Baron and OLH in 1813. Retired in 1829, he died in 1848.

The 5th Hussars were at first with MacDonald and Exelmans in the 2nd Provisional Corps. Officers and 66 men were sent to Bordessoulle.

The regiment was at Mormant, Nangis and Montereau. It remained at Troyes then took part in the defence along the Seine. On 20 March, the regiment was with Exelmans at Arcis-sur-Aube where two officers were wounded. It took part in the Battle of Saint-Dizier which was the last victory in this campaign. Napoleon now moved down towards Paris to try and stop the Allies' advance. Squadron Commander Nadaillac, with 7 officers and 75 men, was with the 1st Provisional Regiment under Colonel Deschamps at Versailles.

The 9th Hussars

Colonel Montagnier: Wounded and mentioned at Marengo, he was awarded the LH in 1804; retired in 1820 and died in 1850.

The regiment had 123 troopers but remained at Schlestadt in order to defend it.

The 11th Chasseurs

Colonel Nicolas: Made a Baron in 1813, served in Belgium in 1815, on the non-active list. Appointed Maréchal de Camp in Spain in 1823, decorated with the Order of Saint Ferdinand in the same year; GdOLH in 1834, he retired the following year. The regiment was mentioned at Vauchamps.

The 12th Chasseurs

Colonel Grouchy: the General's son, he was with the Army of Italy. Wounded at Waterloo where he lost his right arm. Left for Philadelphia in the USA, they returned in 1820. Made Maréchal de Camp in 1831, GdOLH in 1834. He was elected deputy in 1849 and Senator in 1852. Raised to the rank of GdCxLH in 1862. He wrote about his father.

The 20th Chasseurs

Commanded by **Colonel Sourd** from 1 January 1814. He was OLH in 1813. He was often wounded including once at La Ferté-sous-Jouarre on 9 February and lost his right arm at Genappe in 1815. He refused to rest and went back to the fight at the head of the 2nd Lancers. CrLH in 1836, retired in 1848. The regiment was at Montmirail, Vauchamps, and Montereau. On 20 February, it comprised 177 Chasseurs.

The 2nd Chevau-Légers Lancers

Made up of elements of the 3rd Dragoons in 1811, the regiment was mentioned at Rheims and Paris.

The 4th Chevau-Légers

Colonel Guesnon-Deschamps: took part in the Russian Campaign, made a Baron in 1813. He retired as Maréchal de Camp in 1815, but this was rescinded and then restored in 1823. CrLH in 1821. Served in Spain where he was awarded the Order of Saint-Ferdinand.

The regiment was formed from the 9th Dragoons. It was mentioned at Champaubert and Vauchamps.

SAINT-GERMAIN'S HEAVY DIVISION

Commanding the 2nd Corps, Saint-Germain also commanded the Heavy Cavalry Division himself.

Blancard: Sabre of Honour in 1802, Baron in 1810, General in 1813. With Oudinot on 9 February to whom he brought 600 horses from Paris together with the Mangin and Dubarail companies. Wounded at Waterloo, CrLH in 1832, Lieutenant-General in 1835, retired in 1848, died in 1853. The brigade was formed from the 1st and 2nd Carabiniers and the 1st Cuirassiers.

The 1st Cuirassiers

Colonel Clerc was a Grenadier à Cheval in the Consular Guard, then Chasseur à Cheval of the Guard. OLH in 1805, appointed the regimental Colonel in 1809, then made a Baron in 1810 and Couronne de Fer. Wounded at Hanau and in front of Paris. Maréchal de Camp in 1814, he did not serve during the Hundred Days. Viscount in 1818, he joined the reservists in 1839, was promoted to the rank of GdOLH in 1844.

In the regiment there was also Squadron Commander Dessaignes who obtained a Sabre of Honour in 1803, was wounded at Austerlitz and in Russia. It was he who brought 9 officers and 136 troopers in January. Clerc went to Metz to the depot to bring back 321 horsemen for the 1st Corps. They served at Craonne, Laon and Rheims. Part of the regiment was in Hamburg.

The 1st Carabiniers

Colonel Comte de Baillancourt (called Courcol): Wounded twice at La Chaussée and near Chalons on 3 Febrary 1814. He resigned on 19 May 1814. In 1823 he was made Maréchal de Camp, CrLH and St Ferdinand; he died in 1826.

The 2nd Carabiniers

Colonel Desève: Appointed in 1813, raised to the rank of OLH, retired in May 1815, died in 1816. On 20 December 1813, the regiment was reduced to 700 men. A provisional regiment was then set up also incorporating Exelmans' corps, itself reduced to the bare minimum.

The incumbent was Major Tarbé: Chevalier in 1810, appointed Major on 26 February. Made OLH in 1814. His portrait has been taken from the notebooks of the Sabretache and dates from before 1810, which explains why he is wearing the uniform of the Carabiniers.

This provisional regiment comprised
- **from 1st Carabiniers:** 9 officers and 90 men.
- **from 2nd Carabiniers:** 10 officers and 176 men.
- **from 1st Cuirassiers:** 8 officers and 129 men.
Coming from the Thiry Brigade (Exelmans' group):
- **from 5th Cuirassiers:** 7 officers and 96 men.
- **from 8th Cuirassiers:** 7 officers and 51 men.
- **from 10th Cuirassiers:** 7 officers and 101 men.
They were with MacDonald and met at Chalons.

Sopransi's Brigade

Sopransi: Born in Milan, aide de camp to Berthier in 1807, Baron in 1810, General in

DRAGOONS

Trooper from the 20th Dragoons.

Officer from the 22nd Dragoons.

Brigadier from the Elite Company of the 22nd Dragoons.

Colonel of the 25th Dragoons.

Trumpeter from the 22nd Dragoons.

Trooper from the 26th Dragoons.

André Jouineau © Histoire & Collections 2005

1813. In the reserve corps at Versailles with Roussel d'Hurbal. OLH and Couronne de Fer, died in 1814. The brigade was made up of 5th, 8th, 10th and 13th Cuirassiers.

The 5th Cuirassiers

Colonel Christophe: Captured at Baylen, he organised the escape from the prison hulk *"La Vieille Castille"*. He was the first man to get into the great redoubt at the Moskova. Made a Baron in 1813, CtLH in 1814, died in 1848.

The regiment was at Vauchamps, Saint-Dizier and Arcis-sur-Aube. It had 160 men on 20 February 1814.

The 8th Cuirassiers

Colonel Lefaivre: Baron in 1813, Maréchal de Camp in 1826, retired the following year, died in 1839.

With the 5th Cuirassiers, the regiment was present at the capture of the Great Redoubt at the Moskova. It charged at Vauchamps, Craonne, Laon, and Arcis-sur-Aube. 98 troopers were present on 20 February.

The 10th Cuirassiers

Colonel de la Huberdière: Raised to the rank of OLH in 1809, made a Baron in 1814, he served in Belgium in 1815; made CrLH in 1832, he retired the following year.

At the beginning of February, the regiment only consisted of 5 officers and 11 troopers; after receiving some reinforcements there were 108 horsemen when the corps was reorganised.

The 13th Cuirassiers

This regiment was formed from the 1st provisional Regiment set up in Spain. It served with the Army of Lyon and not in Champagne; it is possible however that a detachment was present there.

MILHAUD'S 5th CAVALRY CORPS

Milhaud: Member of the Convention, voted for the death of Louis XVI; Italian Campaign, appointed General in 1800, then Major-General in 1806; made a count in 1808, raised to GdOLH in 1810; Appointed to command the 5th Corps in place of Pajol on 11 November 1813, he was at Saint-Dizier on 25 January 1814, Brienne, la Rothière, Mormans on 17 February, Troyes on 4 March and Saint-Dizier again on 26 March. He commanded a cavalry corps during the Hundred Days at Ligny and at Waterloo. Outlawed, he was pardoned in 1817; retired in 1832, he died at Aurillac in 1833.

On 20 February, the corps numbered some 4 741 horsemen.

PIRÉ'S LIGHT DIVISION

Piré, Comte de Rosnyvinen: An émigré, he landed at Quiberon. He returned to the army

Cuirassier from the 4e régiment. (RR)

Major Tarbé from the 2nd Carabiniers Regiment is here wearing the uniform of Squadron Commander (a model dating from before 1810). (Les Cahiers de la Sabretache)

General Milhaud, commanding the 5th Cavalry Corps. (RR)

in 1800, served on the General Staff in 1805 at Austerlitz; aide de camp to Berthier. Made a baron in 1808 and General in 1809. He fought alongside Lasalle at Wagram. He was promoted to Major-General in 1813. Fought under Grouchy at Brienne, he was with Milhaud at La Rothière, Mormans, La Ferté-sur-Aube and Saint-Dizier on 26 March. He distinguished himself at Quatre-Bras, Waterloo and Rocquemont. Outlawed he went into exile in Russia and returned in 1819. GdOLH in 1834, he retired in 1848, died in 1850.

His chief-of-staff was **Petiet** who came from the 2nd Lancers of the Guard. He was mentioned at Brienne and Nangis where he was wounded twice and captured 14 cannon.

Subervie's Brigade

Subervie: Aide de camp to Lannes in Italy, he was with Lasalle in Spain. Made a Baron in 1809, then a General in 1811; wounded twice at the Moskova; awarded the Order of the Couronne de Fer in 1813. He led his brigade at Saint-Die, Brienne, Champaubert and Montereau. Wounded three times at Paris, promoted to Lieutenant-General in 1814, he commanded a light cavalry brigade at Waterloo in Piré's Division. After taking part in the 1830 revolution, he was elected Deputy for Lectoure in 1831, 1834, 1837, 1846 and 1848. GdCxLH, then Grand Chancelier in 1848.

The brigade was made up of the 3rd and 13th Hussars as well as the 14th Chasseurs.

The 3rd Hussars

Commanded in January by **Colonel Rousseau:** OLH in 1813, retired on 21 February 1814. He was replaced by Colonel Moncey: Comte, served at Belfort in 1815, became a Colonel of the Gendarmerie.

The regiment was at Brienne but distinguished itself especially at Montereau where it arrived at 8 p.m. and led the famous charge by Pajol against the Wurtemburgers who were trying to cross the bridges. In 1815, the regiment was with the corps in the Jura; it was mentioned near Belfort on 27 June 1815, as was its Colonel.

298 horsemen were present in the squadrons on 20 February.

The 13th Hussars (the former "Jérôme Bonaparte" Westphalian Regiment)

Colonel Brincard: Commanded Jerome Bonaparte's Hussars. On the non-active list at the end of 1814 and did not serve during the Hundred days. Made a Baron in 1817, OLH in 1820, he took part in the Spanish expedition in 1823, the year of his death.

Renamed the 13th Hussars in January 1814, the regiment was at first with the Brayer Division in MacDonald's 11th Corps, under Molitor. It fought at La Chaussée on 3 February. On the 20th, it changed to the 5th Corps. It was sometimes confused with the 3rd Hussars which was part of the same corps. It was this 3rd Hussars which charged at Montereau, also in Subervie's brigade with the 14th Chasseurs. According to the regimental histories, Koch only gives the 3rd and 13th Hussars with Subervie, together with the 14th Chasseurs.

The 13th Hussars were mentioned at Maison-Rouge with Molitor covering the 149th, still with MacDonald. On 1 March, it only had 18 officers and 310 men left. On the 25th, it took part in La Fère-Champenoise by falling back towards the marshals. It only had 13 officers and 70 men on 5 May 1814.

The 14th Chasseurs

Colonel Lemoine or **Lemoyne:** Wounded at Ulm and Austerlitz, awarded the LH in 1804, then made Chevalier in 1809, OLH in 1813. Permitted to withdraw in May 1815, he retired in 1821. He was Mayor of Gland (Aisne department) until 1852.

The regiment arrived at Montereau on 18 February in the evening. It carried on towards Troyes and was at La Ferté-sur-Aube on 27 February, then at Saint-Dizier on 26 March. It mar-

DRAGOONS

The 1812 Regulations replaced the French-style coat with the jacket but kept the same distinctive colours. The equipment, the weapons and the saddles were unchanged. The trumpeters wore coats bearing the Imperial livery. There were two types of uniform: the coat with livery, which fastened straight; and the coat for the troopers with braid on the lapels, the sleeves, the turnbacks and the pockets with the livery as drawn by Carle Vernet.

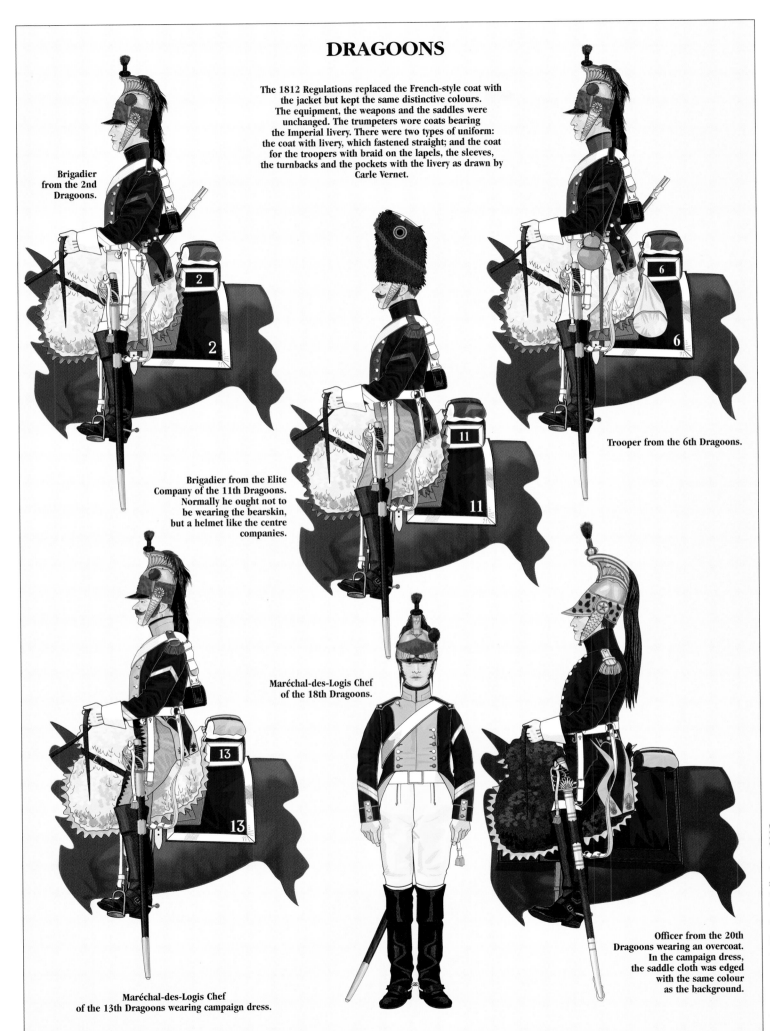

Brigadier from the 2nd Dragoons.

Trooper from the 6th Dragoons.

Brigadier from the Elite Company of the 11th Dragoons. Normally he ought not to be wearing the bearskin, but a helmet like the centre companies.

Maréchal-des-Logis Chef of the 18th Dragoons.

Maréchal-des-Logis Chef of the 13th Dragoons wearing campaign dress.

Officer from the 20th Dragoons wearing an overcoat. In the campaign dress, the saddle cloth was edged with the same colour as the background.

André Jouineau © Histoire & Collections 2005

Carabinier Trumpeter in 1812; he is riding the traditional white horse which was a feature of his function. Drawing by JOB. (RR)

ched to Fontainebleau from 29 to 31 March. The 14th Chasseurs had three squadrons totalling 17 officers and 272 Chasseurs.

Du Coëtlosquet's Brigade

Comte du Coëtlosquet: aide de camp to Lasalle in 1806. He was appointed General in 1813 and was given the command of the reserve division at Versailles with Pajol on 13 January He was at Montmoreau where he commanded a provisional brigade. He served in 1815 at la Rochelle. He was one of General Rigau's judges in 1816. Appointed Lieutenant-General in 1821, he was awarded the CrSL in 1823, was Interim Minister of War and Conseiller d'Etat in 1828. He opposed the insurgents in 1830 and was retired in 1831.

The brigade was made up of the 26th and 27th Chasseurs and it was also with Pajol's corps before this was disbanded.

The 26th Chasseurs

Colonel Robert-Dubreuil: Baron in 1810, aide de camp to Beillard the following year. Raised to the rank of OLH in 1812 then CtLH in 1813. He commanded the regiment from 5 February 1814 and fought at Bar-sur-Aube on the 27th. He was with the 2nd Chasseurs in 1815 then put on the non-active list. He died in 1817. The regiment numbered 351 Chasseurs in its ranks on 20 February.

The Duc d'Arenberg's 27th Chasseurs

The Duke of Arenberg created his regiment of Belgian Chevau-Légers in 1806, which became the 27th Chasseurs in 1808. The Duke was wounded and captured in 1811 in Spain by the English and was only freed in 1814, so he did not take part in the French Campaign. He was the 2nd Prince of Recklinghausen. In 1813 Strub was also mentioned but he was captured in October 1813.

The regiment had 357 Chasseurs on 20 February. It was at la Rothière, Nogent, Bar-sur-Aube and Saint-Dizier.

BRICHE'S HEAVY CAVALRY DIVISION

Briche: General and Baron in 1809, served in Spain. Appointed Major-General in 1813, he commanded Victor's 3rd heavy Cavalry Division in January 1814. With Grouchy at Brienne, he commanded under Milhaud at la Rothière, Mormans, La Ferté-sur-Aube on 27 February. He was arrested by his soldiers and dismissed in April 1815. He was made a count and awarded the CrSL in 1816, the GdOLH in 1821. On the active list in 1823, he died in 1825.

Montélégier's brigade

Bernon de Montélégier was made a general in 1813; wounded in 1813 at Brienne, he

distinguished himself at Mormans. Aide de camp to the Duc de Berry, he followed him to Ghent. He was made a Viscount in 1818, GdOLH in 1820, Lieutenant-General in 1821 and CSL in 1825, the year of his death.

The 2nd, 6th and 11th Dragoons formed this brigade.

The 2nd Dragoons

The regiment had 360 men on 20 February. They were mentioned at Saint-Dizier and Brienne.

The 6th Dragoons

Colonel Mugnier: served with the Chasseurs of the Guard in 1813. He commanded the 13th Dragoons in 1813 and 1814. He returned from Spain where he had been made an OLH in 1809 and a Baron in 1816.

On 24 December 1813, the regiment took part in fight at Sainte-Croix with the 2nd and 11th Dragoons against Frimont and the Cossacks of the Guard whose Colonel was captured. The regiment had 352 Dragoons in January; On 25 January, it was present at the taking of Saint Dizier where Landskoï and Szezbatov were beaten; on the 29th at Brienne where the castle was taken by the Infantry of the Young Guard; on 1 February at la Rothière. On 17 February, the 6th Dragoons was at Mormans with Victor and Kellermann alongside Treillard's Spanish Dragoons (4th, 14th and 16th). Piré and Briche were on the left and Kellermann on the right with the 4th and 16th Dragoons. A Russian square was driven in on two sides and captured and the road to Montereau was open for the battle on the 18th. The Generals hugged each other in the centre of the collapsed square. A sapper from the regiment took the decorations from a Russian General. At Saint-Dizier on 26 March, Sebastiani and the cavalry of the Guard found a ford and then distinguished themselves. On 28 March Napoleon decided to march on Paris, abandoning the idea of going to his eastern strongholds. Sixty wagons which were stuck in the mud were abandoned. On the 30th, they went through Troyes and bivouacked at Sens. On the 31st, the Allies entered Paris.

A detachment which came from the depot at Epinal, commanded by Squadron Commander Gillet numbered 15 officers and 214 horsemen. They took part in the Battle of Rheims and were engaged at Fère-Champenoise then at Meaux. They reached Versailles on 26 March with 4 officers, 2 NCOs and 125 men.

In 1815, the regiment was at Ligny and Wavre.

The 11th Dragoons

Colonel Thevenez d'Aoust: Wounded eight times at Hohenlinden where he received a Sabre of Honour. He was in the Chasseurs of the Guard in 1802. Wounded twice in Spain, he was awarded the LH in 1810, made a Baron in 1813. Retired for health reasons in 1815, he was made CtLH. The 380 dragoons in the regiment were at Saint-Dizier, Brienne, la Rothière and Montmirail.

Ludot's Brigade

Ludot was a nephew of Danton, in Cayenne in 1796, General in 1813, returned from Spain and fought at Mormans. He replaced Briche and was made a Baron in 1804, the CtLH in 1815. He served during the Hundred Days and retired in 1819.

The 13th and 15th Dragoons formed the brigade.

The 13th Dragoons

Colonel Ligniville (Comte de): Wounded at Austerlitz and at Essling, made a Chevalier in 1809 and made a Colonel on 6 February 1814. He was in Spain in 1823 and was appointed Maréchal de Camp in 1825. He was Inspector-General of Colonial Troops and CrLH in 1837.

On 24 January 1814, there was a fight at Saint-Dizier which the Emperor had had attacked. The infantry took the position and the cavalry from Milhaud's 5th Corps scattered Landskoï's corps. The regiment was at Brienne and La Rothière; it was mentioned at Mormans where the Dragoons of the 13th drove in the last enemy square with the support of the 4th and 16th Dragoons from Ismert's brigade in Treillard's Division. They fought their last battle at Saint-Dizier on 26 March. There were 297 Dragoons on 20 February.

The 15th Dragoons

Colonel Boudinhon-Valdec: A veteran of Austerlitz, OLH in 1813; fought at Brienne where he was wounded, then at La Rothière. Made a General on 6 February 1814, he was at Versailles on the 20th and retired in 1833.

On 24 January 1814, 369 Dragoons were present in the regiment for the battle of Saint-Dizier; they were also at Brienne on 29 January and at La Rothière on 1 February. The regiment fought at Mormans on 17 February where it drove in some Russian squares. On 26 March, the regiment fought at Saint-Dizier.

LHERITIER'S HEAVY CAVALRY DIVISION

Lheritier: Italian Campaign, fought at Marengo, Baron in 1808, made a General in 1809, then Major-General in 1813. He served under Grouchy at Brienne then under Milhaud at la Rothière and at Saint-Dizier on 26 March. CtLH in 1814, he served during the Hundred Days and was wounded at Waterloo. On the active list in 1828, he died the following year.

CHASSEURS À CHEVAL

Brigadier from the 10th Chasseurs à Cheval.

Trooper from the 12th Chasseurs à Cheval.

1812-model standard of the 14th Chasseurs à Cheval. On the reverse side there are the names of the battles – ECKMUHL and WAGRAM. There were also a golden bronze eagle, a tricolour cravat and a gold cord.

L'EMPEREUR NAPOLÉON AU 14ÈME RÉGIMENT DE CHASSEURS À CHEVAL

Trumpeter from the 11th Chasseurs à Cheval.

Maréchal des Logis from the 14th Chasseurs à Cheval.

Major from the 23rd Chasseurs à Cheval. The rank of Major corresponded to that of Lieutenant-Colonel with the function of second-in-command. The officers of the Chasseurs à Cheval normally only wore one epaulette, on the left; however quite a number can be seen to be wearing both epaulettes of rank.

Trooper from the 16th Chasseurs à Cheval.

André Jouineau © Histoire & Collections 2005

Top, left:
Colonel Shee commanding the 13th Chasseurs. He successfully charged at Montereau.
(RR)

Top right:
General Ameil. He commanded the 2nd Brigade of Jacquinot's Division.
(RR)

Opposite:
General Lhéritier commanded a division of Milhaud's 5th Corps.
(RR)

Lamotte's Brigade

Lamotte: Oudinot's aide de camp in 1801, Baron in 1808, General in 1809, Lieutenant-General in 1814. Dismissed for having wanted to surrender Bayonne in 1805. In the reserve in 1831, died in 1836. He replaced Briche who was ill on 23 March and took command of the brigade. The Brigade was made up of the 18th, 19th and 20th Dragoons.

The 18th Dragoons

Colonel Dard: Italian and Egyptian Campaigns, OLH in 1809, Colonel in 1812 then Baron and Couronne de Fer in 1814. He led his regiment at Champaubert, Montmirail, Vauchamps, Mormans, Arcis-sur-Aube and Saint-Dizier. Maréchal de camp in 1815, but his appointment was cancelled by the King. He was retired in 1822 and died in 1828.

The regimental depot was transferred from Haguenau to Versailles. On 9 February, the squadrons numbered 253 men; in January, there were 18 officers and 232 Dragoons. On 3 January, the 18th Dragoons were at Saint-Dié then at Saint-Dizier, Brienne, la Rothière, Mormans and Bar-sur-Aube. On 26 March, the regiment was at Saint-Dizier then returned to Fontainebleau. The regiment was disbanded on 27 August but was re-formed and served in 1815.

The 19th Dragoons

Colonel Mermet: a pupil of the regiment, then drummer, he served successively in the 7th, 10th and then the 9th Hussars. Colonel in 1811, he was made an OLH in 1814. After serving in 1815, he was on the non-active list. Made a hereditary Baron in 1818, he died in 1820.

The 19th Dragoons were at Saint-Dizier, Brienne, la Rothière and Mormans. On 26 March it was in the second fight at Saint-Dizier that it was mentioned.

On 20 February there were 296 men in the regiment.

The 20th Dragoons

Colonel Dessargues: OLH in 1809, appointed Colonel in 1811, Baron in 1813. On the non-active list, he retired as Maréchal de Camp in 1824. He was made CrLH in 1837.

The regiment was mentioned at Vauchamps; it had 196 men on 20 February.

Collaert's Brigade

Collaert: Born near Liège, awarded a Sabre of Honour in 1801. General in Holland with Louis Bonaparte, commanded the Guards. Went into French service in 1811 and was awarded the Ordre de la Réunion in 1812. He resigned in 1815 and served the Prince of Orange who made him Cr of the Order of William. He died from a wound received at Waterloo.

The brigade comprised the 22nd and 25th Dragoons.

The 22nd Dragoons

Colonel Adam: OLH in 1813, Couronne de Fer in 1814, then CrLH in 1831, died in 1853. The regiment was mentioned at Brienne where it captured a general and a number of prisoners. It was also mentioned at Saint-Dizier.

The 25th Dragoons

Colonel Canavas, called Saint-Amand, came from the Dragoons of the Guard. Appointed to the 25th Dragoons on 31 January but remained on the staff. Served in Belgium in 1815. Promoted to CrLH in 1835, he joined the reserve in 1839.

Squadron Commander **Cazener** was the acting commanding officer. He was already in command since Leipzig following the death of Colonel Montigny.

Colonel Comte d'Hautefeuille: Made a Colonel on 6 February 1814, he only joined his unit on the 21st, after Montereau. CrLH in 1821, Maréchal de camp in 1823 and in the reserve in 1841.

The regiment comprised: 25 officers and 238 troopers with 1 officer and 18 men in the little depot at Rockenhausen.

On 25 January the regiment took part in the first engagement at Saint Dizier. On the 28th the depot had already sent 3 officers and 114 men for the 1st Corps. On 1 February at la Rothière, the regiment was on Victor's right and were driven back losing several pieces and retreated back to Brienne and Lesmont where the corps passed through on the 2nd.

On the 4th, Colonel Planzeau brought 2 officers and 40 men. On 5 February, the Dragoons of the 25th were at Nogent with Oudinot and were sent 3 officers and 87 men. On the 11th they were towards Provins. On the 127th they distinguished themselves at Mormans and Schwarzenberg started his retreat to Troyes. The 25th took part in chasing him. Colonel d'Hauteville arrived. On 21 February, the regiment numbered 26 officers and 351 men; they fought on the 26th at Saint-Dizier and distinguished themselves alongside the 22nd.

On the 27th, MacDonald was appointed Senior Commanding Officer. With him were Oudinot and Gérard who had replaced Victor, plus the 2nd, 5th and 6th Cavalry Corps.

The enemy was reassured and resumed their offensive.

On 1 March the regiment fell back on Bar-sur-Seine and withdrew towards Sens; it had 22 officers and 320 men. Colonel Christophe from the 5th brought an officer and 11 men. On 25 March a new detachment was caught in the Battle of Fère-Champenoise. On the 26th, the 25th fought at Saint-Dizier against the Russian Guard where it was mentioned with the 22nd. It was their last victory.

The depot at Verdun had been moved back to Moret on 27 March with 16 officers and 227 men after having sent a number of detachments of recruits forward.

On 4 April the regiment was at Fontainebleau: there remained 22 officers and 246 men with those of the 22nd. They were shared out among the 19th and the 20th Dragoon regiments.

KELLERMANN, COMTE DE VALMY'S
6th CAVALRY CORPS

Kellermann: Son of the Marshal, was a General in 1797; a hero of Marengo, appointed Major-General in 1800, wounded at Austerlitz. He was present at Mormans, Bar-sur-Aube, and Saint-Dizier on 26 March. He was made a Grand Cordon of the LH and Cr of the Couronne de Fer in 1814, then a Peer in 1815. He fought at Quatre-Bras and at Waterloo at the head of his Cuirassiers. Made a Marquis in 1817, he was Duke of Valmy on the death of his father.

Bataille de Tancarville: Aide de camp to Kellermann in 1800, he was Chief-of-Staff and OLH in 1813, then Baron in 1814. He served with the 3rd Corps in 1815. He retired in 1833.

Larriu: Italian Campaign, he was Chief-of-Staff of the 4th Division of the 6th Cavalry Corps in 1814. Made a Maréchal de Camp in 1815, he was demoted to Colonel but was appointed Maréchal de Camp again in 1831. He retired in 1834.

Lavoy: Chevalier in 1810, he was promoted to CtLH in 1813. He commanded the artillery of the 6th Corps. Retired in 1816.

The 6th Corps numbered 6 365 horsemen on 20 February.

JACQUINOT'S LIGHT DIVISION

Wolff's Brigade

Wolff: A converted Jew, he was aide de camp to Jerome in 1813 and then during the Hundred Days. Made a Baron and General in 1813, he was on the non-active list on 18 July 1815. Promoted to GdOLH in 1829, he was appointed Lieutenant-General in 1835 and retired in 1848.

The brigade was made up of the 2nd, 4th and 12th Hussars, of the 9th, 21st and 22nd Chasseurs as well as the 9th Chevau-Légers Lancers.

The 2nd Hussars

Its Colonel, **de Séganville**, was a Scout in Italy and aide de camp to Bessières. Made a Baron in 1809, Colonel in 1813, he served in the Jura in 1815 and retired as Maréchal de

Camp in 1823. He was CrLH in 1832.

The 2nd Hussars were mentioned at Montereau and at Rheims.

The 4th Hussars

Colonel Christophe: Baron in 1813, he was at Lyon on 18 March and was promoted to CrLH in 1814. He joined the Gendarmerie, appointed Honorary Maréchal de Camp in 1830 then retired in 1831.

The 12th Hussars

A part of the regiment was with the Army of Lyon, it was mentioned at Macon and Limonest.

The 9th Chevau-Légers

Their Colonel was **Gobrecht** but he was captured at Dresden and only returned on 1 May 1814. He returned to the Jacquinot Division in 1815 and was at Waterloo. **Colonel Fredro,** awarded the LH in 1812, was in command in 1813, but he was captured at Kulm. He became an ordnance officer to the Tsar, and General in 1816. He died in Paris in 1845.

This regiment was created by transforming the 31st Chasseurs. It was reformed by absorbing elements from the 7th Chevau-Légers. It had 116 men on 9 February, i.e. 238 lances for the two regiments united (7th and 9th Chevau-Légers). The regiment was mentioned at Vauchamps and Fère-Champenoise.

The 21st Chasseurs

Colonel Duchastel: Wounded in Andalusia, he remained with the Army of the Pyrenees. Only a detachment took part in the campaign in Champagne.

Amiel's Brigade

Amiel: Wounded in 1806, he was made CtLH in 1809 and General in 1812. He rallied Napoleon in 1815. Arrested on 10 March, he was freed by the Emperor on the 20th, served at Waterloo as Major-General. Outlawed, he went mad and exiled himself in Hanover. Condemned to death in his absence, he was pardoned and retired in 1821. He died in 1822.

The brigade consisted of the 4th, 5th, 10th, 15th and 28th Chasseurs and a detachment of the 13th Chasseurs. These were parts of regiments, mainly joined together. Some were mentioned in Pajol's Corps.

The 4th Chasseurs

Colonel Heljon de Villeneuve, Marquis de Vence: Made a Baron in 1809 and Colonel in 1813. He distinguished himself at Montmirail and Arcis-sur-Aube. GdOLH in 1825, he was made a hereditary Pair de France in 1820.

The regiment had 123 horsemen on 20 February.

The 5th Chasseurs

This regiment has already been presented as being in the Merlin Division of Doumerc's 1st Corps; it was assigned to the 6th Corps on 6 February.

The 10th Chasseurs

Colonel Houssin de Saint-Laurent commanded the 10th Chasseurs but he was with Soult in the Army of the Pyrenees.

The regiment was with Arrighi who covered the retreat until Chateau-Thierry which it reached on 7 February. On the 18th, the regiment charged at Montereau under Delort.

When it was reorganised on 19 February, the regiment was given over to the 6th Corps in the Ameil Brigade with only two squadrons, but reinforced with men from Pajol's division which had been disbanded. On 3 April the regiment was at Fontainebleau.

The 13th Chasseurs

Colonel Shee, Count of Kilkenny: An Irishman who first served the English but went over to serve France in 1806. Aide de camp to Clarke then Berthier in Spain in 1808; made a Baron in 1809. In 1811 he was awarded the order of the Couronne de Fer and made a Colonel. OLH in 1814, he served in the Jura in 1815. Maréchal de Camp in 1817, raised to CrLH in 1820 and retired in 1848.

The 13th Chasseurs was split up into several elements. Detachments from the 5th and 6th Squadrons were with the Army of the Pyrenees, one detachment was with the 5th Corps, one squadron was training at the Versailles depot (probably the 4th) and one was with Pajol's Corps. This squadron, the 6th, was reinforced with the remnants of the brigade's other regiments making a total of 20 officers and 180 Chasseurs. They were at Montereau on 18 February. On the day after that battle, the cavalry was reorganised and Pajol's Corps was disbanded; two companies coming from Versailles joined the regiment with 4 officers and 153 men; the rem-

General Kellermann, commanding the 6th Cavalry Corps.
(RR)

nants of the 5th, 10th, 15th and 28th regiments completed the 13th Chasseurs which then joined Kellermann's 6th Corps in the Jacquinot Division and Amiel Brigade. Two detachments came up to reinforce the regiment in February and March; others were absorbed on the way into other regiments before they could reach their destinations.

At the Battle of Montereau it was said that Colonel Shee charged at the head of the 13th and 14th Chasseurs, the latter arriving towards 6 p.m. In fact this charge was made by various elements assembled from the 4th, 5th, 10th, 13th, 14th, 15th and 28th Chasseurs. Likewise, the 13th Chasseurs are often confused with the 13th Hussars which were in the 5th Corps under Subervie.

On 27 February, the 13th Chasseurs were at Bar-sur-Aube. On 20 and 21 March they were at Arcis-sur-Aube; they then marched towards Saint-Dizier. On 2 April, when they returned to Paris, there were 13 officers and 98 men left. The regiment was mentioned as present at Chateau-Thierry and Craonne.

The 15th Chasseurs

Colonel Faverot de Kerbrech: Baron in 1813, CtLH and Maréchal de Camp in 1821. He was in Spain with the main part of the regiment. Two squadrons were in Champagne with Major Rougiot coming from the depot, then with Major Salomon in 1814. They fell back with MacDonald. They were at Brienne and la Rothière but only a reinforced squadron remained which reached Meaux with the Marshal. They joined Amiel's Brigade and went to Montereau then to Troyes and finally at Arcis-sur-Aube. They then retreated to Paris where there were only 37 Chasseurs left.

The 28th Chasseurs

Colonel Courtier: Wounded at Hamburg in 1813, he was not with the army but with Davout. Wounded at Waterloo, made CtLH in 1821 then retired in 1834.

The chasseurs in this regiment came mainly from the 3rd Provisional Regiment which was at Hamburg. A small detachment could have taken part in a provisional regiment without there being any casualties reported.

TREILLARD'S DIVISION (the Spanish Dragoons)

Treillard: General in 1799, made CtLH in 1804, then fought at Austerlitz. Major-General in 1806, Baron in 1810, he arrived from Spain on 16 February. Mentioned at Mormans on the 17th, at Saint-Dizier on 26 March, he served in 1815 and retired afterwards.

Ismert's Brigade

Ismert was a veteran of Marengo and Austerlitz. Made OLH and baron in 1808, General and Couronne de Fer in 1813. He was at Mormans and Bar-sur-Aube. He served in 1815 then retired; he was 60.

The brigade was made up of the 4th, 14th and 16th Dragoons.

The 4th Dragoons

Colonel Bouquerot: OLH and Baron in 1814, he served during the Hundred Days, wounded at Ligny; made Maréchal de Camp in 1831.

The 4th was mentioned at Mormans for having taken 14 cannon and 600 Dragoons prisoner. It was also at Bar-sur-Aube, Sézanne and Fère-Champenoise.

The 14th Dragoons

Colonel Séguier: LH in 1808, he was mixed up in the Malet Affair in 1812 when he rose up against the General. Made a Baron in 1813 then OLH in 1814, he was aide de camp to MacDonald. Wounded at Arcis-sur-Aube, he served in Belgium in 1815, then retired the following year.

The regiment was mentioned at Montereau, Bar-sur-Aube and Arcis-sur-Aube.

The 16th Dragoons

Colonel Prévost: OLH in 1813, he served in 1815 then retired in 1821.

It seems that this Colonel was with the 11th which had been formed with elements from the 16th.

The 16th Dragoons were mentioned at Champaubert, Vauchamps and Arcis-sur-Aube.

Ormancey's Brigade

Ormancey: CtLH and Baron in 1808, he was promoted to General in 1810; he was wounded at Bar-sur-Aube. He was with the remounts in 1815, then retired.

The brigade was made up of the 17th, 24th and 27th Dragoons.

The 17th Dragoons

Officer from the 3rd Hussar Regiment in 1814.
(RR)

The return of the Spanish Dragoons caused as much enthusiasm in the army as in the population. Treillard's Division which reached Champagne in February was assigned to the 6th cavalry Corps.
(A. Lalauze)

Colonel Lepic: Son of the General, made OLH in 1808 then Couronne de Fer in 1813. He was promoted to Colonel the same year. Wounded at Arcis-sur-Aube where he captured a flag, he was made a Baron. He retired as Maréchal de camp in 1827.

The 24th Dragoons

Colonel Debussy: Promoted to OLH in 1807 and retired in 1815.

The regiment was mentioned as having only a single detachment present during the Campaign.

The 27th Dragoons

The regiment was mentioned at Virrey-sur-Barre where an officer was killed and another wounded. At Bar-sur-Seine, an officer was wounded as was another at Provins on 11 March. At Arcis-sur-Aube, two officers were reported wounded.

ROUSSEL D'URBAL'S HEAVY DIVISION

Roussel d'Urbal: Viscount, a former émigré who served Austria with Lichtenstein against France. He returned to serve France in 1811 as a General; promoted to Major-General in 1812, then Baron in 1813.

He was at the cavalry depot at Versailles on 17 January 1814, then at Troyes, Craonne, Laon and with Belliard at Fère-Champenoise and Sézanne. He took part in the defection of Marmont's Corps. The following year he was present at Waterloo where he was wounded. Made CrSL and GdCx of Saint-Ferdinand of Spain in 1823, and GdOLH in 1846. He died in 1849.

His chief-of-staff was **Adjudant-Commandant Biarnois de Baine:** OLH in 1814, retired in 1822.

Sparre's Brigade

Sparre (Comte de) Equerry to Napoleon, made a Baron in 1811, then General in 1812. He returned from Spain on 16 January 1814, wounded at Craonne and replaced by Rigau. Lieutenant-General in 1814, Pair de France in 1819 and Gentleman of the King's Bedchamber in 1826. Awarded the CrSL in 1828.

The brigade was made up of the 5th and 12th Dragoons.

The 5th Dragoons

Colonel Morin was made a Baron in 1813. He came from the 3rd Provisional Regiment; he was seriously wounded at Vauchamps on 14 February and died from his wounds on the 20th. He was made CtLH posthumously.

The regiment was mentioned at Vauchamps, Craonne, Fère-Champenoise and Paris.

The 12th Dragoons

Colonel Bessard-Graugniard: Made Colonel in 1812. Wounded in front of Paris, he was made OLH in 1814 then retired. The 12th Dragoons were mentioned at Paris.

Rigau's Brigade

Rigau: A Marengo veteran, made CtLH in 1805, General in 1807, Baron in 1809. He distinguished himself at Arcis-sur-Aube. He sheltered the fleeing Lefebvre-Desnoëttes in March 1815 and wanted to arrest Victor. He took part actively in the Hundred Days where he rallied his two regiments to the Emperor with the cry "He who loves him follow me!" Captured at Chalons-sur-Marne and outlawed, he was condemned to death in his absence. He sought refuge in 1817 in the Champ d'Asile in Texas where he died in 1820. He was mentioned in Napoleon's will.

The brigade was made up of the 21st and 26th Dragoons.

The 21st Dragoons

Colonel Saviot: A veteran of the Italian campaign and Hohenlinden where he was wounded. Decorated with the Couronne de Fer in 1807, he was made a Colonel and OLH in 1813. He served in Belgium in the 8th Dragoons during the Hundred Days, then was put on the nonactive list. Retired in 1821, he died in 1830.

The regiment was mentioned at Troyes and Montmirail where Captain de Cordès was successful against the Prussians.

The 26th Dragoons

Colonel Besnard: Aide de camp to Louis Bonaparte in Holland, he was appointed to the regiment in 1813; he was made OLH in 1814.

The regiment was mentioned at Sens, Craonne, Laon, Fère-Champenoise and Paris.

On 10 March, Victor was at Nogent where he fought well, but he had to fall back on the 11th. On 15 March, the regiment was with MacDonald at Provins.

On the 17th it was the fight at Mormans where Piré, Briche and Treillard distinguished themselves and the Dragoons followed through to Nangis and Montereau which was another victory. Schwarzenberg, pushed around as Blücher had been, fell back on Troyes and beyond. As Schwarzerberg had fallen back to his base area around Arcis-sur-Aube, there was a relative calm which allowed the troops to rally. On the 21st the regiment was reduced to 26 officers and 351 Dragoons.

It marched with two squadrons (260 troopers) towards MacDonald. On the 22nd, the two armies observed each other, as there was the possibility of an armistice. But the respite was not long since Napoleon still wanted to fight and the army set off again. On the 23rd at Bar-sur-Aube, Oudinot hoped to hold out in front of the River Aube. He was attacked by Wittgenstein and de Wrède. Kellermann came to rescue him with Treillard but the charges were driven off with heavy losses.

It was then that Ormancey was wounded and replaced by Rigau. Likewise Ismert was sent to Roussel's Division. Schwarzenberg moved off again in the direction of Paris.

INFANTRY OF THE LINE

The reforms caused by the 1812 regulations by Major Bardin (who commanded a Guards Tirailleur Regiment during the French Campaign) were applied generally and greatly changed the infantryman's image compared with the last change dating back to 1786. The weapons remained unchanged however.

Fusilier.

According to regulations, Voltigeurs left their sabre-briquet and fringed epaulettttes.

Sergeant and soldier from a Grenadier company. They kept their fringed epaulettes but they no longer wore the bearskin, but a shako with red braid.

Fusilier drummer wearing a coat with the Imperial livery.

Fusilier.

Voltigeur bugler. He should be wearing a coat with the livery.

Corporal Pennant-Bearer.

André Jouineau © Histoire & Collections 2005

THE MARSHAL'S CORPS
(THE INFANTRY CORPS)

This situation of the French troops has used the original edition of Koch, a Major on the General Staff who was a witness and a historian and who, in his 1819 edition, presented a collection of plates giving detailed tables of the troops engaged together with three maps.

Just as we did, he ran into the problem of the discrepancies which appear during the whole campaign, particularly with the French who brought up reinforcements from Paris, Versailles and Spain. These reinforcements were often made up of detachments from the regimental depots or from regiments which had detached smaller elements which were then amalgamated; so much so that regiments were divided and appeared on different fronts and in different corps in Spain, in the north with Soult, or in Champagne.

The Marshals managed with greatly reduced corps strengths; the regiments were

1. *Marshal Victor commanded the 2nd Infantry Corps. His attitude at Mormans and Montereau however caused Napoleon to remove him from his command.*
2. *General Pachtod was a hero of Fère-Champenoise where he commanded a division of National Guardsmen.*
3. *General Gérard, already brilliant at La Rothière, replaced Victor after Montereau.*
4. *General Pajol commanded the corps which defended the Seine and Yonne valleys before it was disbanded following on the Battle of Montereau.*
5. *General Dubesme.*
(All photos: DR)

mostly often made up of detachments from the depots or from Spain, or from elsewhere, thanks to forced conscription.

These conscripts who were taken from their families sometimes deserted en route but they came in great numbers. At their age, war was attractive since it got them away from their routine. It was adventure. In tatters, badly equipped, unpaid, subjected to awful marches, they lacked supplies except when the peasants helped them. However, some of them came of their own free-will convinced that they had to get rid of the terrible Cossacks who were looting and committing atrocities. They were simply patriotic, that feeling which after the massacres of 1914-1918 and the 1940 debacle is tending to disappear. Formerly, the deserters and those who were unfit for service were very much criticised; it was unthinkable, it was shameful. This was part of a whole set of values which were passed down from father to son, and also by the teachers whom we respected and admired. We have seen these principles deteriorate progressively and then this process gather momentum and in 1968, finish with the famous slogan "it is forbidden to forbid". Laxity has spread to give the present state of affairs. All sorts of wheeling and dealing has developed all the more easily as it started in upper classes and has spread down with no shame. Money rules everything. Honesty is no longer respected as a value; it is now a race to become rich and get the power that goes with wealth.

Back to our Marshals: they had made brilliant careers and obtained titles and wealth, sometimes acquired in rather doubtful circumstances. In 1814, wealthy and titled, they were part of the power system and as careerists they knew how to recognise which way the wind was

blowing, and the wind had turned in Russia, in Spain and at Leipzig. The invasion smelled of defeat and their enthusiasm for victory was faltering.

Their attitude could be seen to be changing; falling back in front of the enemy masses became normal practice. As a result there was not much action from the troops in the north and those, with Augereau, in the south.

Ironically, it was Marmont who fought best until he turned bad at Essonnes, well helped along the way by Souham.

The others did their best, but it was the Guard in particular which did not flinch, and showed how it could still win against double the odds. It has to be admired all during this campaign for its loyalty and its worth in the fighting, but also because it structured and trained the surprising conscripts.

VICTOR'S 2nd CORPS

Victor with his 2nd Corps was part of the central group. On 25 January 1814, he was accompanied by Milhaud's 5th Cavalry Corps. Maréchal Victor was replaced by Gérard at the head

of the 2nd Corps after Montereau where he dilly-dallied too much. The chief-of-staff was **General le Camus,** called Camus. CtLH in 1804, he was made a General in 1806, Baron in 1808. Wounded at Craonne, he could not stay at his post and was taken off the active list in July 1814. He served during the Hundred Days in the Var Dapartment. Retired in 1825, he died in 1845.

The Marshal's aide de camps were:

Auguste and **François Leroy-Duverger**. François was killed at Brienne. **Malaudant, Luzignan de Cerze**

General Mongenet commanded the artillery: A Knight of Malta, he was with Kléber in Egypt in 1800. Appointed General in 1813, he was also promoted to CtLH. After serving in the Army of the Alps in 1815, he retired the following year.

Commanding the Engineers was **Dufriche de Valazé:** He was the son of the Convention member; he was at the Ecole Polytechnique in 1798. He was at Austerlitz.

Bedos was the Chief-of-Staff of the 4th Division. Knighted in 1809 and OLH in 1813. Wounded at la Rothière, he was in the Var Department in 1815 and retired in 1825.

General Gérard was given command of the 2nd Corps after the Battle of Montereau.

Gérard: Former aide de camp to Bernadotte. General in 1808, he was appointed Major-General in 1812 and GdCx of the Réunion in 1813. He commanded the reserve at Paris and fought at Brienne, la Rothière, Lesmont and Nangis where he was wounded. He replaced Victor at Montereau on 18 February. He was also at Nogent on 16 March and Saint-Dizier on the 26th. He was made GdCxLH in 1814.

After fighting at Ligny, he tried to convince Grouchy, on 18 June to attack the cannon in vain. Wounded at Wavre, he was saved by **de Perron**, his aide de camp. Exiled, he returned in 1817. He was elected Deputy for Paris in 1822, 1827 and 1830. Maréchal de France in 1830, he was at Antwerp in 1832, was made GdCX de Leopold and Peer in 1833. He was appointed Minister in 1834 and Grand Chancelier of the LH in 1836. He was a Senator in 1852, the year of his death.

Gérard's Chief-of-Staff was **Saint-Rémy.** He came from the reserve in Paris. Made a General on 23 March 1814, then in 1830. Retired in 1832, made CrLH in 1838.

Gueully (Comte de Rumigny)**:** Aide de camp in 1813, Colonel in 1814, he served with Gérard in 1815. Aide de camp to the Duc d'Orléans in 1819, then to Louis-Philippe in 1830.

He was in Belgium in 1832, then in Algeria where he was wounded. He was made GdOLH in 1833, Lieutenant-General in 1840, Governor-General and chief of the Army in Algiers in 1841. He accompanied the King into exile and was retired in 1848. He was the author of Memoirs published in 1921.

The 2nd Corps consisted of the Huguet-Chataux and Duhesme Divisions.

LIGHT INFANTRY

Chasseur.

Voltigeur.

Carabinier.

Voltigeur Corporal.

Chasseur wearing marching dress.

Carabinier Sergeant-Major.

Musician from the 5th Light Infantry Regiment.

Drummer from a Chasseur company.

André Jouineau © Histoire & Collections 2005

INFANTRY OF THE LINE

Subaltern.

Sapper.

1812-model flag: the reverse side was identical. The names of the regiment's battles are marked on the reverse side: ULM, AUSTERLITZ, JENA, EYLAU, ECKMUHL, ESSLING and WAGRAM.

L'EMPEREUR NAPOLÉON AU 18ME RÉGIMENT D'INFANTERIE DE LIGNE

Infantry regiment colonel in full dress.

Subaltern wearing an overcoat.

Fusilier in marching dress and wearing a Pokalem.

Officer wearing a greatcoat.

Grenadier and Fusilier wearing greatcoats. The greatcoats were often of various shades of grey, beige or even brown. At the end of the Empire, they were shorter to save money.

LIGHT INFANTRY

Subaltern wearing campaign dress.

Subaltern wearing service dress.

Colonel wearing full dress.

ULM FRIEDLAND ESSLING WAGRAM

L'EMPEREUR NAPOLÉON AU 9EME RÉGIMENT D'INFANTERIE LÉGERE

1812-model flag.

Chasseur in a greatcoat.

Sapper.

Voltigeur wearing a greatcoat.

The great 1812 reform applied to all the Imperial army. As a result the silhouette of the Light Infantryman was also modified, at least basically.

Drummer from a Grenadier company.

André Jouineau © Histoire & Collections 2005

Grenadier of the Line and Light Infantry Carabinier.(RR)

THE HUGUET-CHATAUX DIVISION

Huguet-Chataux: Victor's son-in-law, made OLH in 1811, and a General in 1813. He took interim command of the Dufour Division but was mortally wounded at Montereau at the head of his 1st Brigade which he commanded personally.

Huguet-Chataux Brigade

The 24th Light
Colonel Plazanet: OLH in 1808 and Chevalier the following year, he was wounded at Bar-sur-Aube on 27 February. He retired in 1818.

The regiment only had one battalion. At Brienne, three officers were wounded; at la Rothière, three officers were killed and five wounded and at Montereau three others were wounded.
The 19th of the Line
Colonel Trupel: OLH in 1810, Réunion in 1812 and Baron in 1813. He was wounded at Waterloo then retired in 1822.

The regiment was at Brienne, Montereau and Bar-sur-Aube.
The 37th of the Line
One battalion was in Champagne with Major Henon. Colonel Fortier was killed in 1813. The regiment was mentioned at Brienne, La Rothière, Montereau and Troyes.

The brigade also included detachments from the 43rd of the Line and some Belgian conscripts.

Adjudant Commandant Michel's Brigade (?)

The 11th Light
This regiment came from the Tirailleurs Corses and the Pô. Major Signoretti was wounded at Nogent on 11 February. The regiment was mentioned at Brienne, had three officers wounded at Montereau and three at Paris.
The 2nd of the Line
Colonel Corvinius II joined the 1st Division on 10 January. Mentioned at Montereau, made OLH in 1814. He fought at Bar-sur-Aube and died on 26 April from wounds received in front of Paris.

The regiment lost four officers killed and seven wounded defending Besançon and two at Magdeburg.
The 56th of the Line
Colonel Delhaye was with Friant at Auerstadt where he was wounded. He was promoted to OLH in 1812. Wounded at Brienne, served in Belgium in 1815 and was retired in December of the same year.

The regiment only had one battalion, commanded by Battalion Commander Oudot who was wounded at Brienne and then killed at Belleville. Two officers were killed and four wounded at Brienne; three were wounded at La Rothière.

DUHESME'S DIVISION

Duhesme was promoted to General in 1794, then Major-General. He is shown on an engraving sounding the charge by beating the drum with the pommel of his sword at the Crossing of the Rhine in 1797. Mentioned at the taking of Naples in 1799, GdOLH in 1804. He fought at Saint-Dizier on 27 January, Brienne, La Rothière and Montereau. He was made a Count in 1814. He was fatally wounded on 18 June 1815 at Plancenoit leading the Young Guard which heroically opposed the Prussian army.

Materre's Brigade

Materre: Colonel in the 4th of the Line, OLH in 1811, promoted to General on 25 February 1814. He was at Saint-Dizier, Brienne and La Rothière where he was left for dead. He took up his command again at Mormans on 17 February and at Montereau where he was wounded again, Bar-sur-Aube on 27 February, Nogent and Saint-Dizier on 26 March. He retired in 1825.

The 20th Light
One battalion
The 4th of the Line
This was made up of two battalions. It was General Materre's original regiment. It was commanded by Colonel Gélibert from 27 February 1814 following Materre's promotion. Retired in 1815, he was made a Baron in 1816 and retired in 1823, then again in 1833. He was promoted to CrLH in 1853.
The 72nd of the Line
Colonel Barthélémy: OLH in 1813, he served at Phalsbourg in 1815 then was retired in 1816. The regiment lost five officers wounded at la Rothière, one killed and one wounded at Montereau, one at Laon, one at Bar-sur-Aube and one at Saint-Dizier.

Voirol's 2nd Brigade

Woirol, called Voirol was Swiss, appointed Colonel of the 18th of the Line on 2 February 1814. Wounded at Bar-sur-Aube, made CtLH in 1814. Retired in 1816, he was made a Maréchal de Camp in 1823 and Baron in 1828; naturalised French in 1838, he was made a Pair de France in 1839. He was mentioned at Brienne, La Rothière and Montereau.
The 18th of the Line
Colonel Voirol's regiment. When it started the campaign there were 53 officers and 1 383 men. After Saint-Dizier, it took part at Brienne in the capture of the Chateau with Ney. At La Rothière, Major Uny barricaded himself in the village: 19 officers and a thousand men were put out of action. On 16 February, the 18th was at Salins, the 18th it was at Montereau; on the 27th it was Bar-sur-Aube and the 14th at Arcis-sur-Aube. On 22 March, the regiment marched on Saint-Dizier against Winzigerode. At Fontainebleau on 6 April, there were only 209 men left in the ranks.
The 46th of the Line
This regiment was commanded by Colonel Régeau: Chevalier in 1809, Colonel and CtLH in 1813, he retired in 1815.

The regiment fought at Brienne, La Rothière, Montereau and Bar-sur-Aube.
The 93rd of the Line
Colonel Marchier: Chevalier in 1809. At Belfort in 1815, CrLH in 1864, died at the age of 102. This regiment was sent to reinforce the Army of Lyon. It no doubt left a detachment behind.
General Forestier: Made a General in 1813, he was fatally wounded at Brienne on 29 January and was replaced.

Six mentions him as being with Duhesme commanding the 3rd Division in the absence of Dubreton. On the other hand, J.- P. Mir puts him with the Young Guard.

Pajol's Corps before it was disbanded during the 19 February reorganisation.

THE SEINE AND YONNE VALLEYS DEFENCE CORPS

Pajol: General in 1807, Major-General in 1812, Count in 1813. Entrusted with covering the Seine and the Yonne with the 2nd Reserve Division at Melun. He was the hero of Montereau. During the Hundred Days, he served at Ligny and Wavre. He was made GdCxLH in 1830 and a Peer in 1831. He took part in the revolution, a confirmed opponent of the Bourbons. He was appointed Governor of Paris. Pajol was one of the great Light Cavalry commanders of the First Empire.

THE NATIONAL GUARD

Pikeman in the Paris National Guard. Because there were no weapons, some National Guardsmen were armed with pikes.

Mobilised soldiers from the National Guard. With mass conscription at the beginning of 1814, in the best of cases, these guards wore a blue tunic, a shako, a cartridge case and a rifle. The belts and straps were black unless white ones could be found.

Volunteer Chasseur from the Meurthe which was made up mainly of gamekeepers, which explains the green coat with a chamois collar.

Volunteer Chasseur from the Meurthe wearing a greatcoat.

Cadets from the Ecole Polytechnique and invalids were used in the defence of Paris to serve the artillery pieces.

Student from the Maisons-Alfort veterinary school which supplied a 300-man strong battalion for the defence of Paris.

André Jouineau © Histoire & Collections 2005

His Chief-of-Staff was **Frachon**: Baron in 1809, Chevalier in 1813 and OLH in 1814. He was with Berckheim on 16 March then with Maurin on 9 April. He retired in 1830.

General Digeon

He commanded the artillery reserve in Paris under Gérard. He was at Montereau. Made a general in 1814, he was GdOLH in 1820 and Lieutenant-General in 1823 in Spain. He died of a stroke in 1836. He is not to be confused with the other general of the same name who commanded the cavalry of the Army of Lyon.

Aides de camp: **Biot** and **Mondragon**.

DUFOUR'S DIVISION

Dufour: CtLH in 1806, General in 1807, Baron in 1812 and Major-General in 1813. He commanded the Paris reserve on 7 January 1814, the 1st Division under Gérard on 19 February. He served in Reille's Corps in 1815 but died in April 1815 of illness at Lille.

Jarry's Brigade

Jarry: Made a General in 1807, then Baron in 1809. He joined the corps on 8 January; then on 14 February, he replaced de la Hamelinaye who was ill. He served during the Hundred Days and died in 1819.

The brigade was composed of detachments from the 2nd, 4th 12th and 29th Lights and from the 32nd and 58th of the Line.

The 12th Light

Formerly the 87th. Colonel Mottet with the main part of the regiment was with the Army of the Pyrenees. Only the 7th battalion was in Champagne under the command of Major Thibault; it was present at La Rothière and Montereau.

Lefol's Brigade

Lefol: General and Baron in 1808, he was made CtLH in 1811 and Major-General in 1813. He replaced Janssens. He was with Ney at Arcis-sur-Aube where he was brilliant on 20 and 21 March. He fought at Ligny in 1815 and retired first in 1816, then again in 1832.

Detachments from the 5th and 15th lights and the 135th of the Line made up the brigade.

LA HAMELINAYE DIVISION

La Hamelinaye was aide de camp to Bernadotte in 1799, then in 1807. GdOLH in 1820, Viscount in 1822, retired in 1832. He replaced Gérard commanding the 2nd Division of the reserve at Troyes on 17 January, but because he was ill he left the army on 14 February and was himself replaced by Jarry. He therefore only had a minor role during the campaign.

PACHTOD'S DIVISION (the National Guard Division)

Pachtod: Born in Haute-Savoie, mentioned at Toulon, made a General in 1795, then Major-General and Baron in 1808, decorated with the Couronne de Fer in 1810, made GdOLH and Count in 1813, he commanded a division of National Guardsmen under Pajol at Montereau and Bar-sur-Aube. A hero of Fère-Champenoise, he was wounded and captured. He served under Suchet in the Alps in 1815. Naturalised in 1816, he retired in 1826.

Audue de Gorgier, Viscount. Pacthod's Chief-of-Staff was killed at Fère-Champenoise.

Delort's Brigade

Delort: see Kellermann's 6th cavalry Corps.

His brigade was made up of:

- the **54th of the Line** with a single battalion made up mainly of conscripts.

- the **3rd Provisional Regiment** made up of a battalion from the Loir and Cher, under the command of Major Derivoire.

- the **1st National Guards Regiment of the Sarthe** under Major Bergeron.

Bergeron: In the Gendarmerie in 1797, made OLH in 1804, retired as Honorary Maréchal de Camp in October 1815. He died in 1824.

Bonté's Brigade

Bonté: Made a Baron and a General in 1811, he was in the Corps from 8 February. Captured at Fère-Champenoise, he was on the non-active list after the campaign. He was promoted to CrLH in 1821. He retired as Honorary Lieutenant-General in 1826 and awarded the Couronne de Fer.

PAJOL'S CAVALRY CORPS

After their General was wounded at Montereau, the cavalry regiments of Pajol's Corps were shared out among the four cavalry corps under Marshal Grouchy.

Delort's Brigade

Delort: not to be confused with the others with the same name. Baron and General in

1811. Returning from the Army of Aragon, he was with the reserve division in Paris on 9 January 1814. Wounded at Montereau, he was appointed Major-General on 26 February and joined the 2nd Cavalry Corps.

The brigade with a strength of about 500 horses, was made up of elements from the 2nd, 3rd and 12th Hussars and the 7th Polish Chevau-Légers.

The 2nd Hussars

See Wolff's Brigade, Jacquinot's Division in Kellermann's 6th Corps.

The regiment was mentioned at Montereau where Captain Ducis captured two cannon and took a number of prisoners.

The 3rd Hussars

See Subervie's Brigade, Piré's Division in Milhaud's 5th Corps. The regiment had a strength of 298 troopers.

The 7th Chevau-Légers

Commanded by Colonel Tewski. The regiment was made up of part of the 1st Vistula Lancer Regiment.

Ameil's Brigade

which joined the 6th Cavalry Corps.

The 10th Chasseurs

See Kellermann's 6th cavalry Corps. There was probably only a detachment of the regiment present. On the 18th, under Delort at Montereau, they came out of the woods at Valence with the Spanish Gendarmes à pied. After the 19 February reorganisation, the regiment joined the 6th Corps, with Ameil, with only the 3rd and 4th Squadrons, reinforced by men from Pajol's units which had been disbanded, together with 3 officers and 120 men sent from the depot at Saint Maixent.

The 13th Chasseurs

See Ameil's Brigade in Kellermann's 6th Corps.

Du Coetlosquet's Brigade

See the 5th Cavalry Corps, (Piré's Division). He commanded a brigade. He joined Pajol on 3 February at Versailles and commanded a provisional brigade made up of the 26th and 27th Chasseurs at Montereau.

Grouvel's Brigade

Grouvel: Chevalier in 1810, General in 1813. He was with Pajol on 20 January in the reserve division; wounded at Laon, he replaced Wathiez then served with Roussel d'Hurbal and his Dragoons on 4 March. He served under Merlin in 1815. Made a Baron in 1816, Viscount in 1824, Lieutenant-General in 1825, GdOLH in 1835, he retired in 1836.

The brigade was composed of Provisional Dragoon regiments from the 4th, 5th, 12th 14th, 16th and 17th Regiments

2nd Provisional Dragoons

Colonel Séguier de Saint-Brisson. See 14th Dragoons, Ismert's Brigade, Treillard's Division, Kellermann's 6th Corps.

5th Provisional Dragoons

Colonel Canavas Saint-Amand. See 25th Dragoons, Collaert's Brigade, Lhéritier's Division, Milhaud's 5th Corps.

6th provisional Dragoons

Colonel Nicolas. See 11th Chasseurs, Dommanget's Brigade, Maurin's Division, Saint-Germain's 2nd Corps.

MACDONALD'S 11th CORPS

MacDonald: He was made Maréchal and Grand Aigle of the LH in 1809. He withdrew towards Meaux on 4 February 1814, was at Nogent on 17 March, Saint-Dizier on 26 March. Made a Peer in 1814, he was Grand Chancelier of the LH in 1815 and followed the King in 1815. In 1820 he was promoted to GdCxSL and died in 1840.

His Chief-of-Staff was **Grundler** who was a General since 1812. He served in 1815 in the National Guards of the Somme. He was made Maréchal de Camp and Count in 1818, GdOLH in 1822, GdCx of Spain in 1823. He took part in the formation of the Belgian Army in 1831.

His assistant was **L'Olivier**, wounded twice and exiled.

His aides de camps were:

Gauldrée-Boilleau: Polytechnicien, he was an artilleryman. He was decorated with the order of the Two Sicilies in 1813 then made a Colonel on 17 February 1814. OLH in 1823, he was Maréchal de Camp in 1835; Lieutenant-General in 1844 and GdOLH in 1850, the year he retired.

Gunkel: A Dutchman, an artillery Colonel who came from the Guard. Awarded the Order of the Réunion in 1812. He resigned in August 1814, served as a General in Holland and retired in 1835. Arrested for a crime, he died in prison in 1859.

THE NATIONAL GUARD

The Paris National Guard is especially known thanks to a painting by H. Vernet of the defence of Paris (30 March 1814) at the Barrière de Clichy (now Place de Clichy). The twelve legions of the Paris National Guard were given the defence of the outside wall of Paris.

Soldier from the Cohort of the 1st Ban ( ) of the National Guard.

Chasseur.

Officer from the Chasseur company.

Grenadiers.

Sapper.

1804-type flag attributed to the National Guard. A flag was attributed to each department with the number in its centre and the initial letter of the department inside the wreaths. No flag of the 1812-type was ever made. This was captured at Rheims in 1814.

FORCE À LA LOY FIDÉLITÉ À L'EMPEREUR

GARDE NATIONALE DU DÉPARTEMENT DE LA MARNE 59

Sergeant-Major from the Chasseur company.

André Jouineau © Histoire & Collections 2005

*Above, from left to right: **Maréchal MacDonald commanded the 11th Infantry Corps.***
General Brayer commanded the 2nd Division in MacDonald's Corps.
Maréchal Oudinot, Duke of Reggio, commanded the 7th Corps.
General Guyer commanded the first brigade of the Pierre Boyer Division.
(Photos: RR)

Marion: Commanded the Corps' Engineers. Wounded at Nogent and made a Colonel; made a Baron in 1820, CtLH in 1834 and Maréchal de Camp in 1839.

The following must also be mentioned:

Amey: Made a General in 1793, he was a Major-General in 1812, wounded at the Berezina. Made GdOLH in 1813, he commanded the 2nd Division in MacDonald's 11th Corps. Captured at Fère-Champenoise, he served in 1815 and retired the same year then again in 1833.

Thevenet was a Marengo veteran who was made Chevalier and OLH in 1809, then General in 1813. He commanded the 1st Brigade of Amey's Division in MacDonald's 11th Corps. Seriously wounded, he was captured at Fère-Champenoise where his square was the last to surrender. He served in 1815, retired in 1825 and was put in the reserve in 1839.

ALBERT'S DIVISION

Albert: Made a General in 1807, Couronne de Fer in 1809 and Major-General in 1812, wounded at the Berezina. Made GdOLH in 1813, he served with MacDonald from December 1813 to April 1814 and was at Chalons and the Ferté-sous-Jouarre. Aide de camp to the Duc d'Orléans, he followed him but returned to the Army of the Rhine in 1815 and defended Strasbourg. He died in 1822.

The division only had 1 444 men and was made up of the 135th, 140th, 141st and 152nd of the Line. The 154th of the Line was probably part of this division.

The 135th of the Line
325 men.

The 140th of the Line
Colonel Ganivet-Desgraviers: Made an OLH in 1813, retired in 1822. 280 men were present.

The 141st of the Line
Colonel Pignet: OLH in 1813, retired in 1815 then again in 1823 as Honorary Maréchal de Camp. Died in 1836.

The regiment had 220 men.

The 152nd of the Line
Probably commanded by **Colonel Reynaud.** Part of the regiment was at Mainz and Strasbourg. There were 279 men present in Champagne.

The 154th of the Line
This regiment is mentioned in the division although it did not exist at the time.

BRAYER'S DIVISION

Brayer: Colonel of the 2nd Lights at Austerlitz. Made a General in 1809, then Major-General in 1813 and wounded the same year. He was at Chalons and Dormans on 8 February. La Ferté-sur-Aube and Bar-sur-Seine on 2 March. He marched with Napoleon on 22 March 1815 and was appointed Governor of Versailles, the Emperor's Chamberlain, Count and Peer in June 1815. Condemned to death and outlawed, he went into exile in the USA. He went to Chile to take up a command in 1818 and returned in 1821. He was made a Pair de France in 1832 and GdCxLH in 1836. His name was mentioned in Napoleon's will.

General de Gency: General in 1795, he was at Marengo. Made CtLH in 1804, he was made a Baron in 1809. He was wounded in front of Chalons-sur-Marne and was promoted to GdOLH in August 1814. Lieutenant-General in 1815. After the Hundred Days he was on the

non-active list and died in 1825. The regiments making up the division were the 19th Light and the 5th, 11th and 107th of the Line. They were 1 446 strong.

The 5th of the Line
This regiment was in Catalonia under the command of Colonel Roussille. A detachment was present in Champagne.

The 11th of the Line
Its commanding officer, Colonel Aubrée, returned from Spain. He was awarded the LH in 1804, made a Baron in 1809 then Couronne de Fer in 1811. He was killed at Waterloo.

The 107th of the Line
Colonel Tripe: OLH in 1804, wounded at la Ferté-sous-Jouarre on 9 February, he marched with the 13th Hussars and Molitor during the retreat. He was in Belgium in 1815 then retired in 1822.

Several dozen Swiss Grenadiers completed the Division.

MOLITOR'S DIVISION

Molitor: General in 1799, he was promoted to Major-General in 1800. He had been at the head of this division since 17 December 1813. He was at Chalons and Troyes. He commanded the corps during MacDonald's absence on 4 April. He was promoted to GdCxLH. In 1815 he served under Rapp. He took part in the Spanish Expedition in 1823 and was made a Pair de France and Maréchal de France. Grand Chancelier of the LH in 1848, he died the following year and was buried in the Invalides.

The division was made up of the 28th Light and the 46th, 70th, 139th and 149th of the Line.

The 28 Light
Under the command of **Colonel Génin**. In fact the regiment was with Soult in the Army of the Pyrenees and took part in the Battle of Toulouse. A detachment was probably assigned to the Molitor Division.

The 46th of the Line
Colonel Régeau: Made a Chevalier in 1809, then CtLH in 1813. He was at Brienne, la Rothière, Montereau and Bar-sur-Aube. He retired in April 1815.

The 70th of the Line
Colonel Dumareix: Baron in 1809 and OLH in 1811, he was at la Rothière and Laon. He retired in 1819.

The 139th of the Line
Colonel Genevay: Made OLH in 1814, he was at Chalons, Chateau-Thierry (the heroism of Captain Cailus), La Ferté-sous-Jouarre, Arcis-sur-Aube and Saint-Dizier. Discharged in 1815, he retired in 1833. He was promoted to CtLH in 1853.

The 149th of the Line
Colonel Cartier was wounded seven times on 13 September 1813, was picked up and captured. His promotion to Colonel of the 149th dated from the 19 September. The detachment of the regiment operating in Champagne took part at la Rothière and at Laon. It was also on the Bray Bridge on 14 March with the 13th Hussars, then at Fère-Champenoise.

OUDINOT'S 7th CORPS

Oudinot: Made a Maréchal in 1809, and Duke of Reggio in 1810. Wounded at Brienne, he was at La Rothière, Mormans on 17 February, Méry on the 22nd, and was beaten at Bar-sur-Aube on the 27th. On 22 March at Arcis-sur-Aube he was hit by a bullet whose impact was softened by the plate of his Grand Aigle of the LH. Pair de France and CrSL in 1814, he was

NB. A number of regiments which were assigned to other theatres of operation supplied reinforcements to Napoleon's army, often from their depots. These detachments would have been under the command of a Battalion Commander. This dispersion explains why it is difficult to classify the various units.

TRAIN, ENGINEERS and SERVICES

Trooper
in the Artillery train.

Trooper
in the train teams.

Engineer Colonel.

Soldier in the Administration
Companies. These troops
did most of the jobs dealing
with supplies
and the administration
of the hospitals.

Imperial
Gendarmerie.

Medical Orderly. Although
they were dressed like infantrymen,
the medical orderlies were
stretcher-bearers, and orderlies
in the military hospitals.

Surgeon,
2nd Class.

André Jouineau © Histoire & Collections 2005

*Above, from left to right: **Maréchal Mortier, Duke of Trevise,** commanded the Imperial Guard.*
***General Friant** commanded the Infantry of the Guard. He distinguished himself during the whole of the campaign.*
***General Cambronne** commanded the second infantry brigade of the Old Guard: the Chasseurs à pied.*
***General Michel** was at the head of the 2nd Guards Infantry Division. When he was wounded he was replaced by **Christiani**. (Photos: RR)*

appointed Minister of State on 13 May. He opposed the return of the Empire in 1815 and exiled himself to his property during the Hundred Days. He was made GdCxSL in 1816, Governor of Madrid and GdCx of Charles III of Spain in 1823 and Grand Chancelier of the LH in 1839. Governor of the Invalides in 1842, he died in 1847.

His aides de camps were:

De Bourcet: he was aide de camp to Oudinot from 1809 to 1818. Made OLH in 1809 then CrLH in 1821. He retired in 1832 and died at Dr Blanche's in Montmartre in 1836.

Jacqueminot, Vicomte de Ham: aide de camp in 1812, he was wounded at Brienne and Bar-sur-Aube. Maréchal de Camp in 1831, he was made GdCxLH in 1846 then retired in 1848.

Le Tellier. In 1812, his sons Victor and Enguerrand.

General Lorencez (Latrille de) Oudinot's son-in-law. Appointed Major-General in 1813, made GdOLH in 1814. On the non-active list after 1815, he was given the CrSL in 1822 and joined the reserve in 1832.

His chief-of-staff was **Monjardet de Saint-Valrin.** He was with Lasalle in Spain at Cabezon in 1808. He was made OLH and appointed chief-of-staff in 1813. He was wounded in Germany the same year. On the non-active list after the French Campaign he retired in 1821 as Honorary Maréchal de Camp.

His assistants on the Staff were **Gault:** Adjutant-Commandant, made OLH in 1814. He could not serve in 1815 because of his wounds. **Vergez:** Commissary for War. **Delamarre:** Friend of the family. **Duchand de Sancey:** Made a Baron in 1813, he was a Horse Artillery Major in the 7th Corps in January 1814, and then served in the Guard in 1815. Maréchal de Camp in 1830, he was made Lieutenant-General in 1840 and was promoted to GdOLH in 1843.

DUFOUR'S DIVISION IN THE PARIS RESERVE.

Already mentioned with Pajol, commanded by General Gérard.

Battalion Commander Gérard (not to be confused with the General) commanded the only battalion (6bis) of the 32nd of the Line present and was mentioned on 6 February: he defended the bridge at Nogent with two cannon and a squadron of Hussars for 12 hours. Lieutenant Bonsirvin was decorated for this fight.

In a letter from a young officer of the regiment one finds the following passage: "Napoleon's popularity is not due to the prosperous Consulate, nor the grandeur of the Empire; it's 1814, defending France from invasion. The humble have to love, they have to admire! These conscripts melted like snow in the forced marches, in the fires of the perpetual campsites, in the fighting every day. Two men only out of three on average had clothes; the uniform only consisted of a grey overcoat and a forage cap with a rather feminine shape, hence the name given to these brave people: the "Marie-Louises". More seriously, only one out of two men had a weapon. Napoleon armed them on the battlefield with their enemies' rifles."

Major Gérard was chosen to defend Soissons because Napoleon had asked Clarke to "not to send me some fool or worn-out man like Moreau to command Soissons, but a young man, Battalion Commander or Colonel, with his military reputation still to be made."

Behind ramparts which could be reached from all sides, with a garrison made up of convalescents, unit-less soldiers and even deserters, with a strength of barely 2 500 combatants, Gérard held out against Bülow's 20 000 men and 54 cannon. He first replied to the negotiators "that he would answer with canon fire". After a bombardment, the assaults were all driven off and Bülow started a siege by opening a trench. After 9 days of open trench work and

irritated by the daily sallies, Bülow changed the siege into a blockade. Soissons was saved but Paris lost.

Oudot: OLH in 1809, he was Acting Commanding Officer of the 1st Brigade of the Paris Reserve. He was killed in front of Paris on 30 March 1814 while attacking Belleville.

LEVAL'S DIVISION

Leval: Made a General in 1795, he was a Major-General in 1799. He took part in the arrest of the Duc d'Enghien in 1804. Made GdOLH in 1808, captured by the English, he led the escape from the Vieille Castille hulk. Sent to champagne on 8 January, he reached Provins on 6 February and was assigned to the 7th Corps. He fought at Champaubert, Vauchamps, Bar-sur-Aube, was wounded at Arcis-sur-Aube, and at Saint-Dizier. He retired in 1816, 1819 and then 1832. The Leval Division was recalled from Spain and was made up of experienced soldiers.

Maulmond' Brigade

Maulmond: CtLH in 1813, he was promoted to General in 1814 and was mentioned at Arcis-sur-Aube. He served in the Gard Department in 1815. He retired in 1826 then 1834.

The brigade was made up of the following regiments.

10th Light: 3 battalions; **3rd of the Line:** 1 battalion; **15th of the Line:** 1 battalion; **130th of the Line:** 1 battalion.

Montfort's Brigade

Montfort was a General since 1811. He returned from Spain and was assigned to the 7th Corps on 22 January 1814. He fought at Arcis-sur-Aube and was made CtLH on 5 April 1814. He served with Lecourbe in 1815. On the non-active list in 1816, he was available in 1821. He died in 1824.

The brigade was made up of the following regiments.

17th Light: 1 battalion; **36th of the Line:** 1 battalion; **101st of the Line:** 1 battalion; **105th of the Line:** 2 battalions; **118th of the Line:** 1 battalion; The **17th Light**.

The regiment only had its 1st battalion in Champagne. On 24 January, Major Barré, who had come from the 14th Light, was promoted to Colonel.

As the division arrived too late for Montmirail, it was committed at Vauchamps alongside Grouchy; it was sent to Troyes on 24 February. On the 26th it was at Bar-sur-Aube where it drove off the attacks, but Oudinot decided to fall back. Montfort attacked a battery sent by Schwarzenberg, and then his brigade covered the retreat. The Leval Division also distinguished itself at Arcis-sur-Aube.

THE PIERRE BOYER DIVISION

Boyer, Pierre: A veteran of Italy and Egypt, he was made a Baron in 1812. He came to Champagne on 16 February and was assigned to Oudinot's 7th Corps. Promoted to Major-General, he was at Méry on 22 February, with Ney at Laon, then at Arcis-sur-Aube on 21 March. He served in 1815 at the Mont-Blanc. Outlawed, he left for Egypt to serve the Pasha in 1824. He commanded a division in Algeria, at Oran in 1830. He was made GdOLH in 1831 and retired in 1848. The General was sometimes nicknamed "Peter the Great."

Gruyer's Brigade

Gruyer was made a General and CtLH in 1813. He was assigned to the 1st Brigade of Boyer's Division in place of Gauthier who was wounded on 17 February. He was wounded at Méry-sur-Seine on 22 February. He served in 1815, was outlawed and condemned to death in 1816; this sentence was changed to 20 years' imprisonment. Pardoned in 1818, he was freed.

Chassé's Brigade

Chassé: A Dutchman, he was made a Baron by Louis, the King of Holland. General in 1810,

THE OLD GUARD - GRENADIERS and CHASSEURS

Grenadier wearing marching dress.

Subaltern wearing an overcoat.

Grenadier Corporal wearing a greatcoat.

Subaltern wearing marching dress.

Chasseurs à pied wearing marching dress.

Chasseurs à pied Sergeant wearing an overcoat.

Grenadier drummer wearing marching dress.

Subaltern in the Chasseurs à pied wearing an overcoat.

André Jouineau © Histoire & Collections 2005

he was made a French Baron in 1811, then OLH in 1813. He was wounded at Arcis-sur-Aube where he sounded the charge with the pommel of his sword to defend the bridge. He resigned at the end of 1814, returned to Holland and served the Prince of Orange at Waterloo. In 1830 he defended Antwerp against Gérard. He was made Grand Cross of the Order of William. He died in 1849.

PACHTOD'S DIVISION

See Pajol's Corps

The division joined the corps. It tried to find Marshals Mortier and Marmont accompanying a convoy and was destroyed at Fère-Champenoise after a heroic struggle.

General Jamin: Commanded a brigade of the Young Guard under Charpentier. On 12 March; he was with Pachtod at Fère-Champenoise where he was wounded and captured. He served at Quatre-Bras and Waterloo. Made a Viscount in 1822, he was Lieutenant-General in Spain in 1823. He took part in the siege of Antwerp in 1832. GdOLH in 1833, he was Deputy for the Meuse Department in 1833, 1834, 1839 and 1846. Peer. He died in 1848.

ROTTEMBOURG'S DIVISION

This division joined the corps later and is described in the chapter concerning the Imperial Guard.

On 6 March, the 2nd Corps protected the crossing over the Seine; the 7th Corps drew out up to Provins where the Rottembourg Division was set up. The decision to fall back was taken.

On 15 March they fought at l'Echelle.

On 21 March, the division distinguished itself brilliantly by defending Arcis-sur-Aube but the French were forced to go back over the bridge which was "strewn with enemy corpses". The fighting lasted until midnight, even after the bridge was destroyed. Major Langlois was killed.

On the 23rd, they marched on Vitry.

On the 26th at Saint-Dizier, Oudinot, at the head of the Leval Division entered the town at the charge. The enemy abandoned its artillery and left 3 000 prisoners.

On the 29th, the order was given to leave in a hurry for Paris which capitulated on the 30th.

MORTIER'S CORPS - THE IMPERIAL GUARD

Chief-of-Staff: **De Lapointe:** Aide de camp to Mortier since 1806, made General and Baron in 1813. He took part in the capitulation negotiations. Made CrLH in 1822, he retired in 1834, and died in 1856.

The marshal's aide de camps were: Adjudant-Commandant **de Beaumetz; Soulier de Choisy**, the General's nephew; **Herissy**, OLH in 1813; Battalion Commander **Richebé**.

Captains **Durbach** and **Lacourte**

General Henrion was in command of the artillery.

THE IMPERIAL GUARD INFANTRY

FRIANT'S DIVISION- THE OLD GUARD

Friant: Joined the Gardes Françaises, made a General in 1794, took part in the Italian and Egyptian Campaigns, Major-General in 1800, hero of Austerlitz under Davout. Made Grand Aigle of the LH in 18025 and Count in 1808. He commanded the Grenadier Guards in 1812 replacing Dorsenne. Wounded twice at the Moskova, he was Chamberlain in 1813. He was with Mortier in 1814, at Champaubert, Montmirail, Vauchamps, Craonne, Laon, Rheims and Arcis-sur-Aube. Peer in 1815, he was wounded at Waterloo and retired on 4 September 1815; he died in 1829.

1st Brigade - Foot Grenadiers

This brigade was commanded by General Petit.

1st Grenadiers

General Petit: Egyptian Campaign, aide de camp to Mireur then Friant. Wounded at Wagram, he was made a Baron in 1809. Promoted to General in 1813, he was the Major of the 1st Grenadiers on 20 November 1813. He distinguished himself at Chateau-Thierry and Montereau. It was he whom the Emperor embraced at Fontainebleau when he abdicated. He covered the retreat in the evening of Waterloo. Retired in 1824, he was Lieutenant-General in 1831, Peer in 1837, GdCLH in 1849, he was elected Senator in 1852; died in 1856 and buried at the Invalides.

2nd Grenadiers

Christiani: Made a General and Colonel Major of the 2nd Grenadiers in 1813. He replaced Michel who was wounded at Montmirail. He fought at Waterloo in 1815. GdOLH in 1831, he died in 1840.

General Rottembourg. (Musée de l'Armée)

Golzio: Veteran of Austerlitz, promoted to OLH in 1813 and made a Baron after Montmirail. He took command of the 2nd regiment. With the 1st Grenadiers at Waterloo, he retired in 1821 with the rank of Lieutenant-Colonel.

Dambly: Wounded at Marengo, awarded a Sabre of Honour at the Mincio, then made OLH at Boulogne. With the 2nd Grenadiers in 1808; joined the 1st Tirailleurs in 1810, he was made Chevalier of the Réunion in 1813 and Chevalier of the Empire in 1814. He returned to the 2nd Grenadiers in 1814 then retired in 1821.

2nd Brigade - Les Chasseurs à Pied

Cambronne commanded this brigade; he was replaced on 8 March by Pelet.

1st Chasseurs

Cambronne: The hero of Zurich, awarded the LH in 1804, then OLH in 1807, Baron in 1810 and CtLH in 1813. General, he commanded the 1st Chasseurs then the 2nd Brigade of the Old Guard the same year. Wounded at Bar-sur-Aube, he was at Craonne and Paris. He accompanied Napoleon to Elba then was made GdOLH, Count and Pair de France Major-Colonel of the 1st Chasseurs, he was wounded and captured at Waterloo. Condemned to death in his absence, he returned to France, was imprisoned then acquitted in 1816. He was put on the non-active list with half-pay in 1818. Made CSL in 1819, then Viscount in 1822. Retired in 1823, he died in 1842.

Pelet-Clozeau: Chevalier in 1811, made a General in 1813, he was at Brienne where he commanded the 2nd brigade of Decouz's Division; he was also at la Rothière, Champaubert, Montmirail, Vauchamps, Montereau, Craonne, Laon, Rheims and Arcis-sur-Aube. Major in the 1st Chasseurs during the Hundred Days, he was at Ligny and Waterloo where he fought at Plancenoit. Lieutenant-General in 1830, he was elected in 1831, 1835 and 1850. He was wounded by Fieschi's bomb. Made a Peer in 1837, GdCxLH in 1849. He was elected to the Senate in 1852 then to the Académie in 1855.

2nd Chasseurs

This regiment was commanded by **Deshayes**, but he was killed at Dresden. Command was given to Varlet, promoted in December 1813. Baron in 1810, OLH and the Réunion in 1813, Maréchal de Camp in 1831; he retired in 1837.

Henrion: One of the heroes of Montmirail.

Dard: Scout in Egypt, he was with the Grenadiers à Cheval at Marengo, awarded the LH in An-XII. With the 2nd Foot Grenadiers in 1809, he was awarded the Order of the Reunion in 1813. He retired on 4 October 1814.

Two battalions of Spanish Gendarmes were incorporated into the Old Guard.

MICHEL'S DIVISION

Michel: Colonel of the 1st Grenadiers in 1807, made a Baron in 1808, General in 1811, Major-General and CtLH in 1813, he was wounded at Montmirail, cared for in Paris, and replaced by Christiani. Made a Count on 23 March. He formed a division in Paris and was wounded again at Pantin. He was killed at Waterloo. Michel actualy was the author of the legendary *mot* attributed to Cambronne.

His Chief-of-Staff was Saint-Charles: OLH in 1813, wounded at Paris.

Christiani's brigade

Christiani was promoted to General in 1813. In 1814 he commanded the Fusiliers and the Italian Velites, then replaced Michel, wounded at Chateau-Thierry on 12 February. He fought at Waterloo. He was promoted to GdOLH in 1831.

THE MIDDLE GUARD
FUSILIERS-GRENADIERS and FUSILIERS-CHASSEURS

Fusilier-Grenadier wearing marching dress. They were all incorporated into the Michel Division of the Guard under the command of Maréchal Mortier together with the Fusilier-Chasseurs.

A Fusilier-Grenadier or Fusilier-Chasseur subaltern wearing a coat which does not enable him to be identified as one or the other.

Fusilier-Grenadier Corporal wearing a greatcoat.

Fusilier-Chasseur wearing an overcoat.

Fusilier-Chasseur subaltern wearing full dress.

Turin Velite wearing a greatcoat. They belonged to the same brigade as the Florence Velites numbering about 500 men.

Turin Velite Corporal.

Turin Velite Drummer.

André Jouineau © Histoire & Collections 2005

The Fusiliers-Grenadiers

They were commanded by **Léglise**: Baron in 1813, he was made CtLH in 1814, then Maréchal de camp in December of the same year. Retired in 1834, he died in 1836.

The Fusiliers-Chasseurs

Major Boudon-Pompejac was in command since 3 January 1814. He was wounded twice at Montmirail as was Battalion Commander Deschamps. He retired in August 1814 because of his wounds. He died in 1843.

Gros' Brigade - The Flankers

Gros: General and Couronne de Fer in 1807, he was made a Baron in 1808. He retired in 1814 then again in 1815.

The Flanker-Grenadiers

Desalons: Baron in 1810, Maréchal de Camp in 1815, rescinded, reappointed in 1823. CrLH in 1828 and retired in 1831.

The Flanker-Chasseurs

Colonel Tessière: OLH, Réunion and Baron in 1813, he was wounded at Montmirail but was nevertheless present at Arcis-sur-Aube. He served with the 4th Voltigeurs in 1815, and then was put on the non-active list. He died at Toulon in 1819.

Battalion Commander Rouillard de Bauval from the Flanker-Chasseurs whose right arm was seriously wounded at Montmirail, marched passed Napoleon and saluted him. The Emperor said to him *"Thank you, Baron"* and the title was confirmed. He refused to be amputated and was saved by his young wife. He fought in 1815. Rouillard de Bauval is shown in a painting saluting the Emperor with his good arm and being made a Baron on the spot.

The Turin Velites under Cicéron and the Florence Velites under Battalion Commander Delaire who was killed in January 1814 at Chaumont.

How the Young Guard Regiments were split up

The Young Guard regiments were regrouped in 6 divisions at the beginning of the campaign. On 5 December 1813, the roll taken was as follows:

TIRAILLEUR DIVISIONS

Barrois' Division: 1st, 2nd, 3rd and 4th Regiments.
Rottembourg's Division: 5th, 6th, 7th and 8th Regiments.
Roguet's Division: 9th, 10th, 11th and 12th Regiments.

VOLTIGEURS DIVISIONS

Meunier's Division: 1st, 2nd, 3rd and 4th Regiments
Decouz's Division: 5th, 6th, 7th and 8th Regiments.
Boyer de Rebeval: 9th, 10th, 11th and 12th Regiments.

By 14 March there had been some changes: in Ney's Corps, Curial had replaced Decouz, killed at Brienne.

The Lelièvre de Lagrange Brigade which was with Marmont's 6th Corps was reinforced on that date with the 1st, 2nd, 3rd and 4th Voltigeurs and the 14th Tirailleurs formed from its 1st and 3rd Battalions and the 3rd battalion of Laurède's 13th Tirailleurs.

THE YOUNG GUARD INFANTRY REGIMENTS

The regiments of the Young Guard were created in January 1809 when the Tirailleur-Grenadiers appeared. After that, the Tirailleur-Chasseurs, the Conscript-Grenadiers and Chasseurs, the Tirailleurs, the Voltigeurs and then the Flankers were created. In May 1811, Napoleon regrouped these regiments under the names Tirailleurs and Voltigeurs. Only the Flankers were not included.

The regiments partly comprised soldiers from units of the Line, but they consisted mainly of conscripts brought in from all departments of the Empire. On the other hand, the cadres came from the regiments of the Old or Medium Guard. These hardened veterans knew how to instil courage and valour into their men.

The uniform was the same as that of the Line regiments. The Tirailleurs had red epaulettes, collars and pompoms; the Voltigeurs had green epaulettes with yellow twisted braid, yellow collars and green pompoms.

The Tirailleurs and Voltigeurs regiments did not have any Eagles.

For the whole of this horrible campaign, the Young Guard was engaged in the front line, always showing how determined and effective they could be. They took part in all the battles and made all the sacrifices from Brienne to Craonne, Laon and Arcis-sur-Aube.

If one tries to place the Young Guard Major-Colonels with their units, one runs into a lot of difficulties because, depending on which sources are used, there were a lot of changes.

I have tried to inventory these units of the Young Guard, hastily got together with selected conscripts; the battalions were then often mixed with Tirailleurs and Voltigeurs. The following details are taken from Lachouque, Quintin, Six and Fins. These are more or less reliable, but sometimes contradictory sources. Indeed, the Young Guard regiments were mixed or regrouped to make up the right numbers; sometimes single battalions were used. Reduced battalions were often amalgamated and their Majors often went from one regiment to another, or were transferred to carry out other functions.

THE TIRAILLEURS

The 1st Tirailleurs

This was formed from the 1st Battalion of Tirailleur-Grenadiers and was commanded by Colonel Darriule who was replaced by Battalion Commander Masson because he was ill. It was then commanded by Major Albert. This regiment could also have been commanded by Battalion Commander Malet of the same regiment who went over to the Chasseurs and commanded the Island of Elba Battalion; killed at Waterloo.

Major Albert: OLH in 1809, Baron in 1813, he served with the 4th Tirailleurs in 1815 then retired the following year.

The 2nd Tirailleurs

Commanded by **Vionnet, Vicomte de Maringoné:** Came from the 2nd Tirailleur-Grenadiers, made Chevalier, Sabre of Honour in 1802; he was wounded three times in 1813 and made Maréchal de Camp on 26 April 1814, then Baron, CtLH and Viscount in 1822. He was awarded the Order of St-Ferdinand in Spain in 1823 where he was made Lieutenant-General. He retired in 1831. His Memoirs were published in 1899 and 1913.

The regiment had a strength of 27 officers and 818 men on 26 January.

The 3rd Tirailleurs

Formed from the 1st Regiment of Conscript-Grenadiers, it was commanded by **Darquier.** Colonel of the 3rd Grenadiers in 1815, he fought at Ligny and Waterloo. He was in Belgium in 1831.

The regiment was mentioned at Courtrai, Laon and Paris.

The 4th Tirailleurs

Formed from the 2nd Conscript-Grenadiers, it was commanded by **Carré** who was made CtLH and Baron in 1813; he was at la Rothière, Laon and Paris. He was made Colonel of the 21st of the Line in June 1814 at Waterloo where he was wounded and captured. He retired in 1823 with the rank of Honorary Maréchal de Camp.

The 5th Tirailleurs

This regiment was commanded by **Colonel-Major Hennequin:** Made a general and CtLH in 1813, he was seriously wounded at Dresden and retired in 1814. He was replaced by Dupré who came from the 5th Tirailleurs; made OLH and Baron in 1813, he fought at Saint-Dizier on 3 February, la Rothière and Arcis-sur-Aube. He commanded the 46th of the Line in 1815 then retired in 1816.

The 6th Tirailleurs

Trappier de Malcolm: already present at Toulon, took part in the Italian and Egyptian Campaigns; made CtLH and Baron in 1813, he was captured at la Rothière. Colonel of the 1st Tirailleurs in Belgium in 1815, he was made Maréchal de Camp in 1832 then retired in 1837.

The 7th Tirailleurs

The regiment was commanded by **Pailhès:** Italian Campaign, made baron in 1813, he fought at Brienne, Bar-sur-Aube on 3 March and Troyes on the 4th. He served with the 3rd Tirailleurs in 1815. Having plotted at Belfort, he was arrested then pardoned in 1824; he was very active in 1830.

The 8th Tirailleurs

According to Lachouque, the regiment was commanded by **Colonel Bardin.** However, Quintin and Fins place him at the head of the 13th in 1813.

Bardin: Commanded the Pupils in 1811, he was a major and CtLH in 1813. He took part in the Antwerp blockade. In Champagne he was wounded at Brienne and Craonne, probably with a part of the regiment. Retired in 1823 as Maréchal de camp, he was the author of the famous "Règlement des Uniformes" (Uniform regulations) in 1812 which was published in 1841.

The 9th Tirailleurs

Lepaige-Dorsenne: Baron in 1810, he was mentioned with the 8th Tirailleurs in 1813. He was seriously wounded at Paris. Commanded the 5th Tirailleurs during the Hundred Days, he received the CtLH then was retired. According to Quintin, the regiment was commanded by Laurède.

The 10th Tirailleurs

Commanded by **Battalion Commander Vesilier** who was at Antwerp, Craonne and Laon where he was wounded. The previous commander of the regiment, Colonel Vézu, died of typhus in 1813.

The 11th Tirailleurs

Vautrin: OLH in 1812, then Baron in 1813, he was at Courtrai, Laon and Paris. Wounded at Waterloo, he lost his left leg and was discharged on medical grounds.

The 12th Tirailleurs

Mosnier: OLH in 1809, Chevalier in 1810, Baron and Couronne de Fer in 1813, he was made a Major the following year. He was with the 2nd Tirailleurs in 1815, he was retired the following year.

The 12th was mentioned at Antwerp, Claye and Paris.

The 13th Tirailleurs

According to Quintin and Fins, the regiment was commanded by Laurède or Bardin.

Laurède: OLH in 1809, Couronne de Fer, Baron in 1814. Wounded near Antwerp, he was at Wynegen and Craonne. He fought at Waterloo and retired in 1821.

The regiment was formed from elements of Joseph's Guards.

The 14th Tirailleurs

The regiment was formed from soldiers of the Spanish Royal Guard. The 14th Tirailleurs were commanded by Major Chevalier who served in Joseph's Guard in Spain. Awarded the Orders of the Couronne de fer, of the Two-Sicilies, he was made OLH in 1814, wounded in front of Paris. He served with the 50th of the Line with the Beaux battalion. Discharged the same year. The regiment fought at Fère-Champenoise and Paris.

The 15th Tirailleurs

Lavigne: OLH in 1809, in 1814 he refused to obey Montbrun and defended Fontainebleau and the palace. Colonel of the 50th of the Line in 1815, he was put on the non-active list the same year and retired in 1823.

The 16th Tirailleurs

Sauset: Baron in 1814, Colonel of the 90th of the Line in 1815. CrLH in 1831, he retired in 1835.

THE VOLTIGEURS

The 1st Voltigeurs

The regiment came from the 1st Tirailleur-Chasseurs.

It was commanded by **Malet:** Italian and Egyptian Campaign, fought at Marengo, made Chevalier in 1810, then OLH in 1813. He followed the Emperor to Elba and was major in the 3rd Chasseurs at Waterloo where he was fatally wounded.

This Malet must not be confused with the Malet of the 2nd Voltigeurs who was a Major and died of his wounds at Montmirail.

Fins mentioned Rosey, but he was killed in 1813. He also mentions **Jouan,** Colonel-Major of the regiment in 1813, lost his left arm at Dresden. He was made a General shortly afterwards. He only reached Briançon where he was appointed in January 1814. He served in the Drôme and the Ardèche until 1815. Retired in 1832. CrLH in 1837, he was also mentioned by Lachouque.

The regiment numbered 25 officers and 822 men on 26 January.

The 2nd Voltigeurs

The regiment was formed from the 2nd Tirailleur-Chasseurs.

According to Lachouque, its commanding officer was **Schramm** but it seems that it was not him because he was captured at Dresden. In Six there are two General Schramm: the first was taken at Dresden, the other commanded at Strasbourg, then retired in 1815. According to Fins from 1813 it was Contamine, but he was Chief-of-Staff of the Dragoons of the 5th Cavalry Corps.

Battalion Commander Marthe was with the 1st Voltigeurs. The regiment started the campaign with 27 officers and 818 men.

The 3rd Voltigeurs

This regiment came from the 1st Conscript-Chasseurs. It was commanded by **Major Hurel,** made a baron and awarded the Order of the Réunion in 1813. He was at the head of the 3rd Voltigeurs again in 1815. He was laid off. Made Maréchal de camp in 1823, received the GdOLH in 1831. Lieutenant-General in 1835, he joined the Belgian Army in 1836.

The regiment only numbered 20 officers and 291 men on 15 January.

The 4th Voltigeurs

The regiment was formed from the 3rd Conscript-Chasseurs. Depending on the sources, it was commanded by Estève or Marguet.

Estève: Baron in 1811, then General and OLH in 1813, made Regimental Major in 1814, he served in Alsace in 1815 then retired, awarded CrLH in 1831, he died in 1844.

Jamin's Brigade was comprised the 5th, 6th, 7th and 8th Voltigeurs reinforced with elements from the 4th.

Le Capitaine's Brigade was made up of the 1st and 2nd Battalion of the 17th Tirailleurs, the 3rd Battalion of the 11th, the 1st Battalion of the 3rd Tirailleurs as well as the 3rd Battalions of the 3rd, 4th and 10th Tirailleurs.

Bigarré's Brigade was made up of the 3rd Battalions of the 3rd, 14th and 11th Voltigeurs plus a battalion of the 9th Tirailleurs.

Two marching regiments were formed up under Grigny accompanied by light artillery, making a total strength of 4 225 men.

THE ROTTEMBOURG DIVISION

Rottembourg: Baron in 1809, he was made a General and Major of the 1st Chasseurs of the Guard, Major-General and Couronne de Fer in 1813, he commanded the 5th Division of the Young Guard with Oudinot then under Mortier to escort the park. He fought under Oudinot at la Rothière and Bar-sur-Aube on 27 February, at Arcis-sur-Aube on 21 March. In 1815, replaced by Jerome Bonaparte, he went over to join Rapp. He was in Spain in 1823, received the CrSL in 1825 then was made GdCxLH in 1828. He retired in 1834 and died in 1857.

On 25 January he commanded the Tirailleurs of the 1st, 5th, 6th, 7th and 8th Regiments, reinforced with 312 Voltigeurs and Flankers.

The division was temporarily attached to Oudinot's 7th Corps.

De Charrière's Brigade

De Charrière: CtLH in 1809, Baron in 1810, General in 1812 and Couronne de Fer in 1813. He was retired in 1815 then put in the reserve in 1831.

On 25 January, the brigade comprised the 1st, 7th and 8th Tirailleurs Regiments, plus 312 Flankers and Voltigeurs.

Marguet's Brigade

Marguet: Italian and Egyptian Campaigns, he was in the 4th Voltigeurs in 1813. Baron, CtLH and General in the same year. Killed at la Rothière, he was replaced by Bauduin. The Brigade was made up of the 5th and 6th Tirailleurs Regiments.

CHARPENTIER'S DIVISION

Charpentier: Italian campaign, General in 1799, Major-General in 1804, Wagram, Count in 1810, GdCx of the Réunion in 1813. He commanded the 1st Provisional Division at Paris then the 7th Young Guard Division on 7 February. At Craonne, Laon, with Mortier at Fère-Champenoise, GdOLH in 1814, retired in 1824.

Gout: Adjudant-Commandant, Divisional Chief-of-Staff, OLH in 1813, Couronne de Fer, he served at La Rochelle in 1815, available in 1819.

Lelièvre's Brigade

Lelièvre, Comte de la Grange: Napoleon's Equerry in 1810. Count the same

Marguet: Made a General in 1813, then Baron and CtLH the same year. He apparently commanded the regiment in 1813.

Battalion Commander Lecomte distinguished himself in front of Compiègne. Major Tessière who came from the Flanker-Chasseurs was wounded at Montmirail. He was with the 4th Voltigeurs again in 1815.

The regiment numbered 27 officers and 1 100 men on 26 January.

Among the officers, note the presence of Battalion commanders Duparque and Royer.

The 5th Voltigeurs

Carrier: Italian and Egyptian Campaigns, he came from the Neapolitan Guard where he was a Maréchal de Camp. He was awarded the LH in 1814. He served under Suchet in 1815 and retired in 1824.

Delcambre was also mentioned. Baron de Champvert, he was made a General in 1813 at Hamburg. He fought at Waterloo. He was made a Viscount in 1824 then GdOLH in 1825. Retired in 1832.

The regiment had 27 officers and 502 men on 26 January.

The 6th Voltigeurs

Castanié: Made a Chevalier in 1810 then CtLH in 1813. Wounded at Brienne where he commanded the 1st Brigade in the 2nd Division of the Young Guard. He was mentioned at Craonne with the 1st Voltigeurs. He was apparently put in the asylum at Charenton then retired. He was made Maréchal de Camp in 1823. Already mentioned with the 2nd Voltigeurs, Contamine was also mentioned here.

On the eve of the Battle of Brienne, there were 26 officers and 521 men in the ranks.

The 7th Voltigeurs

This regiment was formed from the National Guardsmen in 1810. It was commanded then by Baron Couloumy, who received the CtLH in August 1813. He was wounded, amputated and captured at Dresden.

Its Colonel, Zaeppfel, came from the 6th Light, already mentioned in connection with Marmont's Corps.

The regiment was commanded by battalion Commander Hubert, and had a strength of 25 officers and 563 men.

The 8th Voltigeurs

Sécretan: Baron and CtLH in 1813, he was sent to the Chasseurs depot and was wounded in front of the Buttes-Chaumont. He was replaced by Varlet: Made a baron in 1810, he served in the 2nd Chasseurs where he replaced Deshaies who was killed at Dresden. He was made OLH and Réunion the same year. Made a Maréchal de Camp in 1831, he retired in 1837. The regiments started the campaign with 23 officers and 487 men. At Paris, Battalion Commander Linard only had 5 officers and 62 men left.

The 9th Voltigeurs

Jacquemard: A Marengo veteran, made a Baron in 1813 and General of the 2nd brigade of Janssens' Brigade on 15th March 1814. CtLH in 1815, he served under Ney. He retired in 1824.

Henrion was also mentioned. Born at Metz, he received a Grenade of Honour and was made OLH in 1807. He was made General commanding the Artillery Train of the Guard, the Artillery of the Young Guard. He was made a Baron and CtLH in the same year. Decorated with the Order of the Reunion in 1814, he was wounded at Brienne and at Arcis-sur-Aube. Made Maréchal de Camp in 1823, he was made GdOLH and retired in 1834.

Not to be confused with the Guards General or the Guards Artillery General of the same name.

The 10th Voltigeurs

Suisse de Sainte-Claire, it commanding officer, was wounded in front of Belleville; he was with the 2nd Voltigeurs in 1815, then laid off.

The 11th Voltigeurs

Penguern: Made a Baron and OLH in 1813, he served with the 6th Voltigeurs in 1815. He was laid off in 1822.

The regiment had 22 officers and 444 Voltigeurs.

The 12th Voltigeurs

This regiment was commanded by Grométy. He took part in the defence of Antwerp, CrLH in 1821, made Maréchal de Camp in 1831, the year of his death.

The regiment distinguished itself at Hoogstraten and Maubeuge.

The 13th Voltigeurs

Rignon: Italian and Egyptian Campaigns, he was wounded at Marengo, was made OLH in 1809, then Couronne de Fer in 1813. In 1815, he was Colonel of the 51st of the Line and was killed at Waterloo.

He was also mentioned as being in Grométy's regiment.

The 14th Voltigeurs

Bouvard: Served in the Royal Guard of Naples then Spain in 1808. He was made a General in March 1814, then OLH in 1815, then laid off and retired in 1825 and in the reserve in 1831. The regiment had 14 officers and 309 men.

The 15th Voltigeurs

Leclerc: Wounded at Laon, he was in the 5th Voltigeurs in 1815, retired in 1823 and again as Colonel in 1830; he was made CrLH in 1852.

THE YOUNG GUARD CORPS WITH NEY

During this campaign, Maréchal Ney showed that he was one of the best leaders of men of his time. At the head of his "Old Moustaches" at Montmirail or the beardless conscripts in his Young Guard Divisions, the Prince of the Moskova set the example, always giving of himself. The last days of this epic and the throes of the abdication revealed another side to this complex character.

Ney's Chief-of-Staff was **Béchet de Léocour:** OLH in 1806, he was first aide de camp to Ney and was made a Baron in 1808; General and Chief-of-Staff, he served in 1815. He retired as Honorary Lieutenant-General in 1825 and 1833.

Semery: Adjudant-Commandant: he was chief-of-staff of the 1st Division of the Young Guard. He fought at Arcis-sur-Aube where he was killed.

Aide de Camp: **Heymès:** Chevalier and OLH in 1813, he was wounded at Brienne. Made a Maréchal de Camp and aide de camp to Louis-Philippe in 1830, he was promoted to the rank of GdOLH in 1836 and Lieutenant-General in 1838.

● MEUNIER'S DIVISION

Meunier: Italian and Egyptian campaigns, he was awarded the Couronne de Fer in 1809 and then was promoted to Major-General in 1813. He was at Brienne and la Rothière, Craonne and Laon. He served at Waterloo in the Young Guard. He was promoted to GdOLH in 1835.

His aide de camp, Abdal, was killed at Rheims on 11 March.

At the beginning the division comprised Young Guard Voltigeurs. It was very sorely tried at Craonne and Laon.

— Rousseau's Brigade

Rousseau: Came from the Fusilier Chasseurs and was made a General and CtLH in 1813. He was at Chalons with Ney and Napoleon at the beginning of the campaign and replaced Boyer on 13 March in the brigade which came up from Spain. Retired in 1825, he died in 1834.

The brigade was made up of the 1st and 2nd Voltigeurs.

— Lacoste's Brigade

Lacoste: Wounded at Toulon, he took part in the Egyptian Campaign. Made a Baron in 1809 and CtLH in 1811. In 1813, he was in the 1st Division of the Young Guard. He was captured in Rheims.

The brigade was made up of the 3rd and 4th Voltigeurs and the 1st and 2nd Tirailleurs.

The 3rd Voltigeurs

These came from the north with Poret de Morvan.

The 4th Voltigeurs

Lachouque and J.P. Mir have said that the 4th Voltigeurs were present, but the regiment was with the Army of Lyon apparently.

The 1st Tirailleurs

These were with the Army of the North with Roguet and Maison. Some of them came down with Poret de Morvan as reinforcements, as did 700 men from the 3rd battalion of the 2nd Tirailleurs and 1 200 Voltigeurs from the 6th and 11th regiments.

The 2nd Tirailleurs

The division also included 155 men from the baggage train and workers.

● CURIAL'S DIVISION

Curial: Italian and Egyptian Campaigns, he was at Austerlitz. Major in the Chasseurs of the Guard, he was promoted to General in 1807, then Major-General in 1809. At Essling, he was at the head of the 1st Division of the Young Guard. He was made GdCx of the Réunion in 1813, then Count and GdCxLH in 1815.

He served under Suchet in the Alps during the Hundred Days. Count, Pair de France, Chamberlain to the King, he voted for Ney to be deported. He was promoted to the rank of GdCx of Saint-Ferdinand in 1823. He died when he fell from his horse during Charles X's coronation. He replaced Decouz who was killed at Brienne. He commanded the 2nd division of the Young Guard, comprising the 5th, 6th, 7th and 8th Voltigeurs which were present at La Rothière, Vauchamps, Craonne, Laon, Fère-Champenoise and La Villette. At Fontainebleau, Curial had had enough and Boyer de Rébeval took his place.

Decouz: A veteran of Toulon and the Egyptian campaign, he fought at Austerlitz. Made a Baron in 1808 and a General and CtLH in 1809. In March 1813, he was a Major in the Grenadier Guards. The same year, he was promoted to Major-General and commanded a brigade of the Young Guard under Barrios. On 25 January 1815, he commanded a division of the Voltigeurs under Ney, but he was mortally wounded at Brienne.

Boyer de Rébeval: Commanded the Fusilier-Chasseurs in 1807. He was made CtLH in 1809 and Major-General in 1813. In Paris, he organised the 2nd Division of the Young Guard on 13 February 1814. He was wounded at Méry-sur-Seine and at Craonne, and served at Laon and Rheims. His division was disbanded on 13 March. He served at Paris with Pajol. He was put on the non-active list in 1815.

— Baste's Brigade

Baste: Engaged in the Royale in 1781, he was present at Aboukir. He left the Navy and joined the Guards in 1804 then served under Dupont at Baylen where he was captured. Colonel of the Sailorss of the Guard in 1809, he was made a Count and CtLH in 1810 then appointed Rear-Admiral in 1811. He commanded the brigade from 21 December 1813, but was killed at Brienne.

The brigade was commanded by General Le Capitaine from 14 March onwards.

Le Capitaine: Sabre of Honour in 1802, he was made CtLH in 1804. Former aide de camp to Joseph, he was made a General and Baron in 1814. He was at Rheims and Fère-Champenoise in Charpentier's Division. He served in 1815 and was killed at Ligny.

The brigade was made up of the 5th and 6th Voltigeurs.

— Pelet Clozeau's Brigade

Pelet Clozeau: see 1st Chasseurs à pied of the Guard.

The brigade comprised the 7th, 8th and 9th Voltigeurs. 153 workers and baggage train men were also part of the division.

Maréchal Ney took temporary command at the head of other units of the Imperial Guard during the campaign. In front of the enemy, the "*Rougeaud*" (the red-faced one) remained the "*bravest among the brave*".

year, General in 1812. At Laon on 9 March, with Curial at Fère-Champenoise, he was made a Peer in 1832, GdOLH in 1836 and Senator in 1859.

The division was made up of Young Guard and conscripts from the 5th, 6th, 7th, 8th, 11th and 14th Voltigeurs and the 3rd Battalion of the 9th Tirailleurs.

On 15 February, Charpentier had 6 000 men with him including the training battalion of the Guard under Colonel Lavigne and twelve 3rd battalions of Voltigeurs and Tirailleurs mixed together, supported by 300 Gendarmes, 3 squadrons of Polish Lancers and 10 cannon. He fell back to Fontainebleau abandoned by Montbrun. Pajol had abandoned Montereau where the Wurtembergers were repairing the bridges.

Montbrun: Brother of the great cavalryman killed at the Moskova, CtLH in 1812, he abandoned Moret leaving Fontainebleau open. Dismissed on 17 February.

Simmer: Baron in 1810, General in 1812, he was with MacDonald from 1813. CtLH in 1813, Major-General in 1815, he served at Waterloo; Deputy in 1828, 1830, 1831, 1837, beaten in 1842.

Other divisions were created, like the Henrion, Jansens and Lefol divisions, but their existence was even briefer.

JANSSENS' DIVISION

Janssens: A Dutchman, he was made GdOLH in 1811. He joined Ney on 16 March with the troops available in the Mézières region. He was wounded at Arcis-sur-Aube and was replaced by Lefol.

Lefol: see Dufour's Division in Pajol's Corps.

Jacquemard's Brigade

Jacquemard: see 9th Voltigeurs. He commanded one of the brigades in the Janssens Division. The division later reinforced Marmont.

Two Divisions of Young Guards (Barrois and Roguet) were assigned to the Army

Maréchal Ney, Duke of Elchlingen, Prince of the Moskova, commanded a corps of Young Guard. He took part in all the fights and justified the opinion which Kléber had of him: "With such men, a general does not have to bother counting the enemy's numbers."
(Musée de Versailles. RMN)

of the North under Maison. This will dealt with later in the appropriate chapter.

Taking into account the garrisons at Soissons, Compiègne and Rheims, the Young Guard numbered 10 609 men on 14 March 1814.

A month later they were shared out differently.

BOYER DE REBEVAL'S DIVISION

Lelièvre de Lagrange's Brigade comprised the 1st, 2nd, 3rd, 4th, 5th, 8th and 9th Voltigeurs

Le Capitaine's Brigade comprised the 10th, 11th, 12th, 13th, 14th and 15th Voltigeurs.

This made a total of 280 officers and 2 100 men for the division.

CHARPENTIER'S DIVISION

Guye's Brigade with the 3rd, 9th and 14th Tirailleurs as well as the 5th *Pupilles*.
Bouvard's Brigade made up of the 1st, 12th and 15th Tirailleurs

ROTTEMBOURG'S DIVISION

Charrière's Brigade made up of 5th and 6th Tirailleurs.
Bauduin's Brigade comprising the 7th and 8th Tirailleurs.

BARROIS' DIVISION

Darriule's brigade with the 2nd, 3rd and 4th Tirailleurs and elements of the 12th and 13th Voltigeurs.

ROGUET'S DIVISION

This comprised the 10th, 11th, 12th and 13th Tirailleurs, elements of the 9th Tirailleurs and 12th and 13th Voltigeurs.

The Sailors of the Guard

The Sailors of the Guard were commanded by Rear-Admiral Baste from 1809. He was killed at Brienne. They distinguished themselves at Champaubert, Vauchamps and Rheims.

Between the two extremes of the 5 December 1813 and the 17 April 1814, the units were very often mixed up and Voltigeurs were often associated with Tirailleurs. Some officers who were mentioned often had another function. Thus Contamine who was the Chief-of-Staff with the Dragoons of the 5th Cavalry Corps, or Tessière who was a Major in the Flanker-Chasseurs. Others changed regiments like Rignon who went from the 10th to the 13th Voltigeurs, Bardin who joined the 8th Tirailleurs from the 13th, Suisse from the 12th to the 10th Voltigeurs, etc.

Moreover these pseudo-regiments melted away like butter under the sun. As with the Infantry of the Line, mixes were made with fractions of regiments, or 3rd battalions or miscellaneous companies. This type of practice was mainly used in the Voltigeurs regiments. The organisation in Paris did what it could to send reinforcements; there was a high turnover in officers and men, but the little army did face up to things, nevertheless.

THE CAVALRY OF THE GUARD

At the beginning of the campaign, the Cavalry of the Guard were commanded by General Count Champion de Nansouty. Born at Chateau-Trompette in 1768, he was a contemporary of Napoleon at Brienne. He was made Grand Aigle of the LH in 1807, then Count and First Equerry to the Emperor in 1808. Wounded at Craonne and ill, he was replaced by Sebastiani who commanded at Arcis-sur-Aube. He died in 1815.

Among his aide de camps were:

Talleyrand-Périgord: Count in 1810, he was Colonel of the 8th Chasseurs in 1812. Maréchal de camp in 1814, he was made Duke of Dino and Duke of Talleyrand in 1817, Peer and GdOLH in 1821. Retired in 1848.

His Chief-of-Staff was **Beuverand, Comte de la Loyère:** Badly treated by his boss, he was raised to the rank of CtLH in 1821 then received the CrSL and was made GdCx of St-Ferdinand in 1823. He retired in 1837.

Assistant-Chief-of-staff: **Bergeret:** Adjudant-Commandant, he was wounded at Craonne. He was in Spain in 1823 and was made CrLH in 1824.

Aide-Major-General of the cavalry: **Belliard:** Italian and Egyptian Campaigns, he was made a Major-General in 1800. He was Chief-of-Staff to Murat in 1805 and Governor of Madrid in 1808. He was made a Count in 1810 and replaced Grouchy on 7 March. He was made a Peer and GdCxLH in 1814. Struck off the list of peers, he was reinstated in 1819. Ambassador to Brussels, he died of a stroke in 1832 while leaving the palace.

INFANTRY OF THE YOUNG GUARD - TIRAILLEURS-GRENADIERS

The Young Guard was affected by the changes in uniform caused by the 1812 Regulations; the new jacket-coat replaced the old coats when these wore out and when new regiments were created.
In January 1814, the Tirailleurs were incorporated into the Guards' reserve under the command of Maréchal Ney.

Tirailleur-Grenadier wearing full dress.

Tirailleur-Grenadier Drummer.

Tirailleur-Grenadier wearing a greatcoat.

Tirailleur-Grenadier wearing marching dress.

Tirailleur-Grenadier Sergeant-Major, Pennant-Bearer of the 5th Tirailleurs belonging to General Rottembourg's 2nd Division.

Subaltern.

Tirailleur-Grenadier Sergeant wearing marching dress.

André Jouineau © Histoire & Collections 2005

From left to right:
General Curial took General Decouz's place at the head of the 2nd Division of the Young Guard when Decouz was killed at Brienne. (RR)
General Poret de Morvan, a Brigadier in Maison's Army of the North, arrived in the Champagne region at the head of a division of the Young Guard. (RR)
General Exelmans behaved brilliantly during the whole of the campaign during which he replaced Pajol. (RR)
General Nansouty commanded the cavalerie de la garde at the beginning of the campaign. (RR)

Exelmans: Aide de camp to Murat in 1805, made a Baron in 1808, Grand Maréchal of the Palace at Naples, Major-General in 1812, Count in 1813. He replaced Pajol who was wounded, and was present at Chalons, Vitry, Méry, Plancy and Arcis-sur-Aube. Accused of treachery because of his correspondence with Murat he was nevertheless acquitted. He rallied in 1815, he captured the artillery of the Duc de Berry. Outlawed, he took part in the 1830 events with Pajol. He was promoted to GdCxLH the Gd Chancelier of the LH in 1849. He was a Senator in 1852, the year he died in a riding accident.

Sebastiani de la Porta: A veteran of the Italian Campaign, he was at Marengo. In 1807, he was ambassador in Turkey and drove back the English. He was made Grand Aigle of the LH in 1807 and Count in 1809. He commanded the cavalerie de la garde at Arcis-sur-Aube and Saint-Dizier where he distinguished himself. Deputy in 1815, he was exiled to England. Re-elected in 1819, he was appointed a Minister then Deputy again in 1831, 1834, 1837, 1840 and 1846. He was made Maréchal in 1840.

Delort: Wounded twice at Austerlitz and twice in Spain, he was made a General and a Baron in 1811. In 1814, commanding a reserve brigade in Paris, he was at Montereau and was made a Major-General. He joined the 2nd Division of the 2nd Cavalry Corps, then the 5th Corps. He was wounded at Waterloo. Elected for the Jura in 1830, he was aide de camp to the King in 1832, then was re-elected in 1834. GdCxLH and Peer in 1837, he joined the reserve in 1841. (Not to be confused with the others with the same name.)

Lefebvre-Desnoëttes: Aide de camp to Bonaparte in 1800, was at Marengo. Colonel of the Chasseurs à Cheval of the Guard, he was made CtLH in 1805, General in 1806, Major-General in 1808, GdCx of the Reunion in 1813, he was wounded at Brienne. He fought at la Rothière then brought up a column of reinforcements including the Henrion Division with its 1 500 sabres as well as the 3rd battalion of the 12th Tirailleurs which had been left at Méry by Charpentier just in time for Arcis-sur-Aube. In 1815 he was made a Pair de France. Appointed Commanding Officer of the Chasseurs à Cheval of the Guard and the Lancers, he was at Quatre-Bras and at Waterloo. Condemned to death in his absence he went into exile in the USA. He was to have returned to Europe on the *"Albion"* but he was shipwrecked and died on 22 April 1822.

Durosnel: Napoleon's Equerry in 1804, he was at Austerlitz. Count in 1808, he was made a Major-General and an aide de camp to the Emperor in 1809. He commanded the Gendarmes d'Elite in 1812. Captured at Dresden he did not take part in the campaign. Made a Peer on 2 June 1815, he was elected a Deputy in 1831, then again in 1834. Aide de camp to Louis-Philippe, he was made GdCxLH in 1832. Pair de France in 1837, he died in 1849.

Arrighi de Casanova: A veteran of the Italian and Egyptian campaigns, he was at Maren-

The Young Guard was the linchpin of the French Infantry.
From left to right: a Flanker, an officer and a soldier from
the Tirailleur-Grenadiers. The regiments of the last two were changed
into Tirailleur regiments. (RR)

INFANTRY OF THE YOUNG GUARD - VOLTIGEURS and FLANKERS

Voltigeur drummer.

Voltigeur Sergeant.

Voltigeur wearing a greatcoat.

Voltigeur subaltern wearing an overcoat.

Voltigeur.

Flanker-Grenadier wearing a greatcoat.

From left to right:
Flanker-Grenadier.
Flanker-Chasseur.
Flanker-Chasseur. drummer.

André Jouineau © Histoire & Collections 2005

From left to right:
*Top: **General Belliard**, Aide-Major-General of the cavalerie de la garde and General **Sébastiani de la Porta** who took over from Nansouty.*
*Bottom: Generals **Arrighi de Casanova** and **Lefebvre-Desnoëttes**. (RR)*

Below:
***General Guyot** replaced Walther at the head of the Grenadiers à Cheval before taking command of the Service Squadrons. (RR)*

go. Made CtLH in 1804, he was at Austerlitz the following year and appointed General in 1807. He commanded the Dragoon Guards. Duke of Padua in 1808, he was made a Major-General in 1809. Under MacDonald in January 1814, he served under Marmont at Craonne and Laon where he was routed at Athies during the night of 9 March. He was also at Rheims and Fère-Champenoise. Peer in 1815, his appointment was rescinded and he was outlawed. He retired in 1819 then again in 1837. He was elected Deputy in 1849; he was a Senator and Governor of the Invalides in 1852. Through his marriage to Anne de Montesquiou-Fezensac, Arrighi was a cousin by marriage to Napoleon.

Boulnois: A veteran of Marengo. Made Baron and General in 1813, he commanded a provisional division sent to join Mortier. He was made Lieutenant-General in January 1815 and CtLH. He retired in 1816. On 29 February he commanded 8 squadrons of the 1st, 2nd and 3rd Scouts, 150 Chasseurs à cheval, 100 Grenadiers à cheval and 50 Gendarmes d'Elite as well as a number of conscripts. In this corps they joined the Poret de Morvan, Christiani and Friant divisions according to the roll taken on the 5 March.

At the end of February, the cavalerie de la garde were reformed into three divisions.

COLBERT'S DIVISION

Pac's Poles (600 men)
2nd Lancers (180 men)

EXELMANS' DIVISION

1st Lancers (600 men)
2nd Scouts (200 men)
3rd Scouts (200 men)
Dragoons (500 men)

LETORT'S DIVISION

Chasseurs of the Guard (800 men)
Grenadiers à Cheval (800 men)
1st Scouts (200 men)
the Empress's Dragoons

The Grenadiers à Cheval of the Guard

Their Colonel, **Walther**, was replaced by **Guyot** then, after Vauchamps, by Laferrière-Levesque. Within their ranks as in the other regiments of the Old Guard there were a lot of holders of awards for Honour.

Guyot: OLH in 1804, he was made a General in 1805, then Major-General, CtLH and Chamberlain in 1811. He commanded the Grenadiers à Cheval of the Guard in 1813 instead of Walther.

He was under Nansouty at Brienne, la Rothière, Champaubert, but Napoleon got angry with him after Vauchamps and had him replaced. The Emperor changed his mind later and put him at the head of the Service Squadrons of which there were 100 Grenadiers à Cheval which always accompanied him. He was at Craonne and Rheims. He chased the Duc de Bourbon in March 1815 then was wounded at Waterloo. He retired in 1816 and again in 1833.

Laferrière-Levesque: Former Guide de l'Ouest, he was at Austerlitz. He was made a Baron in 1808; he was wounded three times in Spain; he was made a General and awarded the order of the Couronne de Fer and that of the Réunion in 1811. He replaced Lepic as Major of the Grenadiers à Cheval and was promoted to Major-General in 1813. Commanding the Cavalry of the Old Guard under Mortier, he was at Montmirail, Chateau-Thierry and Vauchamps. He was in Rheims with Corbineau on 5 March. At Craonne on 7 March, he lost his left leg. He was elected Deputy in 1815, was made a Peer in the same year then GdCxLH and SL in 1821 and Peer again in 1832.

Chastel: Italian and Egyptian Campaigns and Austerlitz, he was in the Grenadiers from 1805. He was made a Baron in 1808, General in 1811 and OLH in 1813. Major in the 2nd Grenadiers, he commanded Compans' Cavalry at Paris.

Delaporte (or de la Porte): Italian Campaign and a scout in Egypt he was already in the Grenadiers à Cheval at Marengo. He was standard-bearer in 1802. Baron, he commanded the 2nd Grenadiers in 1814. He served during the Hundred Days and was wounded four times at Waterloo. He was Mayor of Saran from 1815 to 1830. Made CtLH in 1831, he was made a Maréchal de camp in 1836.

Juncker: Made OLH in 1813, Réunion in 1814 and CtLH in 1836. Maréchal de camp in 1846, he retired in 1848.

D'Harembert: OLH in 1814, he was the Colonel of the 15th Chasseurs in 1825.

Bouvier-Destouches: Had his fingers frozen in Russia but returned to service in February 1814. He was wounded and captured at Craonne.

Jamin de Bermuy: Aide de camp to Joseph in Naples and Spain, he was made a General in France on 20 January 1814. He was at the Versailles depot on 8 February and then was Major of the Grenadiers à Cheval on 16 March 1814. Made OLH in 1815, he was killed at Waterloo.

Goubet: Sabre of Honour in 1804, he was made OLH. He fought at Austerlitz and joined

THE OLD GUARD CAVALRY

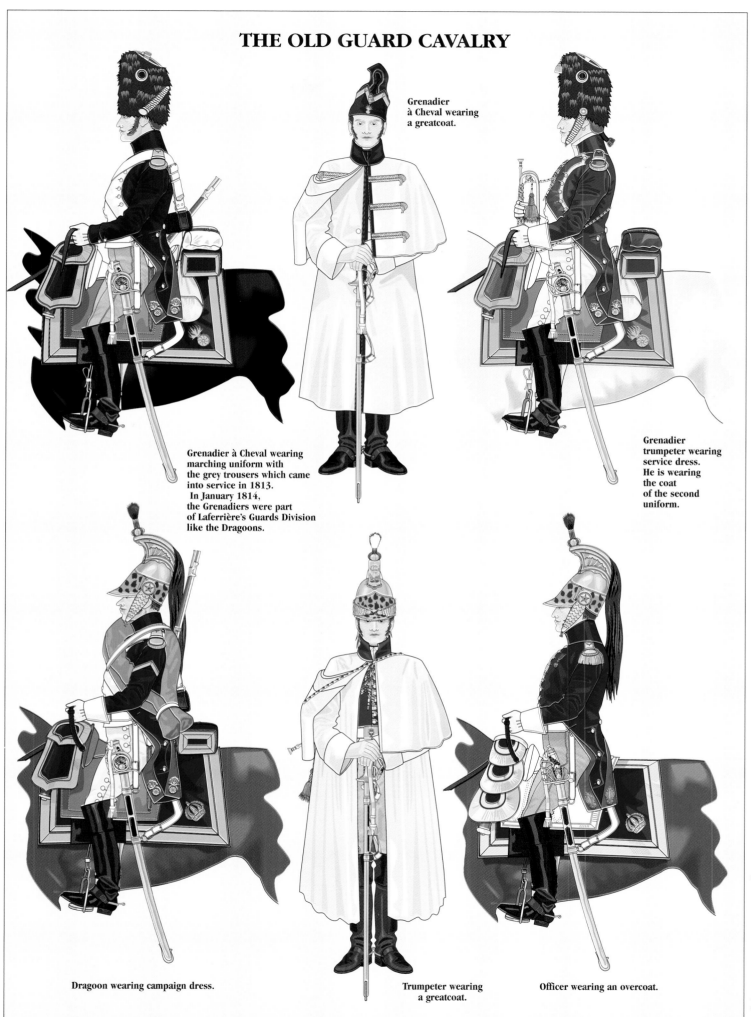

Grenadier
à Cheval wearing
a greatcoat.

Grenadier à Cheval wearing
marching uniform with
the grey trousers which came
into service in 1813.
In January 1814,
the Grenadiers were part
of Laferrière's Guards Division
like the Dragoons.

Grenadier
trumpeter wearing
service dress.
He is wearing
the coat
of the second
uniform.

Dragoon wearing campaign dress.

Trumpeter wearing
a greatcoat.

Officer wearing an overcoat.

André Jouineau © Histoire & Collections 2005

Trumpeters in the Empresses' Dragoons. (RR)

The Chasseurs of the Guard

This was Napoleon's favourite regiment. It served everywhere with redoubtable effectiveness. Lion was its Colonel.

Lion: Baron in 1809, he was Colonel of the Chasseurs of the Guard and General in 1813. He was wounded at Vauchamps. He refused to join Lefebvre-Desnoëttes' attempted uprising on 11 March 1815 and was appointed in his place. He was made Lieutenant-General on 21 June 1815 and made GdCxLH on 1825. After joining the Gendarmerie, he joined the reserve in 1839.

His aide de camp was his nephew Lacouster, a Lieutenant in the Chasseurs of the Guard in 1813, awarded the LH. He was in the Chasseurs again in 1816.

On 18 September 1805, the Velites were created with four companies of Chasseurs. Mortier's Guides and Murat's Chevau-Légers were added to the Chasseurs in 1808 and 1809. In 1811, the Velites were assigned to the Lancers of the 2nd Regiment. Guyot was their Major. In 1813, the Company of Mamelukes with 350 men became the 10th Squadron of the Chasseurs Regiment which grew to ten 250-man squadrons. In order to be part of the Old Guard they had to have had ten years' service and several campaigns. On 17 March, the Chasseurs à Cheval Regiment of the Young Guard was created for the new recruits.

Among the Chasseurs the following should be mentioned:

Rabusson: A Marengo veteran, he was wounded fifteen times at Eylau. A hero of Méry, near Arcis-sur-Aube. In all he was wounded twenty-two times and retired in May 1815. He was made CrLH in 1822, and Maréchal de Camp in 1826. He died in 1848.

Lafitte: Italian Campaign, he was awarded the LH in An-XII, was made OLH in 1808 as he was a hero of Spain. He was made a Baron at Montereau. He served during the Hundred Days and was wounded at Waterloo. He retired and was made CrLH in 1831.

Parquin: Wounded six times in 1807, he took a Portuguese flag on 22 April 1812. He was awarded the LH in 1813. He saved Oudinot at Leizig and was made Captain in the 2nd Chasseurs of the Guard in December 1813, then joined Kirmann and his Mamelukes on 14 February 1814. He was assigned to the 11th Company of the Chasseurs of the Guard; this company associated with the 5th, formed the 5th Squadron of the Old Guard commanded by Klein de Kleinengard, Lion's brother-in-law (who was a General in 1840). They were at Montmirail, la Ferté-sous-Jouarre on 2 March, Laon on 9 March, Arcis-sur-Aube and Saint-Dizier. He retired in 1823 and was made OLH in 1831. Sentenced to twenty years' imprisonment in 1840 for the landing at Boulogne, he died in prison at Doullens in 1845. Parquin was the author of famous Memoirs.

The Mamelukes

They formed a squadron, the 10th in the Chasseurs à Cheval Regiment of the Guard.

Their CO was the Alsatian Kirmann. At Erbach in 1800, he took 500 Austrians, then 12 more and killed five others which earned him a Sabre of Honour. He was OLH in 1804. He was made a Baron in 1810. He was wounded several times in 1813, saved once by Captain Abdallah d'Asbonne; he served at Waterloo and retired in November 1815.

On 1 November 1813, there were only 209 Mamelukes left. With Colbert they charged at Montmirail then at Chateau-Thierry. They were mentioned at Saint-Dizier on 26 March and Parquin took part in their charge against 18 of Winzigerode's cannon with Lefebvre-Desnoëttes. Nacco Lolio, one of three Albanians in the squadron was captured in front of Méry on 20 March. In 1814, there were only a third of real Easterners left, as 205 men from France and other conquered countries had been used to complete the unit (Brunon).

---

the Grenadiers à Cheval of the Guard in 1806. Retired in 1814 he was recalled to his regiment on 1 March 1814. He retired after Waterloo.

The Grenadiers à Cheval distinguished themselves at Chateau-Thierry alongside two of General Petit's battalions, against Prince William of Prussia who was trying to protect the approaches to the bridge but who was overwhelmed. They were always used in the decisive actions and in the service squadrons.

The Cavalry of the Guard always marched together. Nansouty was replaced by Sebastiani who was in command for the big fight at Arcis-sur-Aube which was marked by the rout of this Guard. This lovely cavalry was rallied by the Emperor himself on the bridge of the town and then drove back the mass of enemy cavalry. The Grenadiers à Cheval came from Méry fighting, helped by Curély with his artillery battery and his 10th Hussars. They rallied at Arcis-sur-Aube.

The Dragoon Guards

Ornano was their Colonel but it was General Letort who commanded them in the field.

Ornano: General in 1811, he was made Major-General the following year and Colonel of the Dragoon Guards. Made GdCx of the Réunion in 1813, he replaced Bessières who had been killed. Commanding the Guard who had remained in Paris, he defended the barrière de Pantin. CrSL in 1829 and Peer, he retired in 1848. GdCxLH in 1850, he was made Grand Chancelier of the LH and appointed Governor of the Invalides. He was made Maréchal de France in 1861.

Letort: Italian Campaign, he was made a Baron in 1810 then General in 1813 and Major-General on 13 February 1814. He commanded the Dragoon Guards from 1813 to 1815. He was at Chateau-Thierry, Craonne, Arcis-sur-Aube and Saint-Dizier on 26 March. He was also made a Count and CrLH the same year. Aide de camp to Napoleon during the Hundred Days, he was killed at Gilly in 1815 while charging the Prussian rearguard. At Montmirail, Letort with his Empress's Dragoons and the 1st and 2nd Scouts broke a lot of Russian squares, captured 30 cannon and took a lot of prisoners.

Pinteville: Major of the Dragoons in 1813, he was seriously wounded and retired with the rank of Honorary Maréchal de Camp in 1815.

The 2nd Regiment of Scouts was attached to the Dragoons.

Made a Major-General in February 1814,
Letort commanded the Dragoon Guards. Parquin,
a Captain in the Chasseurs à Cheval of the Guard was the author
of famous memoirs. (RR)

THE OLD GUARD CAVALRY

Chasseur à cheval wearing campaign dress.

Trooper from 2nd Chevau-Léger wearing campaign dress. The shapska is covered with an oilskin, the greatcoat is worn saltire-wise.

Trooper from 1st Polish Chevau-Léger wearing full dress.

Trumpeter from the 2nd Chevau-Légers in campaign dress.

Trumpeter from the Chasseurs à Cheval.

André Jouineau © Histoire & Collections 2005

Trumpeter from the 2nd Regiment of the Lancers of the Guard
(Plate by Lucien Rousselot, Author's Collection)

The Lancers

The 1st regiment: Krasinski's Poles

Krasinski: Wounded at Madrid, Wagram and the Moskova, he was made a Count and CtLH in 1811 then Major-General in 1813. Wounded at Arcis-sur-Aube, he was awarded the Ordre de la Réunion in 1814. After the Abdication, he took his men back to Poland. Appointed Marshal of the Diet in 1818, he was aide de camp to the Tsar and decorated with the Order of St-Andrew.

Konopka: First major, General in 1811. Formed and commanded the 3rd Lancers in 1812, but was captured in Russia and served there later.

Dautancourt (or d'Autancourt): He was present at the execution of the Duc d'Enghien in 1804. He was made Second Major in 1807, Baron in 1809 then General and First Major of the 1st Polish Chevau-Légers in 1813. He commanded the 2nd Horse Guards Division and was at Brienne, la Rothière and Montmirail with a brigade of Dragoons and Grenadiers à Cheval. He was made CtLH in 1814. He commanded the Gendarmerie d'Elite in 1815 and then was put on the non-active list. He retired in 1825.

The regiment fought at Brienne with Lefebvre-Desnoëttes who was wounded and replaced by Colbert. At Montmirail, Dobiecki took a Prussian battalion and was made a Squadron Commander on the battlefield. After Chateau-Thierry, the regiment charged at Vauchamps alongside four regiments of Cuirassiers. Pac joined them on 5 March with reinforcements and took part at Berry-au-Bac where the Poles took the bridge and pushed forward to Corbeny against Czermitchev's Cossacks. Skarsinski who was brilliant was mentioned; the lances of the Cossacks were picked up by Dautancourt. At Craonne Girardot, the Chief-Surgeon was wounded and was made a Baron when he marched past the Emperor and saluted him with his good arm. The Poles were at Rheims on 12 and 13 March. Then they marched to Saint-Dizier after Arcis-sur-Aube where the regiment suffered on 20 March and where Pac was wounded. The Poles returned to Paris with Dautancourt and positioned themselves in front of Pantin, the batteries of the Porte de la Chapelle, then at Aubervilliers, Clignancourt and Montmartre. Counting the 3rd Scouts, there were only 700 left. They were at the barrière des Martyrs   a n d then fell back on the Boulevard des Italiens. At Fontainebleau, the Island of Elba squadron was organised under Cambronne with Jerzmanovski.

General Edouard de Colbert commanded the Red Lancers, the 2nd Guards Lancer Regiment. (Drawing by J. Girbal, Author's Collection)

The 2nd Lancers: the Red Lancers

They came from the King of Holland's Guard and were Edouard de Colbert's famous Red Lancers.

Colbert-Chabanais (called Edouard de): Made a Baron in 1808, General in 1809 then Major-General in 1813. Under Nansouty, he was present at la Rothière, replaced Lefebvre-Desnoëttes who was wounded; he fought at Champaubert, Montmirail, Chateau-Thierry, Nangis towards Craonne with Parquin, Rheims and Arcis-sur-Aube. In 1815, at Quatre-Bras he charged the English squares at Waterloo in spite of being wounded in the arm. Imprisoned, he was freed and put on the non-active list then in the reserve in 1833. Wounded by Fieschi's bomb in 1835. Made GdCXLH in 1837, he retired in 1848 and died in 1853.

His aide de camp was **Bro**: Made a Chevalier in 1810. Became a Captain in the Chasseurs à Cheval of the Guard, he then joined the Red Lancers. He was wounded twice at Waterloo. He was made Maréchal de camp in 1832 at Alger, then GdOLH in 1837 then Lieutenant-General in 1843. He died in 1844.

The following were with him: **Du Bois:** A Dutchman, he commanded this regiment of the

General Dautancourt was the Senior Major in the 1st Regiment of Polish Chevau-Légers. (RR)

Wounded at Arcis-sur-Aube, General Krasinski nevertheless remained at the head of his Polish Lancers until the end of the campaign when he returned to Poland. (RR)

THE YOUNG GUARD CAVALRY

Dragoon from the Young Guard squadrons.

Chasseur à Cheval from the Young Guard Squadrons. The uniform was the same as that of the Old Guard Squadrons, except for the head dress, the equipment, the weapons and the saddles.

Grenadiers à Cheval in service dress. Velite from the so-called squadrons of the Young Guard, created following on the Grenadier Regiments. He is wearing the same uniform but without the aglet.

GUARDS OF HONOUR
They were created in 1813 and recruited among the noble and bourgeois families of the Empire and had to bear the cost of their own equipment. Incorporated into the Defrance division, their most famous feat of arms was the charge at Rheims on 13 March 1814.

Maréchal des Logis from the 4th Regiment.

Trooper from the 3rd Regiment.

Trumpeter in the Chasseurs à Cheval of the Young Guard squadrons. He has kept the pelisse and the colback of the Old Guard which he was probably in before.

Subaltern wearing a frock-coat.

André Jouineau © Histoire & Collections 2005

Left: The 1st Scout Regiment was attached to the Grenadiers à Cheval of the Guards. (RR)

Right: General Testot-Ferry commanded the 1st Scout Regiment of the Guard. (Aquarelle by P.Benigni, RR)

Below: The 3rd Scout Regiment was made up of Poles and assigned to the Lancers of the Guard. (Aquarelle by P.Benigni, RR)

Guard in Holland. He was awarded the Order of the Couronne de Fer in 1809 and the Réunion in 1812. He was made a Baron the following year. In France he was made a Major, then General and OLH in 1814. He resigned after having served during the Hundred Days and remained in Paris with Pully who liked his company. He returned to Holland where he was made General-Major in 1819 then Baron in 1820.

De Tiecken de Terhove: Awarded the Order of the Réunion and the LH in 1812. A hero at Brienne, he was made OLH in 1814. He was Colonel and commanded the 5th Light Dutch Dragoons at Waterloo. A Belgian Lieutenant-General, he was aide de camp to Leopold in 1830 and made Baron in 1847.

With Colbert the Red Lancers took part in most of the battles of the campaign in a brilliant manner. The two Spies brothers were killed one at Craonne and the other in the ranks of the 3rd Scouts.

After this campaign a lot of officers resigned and returned to Holland. A number of them served against their former comrades at Waterloo.

The Scouts of the Guard

The 1st Regiment

The regiment was attached to the Grenadier Guards under Guyot.

It was made up from the Gardes d'Honneur which furnished 337 men from the 1st, 3rd and 4th Regiments. The officers came from the Old Guard mainly, whereas the men were considered as being part of the Young Guard.

To complete the Scouts Regiments, recruitments were made everywhere even among the coachmen. There were 35 men from Joseph's Guard in Spain and Gendarmes or Chasseurs of the Guard; there were also Coastal Artillery gunners and even a sailor with three years' service.

The Colonel-Major of the regiment was **Testot-Ferry:** He was Marmont's aide de camp in 1804. OLH and the Réunion in 1813, he commanded the 6th Squadron of Dragoon Guards, called the second regiment of the Young Guard, then the 2nd Squadron under Letort and Major Pinteville. His horse was killed under him at Hanau and he received 22 sabre blows, but he was saved by his helmet. He took part in most of the fighting of the campaign and the victories at the beginning.

On 6 March a detachment came up in reinforcement and joined the regiment. At Craon-

THE YOUNG GUARD CAVALRY

Guards of Honour: Trooper and trumpeter from the 3rd Regiment wearing campaign dress and their pelisses. The Guards of Honour had one particularity concerning their uniforms: they wore the two plaited cords of the shako on the front and the flounders on the left.

1st Regiment of Scouts: half comprised elements from the Old Guard wearing the uniform opposite, and the other half was made up of elements from the Young Guard wearing a uniform similar to the Chasseur à Cheval of about 1810.

The Scouts
The Imperial Decree dated 9th December 1813 created three 4-squadron regiments of Scouts attached respectively to the Grenadiers à Cheval, the Dragoons and to the Polish Lancers.

3rd Scout Regiment or Scout-Lancer wearing campaign dress.

2nd Scout Regiment or Scout-Dragoons.

3rd Scout Regiment wearing full dress uniform.

André Jouineau © Histoire & Collections 2005

ARTILLERY

An eight-pounder limbered up.

Horse Artilleryman according to the 1812 Regulations.

Gunner.

Drummer.

Artilleryman wearing a greatcoat.

Artilleryman wearing a uniform according to the 1812 Regulations.

Subaltern in the Artillery.

Colonel in the Artillery.

Horse Artilleryman wearing campaign dress.

THE GUARDS ARTILLERY AND TRAIN

Young Guard gunner.

Horse Artillery trooper and officer wearing tail coats.

Artillery Gunner of the Old Guard wearing a greatcoat.

Team crew and artillery train crew from the squadrons recruited from 1813.

Subaltern from the Artillery of the Young Guard wearing an overcoat; most officers were mounted.

Young Guard gunner wearing a greatcoat.

André Jouineau © Histoire & Collections 2005

*Above: **A Scout from the 2nd Regiment doing sentry duty.
A number of men in each company were armed
with a carbine and not a lance, as here.**
(Aquarelle by P.Benigni, RR)*

*Below: **Guillaume Victor Lecoq de Bieville,
a trooper in the 1st Guard of Honour Regiment.***
(RR)

ne Testot-Ferry distinguished himself, his scouts charged the enemy batteries alongside Laferrière-Levesque but the latter lost his right foot blown off by a cannonball. He had to be amputated. Testot-Ferry replaced him and continued the charge supported by Boyer and especially by Drouot's artillery. The Colonel's horse was killed under him, but next to him, Squadron Commander Kister was killed by a cannonball and Testot-Ferry took his horse so that he could continue the charge. He lost his new horse when he reached the artillery, his clothes were in tatters. The Russian artillery batteries were captured for the loss of 800 men out of action; moreover this very costly battle simply opened up the road to Laon, where the Army of Silesia was concentrated. It drove off all Napoleon's assaults and Marmont's night-time rout at Athies forced him to retreat.

During the attack on Rheims on 13 March, the Scouts were brilliant with the Guards of Honour under Ségur. It was he who led the charge which was so beautiful and effective and which earned him the title of Baron on 16 March.

At Arcis-sur-Aube, while Ney was holding out magnificently in Torcy where he resisted until midnight, the Colonel lost his horse killed in the middle of the fighting. He was stuck under his horse. He was immediately surrounded by the enemy and taken prisoner to Poison-les-Fays near Langres. There he found help in the person of the local schoolmaster, Joseph Edme, who got the guards drunk and enabled Ferry to get away in disguise and was led by French guides disguised as Cossacks. The Colonel reached Sens then la Chapelle-la-Reine where he joined his family. He was made CtLH in December 1814, aide de camp to Marmont, Maréchal de Camp in 1826, he retired in 1827. (A biography has just been published by his descendant, Olivier Giatard: it is very complete and very interesting).

As a main arm, the Scouts had a lance without a pennant; they were also armed with pistols and a carbine for the second rank.

Their uniform was close to that of the Guards of Honour with a few small differences in detail. Their shako was black instead of red with red braid at the top made of a series of rings. In theory, the officers wore their colback with silver braid. They rode small Camargue or Ardennes horses. The trumpeters came from the Pupilles of the Guard.

The 2nd Regiment

The regiment was attached to the Dragoon Guards.

It was commanded at the beginning of the campaign by **Leclerc** who, promoted to General, was replaced by Hoffmayer who himself came from the 2nd Dragoons.

Hoffmayer: Wounded twice in Russia, he was made OLH and Baron in 1813. He joined the Dragoon Guards during the Hundred Days and then was put on the non-active list. Retired in 1822, he took part in the 1830 Revolution with Fabvier.

There were two brilliant Squadron Commanders in the regiment.

Parisot: Guide in Italy and then in Egypt, he was awarded the LH in An-XII. He was made OLH in 1810 and awarded the Order of the Réunion in 1813. In 1815, he was with the 8th Chasseurs.

Lebrasseur: He was Grenadier à Cheval at Marengo. After serving in 1815, he was dismissed then retired as Lieutenant-Colonel in 1823.

On 4 February, the regiment had 28 officers and 502 men. They took part in all the Dragoon and cavalerie de la garde fighting. They were at Brienne and charged with the 1st Scouts at Montmirail. On 7 February they joined the Dragoons. On the 12th they were at Chateau-Thierry. On 5 March there were only 200 left.

The 3rd regiment

They were attached to the 1st Lancers of the Guard.

Most of the men were Poles. Squadron Commander **Skarzinski was very** brilliant. They were in the Young Guard as were some Krakus depending on General Pac, commanding the Polish cavalry of the Line. On 8 March there were 66 officers and 794 men among whom 243 Frenchmen (Brunon). A squadron was at Champaubert, almost certainly the Lancers described as being with Picquet. The 3rd Scouts and the 1st Lancers in fact formed a single regiment under General Krasinski. On 1 May 1814, they were released from their oath by Napoleon, the men of the 3rd Scouts, led by Zielonka, their Squadron Commander, returned to their country and the Russian Empire.

General Pac: General in 1812, always with Napoleon. He was made Major-General in 1814. He commanded the Lancers and the 3rd Scouts. At the head of the Lancers at Craonne and Laon, he was wounded at Arcis-sur-Aube. He resigned in May 1814, returned to Poland and became a civilian. Senator in 1819, a member of the Provisional Government in 1830, he emigrated to Turkey and died there in 1835. He brought a large number of reinforcements and was mentioned at Berry-au-Bac.

The Guards of Honour

They were created by a decree dated 31 March 1813. They had to form four regiments of men from rich or noble families who had until then escaped conscription by paying to be replaced. These horsemen had to furnish their own clothes, equipment and mounts. They had

Left: **General Berkeim.** *(RR)*

Right: **Pange, Colonel-Major of the 2nd Guard of Honour Regiment.** *(RR)*

Below: **Colonel Belmont Briançon, Colonel-Major of the 3rd Guards of Honour. He was killed at the Battle of Rheims.**
(Painting by Horace Vernet, RR)

the structure and the pay of the Guards. The Emperor hoped thus to levy 10 000 horsemen for a minimum cost.

The four regiments were organised more or less well; their colonels were chosen from among the Brigadiers or the Major-Generals.

These regiments were presented with those of the Guard but their belonging to this corps is controversial.

The 1st Regiment

Its **Colonel was General Count Randon de Pully.** He was 63 and had started as a Musketeer of the King in 1769. Maréchal de camp in 1792, he was made a Major-General in 1793 then obtained a command in Italy. He was at Raab and was made a Count in 1809. He commanded this regiment at Versailles where he supervised the corps' organisation in 1813. In combat it was the Second-Colonel, Picquet, who was in command.

Picquet: Aide de camp to Murat in 1807, he was made a General in 1813. He was at Brienne, la Rothière, Champaubert and Rheims where he was wounded. GdOLH in 1815, he was wounded again at Waterloo. Inspector for the Gendarmerie in 1830, he was appointed Lieutenant-General in 1831. He died in 1847.

He commanded a brigade of Defrance's Division, with the 1st and 2nd Regiments, plus the 10th Hussars (de Curély).

The Colonel-Majors were De Castellane who replaced Colonel Brincard who had joined the 13th Hussars; and de Mathan who had been made Colonel-Major on 8 April 1813. He was made CtLH in 1814 then Marquis and Pair de France in 1815. He was put in the reserve in 1839. The regiment was completed with men from Joseph's Guard. Three squadrons were on the Rhine and took part in the campaign. 440 horsemen, under-equipped, were at the Deux-Ponts depot. A squadron was at Antwerp in the Army of the North with Maison.

One squadron was commanded by **Etienne de Pully:** LH, son of the General, he was at Mainz.

On 1 April there were only 9 officers and 26 men left.

The 2nd Regiment

This regiment's Colonel was Major-General Count Lepic, but he was ill and controversial so General Valin, the Second-Colonel was in command.

De la Pommeraye: Awarded the LH, he left on 25 June 1813 and was left in Mainz during the blockade.

Most of the regiment was blocked in Mainz, under Morand. 100 Guards were with General Broussier and Colonel Thurot in Strasbourg with the Guards of the 4th Regiment; others were with the Army of the North.

The 3rd Regiment

Colonel Segur was in command and led the regiment himself into combat. The Second-Colonel was Vincent. Colonel Belmont-Briançon was Colonel-Major and was killed at Rheims.

De Ségur: Count in 1809, he was appointed Duroc's assistant and General in 1812. He fought at Montmirail and was the hero of Rheims on 13 March, when he was seriously wounded. He served in 1815. Lieutenant-General and Peer in 1831, he was promoted to GdCxLH in 1847. After retiring in 1848, he died in 1873. De Ségur was the author of memoirs and his account of the French Campaign is very precious.

Vincent: Made a General in 1813, he served under Mortier at the end of February and commanded at Chateau-Thierry. He was Made CrLH in 1814, Equerry in 1820 and CrSL in 1823. Lieutenant-General in 1825, he retired in 1837.

The 3rd Guards of Honour started the campaign with 235 horsemen present. Part of the regiment was with the Army of the North under Maison.

De Ségur commanded this regiment which was often brigaded with the 4th. He described their action in his Memoirs with in particular their role at Montmirail where they supported Dautancourt's charges against Sacken's right wing around Marchais. They distinguished themselves at Chateau-Thierry and it was at Rheims that they lived their great moment of triumph and glory.

The 4th Regiment

General de Bonaldi de Saint-Sulpice was its Colonel. The Second-Colonel was Merlin and the Major was Joseph de Monteil, a former Cuirassier from the 1st Regiment.

Merlin: No relation to the General in the 2nd Corps, he was made a General in 1813, served under Subervie in 1815 and then was outlawed. Lieutenant-General in 1832, he was made GdOLH in 1837. He retired in 1848.

The regiment had a strength of 234 men.

The Guards of Honour formed a division commanded by General Defrance who succeeded General Berkheim.

Defrance: Major-General in 1811, he was at la Rothière, Montmirail, Chateau-Thierry, Rheims and Arcis-sur-Aube. He retired in March 1815. He became Equerry to the King and CrSL in 1820 and was made GdCxLH in 1829.

Berkheim, Baron de: Equerry in 1805, he was made a General in 1809, then CtLH and Major-General in 1813. He served in the 2nd Cavalry Corps on 14 February then was under Belliard on 17 March with whom he fought at Arcis-sur-Aube. With Rapp in 1815, he was elected Deputy then re-elected the following year in 1816. He died in 1819.

Dejean: Commanded the 1st Brigade in 1813. Lieutenant-General in 1817, he was aide de camp to Napoleon in 1815 and served at Ligny. Exiled, he returned in 1818. Made a Peer on the death of his father, he was in Belgium in 1830. In 1844 he was promoted to GdCxLH.

Le Berton was the division's Chief-of-Staff. He was made OLH in 1804 and Chevalier de Bellefontaine in 1810. He was wounded at Rheims.

Piquet's Brigade

Piquet: General in 1813, Second-Colonel of the 1st Guards of Honour on 15 December 1813. He was Champaubert and Rheims where he was wounded. OLH in 1814, wounded at Waterloo, GdOLH in 1815. Inspector for the Gendarmerie from 1820 to 1830, Lieutenant-General in 1831, he was in the reserve in 1840.

The brigade was made up of the 1st Regiment of the Guards of Honour and Curely's 10th Regiment of Hussars.

Curely: Awarded the LH in 1806. After serving under Lasalle he was aide de camp to Colbert in 1809. He distinguished himself at the Berezina; then he was wounded several times in 1813. He was at la Rothière, Montmirail, Craonne, Laon, Méry where he disengaged the Guard, and Saint-Dizier. For his brilliant exploits at Chateau-Thierry, he was promoted to General on the battle field. He served with Roussel d'Hurbal at Waterloo and then was put on the non-active list.

De Ségur's Brigade

This was made up of the 3rd and 4th Guards of Honour Regiments together with the remnants of the 2nd, 3rd and 4th Regiments.

THE GENDARMERIE D'ELITE

Henry: baron in 1809, he was made a General and CtLH in 1812; retired in 1815.

Deschamps: Fourrier of the Palace from 1806 to 1814; he was made a Chevalier in 1812 and OLH in 1814. He accompanied the Emperor to Elba. In 1815, he was at Versailles and was promoted to Colonel.

Retired as a Lieutenant in 1818, he was re-instated with the rank of Colonel in 1831 and then retired in 1832.

THE ARTILLERY

THE ARTILLERY OF THE GUARD

Sorbier: General since 1797, he was made a Count in 1808 and Gd Cordon of the Couronne de Fer in 1809. Appointed Commanding Officer of the Guards Artillery, he replaced Lariboisière on 14 August 1809. He was Commander-in-Chief of the artillery in Champagne and was awarded the Gd Cordon of the LH in 1814. First he was a Deputy in 1815, and then he was exiled in 1815 and 1816 to Cognac; retired in 1815.

Maillart de Liscours: Aide de camp to Sorbier he was in the Guard since 1806.

Drouot: First at the Chalons School, he was at Hohenlinden. In 1808, he was the director of the Guard Depot. He was wounded at Wagram and mentioned for his famous large battery. He was made a Baron as a result.

General and aide de camp to Napoleon in 1813, he was mentioned at Hanau where his action was decisive again. He was at la Rothière, mentioned at Montmirail especially against the Prussians; he was even more effective at Vauchamps, Craonne, Laon. Made a Count on 22 March, he was Commander-in-Chief of the Guards Artillery on 25 March. He remained with Napoleon and became Governor of the Isle of Elba. Commander-in-Chief of the Guards during the Hundred Days, he was outlawed on 24 July 1815, then acquitted in 1816. He retired in 1825 and promoted to GdCxLH and made Pair de France in 1831. He died, blind, in 1847.

Dulauloy: Major-General in 1803, he was made Count in 1811 then took part in the Russian Campaign where he commanded the Artillery of the Guard. Chamberlain and Counsellor of State to Napoleon in 1813, he was made a GdCx of the Réunion and Couronne de Fer in 1814 then GdCxLH and Pair de France during the Hundred Days. He retired in 1832.

Desvaux de Saint-Maurice: Aide de camp to Marmont in 1805, he was a General in 1809 and commanded the Horse Artillery of the Guard. In 1813, he was made a CtLH and Major-General. He commanded the Artillery in the Army of Lyon in 1814. He was killed at the beginning of the battle of Waterloo.

Griois: Italian Campaign, he took part in the Russian Campaign. Made CtLH in 1813, he was made a Major in the Horse Artillery of the Guards and Baron and Couronne de Fer. He retired in 1822 with the rank of Maréchal de camp, even though he had been promoted to this rank back in 1813.

Lallemand (Henry): He was Dulauloy's Chief-of-Staff in the Horse Artillery of the Guards. With his brother, a Cavalry General, and Lefebvre-Desnoëttes they tried to take over the depot at la Fère when they learnt of Napoleon's return. Wounded at Waterloo, he was condemned to death together with his brother. He followed him to Texas where he founded the *"Champs d'Asile"*. Henry Lallemand married and remained in the USA near Philadelphia.

Headquarters of the 2nd Regiment of the Gardes d'Honneur. (Painting by Jacques Girbal, Author's Collection)

Above, left to right:
General Drouot was probably one of the most competent men in the Imperial armies.

General Desvaux de Saint-Maurice commanded the Horse Artillery of the Guard.

Opposite, left:
General Sorbier commanded the artillery in Champagne.

Opposite, right:
Navy Gunner and Old Guard Gunner.
(All photographs RR)

Boisselier: Guide in Italy, he joined the Artillery of the Guard in 1800. Made OLH in 1809, Squadron Commander and Baron in 1813 then finally Colonel and Chevalier in February 1814, he died at Craonne after having both his legs broken.

Boulart: Born at Rheims, he was Battalion Commander at Essling, went to Moscow in 1812 then commanded the Artillery of the Guard in 1813. He was mentioned at la Rothière and Montereau.

Henrion: Awarded a Grenade of Honour in 1802, he was allowed to join the Guard in 1808 and was made a Baron in 1813. He was made CtLH in 1813 and decorated with the Order of the Réunion in 1814. Major in the Artillery of the Young Guard, he was wounded four times. In 1815, he served on the Rhine with Rapp. He retired as Maréchal de camp in 1823 then in 1835. Not to be confused with the Colonel of the 9th Voltigeurs.

Doguereau: Egyptian Campaign where he was wounded twice. He was OLH. Colonel in the Guard, he was made Maréchal de camp in 1814 and then CrLH. He served in 1815. Made GdOLH in 1831, Lieutenant-General 1832, he was elected a Deputy and re-elected in 1839. He was made GdCxLH in 1843.

Mancel: Left the Ecole Polytechnique in 1802. In 1813, he was made Squadron Commander in the Guards Artillery. At Vauchamps, with Lieutenant Coessin, he lost two cannon which caused Guyot to be replaced by Exelmans after Napoleon's terrible wrath. He was wounded at Montereau and discharged in 1825.

Pion des Loches: Battalion Commander, he was aide de camp to Drouot in 1814. He was made Colonel and Equerry in 1815. He opposed Lefebvre-Desnoëttes' and Lallemand's attempted seizure of the depot at La Fère.

Guerrier: Aide de camp to Dulauloy in 1807, he was made Squadron Commander in 1,813 in the Guard. He was killed at Rheims.

Bon de Lignim: He was made Major of the 1st Regiment of the Artillery Train of the Guard in 1813 and Baron. Made CrLH in 1821, he retired in 1848.

Cappelle: Aide de camp to Dulauloy three times; he served in the Artillery of the Old Guard. He commanded the 2nd Artillery Regiment.

Couin: Son of the General, he was a Battalion Commander in the Artillery of the Guard.

Doncoeur: He was the officer in charge of clothing in the Gendarmerie d'Elite. He was made OLH in 1813 and served in the Artillery in 1814 then retired in 1816.

Lachouque also mentions the following: Battalion Commanders Leroy and Demaidy with the train, Le Français, de Montravel, Leclerc, de Lemud, Squadron Commander, etc.

THE ARTILLERY OF THE LINE

Ruty: Egyptian Campaign, he was made a General in 1807, Baron in 1808 then Count and Major-General in 1813. Chief-of-Staff for the Artillery, he was the Adjudant at General Headquarters in 1814. He was GdOLH in 1814, Pair de France in 1819 and CrSL in 1825. He died in 1828.

Couin: Italian and Egyptian Campaigns, he was at Arcola. Made CtLH in 1804, General in 1810. Under Grouchy he commanded the Artillery of the 5th Cavalry Corps In 1814. He was not able to get his guns out of the mud and follow the cavalry to Vauchamps where he could have increased the number of prisoners and the importance of the victory. He retired in 1814 then again in 1832.

Saint-Cyr-Nugues: Aide de camp to Suchet, he was made a Baron and General in 1811. In 1814, he was with the Army of Aragon and Catalonia, where he was Suchet's Chief-of-Staff. He was made CtLH. During the Hundred Days, he served again with Suchet.

He took part in the expedition to Spain and was made GdOLH in 1823. He was at Antwerp in 1831. Made GdCxLH in 1833, he joined the reserve in 1840.

Scheille: Awarded the LH in 1813, he was Colonel in 1814.

THE ENGINEERS

The Engineers were commanded by Léry, a General since 1796; he commanded the Engineers in Spain. He was made a Baron in 1811, Grand Cordon of the LH and CrSL in 1814 and Viscount in 1818.

Rogniat: Born in Metz, he took part in the sieges of Danzig and Stralsund. In Spain he directed several sieges. He was made a Brigadier in 1809 and then Major-General in 1811. He was Commander-in Chief of the Engineers instead of Haxo in 1813. In 1814, he was at General Headquarters but was blocked in Metz. He served at Waterloo. Made GdCXLH in 1820, he was a Viscount in 1822, CrSL in 1827 and Pair de France in 1831. He died in 1840.

Boissonet: Made OLH in 1804. Major in the Engineers of the Guard in 1812, he was Chief-of-Staff of the Engineers in 1813. He served in 1815; made Maréchal de camp and retired in 1824.

Paulin: "Polytechnicien", he was Bertrand's aide de camp. In 1814, he was made a Colonel Director of the Engineers' Depot. He was at Lyons in 1815. Baron in 1829, he was made CrLH in 1831 and Maréchal de camp in 1839. His souvenirs were published in 1895.

Radepont: Born in 1791, he went to the Ecole Polytechnique in 1809 and left Second-Lieutenant in 1812. In 1813, he was at Lützen, Bautzen, Dresden, Leipzig, Hanau; obtained the rank of Captain and was made Chevalier of the LH. In 1814, he commanded an Engineers Company at Brienne, Craonne, Laon, Montereau and Méry where he was wounded, and at Arcis-sur-Aube. He was given leave of absence in April 1814. He served in 1815 then was put on the non-active list.

Recalled in 1817, he was made a Chevalier of SL in 1828 and OLH in 1839. He was appointed Chief-of-Staff of the Engineers in 1848. Commandeur of the LH in 1851, he died in 1874.

Meissonier

The events which took place in Champagne and around Paris are etched in everybody's memory. This is not the case with the operations on the other fronts. Marshal Soult and his Army of the Pyrenees were far from the capital. But General Maison with his Army of the North and Augereau and his Army of Lyon were directly involved in the Emperor's strategies; the former was to serve as a shield against the forces coming down from Northern Germany and Holland; the latter had to beat the forces facing him and then operate in the rear of the Coalition advancing on Paris.

MAISON'S ARMY OF THE NORTH

Above, from left to right:
General Maison, commanding the Army of the North. *(RR)*

General Poret de Morvan, commanding the 2nd Brigade of Barrois' Division. He was sent to Champagne at the head of a division of the Young Guard.
(RR)

The troops making up the Army of the North and facing Bernadotte, the Crown-Prince of Sweden, were commanded by General Maison.

Maison: Aide de camp to Bernadotte in 1804, he was made a General in 1806 and became his Chief-of-Staff in 1807. He was made a Baron in 1808 and Major-General in 1812, Count in 1813, Peer and GdCxLH on 22 July 1814. Napoleon struck him off the LH on 18 April 1815. He was made a Marquis and GdCxSL in 1818. Commanded in Morée in 1828, he was promoted to Maréchal de France in 1829 and appointed Minister 1830 and 1836. He was also GdCx of the orders of Spain and Belgium. He died in 1840. His links with Bernadotte enabled some rather curious contacts to be maintained.

On his staff, one is surprised to meet: **Habaiby** of the Mamelukes. He was mentioned at the Battle of Coutrai, made a Colonel and was awarded the LH in November 1814. He commanded Melun, then retired in 1829. He went to Algeria with Clauzel as an interpreter in 1831, and then retired the same year.

● ROGUET'S DIVISION

Roguet: Italian Campaign, he was appointed General in 1803, then Baron in 1808. He was a hero of Krasnoia with the Young Guard. He was made a Major-General in 1811 then Chamberlain in 1813. He commanded the 6th Division of the Young Guard in Belgium where he was mentioned at Courtrai on 30 March. He was made a Count in 1814 and served as a Colonel of the 2nd Grenadier Guards at Waterloo in place of Friant. Retired in 1824, he was promoted to GdCxLH and Peer in 1831. He joined the reserve in 1839.

The division had a strength of 8 000 men.

— Flamand's Brigade

Flamand: He was made a Baron in 1811, CtLH and General in 1813. Couronne de Fer, wounded at Antwerp. He commanded the Guards depot. He was retired in 1815 because he was infirm.

The brigade was made up of the 12th and 13th Tirailleurs Regiments.

— Aymard's Brigade

Aymard: A veteran of Rivoli and Austerlitz, he was made a Baron in 1808 and General in 1813. He was at Gand then at Courtrai on 30 March. He left for Algeria with Clauzel as an interpreter in 1831. He was made a Lieutenant-General in 1832 then Peer in 1834 and GdCxLH in 1841. He retired in 1848.

The brigade comprised the 12th and 13th Voltigeurs Regiments.

● BARROIS'S DIVISION

Barrois: A Marengo veteran, he was a General in 1807, Baron in 1809 and Major-General in 1811. In 1814, he commanded the 4th Division of the Young Guard; made a Count the same year. He was with the Tirailleurs of the Guard at Ligny and at Waterloo where he was wounded at Plancenoit. Marshal of Portugal in 1833 in GdCxLH in 1836, then retired in 1848.

Solignac: Marshal Jourdan's brother-in-law. Took part in the 18 Brumaire among the 500 where he protected Bonaparte. He was made a General in 1799, Major-General in 1808, then Baron in 1811 but was dismissed for financial problems. He was made Cr of the Couronne de Fer in 1814. He fought at Courtrai, rejoined Napoleon on 22 June 1815 but was outlawed on the 25th and returned in 1819. He was made GdOLH in 1831. In 1834, he accused Soult of disliking him for financial reasons.

The division had 3 500 men.

— Darriule's Brigade

Darriule: A veteran of Italy and Egypt, he commanded the Kremlin in 1812. He commanded the 1st Tirailleurs Regiment in Barrois' Division in 1813; he was appointed Baron and General the same year. He served at Courtrai on 30 March.

He was in the National Guard in Paris on 16 April 1815, and then put on the non-active list on 1 August. He was made GdOLH in 1831 and appointed Lieutenant-General in 1832 and Peer in 1837. He retired in 1848.

The brigade was made up of the 9th and 10th Tirailleurs.

— Poret de Morvan's Brigade

Poret de Morvan: CtLH in 1813, he brought down reinforcements into Champagne on 20 February. Under Mortier he fought at Craonne and Laon where he was wounded.

He commanded the 2nd Grenadier Brigade on 11 March but his division was disbanded on 12 March. Colonel in the 3rd Grenadier Regiment of the Old Guard in 1815, he fought at Ligny and Waterloo. He served in Algeria in 1830 then in Belgium in 1832.

On 31 January, Porvet de Morvan at the head of Barrois' 2nd and 3rd Tirailleurs, and Grométy's and Bignon's 12th and 13th Voltigeurs, supported by the 10th Tirailleurs, opened the way towards Lille and Maubeuge to force the blockade of the town.

The brigade comprised the 2nd and 4th Tirailleurs Regiments.

● AMBERT'S DIVISION

Ambert: General in 1793, he was made a Major-General the same year. He was with Maison in the 2nd Division in 1814; he evacuated Breda and Merxheim then defended Antwerp. He retired in 1832.

— Gilly's Brigade

Gilly: General in 1793, he was made a Baron in 1808, Major-General in 1809 then GdOLH in 1811. He was with Decaen in Holland in 1813. Outlawed and condemned to death, he went into exile in the USA but was pardoned in 1820 and returned. Retired in 1825.

The brigade was made up of a battalion of the 131st of the Line, plus a detachment of miners and veteran Sappers, 157 artillerymen, 1 389 pioneers of which 931 were unarmed Frenchmen.

— Ducos' Brigade

Ducos: A veteran of Italy, he was a General and Deputy in 1802. He was made CtLH in 1808, then Baron in 1810. He was at Longwy in 1815 and retired in October of the same year.

The brigade was made up of a detachment of 131st of the Line, of draft dodgers, veteran gunners and coastguards and 138 Gendarmes.

Lauberdière: Promoted to General in 1807, made a Baron in 1808. At Wesel in 1814, he was made a Major-General and CrLH. Served at Rouen in 1815. This General was mentioned apart and was accompanied by 845 Customs men and 138 Gendarmes in Holland.

● CASTEX'S CAVALRY

Castex: Made a General in 1809, he was wounded at the Berezina in 1812 then made a Major-General the following year. He served with Lecourbe in 1815. He was made GdOLH in 1820, Viscount in 1822, he was in Spain in 1823, GdCx of St-Ferdinand and was elected a Deputy in 1824. He was promoted to GdCxSL in 1827. He died in 1842.

The division numbered 900 horsemen and a squadron of Guards of Honour.

— Meuziau's Light Cavalry Brigade

Meuziau: General, he was the Major of the Chasseurs à Cheval of the Guard in 1813. He accompanied Barrois, commanding a division of Chasseurs, then he went over to serve under Girardin in the 5th Corps on 16 March. He was with Rapp in 1815, and then retired in 1825 as Honorary Lieutenant-General. GdOLH in 1831 and retired definitively in 1833.

— Lalaing d'Audernarde's Brigade

Lalaing d'Audernarde: Baron in 1809, he was made a General in 1812. Major of the Lancers of the Guard. He was under the command of Maison at Courtrai on 7 and 26 March 1814. Made a Lieutenant-General in Spain in 1823, he was made GdCx of Charles III, Peer in 1837 then GdCxLH in 1847. He retired in 1848 and died in 1859.

The brigade was formed of various elements of the 3rd, 4th and 14th Cuirassiers brought together. Units from the Army of the North moved south to join Napoleon's main army, in particular men from the Young Guard.

Operations on the Northern Front

This zone was under the command of Bernadotte who had problems with Norway which was beginning to be troublesome; but he still hoped to be a candidate for Napoleon's succession. He continued his intriguing in France with Benjamin Constant and Mme de Staël. He also had problems with the Allies who did not trust him, like the partisans of the Bourbon faction. He could however count on the support of the Tsar. The Swedish Crown Prince set up his headquarters in Liege which the Swedes only reached at the end of February. Winzigerode's and Bülow's corps together with the 3rd Line Reserve Corps from Holstein (i.e. Tettenborn, Voronstov, Stroganov) were very quickly taken from him and transferred to the Army of Silesia which was having a hard time against the Emperor. Bernadotte only had 35 000 Swedes and the men of the Duke of Weimar who were the Germans under Walmoden and his Saxons. But from the beginning of March even the Duke of Weimar was attached to Blücher.

The English Corps operated with Antwerp as its eternal objective. General Graham attacked Berg-op-Zoom on 8 March with 4 800 men. He had a lot of allies inside the town which Bizanet held rather weakly. Generals Skerret and Goore were nevertheless pushed back and more than 2 000 men were taken and two generals killed. The detachment of Coldstream Guards was badly mauled. The French attempted very vigorous sorties from Antwerp and Maubeuge where Gilly distinguished himself.

The Duke of Weimar was supported by Thielman's 15 000 men, thereby having 27 000 men of which 3 000 cavalry and 41 cannon, with Ryssel and Borstell, three English detachments and Lecoq's Saxons under his command.

From Antwerp to Lille

General Lebrun, the Duke of Plaisance, was Governor of Antwerp. The Prussians attacked. Thumen directed the frontal operations; Krafft and Oppen attacked the town from the rear. Lebrun got Aimar to fall back. Roguet sent Squadron Commander Briqueville and a hundred Lancers to charge supported by a battalion of 12th Tirailleurs and one from the 13th Voltigeurs. They pushed the Prussians back into the neighbouring marsh which they thought was frozen. 100 were drowned and 60 captured. The English were supposed to take part but were slowed down by their cannon but they did make Ambert move back towards the stronghold; they ran into Roguet instead who stopped them. During the night of the 2nd and 3rd, the Allies set up their artillery and started to bombard the town.

Carnot arrived to replace Lebrun as Governor of the town. He put some order into things and called Roguet back inside; the fires from the incendiary shells were put out everywhere. The Allies, lacking ammunition, pulled back on the 6th. Maison decided to fall back on Brussels.

Chambarlac was sent to guard the Tournay Bridge with 1 200 men from the depots and 150 Guards of Honour from the 1st Regiment whilst waiting for Ledru's reinforcements. General Penne was sent to Mons. Admiral Missiessy put his boats out of harm's way.

Bulow reached Malines and Winzigerode reached Namur, but they were called down to the south, to join Blücher. The local population turned towards the Duke of Orange and the Allies. The French had to abandon Brussels. On 3 February, Penne attacked at Mons and had to fall back on Valenciennes. Maison sent Castex to help him. On the 4th, Maison had his headquarters set up at Tournay. The Prussians were relieved by the Saxons: Gablentz replaced Krafft who reached Brussels on the 10th. Bulow let Zielinski's Brigade blockade Gorcum then he headed for Laon which he reached on 24 February.

Maison found himself in front of the Duke of Weimar who had the Anhalt-Thuringia Brigade at his disposal together with Zielinksi's Brigade, made available by the capitulation of Gorcum. Carra-Saint-Cyr's Division which was at Valenciennes ran into Lecoq on the Tournay road and dispersed him. He called Borstell to his help. Maison headed for Courtrai which was occu-

Bernadotte, Crown-Prince of Sweden, had been made a Maréchal de France in the first series of promotions in 1804. (RMN)

pied by Barrois, but who was threatened by Schon's 6 battalions and 2 squadrons who were joined by the Duke of Weimar.

On 30 March Solignac left Gand and reached Courtrai. Thielman therefore marched there supported by the Saxons and covered on his left by Hellwig's partisans. Maison formed up his troops and sent Solignac and Barrois to turn the enemy's flanks. The enemy started to fall back too late because Roguet with the 10th Tirailleurs in the lead attacked them in the centre. D'Audenarde launched his Chasseurs against the Cuirassiers who were driven off and the Saxons fled pursued by Darriule. Three cannon and more than 800 of Thielman's men were killed or captured.

The Allies attacked Maubeuge where Colonel Schouller held out marvellously and drove off the enemy attacks. Maison reached Lille on 6 April where Barrois entered first. There were only 6 400 men left with Roguet and 3 599 with Barrois, but they had accomplished their mission. Belgium was lost but it did take the Allies two months to get hold of it.

The French Generals in this Army

Penne: Was made a Baron and Couronne de Fer in 1810. He was made a General in 1811, then CtLH in 1813. He commanded Maison's 3rd Brigade and was at Mons, Courtrai, Gand and Valenciennes. He served during the Hundred Days and was mortally wounded at Ligny.

Missiessy: Was in the Antilles in 1805. He was made a Rear-Admiral in 1809, GdCx of the Réunion in 1813, and GdCxLH in 1814. He was made GdCxSL in 1820, Cr of the Saint-Esprit in 1827, and retired in 1832.

Bizanet: General in Italy in 1793, he was made a Major-General in 1794, but he resigned in 1796. He drove Graham back on 8 and 9 March 1814, at Berg-op-Zoom. He served at Toulon in 1815. He was taken back in 1831 then retired in 1833.

Carra-Saint-Cyr: General in 1795, he was made a Major-General in 1803. He commanded the 3rd Division under Maison at the end of 1813, was made a Count in 1814, was retired in 1815, then again in 1833.

Ledru des Essarts: Made a General for his conduct at Austerlitz, he was a Baron in 1809 and Major-General in 1811. Under Maison in 1814, he was with the 3rd Reserve Division in Paris on 22 March 1814, under Compans at Meaux on 27 March. He defended Paris and opposed Marmont's and Souham's defection. He served with Suchet in 1815; he was made GdCxLH in 1827, retired in 1832, and made a Peer in 1835.

Chambarlac de Laubespin: Italian Campaign, he was at Arcola and Marengo. He was made CtLH in 1804, he was in command at Cambrai on 10 February 1814. Retired in 1815.

Schouller: From the Ecole Polytechnique, an artillery Colonel, he was mentioned at Maubeuge. Made GdOLH in 1847, he joined the reserve in 1853, the year of his death.

BERNADOTTE'S NORTHERN ALLIED ARMY

THE SWEDISH ARMY

The Swedish Army was under the command of Marshal Count Stedingk.

● **POSSE'S DIVISION**
— **Schulzenhain's Brigade**
Life Guards, 2nd Guards Regiment, Grenadier Guards, Queen's Guards
— **Lagerbring's Brigade**
Uppmand, Sudermanie and Jonkoping Regiments
● **SAENDELS' DIVISION**
— **Brandstroem's Brigade**
Western Gothia, Westmanland and Nerike Regiments
— **Reuterskoeld's Brigade**
Skaraborg and Elfsborg Regiments
2nd Battalion of Voermeland Chasseurs
● **BOYE'S DIVISION**
— **Colonel Hederstierna's Brigade**
Kroneberg, Kallmar and Southern Scania Regiments
● **SKIOELDEBRAND CAVALRY DIVISION**
Cuirassiers of the Guard, Scania Carabiniers, Dragoons Guards and Esmaland Dragoons
Moerner and Scania Hussars, Pomeranian Chasseurs
The Swedish Army therefore had 28 battalions, 32 squadrons and 62 cannon.

WINZIGERODE'S RUSSIAN CORPS

This was with Bernadottes's Northern Army, but was transferred to the Army of Silesia with Bulow's Corps and reinforced it near Soissons which they forced to capitulate. This corps sacrificed itself after Arcis-sur-Aube to trick Napoleon who was trying to draw the Allies away from Paris and they were defeated at Saint-Dizier on 26 March [1].

● **COUNT OBURK'S DIVISION**
(With Generals Jurkovski and Balk)
— **Pahlen's Brigade**
Elisabethgrod, Pavlogrod and Sumz Hussars
— **Drewitsch's Brigade**
Nieginsk Chasseurs and Finnish Dragoons
— **Majewski's Brigade**
13th Chasseurs
— **Galanthe's Brigade**
Polish and Volhinia Uhlans
— **Sagratzki's Brigade**
Nieginsk Chasseurs
Jakutov's Volunteer Cossacks
The division was reinforced with 12 cannon.
● **CZERNICSCHEV'S COSSACK DIVISION**
— **Lapuchin's Brigade**
Ilowaski 4th and Dioetschkin Regiments
— **Benkendorf's Brigade**
Sisoeva 3rd, Girowa and Grekov 18th Regiments
— **Stall I Brigade**
Cossack regiments: 1st Bug,

1. Koch has given us two versions of the make up of Winzigerode's army each with a different distribution for the various regiments. We give here the version which is closest to other existing sources. The second version gives a third division under General Benkendorf; moreover the regiments are shared out differently. It is clear that the organisation of the Cossack units was much vaguer than that of the regular units.

1st Baskir and Andrejanov
Paulogrod Hussars
— **Patton's Brigade**
Tula Regiment
2nd Chasseurs
There 10 light cannon with the division.

VORONSOV'S BATTLE CORPS
(3rd Infantry Corps)
● **LAPTIEV'S DIVISION**
— **Rudinger's Brigade**
Newsk, Petrowsk and Lithuanian Regiments
— **Rosen's Brigade**
Podolsk Regiment
44th Chasseurs
● **WUITSCH'S DIVISION**
vSwarikin's Brigade
Schirwansk and Butirsk Regiments
19th Chasseurs
— **Krabowski's Brigade**
The Umfsk Regiment
13th and 14th Chasseurs
● **VORONZOV'S DIVISION**
This division started the campaign in Holstein.
— **Panteleiev II Brigade**
Popov 13th and Panteleiev II Cossacks
— **Drewitsch's Brigade**
The Isumz Hussars
The Riga Dragoons
— **Krasovski's Brigade**
13th and 14th Chasseurs
— **Harpe's (or Laharpe) Brigade**
Navaginsk and Tula Regiments
Grenadiers from the 9th, 15th and 18th Divisions
30 cannon were with this corps.

STROGANOV'S CORPS
This corps was detached from the Army of Poland.
— **Sanders' Brigade**
Smolensk and Narva Regiments
— **Schwetschin's Brigade**
Alexopol and New Ingria Regiments
— **Glebov's Brigade**
6th and 41st Chasseurs Regiments
— **Scheltuchin's Brigade**
Pensa and Saratov Regiments
The total strength of Winzigerode's Corps was 36 battalions, 84 squadrons and 162 cannon.

GRAHAM'S ENGLISH CORPS
This corps operated towards Antwerp.
— **Cooke's Guards Brigade**
3 battalions of Foot Guard Regiments
— **MacKenzie's Light Brigade**
35th, 52nd, 73rd and 95th Foot
— **Skervet's 1st Brigade**
37th, 44th, 55th and 69th Foot
— **Gibb's 2nd Brigade**
25th, 33rd, 54th and 56th Foot
— **Cavalry**
500 Hussars from the English depots.

— **Artillery Reserve**
4 batteries, i.e. 22 cannon.

BULOW'S 3RD PRUSSIAN CORPS
This corps was with the Army of the North to begin with, and was then assigned to the Army of Silesia under Blücher, was directed towards Soissons and fought at Laon under his command.
● **ZIELINSKI'S DIVISION**
— **Sieholm II Brigade**
East Prussian Grenadiers
1st East Prussia Regiment
— **X's Brigade**
East Prussia Militia
Hussars of the Guard
● **THUMEN'S DIVISION**
— **Stutterheim's Brigade**
East Prussia Chasseurs
4th East Prussian Regiment
5th Reserve Regiment
— **X's Brigade**
2nd Pomeranian Militia Regiment
1st Cavalry Regiment belonging to this Militia
● **BORSTELL'S DIVISION**
— **Schon's Brigade**
Pomeranian Regiment and Grenadiers
2nd Reserve Regiment
The Elbe Regiment
● **KRAFFT'S DIVISION**
— **Zastrow's Brigade**
Colberg Regiment
9th Reserve Regiment
— **X's Brigade**
The New Marches Militia
1st Pomeranian Militia Cavalry Regiment
● **OPPEN'S CAVALRY DIVISION**
— **Treskov's Brigade**
The Queen's Dragoons
2nd West Prussian Dragoons Regiment
The Brandenburg Dragoons
— **Hobe's Brigade**
West Prussian Uhlans
2nd Silesian Hussar Regiment
Pomeranian Militia Cavalry
— **Sidov's Brigade**
2nd and 4th Militia Regiments of Electoral Prussia
Colomb's and Lutzov's Partisans
Bulow's Corps numbered 44 battalions, 52 squadrons and 96 cannon.

THE DUKE OF WEIMAR'S SAXON CORPS
● **LECOQ'S DIVISION**
— **1st Cavalry Brigade**
Headquarter Dragoons, Cuirassiers, Uhlans and Hussars
— **2nd Infantry Brigade**
Chasseurs
Grenadiers
1st Infantry Regiment of the Line
● **RYSSEL I DIVISION**
— **1st Brigade**
2nd and 3rd Infantry Regiments of the Line
— **Gablentz's 2nd Brigade**

1st and 2nd Light Infantry Regiments
● **PAUL OF WURTEMBERG'S DIVISION**
— **Eglofstein's Brigade**
Weimar Chasseurs
Gotha, Schwarzburg, Anhalt-Dessau and Anhalt-Bernburg Regiments
● **THIELMANN'S DIVISION**
— **Liebenau's Brigade**
1st and 2nd Saxon Militia Regiments
— **Brause's Brigade**
3rd and 4th Saxon Militia Regiments
— **Cavalry Brigade**
1 squadron of cavalry of the Line
The Bialov Cossack Regiment
● **THE HANOVERIAN DIVISION**
— **Esdorf Brigade**
Bremen and Verden Hussars
Esdorf Hussars
— **Killmansegg's Brigade**
The Hanoverian Volunteer Chasseurs
Launburg, Verden and Luneburg Regiments
2 Light Battalions
— **Aurenschild's Brigade**
7 batt. and 8 squ. of the Russo-German Legion
— **Tettenborn Brigade**
4 Cossack Regiments
This made a total of 45 battalions, 41 squadrons and 88 cannon for the Duke of Weimar's Corps.

THE DUKE OF BRUNSWICK'S 2nd GERMAN CORPS
● **OLTERMAN'S DIVISION**
This division consisted of the Brunswick contingent.
— **Westphal's Brigade**
Hussars, Uhlans and Chasseurs d'Elite
— **Buttlar's Brigade**
3 Light Battalions
— **Specht's Brigade**
3 battalions of the Line
— **Biers' Brigade**
4 Militia battalions
● **WITZENLEBEN'S RUSSIAN DIVISION**
This division incorporated the contingents from the Hanseatic towns.
— **Lieutenant-Colonel Deluis' Brigade**
Hamburg, Bremen and Lubeck Regiments
— **Major von Arnim's Cavalry Brigade**
Hamburg, Bremen and Lubeck Regiments
● **DOERENBERG'S DIVISION**
This division was made up of troops from Hanover.
— **Killmansegg's Brigade**
The Cumberland Hussars and 2 Infantry Regiments
— **Lyon's Brigade**
10 Militia Battalions
Two independent brigades, directly under the command of the Duke of Brunswick were also set up. The first consisted of two Oldenburg Battalions commanded by Lieutenant-Colonel Werdenberg and the second consisted of four Mecklenburg-Schwerin battalions as well as some Chasseurs à cheval commanded by General-Major Fallois.
The German Corps under the Duke of Brunswick had a total strength of 52 battalions, 13 squadrons supported by 64 cannon.

THE ARMY OF THE NORTH

Bernadotte's Swedes

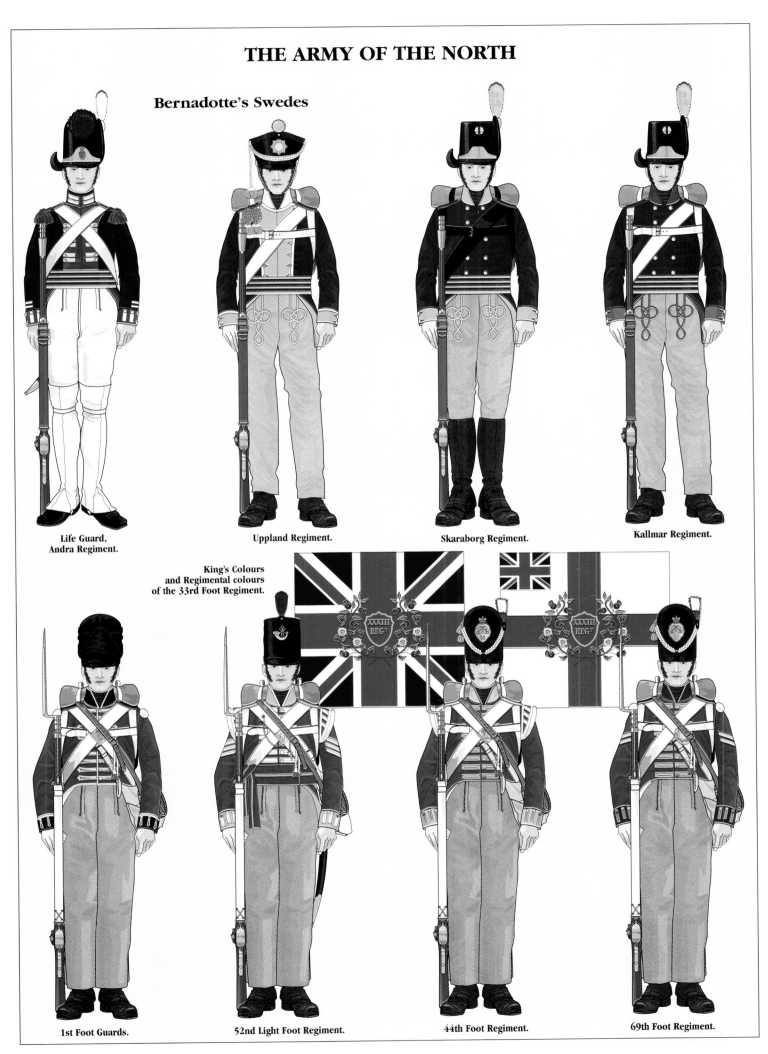

Life Guard,
Andra Regiment.

Uppland Regiment.

Skaraborg Regiment.

Kallmar Regiment.

King's Colours
and Regimental colours
of the 33rd Foot Regiment.

1st Foot Guards.

52nd Light Foot Regiment.

44th Foot Regiment.

69th Foot Regiment.

J. Guerre gives precious details about this Army of Lyon. This writer immediately states that he is anti-"Buonaparte" but he does describe the different phases of the fighting well. A very complete book has been written by Ronald Zins on this subject (Editions Horace Cardon, publishers). He gives a lot of details about this campaign and about the corps present and also gives the differences with Koch's report which is still the basic tool, but which we have modified to take into account the large amount of official local correspondence published by Zins for the dates 15-29 January, 12-25 March and finally 10-15 April 1814.

Bubna led the Allied vanguard and started by taking Geneva and its resources. From there he infiltrated into France towards the River Rhone. At Lyon, everybody was frightened. Augereau had only feeble resources, the town only having 32 Guards of Honour from the 4th Regiment, 30 Gendarmes and 60 Hussars from the 1st Regiment. Mr Charrier-Sainneville was the strongman on the local council and he relied on the local National Guard which was of good quality. Senator Chaptal arrived with full powers which he did not use. On 12 January 1814, General Musnier came to take command.

Bubna occupied Chambéry and Bourg-en-Bresse, then headed for Macon and moved up to threaten Lyon with his 15 000 men. All the town's administrative archives were evacuated. Augereau was designated as commander of the Army of Lyon which did not really exist. With Chaptal, he went scouring the neighbouring departments looking for men. Musnier had to face and try and stop the enemy; he eventually fell back on Saint-Etienne. An Austrian officer, who turned up [to negotiate] and seemed to be provocative, was handled roughly and sent packing. From Valence, Augereau sent 700 men from the 16th and 140th of the Line to Lyon and one 4-lb canon as well as all the powder available. They arrived on 19 January to great acclaim. On the 21st, another column arrived with 400 men from the 32nd Light, 95 Hussars from the 1st Regiment and one canon. At Vienne they were reinforced with 90 Chasseurs of the 4th and 31st and two companies of Gardes-Chasses. The marshal marched at their head, to great applause. Calm returned.

The order to march on Geneva arrived. Augereau was still too weak, had no money and asked for reinforcements. He received one of Suchet's divisions, moving up from Catalonia: Beurmann's Division with four columns, including that of General Gay. It only arrived on 19 March with about 9 600 men. Augereau received rifles from Saint-Etienne; some Catalans arrived on the 9th, then on 23 February, 24 cannon were gathered together.

The Army of Lyon took shape. Its mission was to prevent the enemy from gaining access to the centre and the south of France. Napoleon wanted to use it to attack the lines of communication of the Army of Bohemia which was now engaged in Champagne.

The Kalmuks in the Russian Cavalry marauding and roaming around the French countryside. (RR)

General Digeon. He came from the Army of Aragon; he commanded the French left wing at the Battle of Limonest. (RR)

What the Army of Lyon consisted of

Marshal Augereau was appointed on 5 January 1814, commanding the Army of Lyon (officially called the Army of the East, or of the Rhone). On the 14th he reached the town. *"He found no army, no fortifications, no supplies; only 18 000 men under the command of General Musnier occupied the town."* (Colonel Bourdeau).

Marshal Suchet who was in command in Catalonia did send him reinforcements. The levy of National Guards in the region got organised as best it could. But this was still insufficient. Augereau complained to Napoleon who replied in a letter dated 21 February: *"You say that the six battalions from the Nîmes division have neither clothing nor training; you've not given me a very good reason, Augereau! I destroyed 80 000 enemy with battalions made up of conscripts without cartridge pouches or good clothing. The National Guards, you say, are pitiable; I've got 4 000 here who come from Angers and from Brittany with round hats, no pouches and wearing clogs, but with good rifles. I've turned this to my advantage; you go on about there being no money; and where do you hope to get money from? You can have some when we get it from our enemies... I'm ordering you twelve hours after receiving this letter to start the campaign. If you are still the Augereau of Castiglione, stay in command; if your sixty years are too much of a burden for you, quit the command and give it to the most senior of your Generals. The motherland is threatened and in danger. It can only be saved by boldness and willpower and not by hopeless dilly-dallying. Be the first under fire. It's no longer a question of behaving as before. You have to put your '93 boots on again!"*

Napoleon forgot the grandiose titles of the Empire. The man he was writing to was no longer the Duke of Castiglione, but the "Augereau of Castiglione". He no longer uses a sovereign's pompous terms, but Danton's blunt speech for mass conscriptions.

In spite of his appeals, nothing was ready when the Austrian General, Ferdinand von Bubna, arrived at the head of the corps which was invading south-east France, through Switzerland, and started moving along the banks of the River Rhone.

Created from the feeble units which were present, the Army of Lyon consisted of the Geneva reserve, the National Guards and the Italian conscripts; Suchet sent him good quality reinforcements with Bardet, Beurmann, Pannetier and Digeon's Cavalry. Among these troops coming from Spain, there were a lot of regiments which provided the Army of Champagne with small detachments, mixed with weak marching regiments grouped together in Provisional Divisions.

Augereau's Chief-of-Staff was General Dessaix.

Dessaix: Italian Campaign, hero of the Allobroges; he fought at Toulon and Rivoli, wounded four times during that campaign. He was made a General in 1803, then Major-General in 1809, GdOLH in 1811. Having freed Chambéry he was called the "Bayard of the Mont Blanc". He covered the retreat to Lyon. Arrested in 1816, he was quickly freed and retired in 1831.

The artillery of the army was under the command of Desvaux de Saint-Maurice.

Desvaux de Saint-Maurice: Major-General, he was killed at Waterloo while commanding the artillery of the Guard.

He had 956 men, of which 120 sailors.

● MUSNIER'S DIVISION

Musnier de la Converserie: General in 1798, a Marengo veteran, he was made a Major-General in 1805. He was made GdOLH in 1810 then Baron in 1811. He returned from Spain on 10 August 1813 and was sent to Besançon to organise the National Guards. He failed at Macon, fought at Limonest and retired in 1832.

Some of these soldiers came from the Army of Catalonia. They were veterans of the Spanish Campaign and formed a kernel of solid troops.

— Ordonneau's Brigade

Ordenneau: Sabre of Honour in 1802, he was made a General in 1813. In February 1814, he returned from Spain where he served under Suchet. Wounded at Bourg-en-Bresse and at Macon, he was at Limonest on 20 March. He was made a Baron in 1817, GdOLH in 1821. He served in Spain in 1823 when he was made Lieutenant-General. He received the CrSL in 1826 and retired in 1848.

*After Zins.

The brigade comprised 4 battalions of the 20th and 67th of the Line.

— Passelac's Brigade

Passelac: Awarded the LH in 1804, Adjudant-Commandant, he came from Suchet on 24 January 1814. He retired in 1822 as Honorary Maréchal de Camp.

The brigade was made up of one battalion from the 32nd Light, and the 2nd, 16th and 24th of the Line.

● BARDET'S DIVISION (called *"de Nîmes"*)

Bardet: Made CtLH in 1805, General in 1807, then Baron in 1811. He was made Major-General on 3 March 1814; he served at Macon and at Limonest. He retired in 1815 after serving at Strasbourg.

— Pouchelon's Brigade

Pouchelon: Italian and Egyptian Campaigns, he was made OLH in 1807, Baron in 1808, General in 1812. He was with Musnier on 2 January 1814 and fought at Nantua and Macon. He did not serve in 1815 and retired in 1816.

— Soyez's Brigade

Soyez: He was mentioned as a Major but was made a General in 1803. He was made CtLH in 1804 then Baron in 1808. He was at Hamburg then inactive in 1814. Six does not mention him as being in the Army of Lyon.

The brigade consisted of 3 battalions.

— Lachèse's Brigade

Neither Quintin nor Six mention Lachèse.
This brigade only had 2 battalions.

● PANNETIER'S DIVISION

Pannetier de Valdotte: Wounded at Rivoli, made a General in 1803, CtLH in 1804, then Count in 1808. He brought 10 000 men from the Army of Catalonia on 15 January. He took Macon on 18 February. He was appointed to join Bardet but could not take up the post because he was ill. Lieutenant-General under Suchet in 1815, he retired in 1825.

— Gudin's Brigade

Gudin des Bardelières: Brother of the General killed at Valutina, he was made a Baron in 1810, then General in 1812. Sent by Suchet on 24 January, he served under Musnier in February. He fought at Limonest, was with Rapp in 1815, made CrLH in 1820, Lieutenant-General in 1821, Viscount in 1822. He was in Spain in 1823, was made CrSL in 1823 and retired in 1848.

The brigade consisted of 2 battalions of the 1st Light and the 2nd and 16th of the Line.

— Estève's Brigade

Estève: Baron in 1811, he was made a General in 1813. He came from the Army of Aragon and served in Pannetier's then in Musnier's Division at Limonest. The hero of Dardilly, he retired in 1825 then again in 1833. Made CrLH in 1831, he died in 1844.

Cavalry

140 Hussars from the 1st Regiment, 64 Chasseurs from the 4th, 31st and 24 Gendarmes were attached to the division.

● MARCHAND'S DIVISION (called *"Grenoble"*)

Marchand: Next to Joubert when he was killed at Novi, he replaced him. Made a Major-General in 1805, he was with Ney in Russia. He chased the Austrians from Chambéry on 19 February and then went to Grenoble. He tried to stop Napoleon in 1815; accused of having surrendered the town, he was acquitted in 1816. He retired in 1825 then in 1832. He was made a Peer in 1837.

— Serrant's Brigade

Serrant: Made OLH and General in 1812, he took Annecy with Dessaix, served at Lyon in 1815. He was put on the non-active list and retired in 1825.

— Barral de Rochechinard's Brigade

Barral de Rochechinard: Emigré, he returned in 1797, married a Beauharnais. He was made OLH in 1804 and Baron in 1809. He commanded the Grenoble National Guards under Dessaix at Macon. He served in 1815 and was put on the non-active list then retired in 1825 and again in 1832.

The division consisted of 9 battalions regrouping the detachments of the 1st, 5th, 11th, 23rd,

*Opposite, from left to right: **Maréchal Augereau, Duke of Castiglione. He was Commander-in-Chief of the Army of Lyon. The Prince of Hesse-Homburg.** (RR)*

60th, 79th and 81st of the Line, the 8th and 18th Light, 96 Gendarmes and 182 men from the irregulars (Zins).

The 5th of the Line had 1 013 men and the 11th 722. 43 troopers from the 4th Chasseurs and 23 from the 31st made up the rest of the division.

● RÉMOND'S RESERVE DIVISION

Rémond (called Remonda): A Swiss, he was made a Baron and CtLH in 1809. He had a very good reputation in Spain and arrived in Lyon in February 1814.

Zins gives complete details of the troops which were formed from the 24th's depot and the 3 000 National Guardsmen from a number of neighbouring departments and even from the Nièvre, Indre and Haute-Vienne Departments.

● DIGEON'S CAVALRY

Digeon: Took two standards at Austerlitz where he was wounded. He was made a General of Dragoons in 1807 then Baron in 1809.

He served with Suchet in the Army of Aragon where he was made a Major-General in 1813. He was at Vittoria four times. He arrived in Lyon on 24 February and fought at Limonest, at Lyon in 1815. He was made a Viscount in 1818, Peer in 1819 and CrSL in 1820. He was aide de camp to the King in 1824, commanding the Guard.

Not to be confused with the Digeon who was the 2nd Corps Artillery General.

— Guillemet's Brigade

Guillemet: A volunteer in 1791, he was aide de camp to Brune in 1796 and 1798. He was made OLH in 1810, then General in 1813. He was with Suchet in Spain, he reached Lyon on 26 March and fought at Limonest. Brune's Chief-of-Staff in 1815. He was laid off on the 1 August of the same year.

The division was made up of troopers from the 1st, 4th and 12th Hussars, of Chasseurs from the 4th and 31st Regiments and of Chasseurs Lyonnais. But the most powerful element was the 13th Cuirassiers. This unit from Spain was made up in 1808 from detachments from the 1st and 2nd Carabiniers, and the 1st, 2nd and 3rd Cuirassiers. The 13th Cuirassiers, worn down by the hard work under the harsh Spanish sun was most likely one of the best regiments that the French army possessed. It was disbanded in July 1814.

The regiment's Colonel was d'Aigremont. He was under Suchet in 1809, made OLH. He was made a Baron in 1811, General in 1813. After serving in the Army of the North in 1815, he was retired in 1826.

The division consisted of 1 725 troopers supported by 6 artillery pieces.

In this division there was Colonel Colbert, the brother of Edouard. He served in Egypt then was aide de camp to Murat in Naples in 1810. He was made Colonel of the 4th Hussars in 1812 then of the 12th in 1813. He was at Macon on 11 March and in front of Lyon on 18 and 20 March. He was made a General in 1814. Present at Ligny in 1815, he was made CrLH in 1831 and Lieutenant-General in 1838.

● BEURMANN'S DIVISION

Beurmann: Wounded at Austerlitz, he was made a General in 1811 and CtLH in 1812. He came from the Army of Catalonia and arrived on 19 March to take part at Limonest the following day. Of his four columns, only the first three arrived in time. He served on the Rhine in 1815 then was put on the non-active list. He was made GdOLH in 1837. He was elected Mayor of Toulon and retired in 1848. His brother was also a General.

Coming from Suchet's army, the 13th Cuirassiers were probably one of the best French heavy cavalry regiments.
(J. Girbal. Author's Collection)

— Ricard's 1st Column

Ricard: Adjudant-Commandant on Suchet's staff since 1813. He was LH in 1809 and Chevalier in 1811. He served in the Alps in 1815 and in Algiers in 1831. He retired in 1835. The column was made up of a battalion of the 32nd Light and one from the 116th of the Line.

— Gay's 2nd Column

Gay: Born in Lyon, he took part in the Egyptian Campaign, he was made a Baron in 1814 and served under Bardet at Limonest. He was in the Alps in 1815, retired in 1825 and again in 1834.

— Colonel Grange's 3rd Column

Grange: At Naples in 1806, he was given the LH in 1807, then the Order of the Two Sicilies in 1808. He was with the Army of Catalonia since 1809 and arrived in Lyon on 11 March 1814. He was at Metz in 1815 and retired in 1823.

The 3rd Column was made up of two battalions of the 102nd and two from the 115th of the Line. In all, the Beurmann Division had a strength of 9 661 men.

The Army of Lyon was built up with difficulty and gathered together 27 000 men.

Augereau attacks

In mid-February, Augereau, made keener by Napoleon's exhortations, went over to the attack. He had 26 000 infantry, 2000 cavalry and 30 cannon under his command. Facing him was Bubna reinforced by the Aloys Lichenstein Division, who had about 20 000 men. Augereau therefore had the numerical advantage but he made the mistake of dispersing his troops. Napoleon enjoined him to re-assemble them together again and to march without delay on Geneva, Basel and Langres in order to cut the lines of communications of Schwarzenberg's Army of Bohemia. The Emperor envisaged a grand manoeuvre which had its place in the overall operations of the French armies whilst Augereau was only thinking of defending Lyon. On the 19th, Macon, Bourg and Chambéry were taken back. Bardet occupied Nantua, Bubna fell back on Geneva which Dessaix was approaching. Augereau sent Bardet to attack the fort at l'Ecluse which was blocking their progress. Supported by the inhabitants, Bardet took the place capturing 130 men, their cannon and ammunition.

He decided to leave the town to counter-attack on 28 February. Dessaix could have beaten the Austrians and returned to Carouge, supported by Marchand; Musnier could have made a breakthrough to les Rousses, but it was already late.

The Prince of Hesse-Homburg moved up in reinforcement with the Army of the South, newly set up by the Allies. There were now 46 000 men for Augereau to face up to.

THE ALLIES' ARMY OF THE SOUTH

This is the army which faced Augereau during the campaign and which was reinforced when circumstances required.

BUBNA'S VANGUARD

He was alone at the beginning, but as Augereau received reinforcements and was able to go over to the attack, Bubna had to be reinforced with units from the Army of Bohemia.

● **Bubna's Light Division (1st Austrian Corps)**
— **Zechmeister's Brigade**
6th Chasseur Battalion
Brooder's Regiment
Lichtenstein's Hussars
One artillery battery
— **Klopfstein's Brigade**
The Wenceslas Colloredo and Kaunitz Regiments
One artillery battery
— **Klebelsberg's Brigade**
Levehner's Dragoons (two squadrons)
The Peterwaradin Regiment
One artillery battery
The Geneva Garrison
The Reuss-Graitz Regiment
Levehner's Dragoons
One artillery battery
Other units which were part of Bubna's Corps were attached to Hardegg's Division, in Hesse-

Homburg's Corps.

THE CROWN-PRINCE OF HESSE-HOMBURG'S CORPS
This corps was sent to reinforce Bubna's Corps.

● **BIANCHI'S DIVISION**
According to Zins, this division was with Bakony; in fact, according to Koch, it was blockading Besançon during the whole of the campaign.
— **Hirsch's Brigade**
Hiller's and Jerome Colloredo's Regiments
— **Haugwitz Brigade**
The Hesse-Homburg Hussars
The Riesch-Simbschen Dragoons
— **Quallenberg's Brigade**
The Esterhazy and Davidovitch Regiments
Three artillery batteries

JEROME COLLOREDO'S CORPS
After the defeats at Mormant and Montereau, this corps was sent to Lyon to reinforce Bubna.

WIMPFEN'S DIVISION
— **The Prince of Coburg's Brigade**
This brigade was taken from Prince Ludwig of Lichtenstein's corps.
Gradiscain Light Battalion
1st Valachian Regiment
Kienmayer's Hussars
One light battery

— **Mumb's Brigade**
Froon's and Devaux's Regiments
— **Wazel's Brigade**
The Argenteau and Ehrbach Regiments
● **WIED-RUNCKEL'S DIVISION**
— **Salins' Brigade**
Prince de Ligne's and Czartorisky's Regiments
— **Quasdonovitsch's Brigade**
Albert-Giulay and Reuss-Plauen Regiments
Two artillery batteries
● **HARDEGG'S DIVISION**
This division came from Frimont's Corps.
Raigencourt's Brigade
The regiment of the German Bannat
The Hesse-Homburg Hussars
Riesch's Dragoons
— **Scheiter's Brigade**
5th Chasseurs
Waradin Kreutzer's Regiment
The Emperor's Hussars
Vincent's Chevau-Légers
Two light batteries
● **WEISSENVOLF'S GRENADIER DIVISION**
These battalions reached the south of France in February.
— **Furtenswertther's Brigade**
The Tzarnotz, Berger, Oklopsia and Obermayer Battalions
— **Wiegel's Brigade**
The Habenay, Portner, Fischer and Ruber Grenadier Battalions
— **Klenau's Brigade**
The Frimm, Moessel and Putéany Grenadier Battalions

— **Luz's Brigade**
The Posmann, Lany and Gromada Grenadier Battalions
● **LEDERER'S DIVISION**
This was from Nostitz's Austrian Cuirassier Corps; these regiments were sent to the Army of the South at the end of February.
— **Rothkirck's Brigade**
Archduke Franz's and Prince Ferdinand's Cuirassiers
— **Kutalek's Brigade**
The Archduke of Lorraine and Archduke Albert's Cuirassiers

PHILIP OF HESSE-HOMBURG'S HESSIAN CORPS
This was first held in reserve at Dijon, then the corps was sent to the army at Lyon.

— **Metschery's Brigade**
The Joseph Colloredo and Zach Regiments
Archduke Ferdinand's Hussars
— **Moser's Brigade**
The Wurzburg and Reuss Regiments
— **The Ysemburg-Budingen Brigade**
The Frankfurt, Ysemburg and Fulda Battalions
— **Schoeffer's Brigade**
1st and 2nd Infantry of the Guard Regiments
— **Gall's Brigade**
The Infantry Regiments of the Hereditary Grand-Duke
Prince Emil's Light Regiment
Chevau-Légers Regiment

The Allies' reaction

Schwarzenberg was always slow and indecisive; he thought that his rear was threatened so he sent powerful reinforcements to save Bubna who was in difficulty. Thus Prince Hesse-Homburg's Corps with Bianchi and Wimpfen, about 60 000 men with 128 cannon, was sent towards Lyon.

Clausewitz thought that it was a big mistake to weaken the Army of Bohemia which had already started retreating. The objective had to be Paris and always be Paris with the maximum forces and as quickly as possible.

Macon was therefore occupied and a column attacked Cluny where de Damas resisted and drove off the attackers with his partisans, two battalions of National Guardsmen (one from the Cher), 22 Dragoons and 30 Light Infantry.

On 11 March Musnier attacked towards Macon but he was beaten in spite of the brilliant help of Colonel Colbert's 12th Hussars, and driven back towards Limonest. The Allies were reinforced with 15 000 men and 84 cannon.

Augereau decide to concentrate his troops but nothing had been prepared to defend Lyon. On 18 March at the fight at St-Georges-de-Reneims, the French resisted the Austrian assaults all day. Pannetier was chased from St-Georges, but retook his position with determination, the attacks being carried out with bayonet charges. On the left Ordenneau resisted brilliantly at the head of his brigade. Augereau decided to fall back on the heights at Limonest where he left Musnier and Pannetier.

10 000 Frenchmen had beaten 35 000 enemy soldiers, and the 13th Cuirassiers and the 7th of the Line distinguished themselves.

The Battle of Limonest

In the night of 19-20 March, reinforcements arrived from Spain and were placed with Digeon, the 12th Hussards and 6 cannon at Grande-Blanche. Estève, one of Pannetier's brigadiers, linked up the two positions.

On 20 March Augereau decide to fight: 18 000 against almost 62 000 men. He deployed his men in an arc to the north of Lyon from Limonest to the Demi-Lune, to the west of the town.

The Austrian right wing under Bianchi made a turning movement and attacked the Demi-Lune. Meanwhile Wimpfen made a diversionary attack on Limonest to fix Musnier's Division. At the same time, the Prince of Hesse-Homburg sent a brigade east to turn the French position at Limonest. Fearing this, Musnier retreated to Lyon, drawing Pannetier who was defending Dardilly with him.

Seeing this, Augereau - and here he was truly the "Augereau of Castiglione" - took command personally of the Pasquier and Musnier Divisions and carried out a vigorous counterattack. He succeeded in staying on the le Duchère Plateau until nightfall well supported by General Digeon's troops who were guarding Demi-Lune. Meanwhile, General Bardet, with 6 000 men succeeded in pushing back the 8 000 men under the Prince of Coburg. But they were too heavily out-numbered: when night fell, Augereau had to evacuate Lyon and march to Vienne. He had lost 1 000 men but the enemy had lost 4 000 casualties and 900 prisoners.

In the night 1 500 of Beurmann's men arrived from Spain to reinforce them. The Marshal had to decide whether to retreat and abandon Lyon or fight to the death and risk leaving the town open to looting and destruction. After consulting the Mayor, Mr d'Albon and his assistants Saineville and Varax, Augereau chose to retreat. During the night, an evacuation in good order begun towards Vienne where new troops from Spain were arriving. Digeon and Rémond formed the rear-guard. On 24 March, Augereau's headquarters were at Valence.

On the Allied side, the Prince of Coburg took St-Etienne and its factory. A column of 8 000 men headed for Marchand and Dessaix; they took Nantua. The Vedel Division coming from Italy came to reinforce the French Generals. Bianchi and Bubna moved towards them to block the way from Italy.

In the mountains, courageous officers carried on the struggle near Marchand until April. On this subject, Lahouque mentions:

Jomard and Major Thiloré of the 79th, Colonel de Cubières of the 18th Light at Carouge with the support of Major Oliver of the 126th, Battalion Commander Robergot of the 18th. He also mentions armed peasants, alone, holding out in the Petit-Chatel fort as best they could.

When all this was over, all the criticism levelled at Augereau seems surprising. After all, in the end, the old Marshal had done his job and obliged the Allies to send more than 60 000 men to fight against his small Army of Lyon.

SOULT'S ARMY OF THE PYRÉNNÉES

A very complete book has been written by Jean-Paul Escalates from whom I have borrowed numerous details. My other source is Och but he does not always agree with Escalates, especially where the distribution of the corps is concerned.

The Commander-in-Chief of the Army of the Pyrenees was Marshal Soul, Duke of Dalmatia. The Chief-of-Staff of the Army was General Azan.

Azan, Comte de la Peyrière: A veteran of Zurich, where he was made Major-General on the battlefield. Commanded the Army of the Midi in 1814 after Soul left. He was made GdCxLH in 1815 and a Peer on 2 June. Laid off in 1816, retired in 1825, he was a Peer again in 1831 and finally retired in 1832. General Tirlet commanded the artillery.

Tirlet: Egyptian Campaign, he was made a Baron in 1810, GdOLH in 1815, Viscount in 1822, GdCx of the Order of Charles III of Spain. He was elected Deputy in 1827, 1831 and 1836. He was made GdCxLH in 1836. He was Pérignon's son-in-law and died in 1841.

General Garbé commanded the Engineers. Garbé: Egyptian campaign, he was made a General in 1809 then Baron in 1812. He fought at Waterloo. He was a Viscount in 1822, GdOLH and Lieutenant-General in 1823, he was in Spain in the same year. Elected Deputy in 1830 and 1831. Colonel Michaux succeeded him at the end of the campaign.

THE LEFT WING UNDER CLAUZEL

Clauzel: Major-General at Saint-Dominica, he was made a Baron in 1810, GdCx of the Réunion in 1813, GdCxLH and Peer in 1815; he was suspended and sentenced to death. He went to the USA. He was pardoned and returned in 1820. Elected Deputy in 1829 and 1830. He commanded in Algeria, he was made a Marshal in 1831. Deputy the same year then in 1837. Governor of Algeria in 1835, he failed at Constantine in 1836. Deputy in 1837 and 1839, he died in 1842.

Clauzel's left wing was made up of the Taupin, Maransin, Harispe and Villate Divisions and had 8 889 men.

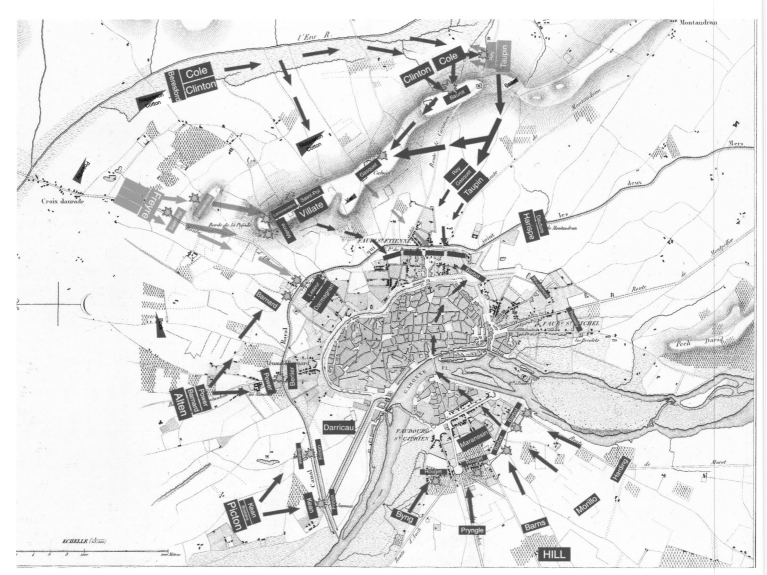

● TAUPIN'S DIVISION

Taupin: A Marengo veteran, he was awarded a Sabre of Honour in 1802. He fought at Austerlitz. He was CtLH in 1805, General in 1807, Baron in 1808 and Major-General in 1813. He was killed at Toulouse on 10 April 1814.

— Rey's Brigade

Rey: Appointed Major-General in 1793, he was at Rivoli, made CrLH in 1814, made a Baron in 1817. He retired in 1826 and again 1832.

The brigade was made up of the 12th Light and the 32nd and 43rd of the Line.

— Gasquet's Brigade

Gasquet: Egyptian Campaign, he was made CtLH in 1809, Baron in 1813, General in 1814. He was wounded at Toulouse. After serving in the Alps, he retired in 1815.

The Brigade was made up of the 47th, 55th and 58th of the Line.

● MARANSIN'S DIVISION

Maransin: General in 1808, he was made a Baron in 1810, then Major-General in 1813. He fought at Toulouse, was made CtLH in 1814, served in the Alps in 1815 and was arrested. He retired in 1825.

— Barbot's Brigade

Barbot: General in 1811, awarded the CrSL in 1815, made a Viscount in 1825 and retired in 1835. The brigade was made up of the 4th Light and the 34th, 40th and 50th of the Line.

— Rouget's Brigade

Rouget: Served in Holland. He was made a General in 1810. He fought at Toulouse, then took part in the Hundred Days the following year. He was made CrLH in 1826 and CrSL in 1829. He retired in 1832.

The 27th, 34th and 59th formed the brigade.

● HARISPE'S DIVISION

Harispe: Made a General in 1807, Baron in 1808, Major-General in 1810, Couronne de Fer in 1811 then Count and GdCx of the Réunion in 1813. He was captured at Toulouse, elected Deputy in 1831, made GdCxLH in 1833, Maréchal de France in 1851, and elected Senator in 1852.

— Dauture's Brigade

Dauture: General in 1813, he was at Toulouse and made CrLH in 1814. He served in 1815, then was put on half-pay. On leave of absence in 1818.

The brigade was made up of the 9th, 25th and 34th Lights.

— Paris' Brigade

Paris: Made a General in 1802, OLH and Baron in 1810, then Major-General in 1813. He was Victor Hugues brother-in-law and died at Perpignan in 1814.

The brigade was made up of the 10th and 81st of the Line, of the 8th Neapolitan, as well as two companies taken from the 114th, 115th, 116th and 117th of the Line.

— Baurot's Brigade

Baurot: General in 1813, wounded and amputated at Toulouse. Made CtLH in 1814, he retired in 1815 and was admitted as a veteran in 1836. The 25th Light, the 115th of the Line and 4 companies from the 117th of the Line made up this brigade.

● VILLATE'S DIVISION

Villate, Comte d'Oultremont: He was made a General in 1803, was mentioned at Elchingen; made a Baron in 1808, GdCx of Baden in 1809, he fought at Toulouse. Peer in 1815, he was in the reserve in 1831.

— Saint-Pol's Brigade

Saint-Pol: His name does not appear in Six or in Quintin. He is mentioned in Escalates. His brigade consisted of the 86th, 96th and 100th of the Line and of the 21st Light.

THE ARMY OF THE SOUTH

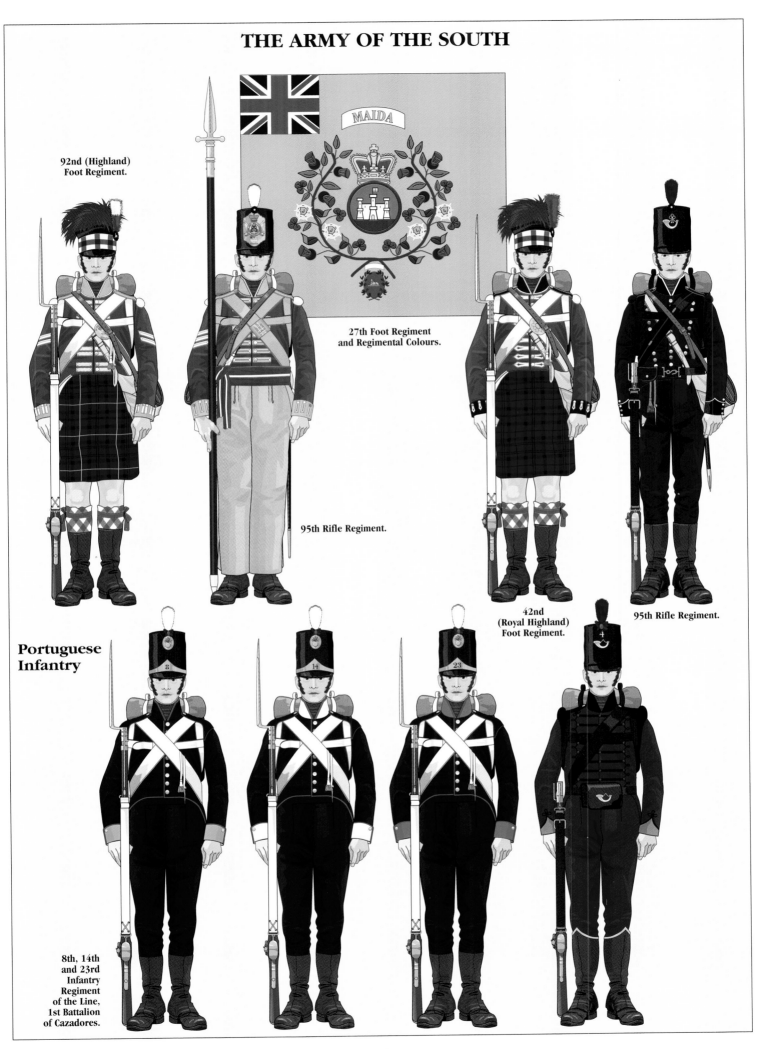

92nd (Highland) Foot Regiment.

27th Foot Regiment and Regimental Colours.

95th Rifle Regiment.

42nd (Royal Highland) Foot Regiment.

95th Rifle Regiment.

Portuguese Infantry

8th, 14th and 23rd Infantry Regiment of the Line, 1st Battalion of Cazadores.

MAIDA

— La Morendière-Ducoudray's Brigade

La Morendière-Ducoudray: Lieutenant at the time of Louis XVI. He took part in the Egyptian campaign. He was made a Baron in 1811, then General and OLH in 1813. He served under Villate in February 1814, wounded at Toulouse, retired in 1815 then in 1832, he died in 1837.

The brigade was made up of 103rd and 119th of the Line and of the 28th Light.

The way the regiments - of which there were sometimes only small sections in the brigades - were shared out in Koch's version, differs from Escalettes' in his book on the Battle of Toulouse.

ERLON'S CENTRE

Drouet, Comte d'Erlon: Major-General in 1803, he was at Austerlitz then in the Tyrol; he was made GdCx of Bavaria then GdCxLH in 1814. He joined Lallemand and Lefebvre-Desnouettes in 1815, was made a Peer in June and mentioned in Waterloo. Outlawed and sentenced to death in 1816, he was pardoned in 1825. He was a Peer again in 1831, he was made a Maréchal in 1843 and died in 1844.

The Comte d'Erlon commanded 9 341 men.

● DARMAGNAC DIVISION

Darmagnac: A volunteer in 1791, he took part in the Italian and Egyptian Campaigns, was made a General in 1801, and was awarded a Sabre of Honour in 1802. He was with the obs-

*Above: **General Harispe**. (RR)*

***General Drouet, Comte d'Erlon,** commanded the centre of the Army of the Pyrenees. (RR)*

ervation corps in the Pyrenees in 1808, was wounded at Medina del Rio Secco and was made a Major-General the same year. He fought at Toulouse, then he was laid off in 1814 then again in 1815. He received the CrSL in 1821, made a Viscount in 1822 then made GdOLH in 1823. Retired in 1831, he was taken back, and died in 1855.

— Chassé's Brigade

Chassé: see Oudinot's 7th Corps, Pierre Boyer's Division.

According to Escalates and Quintin, the brigade was commanded by Leseur.

Leseur: Made Adjudant-Comandant in 1809, he was made OLH in 1813 and in 1815 Maréchal de Camp and was in command at Marseilles in 1815. He was laid off on 1 August and committed suicide in 1818. The brigade was made up of the 16th Light and 8th, 28th and 54th of the Line (according to Och).

— Gruardet's Brigade

Gruardet: Italian and Egyptian Campaigns, he was wounded at Arcola and at Cairo. Appointed General in 1811, he was seriously wounded at Orthez and retired in 1815.

According to Escalates and Six, this brigade was commanded by Menne who also, apparently replaced Chassé who had gone to Champagne.

Menne: Was made a baron in 1808, then General in 1811, he served in 1815 and retired in 1826 then again in 1831.

According to Och, the brigade comprised the 31st Light and the 51st and 75th of the Line. Escalates mentions the 118th and 120th of the Line.

● ABBÉ'S DIVISION

Abbé: Awarded a Sword and Pistols of Honour in 1799, he was made a General in 1807, CtLH in 1808 and Baron in 1810. He was brilliant at Bayonne in 1814, served at Belfort the following year, retired in 1816 then again in 1832.

Only Och mentions this division.

— Beuret's Brigade

Beuret: Baron in 1809, made a General and CtLH in 1813, he fought at Bayonne and at Toulouse. He served in the Alps in 1815. He was made a Viscount in 1817 and retired in 1826.

The brigade was made up of the 27th Light and the 63rd and 64th of the Line.

— Maucomble's Brigade

Maucomble: Was made a Baron in 1810 then appointed General in 1813. He fought at Bayonne, served during the Hundred Days, was made a Viscount in 1822, then GdOLH in 1831 and retired in 1838.

The 5th Light and the 94th and 95th of the Line made up this brigade.

● DARRICAU'S DIVISION

Darricau: Italian and Egyptian Campaigns, he was made a General in 1807, was awarded the Couronne de Fer in 1811 and made GdOLH in 1815. He served during the Hundred Days and was laid off at Dax.

— Fririon's Brigade

Fririon: Made a General in 1800, he escaped at la Romana in 1808, was made Major-General in 1809, organised the Paris reserve in 1815, was made GdOLH in 1821. He commanded the Invalides in 1832.

The brigade was made up of the 6th Light and the 69th and 76th of the Line.

Maréchal Soult, Duke of Dalmatia. He led the retreat of the French Army from Spain masterfully, giving the Anglo-Allied armies a hard time in spite of being out-numbered. (RMN)

The 69th was mentioned at Achistof on 10 November 1813. At Gorospile, Colonel Guinand was killed. On the 14th there were 294 men left. Capitaine Marcel was mentioned at Cambo as was Lieutenant Gouley, who was already a hero of Tolosa. Hervé was appointed Colonel of the regiment on 22 December. At Toulouse, Darricau defended the canal; on 10 May 1814, the 69th's two battalions only had 806 men left.

— Berlier's Brigade

Berlier: OLH in 1806, he was made a General in 1811. He fought at Orthez and at Toulouse then served in 1815. He was given leave of absence in 1818.

The brigade was made up of the 36th, 39th and 65th of the Line.

Jean-Paul Escalates adds the following division:

● TRAVOT'S RESERVE DIVISION

Travot: Took Charette in 1796, made a Major-General in 1813, made a Peer on 2 June 1815 and served in the Vendée. He was sentenced to death but this was changed to 20 years' imprisonment; he finished in an asylum in 1817, and was pardoned in 1819.

— Pourailly's Brigade

Pourailly: His brother was killed at Castiglione. He was made a Baron in 1808, General in 1811, CtLH in 1813, served in Paris in 1815 and was then laid off then retired in 1825.

The brigade was composed of detachments from the 1st, 10th, 33rd, 63rd and 70th of the Line and the 2nd, 4th and 9th Light.

— Wouillemont de Vivier's Brigade

Wouillemont de Vivier: General in 1800, he was made CtLH in 1804 then Baron in 1813. He commanded the National Guardsmen of the Hautes-Pyrénées in place of Maransin

REILLE'S RIGHT WING

Reille: A veteran of Toulon and Italy, fought at Rivoli. He was aide de camp to Masséna in Italy then in Zurich and Genoa where he was mentioned. He was made a general in 1803, Major-General in 1806. He received the Couronne de Fer in 1807 and was made Count in 1808. Aide de camp to Napoleon in 1807 and 1809, who sent him to Antwerp to keep an eye on Bernadotte. He was made GdCX of the Réunion in 1813, GdCxLH and Peer in 1815. He commanded a corps at Quatre-Bras and at Waterloo. Gentleman of the King's Bedchamber in 1820, he was appointed Maréchal and elected Senator in 1847. He was awarded the Military medal in 1852. He was Masséna's son-in-Law.

● FOY'S DIVISION

Foy: General in 1808, Baron and Major-General in 1810. He was made GdOLH in 1814, served at Quatre-Bras and at Waterloo. He was elected a Deputy in 1819 and 1824. He died in 1825 and his funeral drew a crowd of more than 100 000 people.

● LEVAL'S DIVISION

Leval: see Oudinot's 7th Corps.
Leval's Division was sent to join the Army of Champagne.

— Pinoteau's Brigade

Pinoteau: Made a General in 1811, he was sent to Champagne and was wounded at Bar-sur-Aube. He was made OLH in 1814 and Baron in 1815. He was exiled and retired in 1832.
The 10th Light and the 3rd and 15th of the Line made up the brigade.

— Montfort's Brigade

Montfort: see Oudinot's 7th Corps, in Leval's Division.
His brigade was made up of the 17th Light and the 101st and 105th of the Line.

● BOYER'S DIVISION

Boyer, Pierre: see Oudinot's 7th Corps.
This division was sent to Champagne at the same time as Leval's.

— Menne's Brigade

Menne: Was made a baron in 1808, CtLH in 1810 then General in 1811, he replaced Chassé with Darmagnac on 22 January 1814; he served in 1815 and retired in 1826 then again in 1831.
The 2nd Light and the 24th and 118th of the Line made up the Brigade.

— Gauthier's Brigade

*Above and opposite,
from left to right and top to bottom:*
The Spanish General, Morillo.
**General Beresford was certainly
the best English Corps Commander.**
General Foy.
**General Habert remained
in the Spanish strongholds.**
**Maréchal Suchet, Duc d'Albufera, commanded the Army of Aragon. He did
not join Soult for the last battle.**
(RR for all photographs)

Gauthier: Was made OLH in 1810, General in 1812, and Baron in 1813. He was with Oudinot on 22 January and was wounded at the bridge at Bray-sur-Seine. He retired in 1815.
The brigade was made up of the 120th and 122nd of the Line.

THE CAVALRY

This was under the command of General Pierre Soult.

● SOULT'S DIVISION

Soult: The Marshal's brother, he was a veteran of Zurich and Genoa where he was captured. He was his brother's aide de camp and made a General in 1807, then Major-General in 1813. He fought at Orthez and Toulouse. He was elected Deputy during the Hundred Days, he served under Pajol. He was made GdCxLH in 1831. In the reserve in 1839.
His division had 2 791 men.

— Berton's Brigade

Berton (called Breton): Baron in 1808, he was made a General in 1813. He was at Orthez and Toulouse. He served under Exelmans in 1815 at Wavre. He was arrested and freed in 1816. He took part in an insurrection in Saumur in 1822, which failed. He was shot at Poitiers on 5 October 1822.
The brigade was made up of the 2nd Hussars, the 21st Chasseurs as well as elements of the 13th Chasseurs.

— Vial's Brigade

Vial: a veteran of the Italian and Egyptian Campaigns, he was made a Baron in 1808, General in 1813, Honorary Lieutenant-General in 1826, made GdOLH in 1850 and put in the reserve in 1853.

The brigade comprised elements from the 5th, 10th, 15th and 22nd Chasseurs.

A reserve brigade was constituted using isolated elements which were gathered together.

In front of Toulouse, the Highlanders launch an assault on the French lines. (RR)

Gudin de Bardelières: See the Army of Lyon.

The 3rd Light and the 14th and 16th of the Line made up this brigade.

— Ordonneau's Brigade

Ordonneau: See the Army of Lyon.

The brigade was made up of the 20th and 79th of the Line.

● LAMARQUE'S DIVISION

Lamarque d'Arrouzat: A veteran of Toulon and Egypt, he was made OLH in 1809, Baron in 1810 and General in 1812. He served in Catalonia and Aragon. He retired in 1825.

— Beurmann's Brigade

Beurmann: See the Army of Lyon.

The brigade was made up of the 23rd Light and the 60th, 69th and 115th of the Line.

● DIGEON'S CAVALRY DIVISION

Digeon: See the Army of Lyon.

— Delort's Brigade

Delort: Went to Champagne on 9 January. See Pajol's Cavalry in Victor's 2nd Corps.

The 4th and 12th Hussars and the 29th Chasseurs made up this brigade.

— Guillemet's Brigade

Guillemet: See the Army of Lyon.

The brigade comprised the 24th Dragoons and the 13th Cuirassiers.

— In the Strongholds

A lot of troops had been left in the strongholds.

Espert de Latour: He had twin brothers and shared this command with Palmarole.

Palmarole: General in 1795, Baron and OLH in 1811. He wanted to serve in 1815, retired in September. He had men in Figuères, Girone and the Cerdagne Brigade.

Habert: General in 1808, he was made Baron and Major-General in Aragon in 1811, Cr of the Réunion in 1813, he was Governor of Barcelona the same year with 6 781 men. He only gave up the city on 28 May 1814 and was made GdOLH. He fought at Ligny and was wounded at Wavre in 1815. He retired in 1824.

This made a total of 15 000 men.

— The Troops not in the Line

About 4 000 men.

Koch gives a total for this army of 37 268 men of which there were 2 500 cavalry.

Augereau asked for reinforcements to resist the Allies and several units left Catalonia with Musnier and Pannetier together with Digeon's cavalry.

In these troops sent from Spain, there were regiments which furnished small detachments to the provisional divisions and which were assembled into skeleton regiments.

● TREILLARD'S DIVISION

— Ismert's and Ormancey's Brigade

These units were sent to Champagne where they arrived on 16 February at Guignes. For these brigades see Kellermann's 6th Cavalry Corps.

These Spanish Dragoons distinguished themselves everywhere; there were the 4th, 14th, 16th, 17th, 21st, 26th and 27th Regiments, making a total strength of 5 699 sabres.

As well the elements already presented, Och gives the figures concerning the other troops.

— Troops not in the Line

- artillerymen, train and workers.
- pontoneers
- Engineers
- Gendarmes and teams

A total of 5 699 men.

The garrisons of the strongholds:
- Bayonne: 12 852 men
- Saint-Jean-Pied-de-Port: 1 562 men
- Navarrains: 1 400 men
- Chateau de Lourdes: 104 men
- Santona: 1 944 men

A total of 17 862 men.

In all the total strength of the Duke of Dalmatia's forces was 36 635 men.

SUCHET'S ARMY OF ARAGON AND CATALONIA

This army did not reach Toulouse in time because Suchet had had to send a lot of reinforcements to Augereau at Lyon and his strength was greatly diminished; he was also disagreed with Soult.

Only the officers who have not been seen previously will be shown here.

Chief-of-Staff: **General Saint-Cyr Nuguès**

Commanding the Artillery: **General Valée**

Commanding the Engineers: **Major Plagniol**

● MUSNIER'S DIVISION

Musnier de la Converserie: see the Army of Lyon.

— Scepeaux's Brigade

Scepeaux de Bois Guignot: Viscount, émigré and Maréchal de Camp with Louis XVI. He returned to serve as Adjutant-Commandant in 1809. Digeon's Chief-of-Staff at Lyon, he did not serve during the Hundred Days. OLH in 1820, he died in 1821.

The brigade was made up of the 1st Light and the 114th and 121st of the Line.

— Pannetier de Valdotte's Brigade

Pannetier de Valdotte: See the Army of Lyon.

The brigade consisted of the 7th, 44th and 116th of the Line.

● MESCLOP'S DIVISION

Mesclop: Served in the Army of the Pyrenees under Harispe. OLH in 1811, he was with Suchet in 1815, then in the reserve in 1839.

— Gudin de Bardelières' Brigade

THE BATTLE OF TOULOUSE, 10 APRIL 1814

Jean-Paul Escalettes gives a number of very precise details when relating the Battle of Toulouse. I will only give a summary of this battle which took place after the Emperor had already abdicated.

After the defeat at Orthez, Soult left the line of the River Adour and fell back on Toulouse which he reached on 24 March. He only had 30 000 infantry and 3 000 cavalry with which to face Wellington's 60 000 men. He therefore had the town fortified and trenches dug along the approaches. He rallied his troops once sheltered.

Wellington was slowed down by his baggage train and only arrived on 27 March.

Soult was expecting Suchet and his Army of Aragon to move up in support. He sent Lafitte

170

THE ARMY OF THE SOUTH

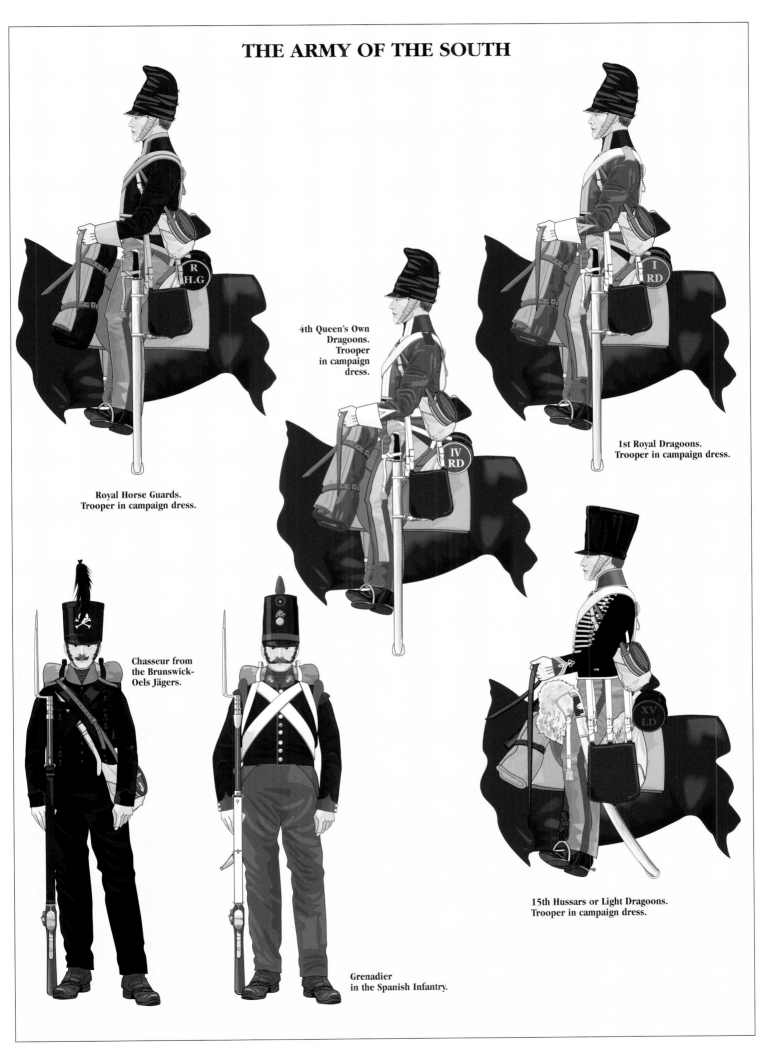

Royal Horse Guards.
Trooper in campaign dress.

4th Queen's Own
Dragoons.
Trooper
in campaign
dress.

1st Royal Dragoons.
Trooper in campaign dress.

Chasseur from
the Brunswick-
Oels Jägers.

Grenadier
in the Spanish Infantry.

15th Hussars or Light Dragoons.
Trooper in campaign dress.

Born the same year as Napoleon, Arthur Wellesley was educated at Eton then at the military academy of Angers. His first fighting was in Flanders, then alongside his brother in India where he beat Tippu Sahib. He landed in Portugal and won the Battle of Vimero in 1808. He disagreed with his superiors and returned to England. He returned in the spring of 1809 and after five years of struggle got the French out of the Peninsula, winning a lot of battles. He was made Count then Marquis of Wellington. After the Battle of Toulouse, he was made Duke. A year later he arrived on the plains of Belgium…
(RR)

to threaten the enemy's lines of communication. Wellington tried to cross the Garonne upstream of the town; then the river was suddenly in spate just after Beresford had got across and this interrupted the crossing for the other troops until 8 April. The French did not take advantage of this opportunity to beat a single isolated English corps. Once crossing the river started again, Freire's Spanish Corps in turn got across, pushing back General Pierre Soult's Cavalry.

The Allies' attack was launched on 10 April

1. On the left bank of the Garonne,

Hill headed for the suburb of Saint-Cyprien held by Reille with Maransin's Division. He led this attack from the Heights of Purpan where he set up his artillery. The Portuguese cavalry supported him. He had 16 628 men of which 4 021 were cavalry. Hill took the first line of defence but was pushed back by Barbot and General Brisbane was seriously wounded. Maransin still had two brigades, Rouget and Barbot, but Soult sent Rouget's Brigade to Harispe.

At 3 p.m., Hill stopped his advance which had halted at the city toll gate.

2. The Pont-Jumeaux

In this sector Picton sent the 45th Foot from Brisbane's Brigade into the attack; Colonel Forbes was killed and Fririon defended effectively.

3. La Croix Daurade

This bridge was of capital importance for Wellington.

Vial's 10th Chasseurs were surprised by the 18th Light Dragoons and the Allies set up a bridgehead. Freire's Spaniards were able to get across supported by a Portuguese battery. Ponsonby followed them. They advanced along the Albi road.

4. Lapujade and Périole

Already engaged, the French Tirailleurs progressively fell back towards Lapujade then towards the northern redoubt at le Calvinet where Freire was driven off. Beresford attacked Lapujade where Lamorendière fought like a lion but was killed and his post captured.

Freire and his Spaniards with Ponsonby advanced and tried to attack Darmagnac, who drove them off vigorously with Leseur's Brigade and his 51st and 75th of the Line. Two Spanish generals were put out of action.

5. Les Minimes (no important action here).

Harispe with Darmagnac and Darricau pushed back the attack. The 69th distinguished itself but von Alten forbade them access to the Croix-Daurade Bridge. The 31st Light held out in the Minimes Convent, protecting the Arnaud-Bernard Bridge.

Two Spanish Generals were wounded.

6. Busca and les Récollets

There was not a lot of important fighting in this sector. The same could be said for the Montaudran sector and the Demoiselles Bridge where Somerset and his cavalry, including the 7th Hussars were driven off by the artillery and the 9th and 21st Chasseurs under Berton.

7/It was along the line of the crests of le Calvinet that the battle was decided. Beresford formed up three columns and went round the crests in a risky movement:

Cole went round the crests, along the foot of the hills with Anson's and Ross' Brigades.

Clinton lined up his elite troops. They were English Riflemen, Portuguese Cazadores and especially Pack's Brigade with his Scots of the 79th, the Camerons, the 42nd, the Black Watch and the 91st, the Argyllshires. Lambert supported Clinton. To do this he advanced the 36th and the 11th Foot, preceded by his 61st which suffered heavy casualties. The Spaniards attacked the other redoubts in order to make things easier for the English.

The Cole and Clinton divisions attacked the la Sypière redoubt on the right of the Calvinet

WELLINGTON'S ARMY

TheChief-of-Staff was **Lieutenant-General Lord Murray.**

LIEUTENANT-GENERAL HILL'S CORPS
At Toulouse, he was placed towards Purpan, on the right wing, facing Saint-Cyprien which was his objective.
● **STEWART'S DIVISION** (with Picton)
— **Barnes' Brigade**
51st, 71st and 92nd Foot
— **Byng's Brigade**
1st, 3rd and 57th Foot
— **Pryngle's Brigade**
28th, 34th and 39th Foot
— **Harding's Portuguese Brigade**
6th and 18th Infantry Regiments, 6th Battalion of Cazadores

BERESFORD'S CORPS
Beresford was certainly Wellington's best general. He marched with the Cole, Clinton, Freire and

> *The Koch and Escalettes versions of the distribution and the make up of the brigades differ. However, the latter seems to be the closest to reality.*

Lambert Divisions for the attack on Le Calvinet, the capital moment during the Battle of Toulouse.
● **COLE'S DIVISION**
— **Anson's Brigade**
27th (Inniskilling), 40th (Somerset), 48th (Northamptonshire) and 2nd (Queen's Royal)
— **Ross' Brigade**
7th (Royal Fusiliers), 20th (East Devonshires) and 23rd (Royal Welsh Fusiliers)
— **Power's Portuguese Brigade**
9th and 21st Infantry Regiments and 11th Battalion of Cazadores
● **CLINTON'S DIVISION**
— **Pack's Brigade** (with the elite)
91st (Argyllshire), 42nd (Black Watch) from Brisbane, 79th (Cameron)
2 companies of Rifles
— **Lambert's Brigade**
was at le Calvinet, making up one of the three columns. 11th (North Devonshire), 32nd (Cornwall), 36th (Herefordshire) and the 61st (South Gloucester) was very often mentioned and was greatly weakened by its head-on attacks against the redoubts.
— **Kempt's Brigade**
43rd and 95th Foot

— **Vasconcellos's Portuguese Brigade**
11th and 12th Infantry Regiments and 9th Battalion of Cazadores
PICTON'S CORPS
Replaced by Brisbane, he was with Beresford for the main attack, and was given the attack on the Pont-Jumeaux and the mouth of the canal.
— **Brisbane's Brigade**
42nd (Nottinghamshire), 74th (Highland Regiment wearing kilts), 88th (Connaught)
— **Kean's Brigade**
5th (Northumberland), 83rd, 87th (Prince of Wales) and 94th Foot
— **Barnard's Light Brigade** (with Picton)
52nd and 95th Foot
● **MURRAY'S PORTUGUESE DIVISION**
— **Da Costa's Brigade**
2nd and 14th Infantry Regiments
— **Buchan's Brigade**
4th and 10th Infantry Regiments and 10th Battalion of Cazadores
● **THE SPANISH DIVISION**
Commanded by Morillo, this division will be presented with the 4th Spanish Army.
Stappleton-Cotton's Cavalry
— **Ponsonby's Brigade**
3rd, 4th and 5th Dragoon Guards
— **Bock's Brigade**

1st and 2nd Dragoon Guards
— **Fane's Brigade**
13th and 14th Hussars
— **Vivian's Brigade**
1st Hussars of the King's German Legion and 1th Hussars
— **Somerset's Brigade**
7th, 10th and 15th Hussars
— **X's Brigade**
3rd Dragoon Guards and 1st Royal Dragoons
— **O'Loghlin's Brigade**
1st and 2nd Life Guards
— **Campbell's Brigade**
4th Dragoon Regiment
— **Barbacena's Portuguese Brigade**
1st, 6th, 11th, and 12th Cavalry Regiments

● **THE ARTILLERY**
This was commanded by Colonel Dickson and had 52 cannon including Colonel Arentschild's 14 Portuguese guns and Gardner's 18 Horse Artillery; the artillery was also equipped with Congreve rockets which were more a source of psychological disorders than real human losses.

The Numbers:
- 25 888 English, 13 404 Portuguese and 12 546 Spaniards.

Above, from left to right:
General Campbell, General Stappleton-Cotton commanding the Anglo-Allied cavalry, General Picton and General Hill.
(RR)

crest. Lambert who was ahead with the 61st was followed by the 11th and the 36th. Colonel Coghlan was killed but the redoubt was taken.

Soult sent Taupin but he manoeuvred badly and arrived in disorder. He was killed. Travot came up to help him and Soult led Gasquet's 55th; he rallied the defenders of the redoubt with the 45th and got the situation under control. Beresford rested his troops around the captured redoubt. Wellington arrived and called up the artillery.

The English attack resumed after a two-hour pause for reorganisation. The Spanish continued to support the main attack by maintaining the pressure on the redoubts to the north of the crests. The Mas des Augustins was attacked by the Rifles, the Cazadores and Clinton's Scots. Dauture defended with the 26th Light and Baurot's 115th, reinforced by the 45th, called up hastily. The English 61st was decimated but was still there.

It was relieved. At the end of five attacks, the redoubt fell. Beresford waited for his artillery before continuing his combined attack with the Spaniards. Soult decided to pull the troops in this sector back. He had trouble getting Clauzel to retreat for his men wanted to defend the Calvinet crests and the last redoubts. They finished by agreeing to fall back on the Canal des Deux Mers.

The 45th fell back last.

The Anglo-Spanish held the crests. No other attack was really attempted. The battle was perhaps interrupted a little too early by Soult. It would not have changed the outcome of the campaign but it could have been a consolation victory for the troops.

Soult retreated on 11 April

Soult was surrounded and only had the Montpellier road to retreat along. The whole region was occupied, there were no more supplies to be found, and the Royalists were beginning to show themselves in the town full of wounded. It was time to go.

The Highlanders trying in vain to take the Matabiau Bridge defended by men from the Darmagnac Division. (RR)

He decided to retreat, leaving 1 500 wounded behind in Toulouse. On the 14th he joined up with Suchet's troops. The French lost 321 killed, 2 369 wounded and 541 prisoners.

The Allies lost 4 458 men of which 2 214 English, 1 727 Spaniards and 607 Portuguese.

The following day, Wellington entered Toulouse and learned of the Emperor's abdication. *"And about time, too!"* he cried out. Today, the name of Toulouse still appears on the colours of 31 British regiments ...

THE SPANIARDS WITH FREIRE
On 17 June 1813, Sir Henry Wellesley, the ambassador to the government in Cadiz told his brother that the Minister of War had replaced Castanos by Freire at the head of the Spanish 4th Army, its second-in-command, Giron also being replaced; and Lacy took command in Galicia. It is Dr Sarramon who pointed out this detail. He also gives the composition of this 4th Army which was under Wellington's direct command. He does not mention the 1st and 2nd Armies and gives, according to Oman and Artèche the situation of these troops as in July 1813.

FREIRE'S 4th ARMY
It comprised six divisions.
● **MORILLO'S DIVISION** (with Picton)
6 battalions of Leon, la Union, Legion Extremena, Doyle, Votoria and Jaen
● **CARLOS DE ESPANA'S DIVISION**
5 battalions of 3rd Guardias Espagnolas, 1st Sevilla, Castilla cazadores, 1st Mallorca and 1st de la Princesa
● **JAVIER LOSADA'S DIVISION**
7 battalions of Toledo, 1st Asturias, Monterey, Rivero, Oviedo and the Leon Volunteers
● **BARCENA'S DIVISION**
6 battalions of the 2nd Asturias, Guadalajara, La Constitucion, and the la Corona, Asturias and Santiago Volunteers
● **PORLIER'S DIVISION**
3 battalions of the 1st Cantabro, Laredo and Cantabrian cazadores
● **LONGA'S DIVISION**
4 battalions of Iberia and one from the Guardias Nacionales
● **PENNE-VILLEMUR'S CAVALRY**
Extramadura, la Rioja, Castilla and Algarve Hussars and the Galician and Cantabrian Grenadiers
— **With Don Julian Sanchez**
2nd Castilian lancers
This made a total of 24 429 men and 3 918 cavalry.
Extra troops came from the Navarra de Mina, Viscaya, Pastor en Guipuzcoa, Pinto Divisions, etc. Finally the army of the Count of La Bisbal, of the Army of Andalusia, the Echevarri and Creagh Divisions and Barcena's Cavalry were probably attached to the 4th Army.
A further total of 13 899 and 828 cavalry.
A number of Spanish units were kept in reserve or used in the garrisons, but Freire was with Beresford for the main attack on Toulouse where he was very useful and effective.
The Spanish were considered as being unreliable, creating an atmosphere of mutiny, according to Koch, who gives the following units which do not seem to have followed Wellington to France.

THE 1st SPANISH ARMY
Commanded by General D. Copons Y Navia, it had three divisions:
● **1st DIVISION** under Baron d'Eroles (3 664 men)
● **2nd DIVISION** (4 396 men)
● **3rd DIVISION** under Brigadier Manso (6 000 men)
It was completed by:
— **Luis de Kraft's Flying Brigade** (2 537 men)
— **Lorenzo Calvo's Elite Corps** (921 men)
— **José Gomez Tortosa's Cavalry Brigade** (537 troopers)
— **San Clemente's Artillery** with 33 cannon and 313 men
This 1st Army therefore consisted of 18 368 men of which 921 were cavalry.

2nd SPANISH ARMY
It was commanded by Major-General Don Xavier Elio and comprised:
● **1st DIVISION**
● **2nd DIVISION** under Brigadier Prieto
● **3rd DIVISION** under Major-General D. Pedro Sarsfield
● **4th DIVISION** under Don Felipe Roche
● **5th DIVISION** under Brigadier Juan Martin
These divisions were supported by
— **The Marquis of Albentos's Cavalry Brigade**
— **Brigadier Tesorio's Artillery** (62 cannon and 907 men)
Lieutenant-Colonel Mariano del Rio's Engineers (394 men)
This made a total of 28 498 men.
The Spanish armies therefore totalled 61 865 men including 1 885 cavalry.

This gives:
22 076 men for blockading the strong points.
39 790 men in the Line against the French.

Some however were kept in reserve in front of Toulouse. They are not therefore mentioned in the detail of the battle.
Koch mentions that Generals Mendizabal and Espeleta were put out of action during their first attack on le Calvinet which was premature and repulsed. These generals are not to be found in Koch's roll but they were most certainly with Freire as was Murillo.

(RR)

HÉROÏC OR PATHETIC?

The invasion of France started in December when the Supreme Commander, Schwarzenberg, at the head of his Army of Bohemia, violated Swiss neutrality, crossed the Rhine at Basel and headed for Champagne, passing along the south of the Vosges. A week later, Blücher and his Army of Silesia did the same thing at Mainz. At the same time, the south of the country was invaded by the English, the Portuguese and the Spaniards under Wellington who marched on Bordeaux then turned towards the pink town of Toulouse. Maison in Holland and Eugene, the Viceroy in Italy also faced enemies coming from the whole of Europe.

What did the Highland warriors, the Swedes, the Bashkirs, the Brandenburgers, the Hungarians, the Andalusians and the Portuguese have in common if not a hatred of the French who, blindly obeying their Emperor whose aims of hegemony seemed to know no limits, had brought war to the whole continent. This hatred of the French and of Napoleon was shared by all the sovereigns: for more than fifteen years, they each kowtowed in turn to this whining Corsican. For the first time, the peoples and the crowned heads of Europe banded together against France and her master. Alone, England, isolated on her island, had conceded nothing since the treaty of Amiens. At first amused by revolutionary France's gesticulations, she started to get worried when France began developing and expanding, before finally going to war against her. Bonaparte's ascension and assumption of power drew Albion into a struggle to the death whose main target was to be first in Europe and therefore in the world.

Napoleon had caught the conqueror's illness, just as his models had before him: Alexander, Caesar and Charlemagne. He had wanted to play out his dream of beating the English and conquering India, in spite of the warnings he was given at Aboukir and Trafalgar. But his dream of the route to India was interlinked to the continental blockade, the Spanish mistake and the Russian Campaign. After the failures came the defeats, the retreats and then the invasion.

Faced with this flood, Napoleon showed how energetic he could be and mobilised all the country's economic and human resources. But France had been was bled white, and there was no longer enough time.

After two months of intense activity, what sort of army would the Emperor be able to draw up to oppose the advancing Allies?

He could count on the unfailing devotion of the faithful in the Guard and the experience of the few veteran troops which had not disappeared in the collapse which had been going on now for the last eighteen months. He could also count on his generals, officers and NCOs, who were of great worth, to structure the conscript masses whose training was done to the sound of the cannon on the battlefield. But these "Marie-Louise" troops were still young and their legs did not have the endurance of their elders, their rifles were cumbersome and their boots heavy on their feet after a day's marching along bad roads. A good number of cavalrymen barely knew how to ride, let alone handle a sabre which was something new to them. Many artillerymen lacked training and experience.

However, no matter how homogenous this army was, it suffered from two major deficiencies which turned out to be fatal in the end.

The first and no doubt the most obvious was the lack of numbers. Except for the south-west where Soult had almost 60 000 to face Wellington with – he was only fighting at one against two -in the rest of France however, the odds were more like one against three, or four or even more sometimes.

There was no point in Napoleon saying when he joined the army on 25 January *"that 50 000 men and me make 150 000 men"*, larger numbers always win, or almost always, in the end.

The second deficiency came from the top of the hierarchy, both civil and military.

Napoleon handing over the Act of Abdication to his Marshals. (RR)

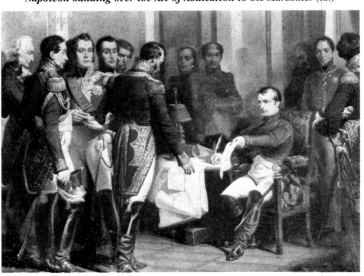

The top dignitaries thought that the Empire was dying and were putting out feelers to the Bourbons so that they would have their place in a restored monarchy. But the exhaustion and discouragement affected most those whom Napoleon had raised highest: the Marshals. These men were tired of the unending wars and the setbacks they had suffered; they wanted to be able to enjoy their possessions and fortunes which they owed to their own worth, but also in particular to this one man: the Emperor. Some of them fought brilliantly, with courage and talent: Soult commanded the army's retreat from Spain with the hands of a master; at the head of the Young Guard Corps, Ney was always in the middle of the fray and constantly reminded the Allies what "Furia Francese" meant; Marmont also fought like a lion but did make mistakes: his incompetence at Athies, his capitulation at Paris and his sorry "Ragusade", the only thing by which history will remember him.

In spite of all these burdens, Napoleon led his little army briskly. For one month, turning round abruptly in the middle of the enemy lines, appearing on one of their flanks, then to the rear of others, he was always one step ahead on the big checkerboard which the Champagne area had become at the time. At the same time Augereau reinforced his army at Lyon, Soult fell back in the south-west as did Maison in the north. In this period of victories, the Allies were prepared to cease hostilities and allow France to keep its 1792 frontiers. From Chatillon-sur-Seine, Caulaincourt transmitted the proposals which had been made to him. After all, they were rather advantageous, considering the state of the country's economy and morale. But Napoleon hedged, still believing he could win a decisive victory, enabling him to negotiate from a position of strength and to obtain an even more favourable armistice or even peace. He was in fact plagued by an illness which has hit many great men: conquest; and his narcissism grew with each success, nourished by the servility of his underlings. Napoleon did not look at what he was doing but instead persisted in looking at what he could do further. He refused to take into account the country's exhaustion and that of his marshals; he could only see his enemies prevaricating.

The worth of his heroic troops, hardened and fanatical veterans of the Old Guard, the ardour and keenness of the conscripts and the Young Guard, dazzled him and drew him in to his headlong flight. The last fights, the last defeats, were but the inexorable continuation of this flight. At Paris the Allies defeated the Marshals; at Fontainebleau, the Marshals defeated the Emperor.

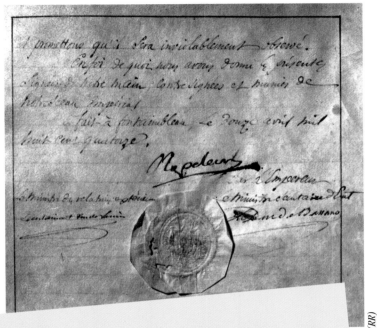

(RR)

(RR)

Heroic or pathetic?

This is the question which one has the right to ask when considering the events which took place all during the French Campaign.

The long marches, the sleepless nights in the cold, in the rain or the snow: these

Below, from left to right:
While he was negotiating with the French plenipotentiaries, Tsar Alexander I learnt of Marmont's defection. The Empire was finished. *(RR)*

Farewells at Fontainebleau. For the last time, Napoleon is acclaimed by his Guard who shout "Long live the Emperor!" *(RR)*

were pathetic. The desperate charges and morrow-less victories: these were pathetic. The death throes of an army which was great yesterday and refused to die today; this was pathetic.

But the men were heroic. They were often very young; when led by their elders or by their commanding officer in person they took positions, overwhelmed columns and broke through squares. The mad and desperate charges whether they were made by hardened troopers or by terrorised but keen novices: this was heroism. The millers' boys who left their work to go and fire alongside experienced soldiers: this was heroism.

It is difficult to describe the symphony which Napoleon played during the winter of 1814, during which he revealed the limits of military genius; but the conscripts did push back the limits of courage, devotion and sacrifice, when faced with the invasion of their country. They are worthy of great respect, they wrote a splendid epic which carried France's prestige to even greater heights.

A WORD ON FRENCH MILITARY TERMINOLOGY

In the many biographical notices to be found in this book (especially pp. 55 to 82 and pp. 101 to 111), the following rules have been adopted.

TRANSLATION OF RANKS

In order to avoid confusion, the French officers rank of '*Chef de bataillon*' (foot troops) or '*Chef d'escadron*' (cavalry) has been translated as 'Battalion commander' or 'Squadron commander' respectively. For the Napoleonic period, this rank could not be translated as 'Major' (in English), as there existed also a rank of '*Major*' (in French) immediately above it. When the rank 'Major' is used in this book, it always refers to the original French rank above Battalion commander and below Colonel – cf. plate p. 23).
- '*Général de brigade*' has been translated merely as 'General', or in some cases as 'Brigadier General' (only in the biographical notices).
- '*Général de division*' has been always translated as 'Major General' in the biographical notices.

- '*Lieutenant général*' (in the Royal French Army) has been translated as 'Lieutenant General'. This rank did not exist in the Army of Napoleon.
- '*Maréchal*' has been retained in French or translated in English as 'Marshall'.
- '*Maréchal de camp*' (in the Royal French army) has been retained in French. This rank did not exist in the Army of Napoleon.

ABBREVIATIONS USED FOR ORDERS AND DECORATIONS

LH : Légion d'honneur *(chevalier de la)*.
OLH : officier de la Légion d'honneur.
CtLH : commandant de la Légion d'honneur.
CrLH : commandeur de la Légion d'honneur *(it replaced the 'commandant' mentioned above, on the 17th February 1815).*
GdCxLH : grand-croix de la Légion d'honneur *(it replaced the 'grand-cordon' on the 21th June 1814).*
GdOLH : grand-officier de la Légion d'honneur.
CrSL : croix de Saint-Louis *(chevalier de la).*
GdCxSL : grand-croix de Saint-Louis.

SOURCES FOR THE UNIFORM PLATES

— *Plate from le Plumet, Rigo,* Generals' ADCs N°243
— *Plate from le Plumet, Rigo,* Ordnance Officer N°43
— *Plate from le Plumet, Rigo,* General Rottembourg N°189
— *Plate from le Plumet, Rigo,* 7th Lights N°71
— *Plate from le Plumet, Rigo,* 5th Lights N° 151
— *Plate from le Plumet, Rigo,* 10th Hussars U26
— *Plate from le Plumet, Rigo,* 8th Hussars U24
— *Plate from le Plumet, Rigo,* 6th Hussars U18
— *Plate from L. Rousselot* n° 80. Infanterie de ligne
— *Plate from L. Rousselot* n° 81. Eta-major et aides de camp
— *Plate from L. Rousselot* n° 71. Les officiers généraux

— *Plate from L. Rousselot* n° 5 et 33. L'infanterie légère
— *Plate from L. Rousselot* n° 28 et 66. L'artillerie à pied
— *Plate from L. Rousselot* n° 36. L'artillerie à cheval
— *Plate from L. Rousselot* n° 7. Les dragons
— *Tradition magazine.* Les cuirassiers 1804-1815, Rigo, Pétard, Pigeard, Malvaux
— *Les équipements militaires,* Tome IV and V. M. Pétard. Editions de l'auteur
— *L'infanterie.* Comandant Bucquoy, Grancher éditeur
— *Austrian army of Napoleonic War.* P Haythornthwaite & B. Fosten. Osprey n°176 et 181
— *Soldat du temps jadis. Les hussards autrichiens.* R. Forthoffer. Planches n°238, 239
— *L'armée russe du Tsar Alexandre 1er.* M. Gayda & A. Kritjitsky.
Editions de la Sabretache, 1950

ACKNOWLEDGEMENTS

I would particularly like to thank my friend *Jacques GARNIER* who helped a great deal during this long work,
together with *Jean-Marie MONGIN*, the king of artists where drawing maps is concerned; also *Denis GANDILHON* who put order back into the text with efficiency and patience.
Thanks to *Alexandre BOBRIKOFF* and *Vladimir GREKOFF* for their help and their kindness.
Thanks also *Jean-Louis VIAU* and *Gérard GOROKHOFF* for their precious help.

Editing by Denis GANDILHON
Design and lay-out by Jean-Marie MONGIN and Denis GANDILHON, photographs by Jean-Louis VIAU
© Histoire & Collections 2005

A book from
HISTOIRE & COLLECTIONS
SA au capital de 182 938, 82 €
5, avenue de la République
F-75541 Paris Cédex 11, France
Telephone (33-1) 40 21 18 20
Fax (33-1) 47 00 51 11
www.histoireetcollections.fr

This book has been designed, typed, laid-out and processed by
Histoire & Collections
and *'le Studio Graphique A & C'*
on fully integrated computer equipment.
Color separation by the *Studio A & C*
Printed by ZURE, Spain,
European Union
November 2005